D0908718

VERA BRITTAIN

For my brother
John Gorham
and in loving memory of our sister
Abigail Gorham
(1943–1976)

VERA BRITTAIN

A FEMINIST LIFE

Deborah Gorham

First published 1996

2 4 6 8 10 9 7 5 3 1

Blackwell Publishers Ltd
108 Cowley Road
Oxford OX4 1JF
UK

Blackwell Publishers Inc.
238 Main Street
Cambridge, Massachusetts 02142
USA

British Library Cataloguing in Publication Data

A CIP catalogue record for this book is available from the British Library.

Library of Congress Cataloging-in-Publication Data
Gorham, Deborah.
Vera Brittain: a feminist life / Deborah Gorham.
p. cm.
Includes bibliographical references (p.) and index.
ISBN 0-631-14715-2 (alk. paper)
1. Brittain, Vera, 1893–1970 – Biography. 2. Women authors, English – 20th century – Biography. 3. Feminists – Great Britain – Biography. I. Title.
PR6003.R385Z67 1996
828'.91209 – dc20
[B] 95-18892
CIP

Typeset in 10.5 on 12.5 pt Sabon
by Best-set Typesetter Ltd, Hong Kong
Printed in Great Britain by T.J. Press Limited, Padstow, Cornwall

This book is printed on acid-free paper

Contents

Plates

Acknowledgements

I visited many archives, libraries and research collections in the course of working on this project. First and foremost I thank the Vera Brittain Archive, William Ready Division of Archives and Research Collections, McMaster University Library, Hamilton, Canada. I have received help from everyone there, but I owe special thanks to Charlotte Stewart, Director, Archives and Research Collections, and to Carl Spadoni, Renu Barrett, Kathy Garay, Bruce Whiteman and Margaret Foley. The following institutions in England allowed me to use archival material: the Hull Central Library; the Public Library in Bridlington; the Imperial War Museum, London; the Fawcett Society Library, London; Somerville College Library, Somerville College, Oxford; the Public Library in Buxton; the Devonshire Hospital in Buxton; the Buxton Museum.

I thank the Social Sciences and Humanities Research Council of Canada and the Office of the Dean of Graduate Studies at Carleton University for funding this research.

Paul Berry, Literary Executor for Vera Brittain and Winifred Holtby and others associated with the Vera Brittain Estate, read this book in typescript in 1994 and kindly granted permission to quote from material to which the Estate and the Executor hold copyright. Paul Berry and Mark Bostridge are the authors of the authorized life of Vera Brittain, *Vera Brittain: A Life*, scheduled to be published by Chatto & Windus in the autumn of 1995.

Since my first meeting with Paul Berry and Mark Bostridge in April 1992, they and I have maintained a friendly correspondence. This manuscript, however, was completed independently and was in production before the authorized life became available.

I thank Shirley Williams (Baroness Williams of Crosby), Vera Brittain's daughter, for kindly meeting with me in June 1986.

Professor Alan Bishop, of the Department of English at McMaster University, whose fine published work on Brittain reflects his extensive knowledge of the Vera Brittain Archive, has been generous with his help. Alan and his wife Judith also offered me warm hospitality on several occasions.

I am grateful to the following colleagues who read and commented on all or part of various versions of this book: Susan Groag Bell, Joyce Berkman, Toby Gelfand, Philippa Levine, Mark Phillips, Harold Smith, Pamela Walker and Angela Woollacott. All offered helpful criticism. In addition to these fellow historians, my brother John Gorham, who is a writer and editor, carefully read and edited the penultimate draft of this book. His thorough and judicious red pencil immensely improved the manuscript. I, of course, am responsible for any remaining errors or weaknesses.

Many friends and colleagues offered various kinds of help and advice. They include Hilary Bailey, Marilyn Barber, Y. Aleksandra Bennett, Aviva Freedman, Roland Jeffreys, Angela John, Raymond Jones, Jane Lewis, Abigail Stewart, John Saville, Marion Shaw and Janice Williamson. I also thank the Department of History and the Pauline Jewett Institute of Women's Studies at Carleton University; Laurie Campbell, Frances Montgomery and Wendy Sinclair of Carleton's library; and many Carleton students and former students.

My thanks go to the following colleagues who invited me to speak on Vera Brittain: Karen Dubinsky, Felicity Hunt, Diana Pedersen, Ruth Roach Pierson; Leslie Howsam and other organizers of the 1993 Victorian Studies Association of Ontario Annual Conference; Alan Bishop and other organizers of the Vera Brittain Centenary Conference, 'A Testament to Vera Brittain', held at McMaster in 1993; Barbara Gabriel, organizer of Carleton University's 1992 *Women and the Arts* series; the Institute for Research on Women and Gender, Stanford University; the Ottawa Historical Association.

I received research and technical help from two research assistants. Dr Beverly Boutilier was not only skilled and competent as an editorial assistant and Apple Macintosh wizard, she was enthusiastic and helpful throughout about the project itself. At other stages, Sarah Namer and Susan Villeneuve also offered excellent help.

At Blackwell, John Davey, Editorial Director, and Tessa Harvey, Assistant Commissioning Editor, have not only played an essential role in negotiations with the Vera Brittain Estate, they have offered judicious and supportive advice throughout the publication process. I also thank Blackwell's copy-editor, Audrey Bamber.

Margaret and James Hepburn have for many years provided a

home-away-from-home for me in London. I am enormously grateful to them and to their family. All the members of my own family have also been enthusiastic supporters of this project. In addition to my brother John, I thank my son David Keith for his unfailing interest and support, and my husband, Toby Gelfand, who has read and commented on several drafts of the manuscript, has listened to me talk (at length!) about Vera Brittain and has offered wise advice and the benefit of his excellent historical judgement.

∞

Some portions of this book are reworked versions of earlier pieces I have published. I thank the publishers for permission to use material from them: 'Vera Brittain, Flora MacDonald Denison and the Great War: the Failure of Non-violence', in Ruth Roach Pierson (ed.), *Women and Peace: Theoretical, Historical and Practical Perspectives* (London: Croom Helm, 1987); '"Have We Really Rounded Seraglio Point?" Vera Brittain and Feminism in the Interwar Period', in Harold L. Smith (ed.), *British Feminism in the Twentieth Century* (Upleadon, Glos.: Edward Elgar, 1990); 'A Woman at Oxford: Vera Brittain's Somerville Experience', *Historical Studies in Education/Revue d'histoire de l'education*, vol. 3, no. 1 (Spring 1991); 'The Education of Vera and Edward Brittain: Class and Gender in a Late-Victorian and Edwardian Family', *History of Education Review*, vol. 20, no. 1 (1991); '"The Friendships of Women": Friendship, Feminism and Achievement in Vera Brittain's Life and Work in the Inter-war Decades', *Journal of Women's History*, vol. 3, no. 2 (Winter 1992).

With the exception of the cover photograph, all the photographs used in this book are from the Vera Brittain Archive, William Ready Division of Archives and Research Collections, McMaster University Library, Hamilton, Canada. I thank the Vera Brittain Archive for permission to reproduce them. The cover photograph is from the collection of the National Portrait Gallery, London, whom I thank for permission to reproduce that photograph.

April 1995

DEBORAH GORHAM
Ottawa, Canada

1

Introduction

On 27 August 1933, readers of the *Observer*'s book page could hardly have missed the large advertisement placed by Victor Gollancz, the most respected and successful progressive British publisher of the interwar decades: 'Tomorrow: *Testament of Youth*: Vera Brittain's autobiographical study of the years 1900–1925'. The advertisement's advance testimonials included one from *The Sunday Times* describing the book as 'likely to make not only a stir on publication but a lasting impression as well', and one from Lady Rhondda, the well-known feminist editor of *Time and Tide*, who said: 'Extraordinarily interesting. I sat up reading it till long past my usual bedtime and have been reading it again all this morning.'[1] On 28 August 1933, Vera Brittain's *Testament of Youth: An Autobiographical Study of the Years 1900–1925* was published.

Vera Brittain (1893–1970) made her mark as a writer, as a feminist activist and as a witness for peace and internationalism. She was a prolific writer, publishing some twenty books and thousands of journalistic pieces over her fifty-year career, but her lasting reputation rests with *Testament of Youth*. Brittain, thirty-nine years old when her most successful book was published, had as a young woman interrupted her studies at Oxford to serve in the First World War as a Voluntary Aid Detachment (VAD) nurse. In the course of the war she lost her only brother, her fiancé and two close friends.

After the war, she completed her studies and began her career as a writer. In the 1920s she published two novels, *The Dark Tide* (1923) and *Not Without Honour* (1924), and two works of non-fiction, *Women's Work in Modern England* (1928) and *Halcyon, or The Future of Monogamy* (1929). She was also an active journalist. But in 1933 she had not yet achieved major recognition as a writer. With *Testament of Youth*, as she herself put it, she crossed the Rubicon from obscurity to fame. The book was an overnight success, selling more than 3,000 copies its first day out.[2] 'Miss Brittain has written a book which stands alone among books written by women about the war',[3] wrote the reviewer in *The Sunday Times*, and Lady Rhondda was not the only distinguished reader who found she couldn't put the book down. Virginia Woolf also found herself caught up in Brittain's narrative even though she was repelled by the book and by its author. 'I am reading with extreme greed a book by Vera Britain [*sic*], called The Testament of Youth [*sic*] . . . A very good book of its sort. The new sort, the hard anguished sort, that the young write; that I could never write . . . I read & read & read & neglect Turgenev & Miss C. Burnett.'[4] *Testament of Youth* was widely and favourably reviewed both in Britain and in North America (where it was published by Macmillan & Co. of New York) and it became a lasting best-seller of the 1930s, entering historical memory as the most important English 'Great War' book by a woman.[5]

Testament of Youth was conceived of and written as a book with a moral purpose and a political message. Brittain believed that the First World War had been a catastrophe for which all those in power, on both sides, had been responsible, a catastrophe that had robbed millions of her generation of their lives, and had robbed the survivors of their youth. She wanted her readers to understand how it was that those who had been young in 1914, as she had been, were so easily caught up in support for the war and she hoped that such understanding would create in her readers a determination to ensure that no repetition of the catastrophe would take place.

Testament of Youth is also a manifesto in support of feminism. Brittain's moving account of her journey from Edwardian 'provincial young ladyhood' to the feminist womanhood she achieved in the 1920s is as central to the book as is its narration of her wartime experiences. Over the course of her long career Brittain made many impressive contributions to the cause of feminism but none was more significant than the passionate advocacy of her most successful book.

As autobiography *Testament of Youth* is a notable achievement. Brittain broke new ground with this book, redefining the genre of autobiography in a way that allowed her to combine personal narrative with historical and political analysis. This was an audacious project. Dominant Victorian and Edwardian assumptions about biography and autobiography sanctioned the telling of life stories only in the case of individuals who were widely recognized as having contributed to public life. Brittain was not such a person, not an individual who 'ought' to have been writing an autobiography. She was a relatively young, relatively obscure writer. Moreover, as a woman, it took courage to assert that her life was important. As one literary acquaintance put it in 1932 when he heard she was working on an autobiography: 'I shouldn't have thought that anything in your life was worth recording.'[6]

But as she conceived of the project, it was precisely because of her youth, her obscurity and her sex that she asserted that her life story was worth telling. As she says in the book's Foreword, her intention was to write 'history in terms of personal life', and while she might be a minor figure, the period through which she had grown to maturity, with its upheaval of the Great War, 'history's greatest disaster', was a crucial turning-point in history.

After the war, Brittain studied history at Oxford because she hoped that history would provide her with an understanding of why the war had occurred. In 1921, as a new Oxford graduate, Brittain had found herself torn between the claims of scholarship and the claims of fiction. As she wrote ruefully to her friend Winifred Holtby: 'Why is it that all my university mentors want me to do research . . . at the expense of fiction, and my literary mentors fiction at the expense of History?' 'How is one to reconcile the two ideals?' Brittain asked Holtby. 'Can both of them be true at once, and each at different times matter more than the other?'[7]

Brittain's youthful faith in an 'ideal of creativity' and in the accessibility of 'historical truth' reflects an ingenuous enthusiasm. At the same time, it prefigures her lasting achievements. As I argue in this study, Brittain did make an important and original contribution to the integration of imaginative and political writing. She did indeed 'reconcile the two ideals' of creativity on the one hand and 'historical truth' on the other. And as I have sought in this book to illuminate her experience and to explore her contributions as writer and activist, I have been influenced and inspired by Brittain's own belief in the value of writing 'history in terms of personal life'.

∞

My first reading of *Testament of Youth* was one of the intellectual milestones of my early adolescence. As a child I had read all the time, and like many bookish girls I found in fiction a liberation from the limitations of my own place, time and sex. When I read *Treasure Island*, I became a boy who imagined he was Jack Hawkins. But such naive androgyny becomes more difficult in adolescence. And that is why *Testament of Youth* was so important to me. *Testament of*

Youth was a book about an exciting and inspiring actual woman, not a fictional character. Vera Brittain was for me a feminist exemplar, a girl who defies the voices which tell her that she will never achieve anything of importance because she is female, and who goes on to become a woman who is able to use her talents and achieve genuine autonomy.

Thirty years later, when as a university teacher of history I began the project of which this book is the outcome I had not only re-read *Testament of Youth* many times, I had read Brittain's other works of autobiography, her fiction, and the commentary on her life and work that was just beginning to appear, and I could situate her as an important interwar British feminist, as an anti-war activist and as a working woman writer. I knew that she would be an exciting subject for research.

Visiting the rich Vera Brittain Archive at McMaster University for the first time was another landmark in my own relationship with Brittain.[8] Reading her wartime letters evoked the freshness of my earliest responses to *Testament of Youth*. It was intensely touching to find, along with the letter her fiancé Roland Leighton sent to Brittain from Flanders on 25 April 1915, the 'Violets from Plug Street Wood', faded but still recognizable, mentioned in the letter.[9]

That dip into the Brittain papers corresponded precisely with my original response to *Testament of Youth*. But it was equally intriguing to find evidence that conflicted with my earliest interpretations of the persona Brittain had created there. The vehemence with which Brittain had broken with her family tradition had appealed strongly to me as a young reader. But the voluminous correspondence between Brittain and her mother, with its minute descriptions of her Oxford experiences, reveals not only that this was a close mother–daughter relationship, but reflects Brittain's continued dependence on the amenities of her upper-middle-class family. She even sent her laundry and mending home: 'Please be careful about the buttons on the blouse. . . . Will you please tell whoever the housemaid is now to mend the two camisoles if they are mendable; I simply cannot sew them up any longer & there is nothing here to patch them up with.'[10] Clearly, my earliest perceptions of the young woman who leaves 'provincial young ladyhood' behind forever in 1914 did not correspond entirely with reality.

The integration between the public and the private, the 'personal' and the 'political' has been a major goal of a generation of feminist scholars. Vera Brittain offers an unusually promising opportunity to study the connection between the public and the private life of a woman who was a public figure, not least because she herself perceived the importance of that connection. Defending the frankness of *Testament of Youth*, Brittain wrote: 'I don't believe we are entitled to keep to ourselves any jot or tittle of experience the knowledge of which can in any way assist our fellow mortals . . . [experience] belongs to the collective effort of humanity.'[11]

But what is 'experience'? Brittain herself believed that she could present it to us through the medium of autobiographical narrative. Can we know the truth about Brittain's experience from reading what she tells us about it? And have we found error when we find discrepancies in tone or in fact between the public narrative of the published works of autobiography and the narrative the historian can piece together from the private papers and other evidence? Recent feminist post-structuralist criticism suggests that we must be sceptical about the relationship between 'truth' and linear narrative. As Nancy K. Miller points out, the critical reader must learn to distinguish 'life from art, nature from imitation, autobiography from fiction' and the distinctions are by no means as obvious as they may at first appear.[12] Bella Brodzki and Celeste Schenck emphasize that the assumption that 'autobiography is a transparency through which we perceive the life, unmediated and undistorted' is based on a corresponding assumption that 'reifies a unified, transcendent self'.[13] Both assumptions, they say, are flawed.

The insight that we are always in the process of constructing a self is a valuable one to remember in an analysis of Vera Brittain. Her project was not merely to construct herself – as we all do – but to use her creative energies to construct a written narrative through which she would present that self to others. Brittain's main purpose was 'writing her own life'[14] not only in her works of autobiography, but also in her fiction and in her informal daily writing of diaries and letters. I examine all these categories of text as evocations of the self. For example, attempting what Nancy K. Miller has called a '*double* reading of the autobiography with the fiction', I analyse the autobiographical content of Brittain's fiction.[15] She was often able in her novels to reveal nuances that remain concealed in the explicitly autobiographical texts.

In creating the narrative which follows, my intention has been to explore the contrasts between the public narrative and the private sources, between for example the portrait of the independent young woman who went off to Oxford and cut her ties with her past, and the young woman who wrote many letters home to 'Dearest mother', sending along with some of them blouses to be laundered and camisoles to be mended. I do not seek to be an omniscient narrator, nor do I point to such discrepancies for the purpose of labelling them errors or omissions. Instead, my intention is to understand why Brittain needed to show one self to herself, in her 'Reflective Record', another in letters, and yet another in accounts constructed for publication.

But I should also emphasise that while I am centrally concerned with analysing the textual evidence for Brittain's multifaceted selves, I also believe that the traditional purpose of biography – the illumination of personality – is still a valid enterprise. Historical biography continues to engage readers because it offers us intimate knowledge of another personality and another period, and that knowledge allows us to know ourselves and our own period better. As Susan Groag Bell and Marilyn Yalom put it in their introduction to *Revealing Lives: Autobiography, Biography, and Gender*, 'it is reassuring to look into a human face . . . [t]he impersonality, fragmentation, and alienation of the postmodern world seem less overwhelming as we follow the vicissitudes of a real person – a brother or sister creature from whom we grasp vicarious validation of our own lives.' Like Bell and Yalom, I reclaim the 'mimetic relationship between literature and life'. Like them, I believe that 'the autobiographical "I," however fugitive, partial, and unreliable, is indeed the privileged textual double of a real person, as well as a self-evident textual construct.'[16]

As a public figure, Brittain was an active advocate for peace and social justice as well as for feminism, but it is with her struggles and achievements as a feminist that this book is primarily concerned. In her private and public life she was representative of the group of educated middle-class women who brought to fruition the goals of Victorian bourgeois feminism in the years following the First World War. Although she was the daughter of a conventional Edwardian family, Brittain discovered the women's movement while she was still a schoolgirl. Throughout her adult life she was sustained by feminist convictions and driven by a fierce desire to achieve personal autonomy. Not only did she achieve such autonomy and build a successful career, she combined the career with marriage and motherhood. She is indeed a fit subject through which to explore both the achievements and the vicissitudes of British feminism in the first half of the twentieth century.

∞

The scope of this book derives from the chronology of Brittain's life up to the publication in 1940 of *Testament of Friendship* and from questions about feminist ideas and feminist experience. The two chapters in Part I: 'Macclesfield and Buxton' deal with Brittain's early life from her birth in 1893 to her departure for Somerville College, Oxford, in October 1914. I analyse the importance of social class and of ideologies of gender in shaping Brittain's family of origin and examine Brittain's acceptance of and resistance to the dominant assumptions that characterized the milieu of her youth.

The three chapters in Part II: '"History's Greatest Disaster": Love and Work in the Great War' deal with the period from October 1914 until the termination of her service as a Voluntary Aid Detachment nurse in April 1919. I explore the influence on Brittain's intellectual development and personality of her first year at Somerville College, of her wartime romance and of her war work.

The three chapters in Part III: '"Lady into Woman": Friendship, Work and Marriage in the 1920s' are concerned with Brittain's friendship with Winifred Holtby, with her emergence as an important post-war equal-rights feminist and internationalist, with her struggles to establish herself as a writer and with her marriage to George Edward Gordon Catlin.

The two chapters in Part IV: '"Having Crossed the Rubicon": the 1930s and After' describe the origins and the writing of *Testament of Youth* and offer an assessment of its lasting importance. I also examine the effect that *Testament of Youth*'s success had on Brittain, discuss her other major literary achievements and political activities in the 1930s, and her transformation after 1936 into a committed peace activist.

Chapter 12 is a brief conclusion.

Part I

Macclesfield and Buxton

2

Origins, 1893–1911

In the opening pages of *Testament of Youth*, Vera Brittain offers her readers the briefest of glimpses of her family history and childhood experience. Her few vignettes emphasize the ordinariness of her family backgound and the stifling nature of the bourgeois milieu in which she grew up. They provide a prelude to that journey of escape from dreary Edwardian provinciality around which she organized Part I of *Testament of Youth*. She concludes her perfunctory discussion of her childhood by commenting: 'I often wonder how many of my present-day friends were themselves limited by a horizon as circumscribed as that which bounded my first thirteen years.'[1] Brittain's stance of ironic distance about her origins is none the less revealing: it points to those aspects of her family background and childhood experience with which she remained uncomfortable, even as an adult. The less foreshortened view of this period of her life presented in this chapter offers insights into the way her earliest circumstances shaped her personality and her social and political outlook and laid the groundwork for the sort of writer she was to become. In the chapter that follows, 'Provincial Young Ladyhood', I analyse Brittain's own representations of her adolescence and young adulthood, examining those aspects she articulated and those she suppressed.

Vera Mary Brittain was born on 29 December 1893 in Newcastle-under-Lyme, a North Staffordshire industrial town on the western edge of the Potteries known for its paper-making factories and textile mills. In the 1890s, Staffordshire's towns and cities along with the rest of the urban Midlands and the northern counties, formed the heartland of Britain's industrial wealth. However, from the perspective of the landed classes and the professional elites which continued to dominate the nation's political and cultural life and to control its intricate web of social hierarchies, the world of industry and commerce was still regarded as socially inferior and culturally unimportant. Brittain tells us that as an adolescent she 'used to believe that such a typically provincial suburb as Newcastle could never have produced any man or woman of the smallest eminence'.[2]

Vera was her parents' first surviving child.[3] Her father, Thomas Arthur Brittain, born in 1864, was a successful young paper manufacturer, as his father had been before him.[4] His company, Brittain's, which grew and prospered in the decades before the First World War, had been based on a foundation of solid family wealth.[5] Arthur Brittain's grandfather, Thomas Brittain, the original founder of the family business, left a fortune of over £100,000 when he died in 1894.[6]

Vera Brittain's mother, Edith Mary Bervon, born in 1868 in Aberystwyth, was one of a family of four daughters and two sons.[7] Her father, John Inglis Bervon, was an organist and composer of church music. During Edith's childhood the family moved several times, as John Bervon sought to improve his circumstances. He left his position as organist in Aberystwyth in the 1860s to accept a post at St Mary's Church in Welshpool. By the 1880s, the family had left Wales and settled in Staffordshire, where John Inglis Bervon worked as an organist and music teacher.[8] In *Testament of Youth*, Vera Brittain describes her grandfather as a 'struggling musician',[9] and he was certainly never wealthy, although he managed to earn a sufficient income to maintain his family in middle-class respectability.[10]

Arthur Brittain and Edith Bervon met when Arthur took singing lessons from his future father-in-law. They were married in April 1891, when she was twenty-two and he twenty-seven. At twenty-two, Edith Bervon was a tall, slim, elegant young woman, with a good amateur singing voice. Thomas Arthur Brittain was the eldest of a family of twelve. Family accounts suggest that as 'the eldest son of an eldest son'[11] he was headstrong and somewhat spoiled, and that until the death of his grandfather he had little say in the running of the family business.[12] His education had been adequate by the provincial standards of the day, but somewhat limited. He had briefly attended Malvern College, a minor public school, and then Newcastle High School, but he had not attended university.

In *Testament of Youth*, Vera Brittain emphasized the social and economic disparity between the Brittain and Bervon families, and says that the prosperous Brittains initially disapproved of their eldest son's marriage. She would later elaborate on this theme in her novel *Honourable Estate*, in which the characters of the wealthy Stephen

Alleyndene and his wife Jessie, whom he meets when she works as a governess in his parents' household, are modelled on her own parents.[13]

But in contrast to the fictional Alleyndenes, the actual marriage of Vera Brittain's parents was in no way a misalliance. While the Brittains were successful business people, Thomas Arthur himself was not a member of the landed upper-middle class (as is the fictional Stephen Alleyndene), nor was Edith a governess in the Brittain household. And although John Inglis Bervon made his living as a musician, he was a church musician of impeccable respectability, and the family outlook was comfortably in harmony with conventional Victorian middle-class values. Indeed, if we view this marriage as a business partnership – and like nearly all bourgeois marriages of the period it was, in part, just such an enterprise – Edith Bervon brought some valuable assets to the arrangement. In her appearance and her patterns of speech, Edith possessed a degree of refinement that surpassed that of most of the Brittain family. For example, Thomas Arthur probably spoke with a Midlands accent, whereas Edith did not.[14] She knew how to dress well and how to decorate a house with flair, and she knew the rules governing social interaction within the provincial circles in which the family would move. She was thus well equipped to act in partnership with her husband in that quest for upward social mobility which was always an important goal of their joint enterprise.

Although many years later, in a moment of intimacy, Edith Brittain would confide to her young daughter that, on her side at least, the marriage had not been a love match,[15] all the evidence suggests that at the time of their marriage, they were a harmonious and happy couple, with shared values and shared aspirations. In 1895 the young couple moved from their 'decorous little villa in the Sidmouth Rd. in Newcastle',[16] to Macclesfield, the Cheshire silk town. Here, they settled into 'Glen Bank', a spacious semi-detached house set in a large garden on the outskirts of the town.[17] Their second child, Edward Harold, was born at 'Glen Bank' on 30 November 1895. They had no further children and we may surmise, as there is no evidence that they suffered from fertility problems, that they conformed to a pattern that was becoming increasingly common among middle-class families, and employed some method of birth control.

In *Testament of Youth*, Vera Brittain described the family home in Macclesfield as typical of the Edwardian provincial middle class: 'Not only in its name, Glen Bank, and its white-painted semi-detachment, but in its hunting pictures and Marcus Stone engravings, its plush curtains, its mahogany furniture and its scarcity of books, our Macclesfield house represented all that was essentially middle class in that Edwardian decade.'[18]

When Brittain wrote that description, she had of course become intensely critical of her Edwardian provincial upbringing but, even then, she allowed that 'I and my brother Edward . . . passed through a childhood which was, to all appearances, as serene and uneventful as any childhood could be',[19] and all the available evidence serves to bear that observation out. The household established by Arthur and Edith Brittain was both secure and serene, with sufficient wealth to maintain a comfortable middle-class standard of life at the outset of the marriage, and, by the Edwardian decade, an upper-middle-class standard; moreover it was a family in which both parents were devoted to their two children.

When the children were very young, the Brittains maintained a domestic staff that included a housekeeper-cook 'Towby', who stayed with them for several years, and was an important part of the children's lives,[20] two maids, and a governess, A.M. Newby, whom Vera Brittain describes in *Testament of Youth* as 'devoted and intelligent' and 'adored'.[21] Glimpses of Vera Brittain's early childhood years can be seen through the surviving correspondence between herself and her parents on the infrequent occasions when Edith Brittain went to visit her relatives, or when Arthur and Edith went on decorous holidays to Brighton or Eastbourne or abroad. These glimpses reveal, on the one hand, the love and gentle serenity of the household, and on the other the care that was taken to ensure that Vera and Edward would remain insulated within their comfortable, well-ordered universe. For example in 1903, when their parents were away on one such holiday, a circus came to Macclesfield. The children both wrote to their mother, asking to be allowed to go, with Vera taking the lead: 'We want to go to the Italian circus very much, please do let us go. It is a shilling each admission and Towby has plenty left over from the housekeeping. It is quite clean & there is nothing objectionable about it, a gentleman told us. . . . Please send a post card . . . saying whether or not we may go . . . there is nothing nasty about it, no freaks or menageries or anything dirty, only acting dogs, ponies, goats. . . .'[22] Edward sent his own supporting letter: 'Do let us go to the Italian circus on Wednesday. . . . Vera is telling you all about it. . . .'[23]

In Charles Dickens's *Hard Times* (1854), the novel's circus people represent a spontaneity and creativity lacking in the emotionally and spiritually dead environment of industrial 'Coketown' and of the Gradgrind household. For Tom and Louisa, the Gradgrind children, the circus represents a world of colour and emotional depth, but their father is horrified when he finds them there, for the circus represents to him the negation of his Utilitarian value system. The oppositional relationship between the Gradgrinds and the circus people represents Dickens's symbolic use of what was a commonplace middle-class mistrust of such potentially unruly folk, and of the gulf between popular and middle-class taste. The incident just recounted from the Brittain family's experience suggests that half a century later such mistrust still existed.

The fictional mid-Victorian characters Tom and Louisa Gradgrind bear little relationship to the real Edwardian children Vera and Edward Brittain (if Mrs Brittain did object to the circus, it would only have been on such matter-of-fact grounds that it might be dirty or frightening), but there is one similarity between their situations. In contrast to Mr Gradgrind who tells Sissy Jupe the circus child that she must 'never wonder', the Brittains had no ideological objection to 'wonder'. However, their household was not designed to encourage it. As a child, therefore, Vera Brittain had to nourish her own creativity.

Her position as the eldest child helped to foster in her a spirit of inventiveness and a sense of the pleasure of adventure. During their early childhood, Vera appears to have been the more forceful and imaginative of the two children. For example, she told her brother stories, inventing a 'mythical community called "The Dicks"'.[24] While there is no indication that as a young girl she felt any less loved than her brother, or constrained in any way by her sex, by adolescence the sex discrimination practised within the family would be painful to her, and there is plenty of evidence that the Brittains' family life both exemplified and encouraged masculine privilege and conventional patterns of behaviour for males and females.[25] Arthur Brittain was occupied with his business, leaving the management of the household to his wife and the female staff. Arthur was strong-willed and used to getting his own way, whereas Edith was gentle and retiring in manner. We can assume that just as the children would have learned lessons about their social position from the careful way in which they were insulated from the dirt and disorder of the outside world, Vera and Edward would also have absorbed messages about gender from their surroundings.

A minor incident when Vera was ten years old demonstrates the way in which she was subjected to conventional assumptions about gender difference. When the senior Brittains were away for a few days, the children and their governess saw a mouse in the nursery.

Vera's letter to her mother, complete with illustration, reads: 'I saw a mouse in the place & Edward saw it in the nursery . . . and Spot came running . . . and he caught it and killed it. . . .' Miss Newby saw fit to add a postscript, explaining that Vera had responded with stereotypically feminine shrieks, and Edward with stereotypically masculine bravery: 'all is going on very comfortably and the children are very well . . . we had a great fright over the poor little mouse . . . Vera *shrieked*, I picked up my dress & rushed away, & Edward was very bold and took the poker and tried to kill it.'[26]

Vera's fear of the mouse suggests one shadow over her childhood that she does explicitly mention in *Testament of Youth*, namely the 'irrational fears which were always waiting to torment me – fears of thunder, of sunsets, of the full moon, of the dark'.[27] But on some occasions she dealt with these fears by experimenting with fearlessness, as when she wrote, when her parents were travelling in Switzerland, asking her mother to send her insects, and suggesting that it was her mother who might be afraid: 'If you find any moths or any pretty insects any pretty beetles or moths please send them to me that is if you are not afraid. . . .'[28]

Fantasy was the most significant way that Vera Brittain dealt with the ripples under the surface of the matter-of-fact happiness that constituted her childhood milieu. The literary sources which nourished this childhood creativity were limited (in *Testament of Youth*, Brittain emphasizes the lack of books in the Brittain household) but significant. Andrew Lang's fairy tales had a profound influence on Vera Brittain that continued to adulthood. She also mentions girls' fiction, like that by L.T. Meade, which she characterizes as 'saccharin', but enjoyed as a child, and Victorian melodrama: she mentions in particular the novels of Wilkie Collins and Mrs Henry Wood. From the girls' stories, as well as from the sensational novels, she would have gained contact with a world of emotions far more heated and violent than those she encountered in actual experience. Much of the girls' literature of Vera Brittain's childhood was influenced by such traditions of Victorian melodrama as the heroine who sacrifices herself for others, the heroine who suffers and is rewarded by love, and the heroine who is seduced and suffers and dies for love.[29] In addition to these limiting and oppressive motifs, girls' fiction also, but to a lesser extent, offered stronger and more self-reliant images of women.

Several 'novels' she wrote as a child show how she used this array of literary genres in combination with her own experience. These are charming relics of the girlhood of someone who would later become a professional writer, but they also reveal how an intelligent girl absorbed and assimilated some of the ideas and images that pervaded Victorian fantasy, melodrama and girls' fiction concerning woman's nature and role. Vera's childhood fictions are filled with violent death and with the motif of self-sacrifice. Vera's favorite character – who bears her mother's name, Edith – can be either heroine or villainess. She dies in one story only to be reborn in the next. The stories all touchingly reveal Vera's love for her home and surroundings: they are all set in or near Macclesfield (a locale which the adult Vera would consider a most unlikely setting for drama or melodrama), which in one story Edith is said to have 'loved and cherished with all her affectionate girlish heart'. There is one school story which nicely mirrors the tone of Edwardian school-girl fiction: 'The school of St Margaret was a country school, and a very good one, too. . . . It then held about twenty-six girls.'[30]

Vera herself did not go to school until 1905, when she was eleven. In that year, the family moved from Macclesfield to Buxton in Derbyshire, which was to be their home until Arthur and Edith moved to London during the First World War. According to Vera Brittain herself, the family made the move 'in order that Edward and I might be sent to "good" day schools',[31] her choice of inverted commas for 'good' displaying her own awareness of the fact that her parents' assessment of Buxton's schools extended beyond a concern with their intrinsic qualities as educational institutions. For middle-class families like the Brittains, a judicious selection of schooling for their sons, and to a lesser extent for their daughters, was one important way to raise their social status.[32] Unquestionably, a desire for upward social mobility did figure in the family's move to Buxton. Their earliest move from Newcastle-under-Lyme to Macclesfield had taken them some distance from the grimy ambiance of urban Staffordshire, and for the sake of his family Arthur Brittain had willingly made the daily railway journey from Cheshire to Hanley, where his business was situated. Buxton, in the Derbyshire Peak District was even farther removed, both physically and psychologically, from the source of the family's wealth.

In the first decade of the twentieth century, Buxton was at the height of its success as a watering town. With its grey stone buildings and its 'bracing' climate it had a northern austerity, but it also offered a certain elegance with its fine eighteenth-century Crescent, its attractive Pavilion and Public Gardens, its Opera House and its collection of expensive hotels.[33] Although never as fashionable as the Continental spas, Buxton did attract a wealthy seasonal clientele,[34] and a group of substantial business and professional families who made the town their permanent home. The Brittains aspired to join this latter group and by 1905 Arthur Brittain had achieved an income which would allow the family to do so. Their new family home, 'Melrose', a spacious, handsome stone house situated in The Park, Buxton's most desirable residential area, provided a good foundation for such acceptance.[35]

Edith Brittain bore the brunt of the responsibility for the work of elevating the family's social status. She engaged in charitable work, she entertained and she entered into the complex rituals surrounding social calls.[36] The education of both children, but especially of Edward, was also part of the family's strategy to gain an unequivocal claim on gentility. In 1908, the Brittains would send Edward to Uppingham, a well-respected public school and, had the First World War not intervened, he would have gone to New College, Oxford. Despite the Brittain family's prosperity, Arthur Brittain's father had not considered a public school or university education essential to his son's future prospects. In contrast, Arthur and Edith believed that these signs of upper-middle-class status were essential for their son and for the family as a whole.[37]

Vera's education was also planned with an eye to social status, although she would not be aware of this until her late teens. In *Testament of Youth*, she says of her Buxton day-school that it 'inevitably described itself as "a school for the daughters of gentlemen"'.[38] 'The Grange', which was the sort of girls' school small enough to be accommodated in a private house, was within walking distance of the Brittains' home, and its headmistress was a family acquaintance.[39] The girls studied arithmetic, French and German, and played hockey and cricket, as well as doing 'drill' – that is, calisthenics. Vera's first report card describes her as 'a very intelligent pupil'.[40]

As the family settled into Buxton, life continued happily for Vera, despite the departure of the children's beloved governess, A.M. Newby.[41] Letters to her mother reveal her as an energetic child with a well-developed sense of curiosity. In October 1905, for example, she wrote to tell her mother that she had been looking at various objects with her 'microscobe' (*sic*). A few months later, when Edith Brittain again spent a few days away from home, Vera wrote a letter proudly reporting her physical accomplishments: 'Today in Drill we had a jumping competition . . . I jumped . . . [O]nly my dress caught after I got over . . . the height was 3 ft. 10 inches. . . .'[42]

While Vera Brittain would later caricature The Grange in her novel *Not Without Honour* (1924) as second-rate and uninspiring, it prepared her more than adequately for her next experience, St Monica's School, in Surrey, which she began attending in 1907. St Monica's had been founded by Louise Heath Jones (1869–1931), who had herself attended Cheltenham Ladies' College, and then Newnham College, Cambridge.[43] Like so many early university-educated women of talent, Heath Jones entered the profession of teaching girls of the middle and upper classes, first as a mistress at St Leonard's School in St Andrews, and then founding St Monica's in 1902. St Monica's was selected for Vera Brittain because her mother's oldest sister, Florence Bervon, was Louise Heath Jones's partner and life-long companion. Intrinsically and in terms of the social status of its clientele, many of whom were wealthy, well-connected families,[44] it was a better school than the Brittains would have been able to find for Vera without the family connection.[45]

When Vera Brittain eulogized her aunt at the time of her death in 1936, she wrote of the 'remarkable friendship' between Florence Bervon and Louise Heath Jones. The relationship was both business partnership and intimate friendship, and it lasted until the latter's death in 1931. Of the two, Florence Bervon was the more conventional and less intellectually complex but she had reserves of emotional and physical strength that Louise Heath Jones did not possess. Her niece would later describe Bervon as 'one of the pioneer women who achieved economic independence long before careers for both sexes became a matter of course',[46] but in fact the limited financial resources of her family had not allowed her to acquire a modern woman's education. It was Louise Heath Jones who had achieved that, and in large part it was Heath Jones whose ideas shaped St Monica's. But Bervon's strength of character and organizational skills also contributed to the joint enterprise. Moreover, soon after Vera left the school, Louise Heath Jones suffered a breakdown from which she never fully recovered, and its day-to-day management passed into the hands of Florence Bervon. Although no evidence exists to support an assertion that the two women actively chose to make a life together in preference to heterosexual marriage, they did create for themselves what Martha Vicinus has called a 'woman-controlled space', a community in which work and home were amalgamated.[47]

In *Testament of Youth*, Brittain would express her ambivalence about the education she received at St Monica's, acknowledging its strengths but at the same time describing it as a finishing school for wealthy girls which failed to prepare her in any direct way for university entrance.[48] Brittain's assessment of the school's conflicting objectives was largely correct. In its early years St Monica's was a small private school catering to a wealthy clientele, but its founders did not believe that their pupils should become mere 'ornaments'. Like other progressive headmistresses of the late-Victorian and Edwardian periods, Louise Heath Jones's attitude toward the upper-middle-class woman's role was a contradictory mixture.[49] She supported advancement for women, but at the same time she supported the older values associated with the Victorian ideal of femininity. St Monica's earnest motto, 'Service and Sanctification', would have suited an Edwardian boys' school, but would never have been adopted by the proprietors of a typical Victorian 'school for the daughters of gentlemen'. It reflects Heath Jones's and Bervon's intention to establish a school for girls that would in part exemplify male public-school ideals of leadership and public service.

St Monica's offered a rigorous curriculum similar to that of a boys' public school, although there was considerably less emphasis on the classics and more emphasis on history and modern literature.[50] However, the school was not, as were some girls' and all boys' schools for children from this social stratum, focused on preparing its pupils for university entrance, and it is in this regard that the views of the school's select clientele probably had their influence. Fitting their daughters for professional occupations was not of primary concern to St Monica's parents, and we can surmise that it was for this reason that the school did not make the organized effort characteristic of larger girls' schools to ensure that its girls would in the normal course of their studies be prepared for public examinations. However, the girls could and did take such examinations.[51]

During her four years at the school, St Monica's had a profound influence on Brittain's development. Entering the school at thirteen, she experienced there the crises of adolescence and began forging an identity separate from that of her parents. She did indeed rebel, rejecting in part, although not entirely, her parents' values. Most notably she developed a sense of herself as ambitious, with a desire for personal autonomy and achievement and with a love of serious intellectual work. Arthur and Edith Brittain had expected that Edward would gradually become more detached from the family when he went to Uppingham, but independence on the part of their daughter they could not, initially at least, either understand or accept. Unquestionably Arthur and Edith would have preferred it had Vera experienced boarding-school as the culmination of her education and returned home at eighteen ready to accept the role of provincial debutante.

St Monica's provided an environment that fostered Vera's developing independence. The school offered subtle but important differences when contrasted with the milieu of her home. The tone of the Brittain household, with its stability and its attention to outward form, was largely set by her mother; and while her father was given to outbursts of irritability, the household was one in which calm, order and harmony were valued over intensity of feeling. St Monica's, while it also valued order and propriety, offered Vera for the first time the possibility of intensity of feeling in human relationships, along with a genuine widening of her intellectual horizons.

Brittain occupied a privileged position in her relationship to the two headmistresses, but also a difficult one. She was, of course, well acquainted with her Aunt Florence before she went to St Monica's, but it appears that Florence Bervon kept a certain distance between herself and Vera, to emphasize that Vera was at St Monica's primarily as a pupil, and not as her niece. This distance is reflected in the fact that Brittain refers to her aunt as 'Miss Bervon' in her youthful 'Reflective Record'. The two headmistresses impressed their personalities on the school community they created in a forceful manner, but also in a way that fell decidedly within the mould of prevailing definitions of femininity. They sought to influence their pupils not merely through moral suasion and intellectual authority, but through their emotions. For example, they introduced a prefect system modelled on that of a boys' public school. Vera was part of this school hierarchy in her final year, but her description of the relationship between teachers and pupils suggests that the prefect system at St Monica's was much less of a rule-governed, masculine-style institution than that experienced by Edward at Uppingham. It was more feminine and more familial. The two headmistresses expected all the girls, but especially the prefects, to be responsible, disciplined and able to set a good example, but they appear to have used emotional persuasion and to have provoked scenes involving tears and remorse to effect changes in individual girls and in the school as a whole to a much greater extent than was common at Edwardian boys' schools.[52]

Brittain quickly proved to be one of the school's most promising pupils, and both headmistresses, but especially Louise Heath Jones, became closely involved in her intellectual development. In *Testament of Youth*, Brittain acknowledges this influence and explains how much she benefited from Louise Heath Jones's remarkable personality. She tells of her commitment to expanding the intellectual horizons of the pupils in her lessons on history and scripture; to informing them of politics and current events by providing them with newspaper articles (the clippings were carefully culled from newspapers, to which the girls were not allowed access); and to introducing them to her quiet, but unmistakable feminism. She even took Vera and a small number of other senior girls to a suffrage meeting in 1911. The meeting they attended was a constitutionalist, not a militant one; even so, Heath Jones was acting with considerable courage in exposing her pupils to suffrage activism during a period when the press was highlighting militant suffragism. This would have been anathema to most of her pupils' parents.[53]

Brittain goes on to explain that Louise Heath Jones introduced her to a wide range of reading and this must truly have been a great release after the limited offerings available to her at home. In *Testament of Youth*, Brittain mentioned three texts of special significance to which she was introduced by Heath Jones. The first was Shelley's poem 'Adonais', 'which taught me in the most startling and impressive fashion of my childhood's experience to perceive beauty embodied in literature, and made me finally determine to become the writer I had dreamed of being ever since I was seven years old'.[54]

The second text was Mrs Humphry Ward's novel *Robert Elsmere* (1888). That successful but controversial novel, which evoked the Victorian 'crisis of faith', remained in 1911 a bold choice for a sheltered girls' private school. In *Testament of Youth* Brittain would claim that *Robert Elsmere* 'converted me from an unquestioning if somewhat indifferent church-goer into an anxiously interrogative agnostic'.[55] As we shall see in the next chapter, the term 'agnostic' suggests stronger religious doubt than she actually experienced during these years, but reading Ward's novel did encourage Brittain to question Anglican orthodoxy.

The third text was Olive Schreiner's feminist classic *Woman and Labour*, the most daring of all of Heath Jones's selections for this favourite pupil. Brittain apparently read it in 1911, the year it was published. In 1926 she would write that, in her evolution towards feminism, Schreiner's work 'sounded with a note that had the authentic ring of a new gospel'.[56] She described her first encounter with the book and with its message 'We take all labour for our province' more fully in one of *Testament of Youth*'s most moving passages:

> Thus it was in St Monica's garden . . . that I first visualised in rapt childish ecstasy a world in which women would no longer be the

> second-rate, unimportant creatures that they were now considered, but the equal and respected companions of men.[57]

It was through Louise Heath Jones, then, that Vera Brittain learned about feminism. This was a crucial formative experience for her. Just as she was experiencing discontent and realizing that the life her parents and her society had in mind for her would be severely limited because of her sex, she was exposed to feminist language and feminist solutions. These enabled the still-adolescent Vera to name her discontent in a manner that offered positive solutions. Historian Philippa Levine has noted the importance of family influence in creating feminist consciousness among some nineteenth-century feminists. In the case of Vera Brittain, who was niece as well as pupil at St Monica's, the extended family that the school represented certainly nurtured her feminist awareness.[58] She acknowledged this herself in *Testament of Youth*: 'the foundations of that conviction [about feminism] were first laid, strangely enough, at a school which was apparently regarded by many of the parents who patronised it as a means of equipping girls to be men's decorative and contented inferiors'.[59]

Louise Heath Jones was not the only St Monica's teacher who had a formative influence on Brittain's development. Equally important was Edith Fry, a mistress hired on a part-time basis by St Monica's in 1910. In 1911, when she began to keep a diary, Brittain recorded the importance that Edith Fry had for her. In her summary of the autumn or 'Michaelmas' term of 1910, she wrote:

> The most important of all terms so far–as it marked the rising of my star. . . . During the term Miss H.J. got a visiting mistress, a Miss Fry –to take her lessons. I never met anyone who so attracted me, both intellectually and otherwise. She is not good looking really, but has one of the most fascinating, clever and sympathetic faces that I ever saw . . . whether due really to her, or whether due to some development that growing out of childhood must bring, I cannot say – I only know that the strange, irresistible, yet beautiful shadows of greater things, which had puzzled yet fascinated me for so long shaped themselves into a world, not of this one, but in it, since I am in it, in which visions and imaginations and ideals became sometimes more real than the everyday world.[60]

Martha Vicinus has analysed the significance of intense relationships between teachers and pupils in girls' boarding schools of the Victorian and Edwardian years. When Vicinus writes of such relationships, that 'differences in age and authority created a distance that intensified desire',[61] she could well have been describing Vera Brittain's feelings for Fry. On a personal and emotional level Fry provided Vera with an example of a woman's life that was very different from the models offered by Buxton. She was 'fascinating, clever and sympathetic', as Vera wrote in her diary, and also, from Vera's limited perspective, somewhat unconventional. She was clearly more open and frank with Vera than any other mistress at St Monica's was, and may have been the first person Vera admired who voiced any criticism of the mores and the milieu in which she had been brought up.

If Vera had a schoolgirl crush on Edith Fry, it was primarily because this teacher offered her an introduction to adult, intellectually stimulating writers, and a chance to discuss them and write about them in a serious way. Edith Fry encouraged her to read Ruskin and Carlyle who, as she confided to her diary, fired her with a new enthusiasm and strengthened her determination to become a writer herself: '[M]y writing tends towards a purpose now–I want to write, but I will not reveal what until the time shall come. I believe this is greatly due to Miss Fry's teaching, and her understanding of Carlyle and Ruskin, about whom she taught us, so differently to the dull, hackneyed type of "literature" that so many English mistresses make use of today.'[62] Years later, Brittain's gratitude to her teacher remained undiminished, despite the waning, by the post-Victorian 1930s, of her admiration for the Victorian literary giants to whom Fry had introduced her.[63]

Edith Fry's reading assignments included the poems of Robert Browning, the *Orestea* of Aeschylus and Thomas More's *Utopia*, all of which, while fine literature and stimulating reading, were choices that did not violate Edwardian convention. In a more daring vein Fry also assigned William Morris and H.G. Wells, writers whose social and political ideas did challenge the verities of bourgeois society. Vera did not approve of Morris. Her essay on his Utopian *News from Nowhere* reveals both her conventional social and political beliefs and her unquestioning acceptance of Victorian moral earnestness. Morris's London, she says, 'is a city of self-satisfaction, living in the gorgeous present, seeing no sanctity in the past. . . . Life is merely an amusing game, in which men's minds have little influence, and where the contemplative life, that "better part" once so highly commended, has no place. The idea that "Life is real! Life is earnest!" seems to have been entirely lost.' She criticizes his socialism ('when competition ceases, most of a country's energy ceases with it') and rejects his suggestion that the cause of crime is to be found in class distinctions, insisting that its causes are to be found in original sin.[64]

If Edith Fry's lessons encouraged Brittain to read a writer like Morris, but at the same time to reject his social criticism, the milieu of the school and her own predilections allowed her to be less conventional concerning feminism, about which she commented in an essay on More's *Utopia*: '[Women's] rights are a burning question not only in their own, but in male minds, and not infrequently their voices are heard in our streets demanding of the age a speedy reparation for the injuries of neglect done to them by the "centuries that are gone".'[65]

Brittain's attachments to Louise Heath Jones and Edith Fry were intense, but it was an intensity of manageable proportions. Her 'disciplined love'[66] for these admired women authority figures contributed to her developing maturity, autonomy and self-control. In contrast, her close friendships with contemporaries at school proved to be so confusing that in recollecting them two decades later in *Testament of Youth*, Brittain pushed them virtually out of sight, saying merely that '[t]he only intimate friends that I made at Kingswood were a small, dark, half-foreign girl, and a pretty, fair sweet-natured Anglo-Saxon, whose names might very suitably have been Mina and Betty. . . . In neither case did the intimacy long survive our departure from school.'[67]

In her autobiographical novel *Not Without Honour*, published in 1924,[68] which opens at a fictional school, Marchfield Priory (a thinly disguised St Monica's), the heroine, Christine, is portrayed as having few school friends. In this fictional recreation of her school-girl self, we are introduced to a young girl who is proud and sensitive and genuinely out of place in the school-girl milieu because her intellectual development and her aspirations are so much at variance with the ordinary, cheerful, unambitious temperament of most of the school's pupils. Christine has an intensity of emotion which she conceals behind an aloof façade designed to repel any approaches toward friendship on the part of her schoolmates. She is the brilliant prizewinner whom the other girls admire but do not really like.

In creating Christine, Brittain incorporated important aspects of her own school-girl personality, but her fictional creation was also designed to evade some crucial aspects of that personality. Unlike the fictional Christine, or the Vera Brittain of *Testament of Youth*, the relationships of the Vera of the diary, not only with her two closest friends, Stella Sharp and Cora Stoop (the first 'Betty' and the second 'Mina' in *Testament of Youth*), but with the entire school community, were often passionate and engulfing, but at the same time sources of pain and confusion. She deeply desired affirmation and admiration, but at the same time, she feared rejection.

These intense friendships helped her to validate her developing feelings of ambition. Influenced by the unresolved mixture of masculine and feminine values to which she was exposed at St Monica's, Vera often expressed her desire for achievement in terms that were passionate, but at the same time considerably more vague than they would have been had she been a talented, ambitious boy. This diary entry, made when she was home for the Christmas holidays in 1910, reveals the flavour of her hopes and feelings: 'Read Tennyson after supper to the accompaniment of Edward's violin . . . thought a good deal about the dream-world and the future, with its longed for independence and wider life.'[69]

While the approval and encouragement of the teachers she admired were important to her, she also needed an intimate friend of her own age with whom she could share these inchoate dreams of a 'wider life'. Her first such confidante was Stella Sharp, who had entered St Monica's in the summer term of 1910. Vera and Stella became intimate friends in the autumn of 1910, the same term in which Edith Fry came to the school and made such a great impression on Vera. The friendship allowed her to talk about her emotional and intellectual feelings for Edith Fry: 'I told Stella a good bit of all this. . . . I found that to know her was to trust her & to trust to love. . . .'[70]

The friendship blossomed throughout 1910, and in fact became so intense that in February 1911 the two headmistresses intervened, feeling that the two girls were spending so much time together that they were neglecting their duties to the school community.[71] They were also worried about the moodiness that Vera had been displaying. Fortunately, both women displayed considerable sensitivity at this juncture, and proved themselves able to give Vera the adult support she needed during this time of adolescent storm and stress: 'to my great joy, they understood as I never knew they would do', she wrote.[72]

Vera defined her friendship with Stella Sharp as one in which she was dominant. When they were still school-girls, she reports scolding Stella for 'slackness'.[73] By 1913, she would write, accurately: 'I am afraid the "passion" part of my affection for her has died out for good and all.'[74] The 'passion' may have dissipated early on, but this friendship endured through the war years and into the post-war decades. Cora Stoop, Brittain's other close school-girl friend who was, like Stella Sharp, from a London family, possessed greater sophistication than either Stella or Vera. Cora is almost certainly the model for the Jewish Rachael in *Not Without Honour*. In her portrayal of Rachael there are disturbing anti-Semitic overtones:

'Rachael Meyer . . . was a Jewess, and though this meant that she was intelligent, it also meant that she was too rich to be anything but lazy.'[75] Vera became friendly with Cora probably during her last term at St Monica's, and the friendship continued to be an intense one after they had left school, until Cora ended it in anger in 1916.[76] In this relationship, Cora was dominant both during their school days and in the years following. Vera was never certain of Cora's affection and frequently felt hurt by what she perceived as Cora's rejection or neglect of her.[77]

From her arrival in 1907, when she was thirteen, until her departure in December 1911, just before her eighteenth birthday, St Monica's provided Vera Brittain with a supportive milieu. It was, first and foremost, the place where she received the foundation of her education. What St Monica's did not provide was help in planning her future. Her parents assumed that on completing school she would come home to Buxton, 'come out', and occupy herself as a 'provincial young lady' until she got married. Originally, they intended that she would leave St Monica's at the end of the school year in 1911. At seventeen, Vera herself, while she had ambitions and already hoped to become a writer, had no clear idea of what she wanted to do after leaving school. She knew that she did not immediately wish to return to Buxton. Stella was to spend a year in Brussels 'finishing' her education, and Vera was greatly disappointed when her parents would not agree that she could do this too. They would offer her only an extra term at St Monica's and, with the urging of her Aunt Florence, Vera settled for this compromise.[78]

Why did the school's two headmistresses (one of whom was Vera's aunt) not suggest to her parents that further education would be an appropriate choice for their daughter? They had given this promising pupil glowing reports throughout her years with them, and they fully acknowledged her writing ambitions. 'Vera should write some day',[79] wrote Louise Heath Jones on one of Vera's last school reports. Heath Jones, having herself attended Newnham, was familiar with the Cambridge and Oxford women's colleges. Finally, they themselves valued achievement and they cared deeply about women's rights. But the fact was that, as an attractive girl from an affluent family with no need to earn her own living, Vera was expected to marry, and it was assumed that marriage must determine her future. This seemed both preferable and inevitable, not only to her parents but to the two unmarried ladies. Heath Jones may have given Vera Olive Schreiner to read, but even she was too firmly enmeshed in the class and gender assumptions of the period to encourage Vera to pursue a path that, while less remarkable than it had been in her own generation, was still unusual. So, in December 1911, just before her eighteenth birthday, Vera left St Monica's, to return home with her strong if unformulated ambitions, to loving but conventional parents who assumed that her formal education was now complete.

3

'Provincial Young Ladyhood', 1911–1914

Vera Brittain came home from St Monica's in December 1911, just before her eighteenth birthday. Her parents assumed that she would now enter into the family's social life as a young adult and she herself anticipated the 'coming out' rituals then considered appropriate for a daughter of the provincial upper middle class: to make her 'debut' at a local ball; to be her mother's companion in the daytime round of calling and entertaining which still formed a major part of the activities of upper-middle-class adult women; to take part in the recreational and charitable pursuits considered appropriate for unmarried young women.

The significance of these activities had altered little over the course of two generations. In 1912 it was as true as it had been at the height of the Victorian era that an attractive, well-educated, appropriately turned-out daughter enhanced a family's social status. And, of course, the major purpose of the rituals of 'coming out' had not changed: in 1912, no less than in 1850 or 1890, a young woman's main business was to marry as well as possible, and her social network existed in order to enable her to do so.[1]

In the years just before the First World War, 'society' in Buxton was still dominated at its highest levels by the landed families from the surrounding countryside, the most prominent of whom were the Dukes of Devonshire, Buxton's original landlords and primary benefactors. These 'county' families presided over such important town social events as the Hunt Ball, but for the most part the Tory landed families kept themselves aloof from the town's business, and Buxton's civic and social life was controlled by its business and professional elite which was Liberal in politics and Anglican in religion. Below them was a solid group of prosperous tradespeople and shopkeepers, which was also Liberal in politics, but non-conformist in religion. At the bottom of the social hierarchy were Buxton's working people.[2]

Civic activities included the work of the Town Council and the management of Buxton's principal charities, the Devonshire Hospital and the newer, smaller Cottage Hospital. In the pre-war decade these remained primarily male preserves but the organisation of day-to-day charitable work and of social events fell largely to the wives and daughters of the male business and professional elite. Such events included once-a-year occasions like the Old Folks' Dinner, the Midsummer 'well-dressing' – an ancient ceremony in which the town's water sources were decorated with flowers – and the Cottage Hospital Ball. Year-round activities included groups like the Mothers' Union.

The town had an active cultural and social life. The new Opera House and the large hotels hosted performances by touring singers and theatrical companies[3] and there were, as well, amateur theatricals and recitals by local talent. The Buxton Cricket, Bowling and Tennis Club was the centre for sport for the well-to-do, along with the golf-links in nearby Fairfield. The most important events of the Buxton social season were held at the large resort hotels. In the years 1912–14 these included the Buxton Hydropathic, the Peak Hydro, the Empire and St Ann's Hotel. The Hunt Ball of the High Peak Harriers and the Cottage Hospital Ball, both held in January, were fixtures of the social calendar, but there were other formal dances, as well as a continual round of private entertaining: 'at homes'; bridge parties; tennis parties; and, in addition, the ritual of calling and returning calls. And in fine weather, there was the church parade in the Buxton Gardens on Sunday where in the Edwardian era 'men wore top-hats and frock coats, and the ladies were . . . swathed in voluminous clothes'.[4]

There was also a more serious side to Buxton life. Liberal politics provided possibilities for activity for both men and women[5] and in addition, with the establishment of a branch of the National Union of Women's Suffrage Societies at Buxton in 1912, the town offered scope for feminist activism. By 1913, the adjacent village of Fairfield even had a branch of the militant Women's Social and Political Union.[6]

In the Brittain family it was Edith rather than Arthur who took the initiative in engaging in social and civic activities in the community. She was active in the Mothers' Union, she arranged musical evenings at her own home and kept a regular 'at home' afternoon. In 1912 and succeeding years, during Vera's period as a debutante, Edith became even more active: during 1913, she served on the Ladies Committee which organized the 1914 Cottage Hospital Ball.[7] In contrast, Arthur, perhaps because his business and his daily commuting between Buxton and Handley took so much of his energies, or perhaps because he was temperamentally unsuited to such activity, did not perform the masculine equivalents of his wife's involvements. He did not, as did other men of his acquaintance, serve on the town council or on the management board of either hospital.

Arthur's reluctance to participate in Buxton's social and civic life must have been distressing for Edith, and for that reason alone she would have been delighted by the prospect of Vera's return from school and entrance into young ladyhood. By 1912, Edith Brittain's efforts to forge upwardly mobile social contacts had been successful enough to ensure that her young daughter would be accepted by Buxton society as a debutante. Vera herself was ready to conform, outwardly at least, to her mother's expectations. At eighteen her personality combined a number of potentially contradictory possibilities. On the one hand she had indeed discovered her fundamental core of seriousness, her commitment to spiritual and intellectual growth and her desire for personal achievement. On the other hand, in outward manner and appearance she had matured into a lively, accomplished, extremely pretty young woman. Even before she left school, she had begun to enjoy mixed parties. In her 1911 diary she mentions several which took place during the holidays of that January: 'We had an "at home" in the evening for grown-up unmarrieds and "flappers". The first thing was a treasure hunt and the second a musical romance competition.'[8] And even before she had left St Monica's, Vera's life-long interest in dress had begun to develop: when she was at home on vacation in 1911 she made frequent references in her diary to new clothes. So in 1912, with her family assuming that she would as a matter of course enjoy the rewards her prettiness and her social grace could bring her, she did not resist. For a brief period her serious but still unformulated plans for her future were shelved, and she entered willingly and even enthusiastically into the life of a provincial debutante.

Vera made her debut at the High Peak Hunt Ball on 9 January 1912,[9] held that year in the grand ball-room of the Buxton Hydropathic Hotel. Vera and her mother had been occupying themselves with her coming-out clothes since the summer, and for the important Hunt Ball her dress – which she would describe much later in *Testament of Youth* as 'the conventional white satin and pearls' – was ordered from London.[10] The debut of their only daughter was a quiet affair, however; perhaps disappointingly quiet for the Brittains. The account of the ball which appeared in the local paper did not, on this occasion, include either a description of her dress or a mention of her name. A measure of Vera's success as a debutante during 1912 is that a year later, in January 1913, she was mentioned in the accounts of both major events of the Buxton season. On both occasions her choice of dress was more assertive than the demure white satin of the year before. To the 1913 Cottage Hospital Ball 'Miss Brittain' wore 'a lovely gown of canary satin charmeuse with gold and jewelled embroidery over which was most gracefully draped sky-blue ninon'. To the High Peak Hunt Ball, held a week later, she wore a 'blue frock with white tunic'.[11]

During the year and a half in which life as a 'provincial young lady' was her primary occupation, these formal dances formed the high point of a busy schedule. Vera went to entertainments at other people's houses and helped her parents to entertain at Melrose; she assisted her mother in receiving callers; she played golf and tennis, the latter at the Buxton Cricket, Lawn Bowling and Tennis Club in the park adjacent to Melrose. On Sundays, along with the rest of the family, she took part in the church parade in the Pavilion Gardens.

Privately, and as a countervailing influence to the bustling social life in which she was involved, she continued to read and to be inspired by what she read: 'I finished *Felix Holt* after dinner. How George Eliot's books do inspire me; they make all good seem worthwhile', she recorded in February 1913.[12] She also continued her study of the piano.[13] But although opportunities for doing so existed in Buxton, Vera did not during these years develop the nascent interest in the women's movement which Louise Heath Jones had sparked at St Monica's. Although Brittain and her family knew several of the people who were involved in the Buxton branch of the National Union of Women's Suffrage Societies, there is no indication that she was ever involved in the group or that she was even aware of its existence.

If she had ventured into this more serious side of Buxton's civic life she might have made congenial friends of her own age. As it was, she made no real friends during her period of young ladyhood in Buxton. She met no one with whom she could enjoy genuine companionship, as she had with Stella Sharp or Cora Stoop, with whom she continued to correspond, but from whom she felt herself increasingly cut off. So that although Vera was a social success, she was lonely and fundamentally dissatisfied with herself and with her prospects for the future. At the end of a June day, when she'd spent yet another long afternoon playing tennis in the company of a girl for whom she felt little affinity, she wrote in her diary: 'I fear I am going to bed in the sort of depressed mood mother often mistakes for discontent, which is really of longing unsatisfied, I don't quite know for what but I think for more fulness of life and love! If *only* I had someone to really love & be friendly with what a different place Buxton would be!'[14]

In this period in which she had no close friends of her own age, Vera directed her expressive nature and absorbing interest in human relationships into several largely one-sided involvements with Buxton people she admired. The two most important were with Joseph Harry Ward, Anglican curate of Fairfield, a village adjacent to Buxton,[15] and Mrs John Harrison, wife of the proprietor of the St Ann's Hotel. In 1913 Vera conceived a passionate admiration for each of them, an admiration which absorbed much of her fantasy life during 1913 and 1914. In both cases, the quality of the fascination resembled her attachment to her St Monica's teacher, Edith Fry. Like Fry, both Harrison and Ward were considerably older than she was, but younger than her parents. Neither was a close friend of the Brittain family. Indeed, both Harrison and Ward appeared to Vera in 1913 to be on the fringes of Buxton society, and this made them especially attractive to her because they represented to some degree a challenge to what she was beginning to reject as Buxton's smugness.

Vera was attracted to Mrs John Harrison because she seemed less constrained and more vivid than the usual Buxton matron and also much less conventional. She was involved, for example, in the work of bringing university extension lecturers to Buxton. Moreover, Vera saw her as having established herself in Buxton society not through her husband, but through the force of her own character and cultural interests. Vera records in her diary that on one occasion – they were playing tennis together – Mrs Harrison told her that at first she had been barred from admission to the tennis club. 'It is disgraceful', Vera comments, 'the way people here – the snobs! – have treated her simply because she had the courage to marry Mr Harrison, who being the proprietor of St Ann's Hotel was lower in the social scale, & of course with these parvenus the fact that he is clever & well-educated doesn't count at all.'[16] From Vera's perspective, championing Mrs Harrison was a way of challenging what she considered to be Buxton's false standards. Vera actually spent very little time alone with her idol – the conversation recorded above was one of their few *tête-à-têtes* – but this actual distance increased Vera's admiration. 'She certainly gets to attract me more & more', Vera wrote, a few days after the tennis game. 'I am by way of feeling quite a g.p. [grand passion] for her.'[17]

Joseph Harry Ward, the clergyman, challenged conservative religious sensibilities in Buxton by his support for the 'Higher Criticism'.[18] For Brittain, Ward's sermons breathed new life into Anglicanism. During this period, Brittain did have strong religious feelings, but she was also having troubling doubts about orthodox, trinitarian Christianity; doubts, we may surmise, that had first been aroused at St Monica's when she read *Robert Elsmere*. The ritual at St John's, Buxton's parish church, did nothing to dispel her spiritual discomfort. For Vera, the sermons of the parish's vicar, the Reverend Canon Scott-Moncrieff, who took up his parish duties in December 1911, the same month that she returned home from St Monica's, seemed stiff, formal and lifeless.[19] 'Felt the usual sleepiness – I may say boredom – in church. Oh! "Church of England", where is the *King*, that I may worship him?', she wrote after one Sunday service in January of 1913.[20] In November of that year she would find an answer. Joseph Harry Ward had arrived to take up the post of curate in Fairfield in January 1913, but Vera only became aware of this new presence when he and his views became a matter for local controversy. He is 'a sort of Robert Elsmere', she wrote, and she had a heated argument with her father concerning Ward's heterodox views.[21] One late November Sunday, she and her mother walked over to Fairfield for Ward's evening service: 'He spoke of Christ having revealed to men their own spiritual nature . . . but it is impossible to reproduce his sermon in a few words. . . . He started to speak containedly . . . & worked up to the highest pitch of fierce earnest enthusiasm when speaking of Christ as the Light of the World.'[22] After this first encounter, Vera became an enthusiastic partisan of Joseph Ward's preaching and for some months she perceived him in voice and appearance as a Christlike figure: 'he seems like his Master', she wrote.[23] In 1913 and 1914 she attended his Sunday evening services regularly.

In August 1911, Brittain had allowed her 'Reflective Record', the journal she had begun keeping in 1910, to lapse. In January 1913, just after her nineteenth birthday, she resumed it. The first entry she made, on New Year's Day, reflects both her pleasure in her social success and her unhappiness:

> We danced the New Year in at the Garnetts' yesterday evening; I don't know why I enjoyed it so much, except that I suppose it is gratifying,

> when there are too many girls at a dance, never to have to dance with girls or sit out. Oh! I was so relieved to hear those twelve strokes which announced the departure of 1912 for good & all. I don't know why it was such a miserable year. . . . It was my year of being eighteen too, which is supposed to be a girl's traditional age for happiness – but it is like me to go contrary to this tradition as to so many others! *I* have been far from blameless; I shudder to think how I have thrown a year away – save in experience, which one cannot throw away! – how little I have read, & written practically nothing, how unenergetic, unenterprising I have been, after so many good resolutions, too, last New Year![24]

While it is evident from succeeding entries that Brittain was not often as miserable during 1913 as she was on that New Year's Day, she did feel an increasing urgency to escape from what she often saw as the pettiness and triviality of Buxton and to plan for her future. Resuming her journal was one major way in which she allowed her more introspective, serious side to reassert itself. In 1913, significantly, Brittain's 'Reflective Record' changed character. In 1910 and 1911 it had been an intimate friend, a place where Vera, when still a school-girl, could unselfconsciously pour out her thoughts and freely express her emotions. In 1913 it continued to serve this function but in addition it became, by gradual degrees, a *writer's* diary as Brittain's childhood love of writing took shape as an adult determination to become a writer: 'I am beginning to be very keen about writing at once, though I suppose this should really be my receptive, not my creative, period. . . . I want to go about armed with a notebook & put down all the things, absurd, pathetic, interesting, original, humorous, satirical, that strike me as being useful for material.'[25] Throughout 1913, she formulated plans for what she called her 'Buxton story',[26] a book she would actually write a decade later; it appeared in 1924 as her second novel, *Not Without Honour*.

Although the diary bears witness to the changes in her inner life, for much of 1913 Brittain's outer life continued to be dominated by dances, parties and amateur theatricals. However, it was over the course of 1913 that she took concrete steps to ensure her escape from the stultifying comfort of provincial young ladyhood and the even more stultifying prospect of life as a provincial matron. In gradual stages she conceived the project of becoming a student at one of the Oxford women's colleges. By the autumn of 1913 this had become a firm goal. In 1913 and 1914 she prepared for the examinations necessary for entrance to Somerville College, Oxford, and by the summer of 1914 she had achieved not merely an offer of admission to Somerville, but an Exhibition.[27]

Going to Oxford did indeed prove to be a pivotal decision for Brittain. Her Somerville years provided her with an essential foundation for the adult life she would construct in the 1920s. Oxford also assumed a prominent place in her narratives of her life. Her journey to Somerville dominates the first hundred pages of *Testament of Youth*. Chapter II of the autobiography, which is entitled 'Provincial Young Ladyhood', is both a portrait of provincial society as it was before the Great War, and a condemnatory judgement upon it. In 'Provincial Young Ladyhood', Brittain fashions Oxford into a symbol representing those 'far countries of loveliness, and learning, and discovery' that she so longed for as a young girl. In *Testament of Youth*, Oxford and learning itself are suffused with the glamour of adventure. The freedom they represent stands in opposition to the narrowness and small-mindedness of Buxton, which serves in the book as the epitome of 'bourgeoisdom'.

As she portrays it in *Testament of Youth*, Brittain's decision to attend Oxford sprang from a passionate desire to escape this deadening provinciality, and the limited definition of woman's role that was one of its essential features. She portrays her struggle to become an Oxford student as an archetypical feminist story. She writes of waging a lonely battle against uncongenial surroundings to attain a goal with which her own parents were not in sympathy, and which Buxton regarded as unsuitable and outlandish. She presents herself fighting single-handedly against prejudice and also to overcome her own ignorance and her lack of appropriate formal education.

Readers of *Testament of Youth* are led to assume that Brittain had conceived her plan of becoming an Oxford student during her final year at St Monica's and that she returned home with an unwavering determination to get there. 'I never ceased . . . to pester my parents to send me to college', she says. 'Each fresh refusal to spend another penny on my education . . . plunged me into further depths of gloom; I felt trammelled and trapped. . . . I had nothing to do and no one to talk to. . . .'[28]

As they are presented in *Testament of Youth*, Arthur and Edith Brittain, while not unkind or unloving, are unsuited to understanding their daughter's intellectual aspirations. They appear as conventional people whose ambitions are limited to achieving an assured position within Buxton's upper-middle-class society and whose views about the roles of men and women conform to Victorian stereotypes about male dominance and female subordination. While they had always assumed that their son would go to Oxford, it had never occurred to either of them that a university education might be suitable for their daughter, even though it was Vera rather than Edward, who had excelled as a scholar: 'The most flattering of my school reports had never, I knew, been regarded more seriously than my inconvenient thirst for knowledge and opportunities; in our family, to adapt a famous present-day phrase, what mattered was not the quality of the work, but the sex of the worker.'[29]

In *Testament of Youth*, this impasse between the determined, self-possessed Vera Brittain and her old-fashioned parents is resolved by the arrival of Sir John Marriott, the Oxford historian, who 'during the Spring of 1913'[30] gave a course of University Extension Lectures in Buxton's Town Hall. Sir John, Brittain tells us, 'represents the deus ex machina of my unsophisticated youth, the Olympian who listened without a hint of patronage or amusement to the halting account of a callow girl's vaunting, ingenuous ambitions. To him I owe my final victory over family opposition, my escape from the alien atmosphere of Buxton, and the university education which for all its omissions did at long last equip me for the kind of life that I wanted to lead.'[31]

It was his influence that persuaded her parents that Oxford was a perfectly respectable and feasible goal for a young woman. The Brittains entertained Marriott after his final lecture: 'On this occasion he returned my weekly essay at home after we came back from the now almost empty Town Hall. His praise moved me to speak, in my parents' presence, of my longing to go to Oxford, and I asked his advice with regard to the first steps to be taken. The genial matter-of-factness with which he gave it seemed to dispel all doubts, and made the customary objections look so trivial that they were hardly ever mentioned again.'[32]

The Vera Brittain of *Testament of Youth* is a mature young woman with an unwavering determination to become an Oxford student, and a clear notion of her goals. But the autobiography was not Brittain's only attempt to recreate her Buxton years. The fictional self-portrait in the autobiographical novel *Not Without Honour* stands in striking contrast to the self-possessed persona of *Testament of Youth*. The novel's central character, Christine Merivale, is much more of an adolescent, and considerably less single-minded. Christine leaves school in the summer term of 1911 to return home to 'Torborough' with a firm short-term plan in her mind, but it is not to attend Oxford, which she thinks would be 'just like going to another school'.[33] Her favourite teacher, Miss Lansdowne (who is unmistakably modelled on Edith Fry), has suggested that she attend a London school of journalism, and live at a student hostel. Miss Lansdowne advises Christine to wait until Christmas, when she will be eighteen, to broach this plan to her parents.

Christine does so, with disastrous results. Her parents respond with uncomprehending hostility. Christine accepts defeat surprisingly quickly, given her intense dissatisfaction with her life at home. Although she is bitter and apprehensive about her future and estranged from both of her parents, Christine is distracted by the pleasures of 'coming out', an event which occurs only a day after the angry family scene over her wish to go to London. We see her dressing for the ball, seduced by her own prettiness, and stirred by imperfectly understood sexual feelings:

> She put the last pin into her hair, and turned to the long glass to survey the effect. . . . Her features softened with pleasure at the sight of her own reflection . . . 'If only Miss Lansdowne could see me now!' Then, unaccountably, she blushed, suddenly observing her long white arms and soft bare shoulders.

In the early chapters of *Not Without Honour*, Brittain portrays Christine and her misery in a sympathetic manner. But in the later chapters, Brittain distances herself from her heroine and adopts an ironic tone. In the middle section of the novel, the author encourages the reader to perceive Christine as a tragi-comic figure, and her experiences as illustrative of the false perceptions arising from the self-absorption of youth. We see her indulging in daydreams and becoming entangled in relationships the nature of which she does not fully understand. In place of any real effort to find for herself a way out of Torborough, and dependence on her family, she decides instead to reform the town: 'she would learn how to waken Torborough from its complacent slumber and make it, by her example, a different town, full of ideals, eager to use its natural advantages for the sake of suffering humanity, instead of exploiting them for the benefit of its prosperous shopkeepers'.[34]

Much of the remainder of the novel is concerned with Christine's naive and unwise attempts to remake Torborough, and with her relationship with Albert Clark, the rationalist curate of Garthington, a character whose original was Joseph Harry Ward. In the final section of the novel, Brittain could not resist resorting to melodrama. Christine and Albert fall in love. Although Christine herself defines her relationship with Albert Clark as a 'perfect spiritual communion',[35] it is not perceived that way by Torborough society, and a budding scandal ensues. Christine's parents remain unaware of their daughter's compromising behaviour with Albert Clark until the truth is revealed to them by a well-meaning acquaintance, who explains to the shocked and angry Merivales that their daughter has become the subject of scandalous local gossip, because she is seen regularly with Albert Clark. She tells them that they 'must send Christine away. . . . A long way off – and at *once*'.[36] She proposes that they send her to Oxford.

At first, Christine rejects this solution:

> As if to support her resolution came the recollection of her father's words. He had shouted something about college – about sending her to Oxford to 'hide her disgrace'! Hateful place, college – like going back to school after all this time of free spiritual growth! No doubt in actual years she was still quite young, but in her mental development she had long outgrown the stage at which people went to college. She wasn't going to college – not she; she'd die before they should send her![37]

But when Albert proves unwilling either to abandon his wife, or to compromise Christine, she does agree to go to Oxford. We meet her at Oxford, at 'Drayton College' in the novel's brief 'Epilogue', in 1914. This is a new Christine; a very different young woman from the passionate, if wrongheaded and self-absorbed, girl of the book's main body. While she has matured intellectually, she has become cynical and shallow, shutting out all feelings, and even refusing to take the war in Europe seriously.

In the last pages of the book she is redeemed, and by Albert himself: he has died a 'hero's' death in the Dardanelles, where he had served as a chaplain. Christine receives a posthumous letter from him. After she had been sent to Oxford, her love for Albert had turned to contempt, because he would not run away with her. His letter causes her to see not only him, but life in general in a more balanced, mature light: 'Although she was hardly conscious of it, the hardness and the bitter cynicism of many months had dissolved into quiet weeping.'[38]

Unquestionably, the account Brittain presents to us in *Testament of Youth* is much closer to her actual experience than that found in *Not Without Honour*. In the autobiography Brittain sets out to recreate her experience as it actually happened. *Not Without Honour*, though it sprang directly out of her youthful experience, is fiction. (There is, for example, not the slightest evidence that there ever was any romantic attachment between Joseph Harry Ward and Brittain, though Brittain was infatuated with him, and her use of his character in her novel indicates that she herself was aware of the fact.) But *Testament of Youth* contains revealing omissions and even some distortions in her retelling of her experience. The very different use of that experience in the fictionalized account allows us to understand some of the thoughts and feelings that she omitted from the ostensibly factual narrative of the years 1912–14.

Testament of Youth accurately reflects Brittain's strong desire for autonomy, her ambition and the genuine if undeveloped feminism that led her to select Oxford as her goal, and that gave her the energy to work towards that goal. But she was not as clear-sighted nor as single-minded as she portrays herself, nor was the achievement of the goal the lone struggle she depicts.

First, although she tells us that she had determined to go to college when she was at St Monica's – she says her 'budding ambition to go to college . . . developed as soon as I discovered that such places as women's colleges existed, and learnt what they stood for'[39] – the evidence from her letters and diaries does not bear this statement out. She did indeed wish to escape from Buxton: 'Unhappy, shut up little Buxton, lying at the bottom of a basin! . . . Oh! to escape from it!'[40] she wrote on one dreary January day. But the idea that a university education might provide a way out became an option she seriously considered only in 1913.

She also distorts the significance of Sir John Marriott and his series of lectures. Her attendance at his University Extension Lecture series was important to her. She worked diligently on the essays she wrote, and she was thrilled when Marriott praised her work: 'I asked for my essay back, somewhat in fear & trembling as I knew how sarcastic he could be. He looked at me in surprise when I indicated which it was. I only put my initials not my name, hoping he wouldn't know the sex of the writer & perhaps he didn't. To my surprise he said "Is *that* yours? It is a *very* good essay indeed". . . I seemed as indifferent as I could manage though the inward elation was at bursting point!'[41] But the confrontation between the worldly, kindly 'Sir John' and Brittain's old-fashioned parents over the question of Oxford, which plays such a pivotal role in the autobiography, is not mentioned in Brittain's diary. The entry for Wednesday, 19th March 1913 does indeed contain a full description of Marriott's stay at the Brittain household, and Brittain did record with great excitement that she was planning to attend the Oxford Summer Meeting of the University Extension Delegacy, and was pleased when Marriott suggested that she try for one of its prize essays, but she does not record discussing the possibility of actually attending one of the women's colleges.

Moreover, the entries for the succeeding days and weeks are full, not of references to the possibility of attending Oxford, but of her triumphs in a local amateur theatrical production, and of her relationships with her family and with Mrs Harrison. She does record on 5 May that she sent her essay on 'The Growth of Pauperism, 1780–1830' to Oxford, 'with an inward prayer for its success – which, however, I dare not & do not expect'.[42]

She won the prize. 'My humble essay!' she wrote in her diary. '[H]ow glad I am I wrote it at Mr Marriott's suggestion. I didn't think I had an earthly chance; it is one thing writing the best papers in a little town like this & quite another entering for a competition open to the whole United Kingdom.'[43]

Winning the prize did lay the way for the real turning point, which came during her visit to Oxford, in August 1913. It was then that for the first time she made serious enquiries about what would actually be required for admission, and it was also then that she selected Somerville as her choice of college. She was too busy to keep up her diary during her visit and in the months immediately following. As she says herself, when she did resume regular entries: 'Of course I stopped writing the record just when everything most interesting was going to happen.' But the brief summary she wrote in the 'Record' does confirm that it was during her Summer Meeting visit that she decided to go to Oxford: 'In August I went with Miss Heath Jones & Miss Bervon to Oxford for the Summer Meeting. There I had heaps of lectures & saw something of Mr Marriott; I stayed behind a day after Miss H.J. & Miss B. & had dinner at his house. It was after this that I finally decided to go to Oxford & Somerville if I can, & I got Daddy to give his permission at last.'[44]

In *Testament of Youth* Brittain allowed no trace of doubt about her desire for a university education to be part of the narrative. But in fact, even in the autumn of 1913, when she was engulfed by the engrossing task of preparing for the Somerville scholarship examination, she was not completely certain that she wanted to become an Oxford woman student. In that same entry of 18 October 1913, in which she resumed keeping her 'Record' after the hiatus of three months, she writes: 'Whether I shall ever go to Oxford, & whether it will be the wisest thing if I do, time will show.'[45] One of her chief concerns was that a university education might be detrimental to her creativity and to her ultimate goal of becoming a writer. She was worried enough about this to confide her fears to Edith Fry, who wrote back reassuringly: 'I don't see why a university course should crush your individuality! . . . yours will survive.'[46]

These doubts may have masked a more pervasive uneasiness about the suitability of a university education for a young women in her position. Given her family's affluence and her own prettiness, vivacity and social poise, Vera Brittain was not a typical early twentieth-century woman university student. Prospective female university students in the years before the First World War tended to be middle-class women who faced the necessity of supporting themselves as single adults and who had been assessed by themselves and their families and friends as unlikely to marry. Indeed, the stereotype of the woman university student suggested that she would become a spinster school teacher. The dreariness of that stereotype was daunting to Brittain, who appeared both to herself and to others as too financially fortunate, too attractive and too talented to need a university education.

The idea that she herself might someday wish to teach in a school was one that she emphatically rejected. After receiving information from Somerville in December 1913 encouraging prospective students to take the degree course in order to increase their chances of obtaining good teaching posts, Brittain expressed her distaste: 'A letter came from Oxford . . . saying that Oxford women students cannot be eligible for the "Teacher's Register" – whatever that may be – unless they take Responsions & the Degree Course. As I have no intention of teaching – rather than be a dowdy, downtrodden undermistress at a small school I would give up working altogether – I don't expect it affects me.'[47]

Brittain's assumption of privilege – social and economic privilege as well as the privilege associated with the beauty and vitality that she knew herself to possess – is expressed in a spontaneous and unexamined way in that entry. The passage in *Testament of Youth* in which Brittain describes her feelings of uneasiness about Somerville when she went up to Oxford to take the scholarship examination conveys her later awareness that as a young woman she had made such assumptions about her own privileged position: 'When, on my first evening at Somerville, I stood timidly at the door of the big dining-hall, heard the shrill clamour of feminine accents from every geographical area, noticed the long-sleeved dowdiness of dinner frocks, and shuddered to see the homely food . . . a suddenly sinking heart threatened me with the fear that even if I succeeded in getting to college, I should never be able to endure it.'[48]

If Brittain overemphasised her singlemindedness in seeking an Oxford education in *Testament of Youth*, she underplayed the role of her parents, and especially of her mother, in helping her to achieve her goal. In *Testament of Youth* she emphasised the difficulties of her situation and her feelings of isolation:

> The mornings I gave to the Scholarship examination, getting up every day at six o'clock and working steadily till lunch-time in a chilly little north-west room. . . . It was on the ground floor and dark as well as cold, but I was not allowed a fire out of consideration for the maids, though we then kept three and a garden-boy. But I gladly endured my frozen hands and feet in order to obtain the privacy and quiet which none of the living-rooms in ordinary use would have given me.

She goes on to record spending 'the greater part of that autumn's tiny dress-allowance on the necessary volumes of Fielding and Goldsmith, Wordsworth and the Cambridge History of English Literature'.[49]

This bleak picture is both overdrawn and incomplete. On the one hand, Brittain exaggerates her lonely isolation: given what we know of the actual Edith Brittain's solicitousness, the 'chilly room' and Vera's endurance of 'frozen hands and feet' are surely hyperbolic. On the other hand in *Testament of Youth* Brittain avoids a full examination of the considerable amount of money it took to become an Oxford woman student in this period. (Her use of the word 'tiny' to describe her sizeable £30 dress allowance is indicative of the way in which she minimizes the important role her family's affluence played in enabling her to become a student.[50]) She also overlooks the practical assistance she received from both parents. It was her mother and father together who found the necessary tutors, and her father who paid for them, during the months she was preparing for her examinations, and of course it would be her father who would pay her college fees and other expenses.

Moreover, throughout 1913 and 1914, Edith and Arthur Brittain gave Vera more than material and practical help. They both entered enthusiastically into the role of proud and supportive parents. For example, when she won her Exhibition in March 1914 Vera noted their great pride in her achievement: 'I was not at all disturbed by the announcement, though Mother got quite flustered in her delight & wanted to tell everyone at once & Daddy seemed quite overjoyed – though I wish they would not make demonstrations.'[51]

Why was Brittain unable to acknowledge in *Testament of Youth* the material and emotional support she received from her parents? It appears that even when she was nearing the age of forty, she had not fully come to terms with her feelings about her family, and especially about her mother. There is a striking contrast between the fragmentary glimpses we are given of her mother in *Testament of Youth* and in her other published work and the loving relationship that emerges from the diaries and correspondence. Brittain's conflictual relationship with her mother stands as an early example of what would become a central experience for many twentieth-century feminists.[52] She was a woman whose aspirations caused her to reject her mother's way of life, but who, on the other hand, felt the force of a strong – if not always easy – attachment to that mother.

In *Testament of Youth*, Brittain handled her ambivalence about her mother by avoiding it. The Edith Brittain of *Testament of Youth* is a shadowy figure throughout – we do not even know her name, because in describing her mother's own family Brittain refrained from revealing that her mother's family name was Bervon, and nowhere does she reveal either her mother's or her father's given names – but the indistinct and fragmentary nature of the portrayal is especially evident in the early sections of the book dealing with the period of Brittain's life up to October 1914, when she entered Oxford. The few things we are told reinforce a view of Edith as insignificant, insipid and fundamentally unimportant. The mother of *Testament of Youth* is a woman whose conventional nature prevents her from understanding or truly sympathizing with her 'modern' daughter's aspirations, although she exhibits a passive kindness.

Yet the evidence, beginning with the strong love for her mother so apparent in the childhood letters and juvenile literary productions, and continuing with the many references to her mother in the 1911–17 'Reflective Record', and the voluminous correspondence Brittain maintained with her mother during her first year at Oxford, during the war years and into the 1920s, suggests that she loved her mother deeply, that she enjoyed many things in common with her, and that her mother's advice, encouragement and pride in her achievements was of great importance to her as she was growing up and when she was an adult.

For the period 1911–14, the diary entries reveal a close bond between mother and daughter. Some of the earliest entries, written while she was still at St Monica's, record her pleasure when her mother visited her at school. And when she was at home, they shared many activities. These included first of all a number of traditionally feminine tasks and recreations. In *Testament of Youth* Brittain describes herself as totally isolated from Buxton's social life – 'I had nothing to do and no one to talk to'[53] – and in *Not Without Honour*, the rebellious, unhappy Christine Merivale balks whenever her mother wants her to help out at a tea party, or with charitable work, or to attend a social function. But the real Vera Brittain experienced no such estrangement either from her mother herself or from the rituals which made up the fabric of their lives. For example, they shared housekeeping tasks and the duties of provincial social life: 'Turned out Edward's room with mother in morning & threw away various old letters, etc.',[54] reads one diary entry for 1911. And two years later: 'Mother rooted around hard all morning owing to the absence of Norah the parlourmaid. I cleaned the silver, which looked infinitely better than it has done for weeks. This afternoon mother went to a bridge at Mrs Whitehead's & I kept her at home day . . . fortunately . . . only the two Duncan girls called and did not stay long.'[55]

Mother and daughter shared an interest in clothes. On 18 March 1913, for example, Brittain recorded in her diary: 'Mother met me in Manchester – I was so glad to see the darling – and we went and did a little shopping.'[56] In these years just before the war, Edith and Vera often 'did a little shopping' and not only in Manchester. In March 1913, for example, they went up to London for a few days, mainly to shop, but also to visit friends, including Vera's friend Stella Sharp. They stayed at the Ladies' Constitutional Club in Kensington Gardens, which Brittain refers to as 'mother's new club', and they did the round of the London shops. At Dunns, for example, they chose styles for their tweeds: 'mother's . . . a Donegal – mine a pretty grey'.[57]

A few months later, in May 1913, she travelled with both parents to Paris. When the three stayed overnight in London, en route for Paris, her father stayed at a hotel but Edith and Vera stayed together once again at the Ladies' Constitutional Club.[58] This was Vera's first trip abroad and she thoroughly enjoyed it, although mother and daughter were limited by Arthur Brittain's unwillingness to participate in much sightseeing. They were 'seriously handicapped without a man', Vera wrote, and forced to resort to a 'touring motor' tour: 'Neither mother nor I can bear such things as "personally conducted tours", but when one is ignorant it is difficult to do without them; they seem a necessary evil to non-millionaires.'[59]

Not only did she accept her mother's judgement on many matters, she was proud of her. For example, on 7 January 1913, the Brittain family sponsored a dance at Buxton's Palace Hotel, and Brittain recorded in her diary: 'Mother looked lovely . . . there was no dress to touch [hers] in the whole room. . . .'[60]

Although the relationship was close and loving during these years when Vera was her mother's constant companion, there were times when Brittain felt impatient with her mother. Her irritation focused not infrequently on what she saw as Edith's excessive preoccupation with order and propriety. For example, in April 1913 Edith spent a few days in Surrey looking after her ailing mother, leaving Vera to preside over the household, including the spring cleaning, a major annual ritual. When Edith returned at the end of the week, she apparently expressed some dissatisfaction with the way in which the spring cleaning had been carried out, and Vera recorded:

> Mother of course found fault with everything she saw at home, & seemed to think everything a complete muddle if she was away. It is characteristic of Mother that though I always want her to come home she always upsets me when she does come; one really feels it is not worth bothering to try & keep things straight in her absence. When Mother wants to be particularly nasty to me she impresses upon me how like I am to the Brittain family; thank goodness, thank goodness I am! *They* at least have a little courage, reserve, self-control, determination & staying-power![61]

But this is one of the few entries in which Brittain expresses real exasperation with her mother, and even this reflects intimacy rather than the ironic detachment that the persona of *Testament of Youth* feels towards her mother. Most of Brittain's diary entries about her mother during the pre-war period reflect either a calm acceptance and enjoyment of the relationship or irritation with what Brittain perceived as her mother's fussiness, overconcern or timidity. Only occasionally does the diary reveal more intense emotions in connection with her mother, but these entries, while few in number, are revealing. One such entry, made in April of 1913, concerns her mother's feelings about her own family and about her marriage. Vera reports that she 'managed to drag from [Mother] a little of the closed book of her early life'. Her mother told her that she hadn't been in love with her father when she married him: 'I only needed her assurance last night to convince me – I really guessed all along – that her marriage with Daddy wasn't a love match on her side.' Instead, she had married to escape the 'poverty and sordidness' of her own family. In the diary entry, Brittain both sympathizes with her mother and asserts that she will not settle for so little: 'It is not for these things that *I* should count the world well lost, I don't feel I could marry a man if there was not romance attached to him, especially if he were impatient & intolerant like Daddy was with Mother. But then I have never known the sting of poverty, so I can't imagine the great joy that release from it must be.'

Brittain concluded the entry with an account of the emotionally charged exchange that took place between her mother and herself after her mother's revelations about her own courtship:

> The history of all these things made it clear to me why Mother finds me difficult to understand & get on with, because the part that is understandable is like Daddy's side, which she always objected to, rather than hers. The sense of loneliness quite overpowered me; there seems so often to be no one here to turn to; Daddy of course is hopeless, far too shrewd, business-like & limited, & Edward is the baby that boys of seventeen nearly always are. So I began to cry weakly at first & then more miserably & entered with Mother into a variety of rather heart-rending explanations concerning difference of temperament. She did seem to want me after all, & to want to make me less lonely. A few hours ago I couldn't have imagined myself either confessing my loneliness to Mother or letting her see my distress, but I am glad of it instead of sorry if only to prove how great a darling I always knew she could be.[62]

In this entry, nineteen-year-old Brittain is expressing a genuine sense of loneliness and an acute awareness of the distance that adulthood had brought to her relationship with her beloved mother. There were substantial reasons why both the older and the younger woman would at this juncture be confronting differences between themselves. Edith was, after all, satisfied with her life as a Buxton matron and we may surmise that she felt at times bewildered by and disappointed with Vera's growing dissatisfaction with that life. But the Brittain of the diary was not suffering from the desolate emotional isolation experienced by the Brittain of *Testament of Youth*. She was, rather, struggling both to acknowledge the parts of herself that were like her mother while at the same time separating herself from what she saw as her mother's limitations. This was a painful and a confusing process but she did not – as does the Vera Brittain persona of the autobiography – have to endure it entirely alone, or without comfort and reassurance from her mother.

In April 1913, when Brittain had that conversation with her mother, she had begun to take her first steps away from Buxton. The process did begin with John Marriott's series of lectures. But what Brittain suppresses in *Testament of Youth* is the significant fact that she did not attend the lectures alone: Edith Brittain accompanied her daughter to all of the lectures and enthusiastically supported Vera's efforts to prepare her bi-weekly essays.[63]

The diary, then, in this instance as in several others, reveals the extent to which Brittain's intellectual growth in 1913 occurred with the support of her family, and especially of her mother. It was her mother, for instance, who appears to have been instrumental in arranging for the Latin lessons she began to take in April 1913.[64] After August 1913, when she was preparing in earnest for admission to Oxford, she tells us in *Testament of Youth* that various of 'my parents' acquaintances' were highly critical of this decision, and that her mother had to bear the brunt of their censoriousness:

> For a few weeks my mother had quite a bad time at the G.F.S. teas and Mothers' Union meetings which she was then accustomed to attending. On these occasions she was invariably tackled by one or two stalwart middle-class mothers who did not hesitate to tell her how deplorable they thought my future plans, and to identify her acquiescence in them with her abandonment of all hope of finding me a husband.[65]

Omitted from the *Testament of Youth* account, but present in the diary, is her mother's spirited defence of her activities, and her own appreciation for her mother's support:

> Mother had a Mothers' Union meeting at Mrs Cox's to-day, which appears to have been quite amusing. At the end of the meeting Mrs Cox suddenly said to Mother 'Is it true that Vera is going to be a lecturer?' Mother very naturally said 'What?' & Mrs Cox continued 'Why, it is all over the town that Vera Brittain is shortly going to begin lecturing!' Mother, with some dignity, drew herself up & replied to the effect that 'Vera Brittain is at present working up for two exams, . . . should she be so fortunate as to pass them, she may go to Oxford the following October.'

Her mother was then asked what Vera would do if she were to get married in the meantime: ' "In that case," replied Mother, still with the dignity which she is able to exercise on other people's behalf but never on her own, "not a moment of what she has done will be wasted, as what she has learnt will be of inestimable benefit to her. . . ." '[66]

The Edith Brittain of *Testament of Youth* is easily dismissed as inconsequential, but in creating this portrait Brittain did not deliberately set out to distort. In her fiction, however, she used her mother as a starting point for some profoundly unsympathetic characters.

The most fully developed such character is the mother in the novel *Not Without Honour*. Mrs Merivale is a shallow, narrow-minded woman who has no interest in her daughter's individuality, seeing her only as an extension of herself, and as an object for display: a pretty 'daughter-at-home' will enhance the family's standing in the community. In her inability to understand her daughter's needs and aspirations Mrs Merivale is revealed not merely as limited, but as without genuine love for her daughter. She is also a silly, censorious snob, who does her best to stifle her daughter's interest in 'Mrs Hastings', the character based on Mrs Harrison. Mrs Merivale says of Mrs Hastings: 'Mrs *Hastings*! My dear child, surely you know that people in our set don't call upon a dentist's wife!'[67] She is equally hostile to 'Mr Clark', the character based on J.H. Ward.

But the diary indicates that Edith Brittain was cordial to Mrs Harrison, and encouraged Vera's interest in her, and Brittain records in the diary that although her father was offended by Ward's rationalist views, 'mother more or less agreed, in her mild way, with Mr Ward'.[68] And Edith Brittain not only regularly accompanied Vera on the lengthy walk to Fairfield on Sunday evenings in 1913 and 1914 to hear Mr Ward preach, she called on his wife, and invited the couple to tea.[69]

The mother figure in *Not Without Honour* was but one of several fictional characters Brittain based on her mother. Daphne's mother in *The Dark Tide* and Ruth's mother in *Honourable Estate* are, like Mrs Merivale, women estranged from their daughters because they are fundamentally shallow and mean-spirited. The negative portrayals resembling her own mother found throughout Brittain's fiction represent split-off fragments of Edith Brittain towards which Brittain felt anger and resentment, a resentment that she had not been able to acknowledge or fully comprehend when she was living at home and the complexities of which she could not acknowledge even as a mature writer.

In *Not Without Honour*, the selfish, social-climbing Mrs Merivale is the repository of Brittain's anger at discovering just how limited her mother's life in Buxton had been, and how trifling was the social success she had struggled to achieve. Brittain was also expressing her anger at the realization that she herself had been used as a valuable possession in her family's quest for upward social mobility, but here too her fictional representation is one-dimensional. Christine Merivale quite consciously rejects her own objectification. In one of the novel's early scenes, Mr and Mrs Merivale, Christine and her brother Derrick walk after church on Sunday on Torborough's

'Terraces': 'She knew that her father and mother were looking Derrick and herself up and down with complacent appreciation, occasionally turning aside to bow with satisfied smiles to an acquaintance, as if crying out, "See what we've accomplished!" to all beholders. . . . [S]he objected intensely to her position as a family exhibit on those dull, hateful Terraces. Above all, she objected to her white coat and skirt, and the ingenuous hat of white muslin with wired bows, which made her feel like a dressed-up doll.'[70]

But did Brittain feel like a 'dressed-up doll' in 1913 and 1914 when she and her family took their fine-weather promenades in Buxton's Pavilion Gardens? If we judge from an entry she made in her diary one Sunday in May 1913, it would appear that Vera, in contrast to the fictional Christine, quite enjoyed these Sunday walks: 'I put on my new white serge and the Paris hat with the white tulle bows, white shoes & stockings & a low necked blouse, and looked quite a dream. The people in the Gardens after Church stared like billy-oh.'[71] On the other hand, against that exhuberantly self-confident diary entry we can put a photograph of Brittain, *circa* 1913, taken against a background of rhododendron bushes in what may well have been Buxton's Pavilion Gardens. In this photograph, Brittain's slight figure is swathed in a high-necked, long-sleeved, beruffled dress. She is wearing long white gloves, white stockings and white shoes. Her face, underneath a large, frilly, decidedly 'ingenuous' white hat, appears wan and forlorn.[72] The juxtaposition of diary entry and photograph suggest that Brittain may at times have felt oppressed, if only on an unconscious level, by her role in a social system of which her mother was an agent as well as a victim. Her anger in the face of that suppressed sense of oppression finds a voice in the fictional Christine, created a decade after Brittain's own years as a Buxton young lady. What Brittain could never confront in her published work – either fictional or autobiographical – was her own acquiescence: that like her mother, she was a potential accomplice in as well as a potential victim of a milieu in which women became objects of display.

Although Brittain was closest to her mother, her relationship with her father was also important to her. During Vera's adolescence and young adulthood, her father was a bluff, successful businessman who assumed that he would be deferred to by his wife, his children and the servants. As a prototypical Edwardian *pater familias*, he was the final arbiter of major family decisions, especially of any involving substantial amounts of money. For example, characteristically, it was Arthur who wrote to Vera at St Monica's in March 1911 to tell her that she could not go to Brussels with her friend Stella Sharp, but that she could stay on for another term at school.[73] And it was her father who provided her with the pleasure of unexpected gifts: 'Joy divine because Daddy has given me £10 out of his "bonus" as a non-birthday, non dress-allowance present, and I shall be able to pay off my debts & have something quite interesting left over', she wrote in her diary on one such occasion.[74] And of course it was her father who had to give his consent before she could go to Oxford.

During her late teens, Brittain's relationship with her father underwent subtle alteration, as both parties adapted to her entry into adulthood. It appears that Arthur's recognition of his daughter's sexual maturity was largely expressed as anxiety. His fears had a specific focus: he worried that Vera might be abducted by agents of the White Slave Trade. Arthur's fear of White Slavery is understandable, since widespread public panic about the White Slave Trade was a frequent motif in sexual discourse during these years,[75] but it irritated Vera. For example, when in March 1913 she went on a journey to visit her Aunt Lillie, she writes: 'Mother of course insisted upon going . . . with me, as Daddy started talking about pepperboxes, & gags, and White Slave Traffic as usual.'[76]

Other diary entries reveal a recognition by both father and daughter of Vera's developing attractiveness. The most explicit entry is this one, from January 1913: 'After tea Daddy retired to bed with a cold, after admiring and playing with my hair, which I was drying in front of the morning room fire after washing. I think all men must be fascinated by a woman's hair, if it have any beauty of its own!'[77]

On this occasion Brittain experienced her father's acknowledgement of her physical attractiveness as affirming, but for the most part, her diary entries suggest that as she grew older, she became increasingly exasperated with her father, and increasingly critical of his conventionality and of his unquestioning assumption of masculine privilege. In November 1913, when father and daughter quarrelled openly about the clergyman J.H. Ward, Vera records with unusual bitterness: 'Finally he ended up by saying that I didn't know what I was talking about, & it was ridiculous a little slip of a girl arguing with him about what I didn't understand etc.' She continues: 'Of course I have always known, but it is no longer doubtful to me, that it is as a plaything or a pretty toy that he spoils & pets me, not as a sensible human being who *counts*, & that he has nothing but contempt for me & my knowledge, just as he has at heart for all women, because he believes them for some unknown reason to be inferior to him. . . .'[78]

On another occasion when they disagreed – again about J.H. Ward she wrote of her father: 'Years – nay centuries – of social & spiritual evolution intervene between him & me. . . . I understand now what has conventionalized, limited & checked the spiritual development of poor Mother.'[79] As an intimate and critical observer of her parents' marriage during these years, she knew that she did not want such a union. In the privacy of her diary, she was her mother's partisan, though we can surmise that Edith herself would not have welcomed such partisanship: in the years before the First World War, she appears to have been quite content with her marriage and to have regarded her husband's uneven temper as a minor inconvenience. Vera notes that her father is 'impatient and intolerant' as a husband[80] and she finds his bluster and irritability childish. For example, on one occasion in 1914 when Edith was away and Vera was taking her place as household manager, she records:

> Daddy, who had arranged to get home at 10:00 arrived instead at 7:30. He was in such a dust when he found the servants all slacking and nothing prepared for him. . . . However, by means of his dinner and a little judicious conversation he soon quietened down after a few of the usual remarks about 'packing them all off', 'shutting the place up' etc. and by the time Mother returned all was calm.[81]

In spite of her new-found adult capacity to judge her father and find him wanting, her feelings for him were by no means completely negative. She was for example proud of his knowledge and skill as a manufacturer[82] and she also acknowledged that he was at heart, 'whatever his limitations', a good man who was usually both fair and generous.[83] And she was gratified that he, as well as her mother, was proud of her achievements. As the following entry reveals, she did not always perceive him as an unthinking patriarch who underestimated her because of her sex: 'This evening Daddy showed his appreciation of my work in general by a long and confidential conversation about prospects, the works & various other matters. He told me he felt inclined to put more & more confidence in me as I was showing myself more & more worthy. . . .'[84]

The fourth member of the Brittain family was Vera's younger brother, Edward. In the public narratives of her life Brittain's portrayal of her relationship with Edward is vivid and moving, but at the same time elusive and opaque. Edward Harold Brittain, then a captain in the 11th Sherwood Foresters, was killed in action on the Italian front on 15th June 1918. His death made it difficult for his sister to write about him and her feelings for him in a way that would encompass the realities of the relationship. Her best-known portrait of Edward is in *Testament of Youth*, where he figures as a faultless war hero and their brother–sister relationship is portrayed as flawless and virtually free of conflict. Less well known is the fictionalized portrait in Brittain's novel *Honourable Estate*, published in 1936, in which she courageously deals with Edward's homosexual experience, but even there she does not fully explore the nuances of the relationship. In fact, the relationship between Edward and Vera, while close and largely harmonious, was not without the inevitable conflicts and ambivalences one would expect of a real sister and brother, rather than of a war hero and war heroine.

As small children, Vera and Edward, less than two years apart in age, had been each other's closest friend and companion. Because of that secure foundation, their fondness for each other successfully weathered the changes that the later years of childhood and adolescence brought with them. Their experience began to diverge when the family moved to Buxton and both children began attending day schools. That their schools would be segregated by sex was of course nearly inevitable: sex-segregated education was the usual pattern for middle- and upper-class families. And if Vera's education was designed to turn her into a proper young lady, Edward's was designed to turn him into a gentleman who would be also a 'manly' man. As the family's only son Edward took precedence over his sister as they grew up: it was he, rather than Vera, who would need to be prepared for achievement in adulthood. Thus, the selection of his public school had far more importance for Edward himself, and for his family, than did the selection of his sister's boarding school. Edward went off to public school in 1908, a year after his sister was sent to St Monica's. Uppingham, the school the Brittains selected for their son, was by 1908 excellent and well-respected. Edward remained there until the summer of 1914, when he left intending to take up in the autumn the place he had gained at New College, Oxford.[85] Edward did well at Uppingham, achieving solid, if not outstanding, academic success, and learning one of the most important lessons public schools were designed to teach: to distance himself to some degree from emotional dependence on his family and to identify with an exclusively masculine upper middle-class group. But as the end of his school days approached he appears to have grown into a gentle young man who remained fond of his family and comfortably close to his sister. Vera's diary entries for the 1910–11 school vacation period, for example, tell us that brother and sister shared many holiday activities, from violin and piano duets to roller-skating.

Vera's and Edward's lives again diverged sharply when Vera left St Monica's while Edward continued at Uppingham, preparing during his final school years for admission to Oxford. At home in Buxton, Vera missed Edward. At the end of his Christmas vacation in 1912–13, she wrote: 'Edward went back to Uppingham to-day. Now the boring time begins. . . .'[86] And a year later, just after she had taken her Somerville admission examination and had won her Exhibition, she turned down an invitation to spend Easter in Surrey with Louise Heath Jones and Florence Bervon 'because I did not want to miss any of Edward's holiday'.[87] Clearly, she loved her brother and valued his company. But she was not uncritical of him. During the Easter holiday of 1913, for example, although she relied on Edward to help her with the Latin lessons she had recently embarked on, she also found that during this holiday period her beloved brother could not assuage her feelings of loneliness and isolation: 'Edward is the baby that boys of seventeen nearly always are',[88] she wrote despairingly in her diary. She was on occasion critical of Edward's appearance, and disappointed when he looked 'plain';[89] and she thought he had a priggish streak: he could be 'pedantic'[90] and even self-righteous,[91] and she could not help resenting his privileged position in the family, both as the boy and as the 'easier' of the two children:

> Edward came home to-day. There are rumours afloat now of his going into the works after all – there is so much money & promise in them that we may someday be really rich, & Daddy naturally wants his only son to have a part in it. Mother wants it too – even if he could get into the Civil Service, she would hate him to go away – had I but been the boy I & my disposition could have been much more easily spared. Poor thing! she admitted to-day that she would much rather have an ordinary daughter – living & sleeping & dying & leaving no impress behind! I suppose I have all the share of enterprise & ambition. . . . Of course E. will go to Oxford in any case.[92]

Yet in spite of these tensions, sister and brother did enjoy real comradeship. For example, when Edward was preparing for his Oxford entrance examinations, he turned to Vera for help with history, a subject that had been more thoroughly taught at St Monica's than at Uppingham.[93] And when Vera decided to prepare for admission to Oxford, Edward gave her both emotional and practical support. For example, during the difficult spring of 1914, when Vera became confused about the examination regulations for the Oxford Senior Local examination, which she discovered to her exasperation she would have to take after she had won her Somerville Exhibition,

Edward was mature enough to ignore the bad temper to which Vera gave way under stress. It was he who smoothed out the difficulties, writing to the examination officials, and driving his sister to town to register for the exam.[94] During this same holiday, he entered into Vera's enthusiasms – for example he walked with her to Fairfield to hear J.H. Ward preach[95] – while Vera, for her part, accompanied Edward on the piano as he worked on a violin sonata he was composing.

Vera's genuine fondness for Edward enabled her to enjoy his successes as he entered the world of masculine privilege. For example, she and her mother travelled to Uppingham to attend Speech Day (the school's annual closing ceremony) in 1913 and 1914. On both occasions, her diary reflects her approval of the masculine public school ethos. She did not begrudge Edward his right to enter into it. What she regretted was that she, as a girl, could not do so. In 1913, she writes, after hearing the boys (dressed in their Officers' Training Corps uniforms) sing their school hymns: '[it] . . . makes me feel most choky. I don't wonder boys love their public schools where they have such a splendid time & where "esprit de corps" seems to be in the very air you breathe. . . .'[97]

In 1914, at Uppingham for Edward's last Speech Day, she wrote even more explicitly in the same vein: 'I can understand perfectly why Edward regrets leaving it so much. For girls – as yet – there is nothing equivalent to public school for boys – these fine traditions & unwritten laws that turn out so many splendid characters have been withheld from them – to their detriment.'[98]

In *Testament of Youth*, Brittain recorded a memorable occasion dating back to her school days at The Grange in Buxton, when her mother and an aunt (probably her Aunt Florence) had reprimanded her severely because she had stopped on her way home from school to talk to her brother Edward and several of his companions. She describes her bewilderment when, at tea time, she was subjected to a barrage of 'inexplicable' disapproval: she did not realize that talking to a group of boys was 'naughty'. She goes on to explain how much more damaging to her 'decency and peace' than any conversation she might have had with Edward's friends was the fact that she was bullied, physically and mentally, by two older fellow-pupils who thrust on her unwanted details about sexuality. She was too ashamed of the fact that the bullies made her cry to tell anyone about these assaults, so they remained a hidden childhood torment.

Even after she had left St Monica's, the realm of sexuality remained confusing and mysterious. While Brittain would later say that she was taught at home and at school to adopt a 'reverent' attitude toward sex, she was offered little explicit information either about her own sexual feelings or about the nature of sexual intercourse.[99] Yet her diary entries from 1911–14 make it clear that she knew she was attractive to men: her own reports of her successes with men, both older and younger, are scattered throughout her descriptions of the dances, tennis games, teas and amateur theatricals. But it appears that she seldom fully enjoyed this success. While she enjoyed receiving male acknowledgement of her attractiveness, she experienced both guilt and repugnance when she glimpsed the threatening possibilities that lay underneath the surface of acceptable interaction between the sexes. For example, on one occasion, after a dance in January 1913, she records her confusion, her resentment of male behaviour, and her uneasy feelings about her own responses:

> Alas! I fear dances have the effect of turning both Ernest's & Maurice's heads. Ernest, after several sentimental remarks, seized hold of me at my bedroom door & tried to persuade me to come with Edward & talk to them in his room while they smoked. Maurice was taken the same way last night . . . he murmured something that sounded like 'Darling' & tried to put his arms round my neck. Oh! they have no right to behave so to a girl much weaker & smaller than themselves. When they behave so I feel ashamed both of myself & of them. They have left me feeling very tired and depressed tonight; I feel that surely they would not take such liberties unless there were some element in me not altogether admirable & worthy of respect. How can I tell wherein it lies and how destroy it! tonight I feel that I am 'born to trouble as the sparks fly upward'.[100]

Two months after this dance, her feelings of confusion about sexuality were so acute that she approached her mother for information:

> On the way to golf I induced Mother to disclose a few points on sexual matters which I thought I ought to know, though the information is always intensely distasteful to me & most depressing – in fact it quite put me off my game! I suppose it is the spiritual & intellectual-development part of me that feels repugnance at being brought too closely into contact with physical 'open secrets'. Alas! Sometimes it feels sad to be a woman! Men seem to have so much more choice as to what they are intended for. Still, I suppose our position improves with the years, & I must be thankful not to have lived in Homeric Greece instead of 20th-century England![101]

In *Testament of Youth*, Brittain would make use of part of this fragment from the diary. However, she uses it, not to say something about the intimate and confusing question of sexuality, but rather about the less charged, more public issues of political feminism. In the course of discussing the inequalities within her own family she says:

> The constant and to me enraging evidences of this difference of attitude towards Edward and myself violently reinforced the feminist tendencies which I had first acquired at school, and which were being indirectly but surely developed by the clamourous drama of the suffragette movement far away in London: 'It feels sad to be a woman!' I wrote in March 1913 – the very month in which the 'Cat and Mouse' Act was first introduced for the ingenious torment of the militants. 'Men seem to have so much more choice as to what they are intended for.'

It may well be that the activities of the militants were having an indirect effect on Brittain during these years, but there is no evidence at all that they were having any direct effect, and certainly this particular passage from her diary, as we have seen, does not have reference to the suffrage struggle at all, but rather to Brittain's nineteen-year-old feelings of ambivalence about sex.[102]

Would Edith Bervon, at nineteen, have asked her mother questions about sex? Probably not. Among respectable Victorian middle-class people like the Bervons, sex was pushed firmly out of sight. And it is unlikely that a Victorian girl would have consoled herself, as Vera does here, with flippant humour. ('It quite put me off my game.') But even in 1913, the subject was still difficult and distasteful for a young woman with Brittain's upbringing, and not only because it was embarrassingly physical: Brittain's repugnance arises largely because of what she believes is implied in sexuality about male power over women. And the subject is so unpleasant and frightening that in March 1913 Brittain does not record exactly what it was she asked her mother, or what her mother's reply was.

A few months later, sexuality would again cause Brittain considerable distress. In June 1913, the son of close family friends, a boy who was, like Edward, at Uppingham, was expelled from the school because he had engaged in homosexual activity. Although Vera's father attempted to exclude his daughter from knowledge of this sexual secret,[103] Edward sent her a letter about it, and when he came home for the summer holiday, he discussed it with her: 'E. says there is only one unpardonable sin at a public school – immorality – and this is the only thing for which a boy is not given another chance. . . . E. & I both agreed that – 's lack of ideals & moral standards . . . was responsible in a great measure for his downfall.'[104]

But what *was* 'immorality'? What precisely was involved in sexual activity, whether homosexual or heterosexual? Brittain still did not know. Characteristically, given her rational bent, she attempted to assuage her uneasiness with information, this time pressing her mother for more explicit information than she had received during their conversation in March: 'Being afraid of my own ignorance in sexual matters, I entered after Edward had gone into an intimate discussion with Mother about the 'open secret' & now *I know*. I feel as if I don't want now ever to marry – it is all such confusion, the union of our physical & spiritual nature & to know just where longing becomes temptation & is wrong. Oh. I wept for the war of physical inclinations with spiritual inspiration, and for the futility of our poor human nature.'[105]

Ironically, given her father's preoccupation with the risks his daughter ran from faceless 'white slavers', the most disturbing manifestation of male sexuality with which Brittain was confronted during these years in Buxton were incidents of what we would today call sexual harassment. In *Testament of Youth*, Brittain mentions an incident from her teenage years, in which she was subjected to sexual assault when travelling home by train from St Monica's to Buxton.[106] In her description, she vividly portrays her fear of the 'leering black eyes, the pawing hands' of this drunken stranger.[107]

On this occasion, Brittain had the presence of mind to run out into the train's corridor and successfully escape her assailant. But when one of the tutors hired to help her prepare for admission to university subjected her to similar behaviour, there was little she could do. In *Testament of Youth*, she mentions her dislike for this 'elderly classical assistant' 'Mr Cheese' without explaining its cause, but it is revealed in her diary: he was making furtive but unmistakable sexual advances to her. She was faced with a distressing dilemma: she needed the man's help with Latin, but this meant enduring his offensive behaviour. She was, fortunately, able to turn to her old St Monica's teacher Edith Fry for advice, but while Fry was comforting, she offered no solutions: 'I told her how I disliked my coaching lessons, and about old Cheese's horrible behaviour. She agreed the position was uncomfortable in the extreme for me & so difficult as I can't give it up, because I can't give a reason & have really nothing *definite* to state. . . .'[108]

The unwanted sexual advances she was forced to put up with from her Latin tutor represent the most unpleasant and frightening aspect of Brittain's experience with sexuality during her years at home in Buxton. She felt both powerless and degraded in the face of his behaviour. But even when she felt more in control of the situation, relations between the sexes seemed to offer little except unpleasantness and confusion. In 1913, a respectable but rather dull and priggish Buxton young man named Bertram Spafford fell in love with Brittain. He proposed to her some time in the summer of 1913.[109] Brittain had no serious regard for Bertram Spafford. On the contrary, she was contemptuous of him and his entire family and regarded his feelings for her as something she could ridicule, in private at least. But while she refused him outright when he proposed, she did not completely discourage him. As she confessed to her diary, she enjoyed the experience of receiving his admiration too much to do that: 'The days are more interesting when I talk to B.S. . . . To fall in love with him would be a perfect impossibility, but it is very easy to be in love with love. To hear a man's voice say "you" in a tone which he uses to no one else on earth, is in itself a gigantic temptation to make him go on saying it like that . . . It is wrong . . . but then I am not good, & in spite of high purposes, only a very human girl.'[110]

But while Brittain did not treat Spafford well, she did not derive much pleasure from her behaviour towards him: she was too serious and fundamentally too moral to enjoy her own flirtatiousness. And although she was in fact too preoccupied with her academic activities in 1913 and 1914 to think very seriously about love, when she did do so, what she wanted was a genuine romance, in which she would be able to enter wholeheartedly. '[I]t leaves me with a very unsatisfied feeling to have met so many stupid & superficial men. . . . How I wish I could meet a good strong splendid man, full of force & enthusiasm, & in earnest about his life! There must *be* such!'[111]

Part II

'History's Greatest Disaster': Love and Work in the Great War

4

Somerville, 1914–1915

When the Great War broke out it came to me not as a superlative tragedy, but as an interruption of the most exasperating kind to my personal plans.

In the spring of 1914 Vera Brittain had successfully transformed her life and was preparing to enter Somerville on her own terms; she would not remain immured in the provincial tedium of Buxton. Instead she would begin a new adventure as an Oxford woman student. As she prepared for Oxford in the spring and summer of 1914, one of the things to which she looked forward most eagerly was the intellectual companionship she expected to find there; and, from April 1914, when Edward brought Roland Leighton home for a visit, Edward's school friend formed part of her own expectations about her approaching new life at Oxford. A few months later, under the as yet unforeseen [illegible]

[illegible]ever, however, in the spring and summer of 1914, when she was attracted to Roland and delighted that this intelligent, witty young man would also be at Oxford, Brittain was happy to get to know him gradually and did not then think of him as a prospect for a romantic passion; but the war's history produced drastic interventions.

Part I of this book is concerned with Brittain's experience during the war years. This chapter is about her first year at Somerville, where for several months she remained largely insulated from the war. The two subsequent chapters take up Brittain's experience of love and war and her representation of that experience in *Testament of Youth* and elsewhere.

When Vera Brittain went to Somerville in 1914, university education for women, while still uncommon, was much more acceptable than it had been for the earliest generation of women students at the end of the 1870s. Oxford and Cambridge had been exclusive

4

Somerville, 1914–1915

When the Great War broke out, it came to me not as a superlative tragedy, but as an interruption of the most exasperating kind to my personal plans.[1]

By the spring of 1914 Vera Brittain had successfully transformed her life and was preparing to enter adulthood on her own terms. She would not remain mired in the provincial tedium of Buxton. Instead she would begin a new adventure as an Oxford woman student. As she prepared for Oxford in the spring and summer of 1914 one of the things to which she looked forward most eagerly was the congenial companionship she expected to find there. And from April 1914, when Edward brought Roland Leighton home for a visit, Edward's school friend formed part of Brittain's reveries about her approaching new life at Oxford. A few months later, under the as yet unforeseen pressure arising out of the war, Vera and Roland would fall deeply in love. However, in the spring and summer of 1914, while she was attracted to Roland and delighted that this intelligent, literary young man would also be at Oxford, Brittain was happy to get to know him gradually and did not then think of him as a prospect for a romantic passion. But the war, 'history's greatest disaster', intervened.[2]

Part II of this book is concerned with Brittain's experience during the war years. This chapter is about her first year at Somerville, where for several months she remained largely insulated from the war. The two subsequent chapters take up Brittain's experience of love and war, and her representation of that experience, in *Testament of Youth* and elsewhere.

When Vera Brittain went to Somerville in 1914, university education for women, while still uncommon, was much more acceptable than it had been for the earliest generation of women students. Until the end of the 1860s, Oxford and Cambridge had been exclusive bastions of male privilege. But beginning with Emily Davies's founding of Girton College, a group of determined reformers had succeeded in making it possible for women to study at both Cambridge and Oxford. With the establishment by 1879 of women's Colleges affiliated with both institutions, the doors of the two universities, if not opened wide to welcome women, were at least unbolted.[3]

It is significant that Brittain never appears to have questioned or even examined the fact that, for her, a university education meant Oxford, one of England's two elite universities. By the early twentieth century, Oxford and Cambridge were no longer the only institutions of higher learning in the country, and several of the newer foundations were not only educating women, but granting them degrees.[4] Brittain's assumption that if she were to seek further education, it would be at one of the two 'ancient' universities (both virtually exclusively the preserves of the middle and upper classes in the years before the First World War) reveals the extent to which she unquestioningly accepted the social stratification that was so deeply ingrained a part of English life.

In October 1914, when Brittain began her studies, Somerville was thirty-five years old.[5] Although it was still a young institution, and women continued to face serious obstacles as students, the College's pioneer days were over. The main buildings had been built, tutors and students had developed a set of traditions, and, along with the other women's colleges, Somerville had a recognized, although limited, place within the University itself. Women students could attend lectures and take the examinations for degrees, although full degree status for women was achieved only in 1920, and even that major landmark did not eliminate discrimination against women within the University community.

Somerville had been since its founding the most austere and intellectual of the Oxford women's colleges. Seven years before Brittain went up, the College had taken a decisive movement towards modernization with the appointment in 1907 of its third principal, Emily Penrose. Brittain would later describe Penrose as the 'first genuine scholar among women principals'. She had herself been a Somerville student, and she was the first woman to receive a First in the degree examinations in 'Greats'. Building on the work already accomplished by her predecessors, she had established and encouraged the development of a highly trained tutorial staff of university women, and she planned ahead for the admission of women to full degree status. Brittain had first encountered Penrose during her visit to Oxford in the summer of 1913, at the interview so vividly described in *Testa-*

ment of Youth, when she had gone to her appointment to enquire about the regulations for admission dressed in a beautiful but inappropriate blue and grey satin evening cloak.[6]

Brittain was part of an entering class of thirty-five students. Their average age was nineteen, making Brittain, at twenty, just a little older than the average. The class contained four Scholarship students and four Exhibitioners; and Brittain, as one of the Exhibitioners, was marked out as a potentially strong student. In social class they ranged from the daughters of army or navy officers or clergymen, to the girl who was the Clothworkers' scholar, and who had attended a Church of England elementary school. But they were, overwhelmingly, a middle-class group.[7]

As Martha Vicinus has pointed out, the early women's colleges were, among other things, communities of women, forming 'an important alternative to the traditional family for single women', and offering 'a unique opportunity for intellectual women to join others who shared their delight in study'.[8] In 1914, Somerville was still small enough to be such a community. The Principal and staff together – the Senior Common Room – consisted of fewer than a dozen women and the students numbered fewer than 150.[9] Over its thirty-five-year history, the College had developed traditions for social intercourse among students, and between students and members of the academic staff. There was a social ritual that was based on a student's place in the hierarchy of experience: the third-year students were the most important; the second-years ranked second in line, and the 'freshers' were definitely the least important.

In her famous essay *A Room of One's Own*, Virginia Woolf draws a telling comparison between the elegance and ease of the luncheon she enjoys at one of the Oxbridge men's colleges, and the unattractive dinner she endures at the women's college, 'Fernham', with its prunes and custard 'stringy as a miser's heart'.[10] Woolf quite correctly points out that the women's colleges could not rival the men's in wealth, tradition or beauty. Still, by 1914 Somerville was not as bleak as Woolf's Fernham. Its buildings and grounds were comfortable and attractive. The College quadrangle was spacious, and the library, new in Brittain's day, was a well-appointed, pleasant place to work. The students' rooms themselves, while bed-sitting rooms rather than the suites to which men students were customarily assigned, provided privacy and autonomy. In their own rooms, and in the College's public spaces, students and staff engaged in a wide variety of social and academic activities. Individual students entertained each other in their rooms with tea and cocoa parties. The College as a whole sponsored all-women college dances, for which the students changed into evening dress, and there were a variety of other Somerville activities, or activities involving the other women's colleges, including athletics, debating and the women's college literary magazine, *The Fritillary*. In fact, in these years just before the granting of degrees for women in 1920, after which the women students were much more closely integrated into university life than they had been earlier, there were numerous flourishing traditions associated with one or another of the women's colleges, or with the women's colleges as a group. Somerville, for example had its mock parliament and its going-down play, and the students kept a detailed record of student activities in a handwritten communal diary, called the Somerville Junior Common Room Log Book. In short, during Brittain's era, the prevailing tone of college life at Somerville appears to have been cosy rather than bleak and intensely intimate rather than lonely.

Brittain was acutely conscious of the fact that her departure for Somerville was a major landmark in her life. On 8 October – a Thursday – she spent the day packing and preparing for her departure. In the evening she wrote in her diary: 'This is an important step, the biggest since I left school, perhaps the biggest I have ever taken.' Even though she remained concerned that she would find college life 'narrow', she hoped both for genuine intimate friendship, and for a widening of her horizons: 'I may begin to *live* & to find at least one human creature among my own sex whose spirit can have intercourse with mine. Any life must be wider than this lived here; Oxford I trust may lead to something, but Buxton never will.'[11]

On Friday, 9 October, she travelled to Oxford by train, arriving at 2:30 in the afternoon, when she immediately went for an initial interview with Emily Penrose. Brittain's intention had been to study literature, but her understanding of the College and University requirements was hazy. Before arriving, she had not even seriously considered pursuing the degree programme. At this first interview with the principal she discovered to her surprise that the College authorities expected her to take the degree course, and she found herself gently but firmly steered in that direction.

She entered at once into the excitement and surprises of her new life. The first few days and weeks were both exhilarating and confusing, as Brittain learned about the College's academic routine, about what work would be expected of her and with whom she would do it, and as she began to make friends and integrate herself into the social life of her new community.

Staff and senior students together organised themselves to ensure that in the first few days of the new term incoming students would be instructed in all aspects of College and University life. The day after her arrival, in the company of several new acquaintances, Vera enjoyed getting to know the town. She visited Blackwell's in search of second-hand books; she toured some of the men's colleges; she visited Lady Margaret Hall, which she thought somewhat grander than Somerville. On the next day – a Sunday – Brittain records that 'the Freshers' had 'hymn practice' and were taught the Somerville Song. They were then taken as a group to the Radcliffe Infirmary where they sang hymns to the patients. Afterward, Miss Penrose discussed with them the relationship between the College and the wider University and they were then given a tour of the library, and taught 'how to use it by means of a system of numbers from 100 to 900'.[12] The following day, the senior student in Brittain's wing of the college residence gave her junior students 'a pantry lecture', and Brittain and Norah Hughes, the first friend she made at Somerville, went off to buy 'still more necessaries, such as notebooks & a Lacrosse stick'. Later, she bought some furniture for her room at a college auction and arranged to rent a piano.[13]

Brittain thoroughly enjoyed her introduction to college life. It was like school, she wrote, but 'on an enlarged scale'.[14] As an Exhibitioner, Brittain, when she entered, was acutely conscious of the fact that she had a special position. She was delighted when she was informed by one of her fellow first-year students during the first days of the term that she had impressed the senior students and was considered to be one of the 'lions' of her year. She certainly hoped to shine, to appear exceptional and 'brilliant', to be a leader rather than a follower, and during her first term she would suffer moments of depression when she feared she would be unequal to the challenges she had set herself.

Although she would not find that 'one human creature among my own sex whose spirit can have intercourse with mine' until her postwar return to Oxford, she took an active part in the life of the College, making both friends and enemies, and her diary during her first year contains copious entries about the personal relationships she formed. A month after coming up, she wrote: 'I have of course got my usual reputation of being insufferably conceited, hard & cold, without a scrap of sympathy or kindness. Alongside of this goes the usual interest in me, & I seem to be a much-discussed person. But if the majority do not love me . . . at least they cannot say I am mediocre & seem to find me original.'[15]

With Norah Hughes, the friend she made the day she arrived, she could enjoy the familiarity of a common background. Like Vera, Norah came from the sort of upper-middle-class family which did not usually send its daughters to university.[16]

> I came across . . . a very interesting girl named Miss Hughes . . . who comes from Winchester, is in the Cathedral set, which she hates, & has been to dances, parties etc. & got tired of them, & is thought pretty mad to go to College by her associates, & altogether seems in something the same box as I am.

She could agree with Norah Hughes about a number of things for example, about 'the stupidity of becoming dowdy just because you worked'[17] – and for the first few weeks there was 'no-one at present I would rather go about with than Miss Hughes'.[18] But there were tensions in this not very deep friendship right from its beginning, and after a few weeks the two were spending less time together: 'Miss Hughes finds me . . . too much in earnest & too little on the surface to please her'[19] Brittain wrote in her diary in early November.

Brittain and Nora Hughes shared the experience of 'provincial young ladyhood'. In Una Mary Ellis-Fermor, another close acquaintance Brittain made during her first year,[20] Brittain met a contemporary who came from a markedly different social background. Ellis-Fermor was a London girl, whose family lived in West Hampstead, and she had attended the South Hampstead High School (a Girls' Public Day School Trust school), followed briefly by Bedford College.[21] As her history indicates, Ellis-Fermor's education had been designed to prepare her for university admission and later for the academic life she in fact took up.

Brittain's friendship for Ellis-Fermor was tinged with rivalry – on both sides. For example, she recorded in her diary, a few weeks after arriving, that Emily Penrose had taken her into dinner: 'It was a little formal as of course she keeps one at arm's length, but it was not at all terrifying.' She adds: 'I think she must be going through the scholarship people. I mentioned this fact to Miss Ellis-Fermor' who, Brittain records, replied that if so, *she* should have been taken into dinner first, as her Exhibition was worth more than Vera's. 'I was inwardly very much amused', Brittain writes, adding that she doesn't know what Ellis-Fermor has to boast about, as she had the very best in coaching, whereas she had had to prepare 'as a leaf in the dark'.[22]

In spite of their rivalrous feelings for each other, Brittain and Ellis-Fermor shared a seriousness of purpose, and their acquaintanceship developed over the course of the year. They gave tea parties together several times, they met frequently and they enjoyed intense discussions with one another about 'such things as standing alone . . . & truth & ideals'.[23] With her, Brittain was able to share her thoughts about Somerville's limitations, thoughts that became increasingly strong as the year wore on. In January, for example, she records discussing with her 'the narrowness of College; their absurd attitude towards work and the time necessary to do it in, about the way in which you are treated like a child here as though you needed to be driven to do what you have chosen'.[24]

By January 1915, Ellis-Fermor had become 'E.F'. and was the college associate with whom Brittain could most freely discuss her intellectual interests. But she was not her most intimate friend, nor the one about whom she felt most deeply. In *Testament of Youth* Brittain refers to 'Theresa S., a fair, gay, half-Belgian girl' as her 'one real friend' among her 1914 contemporaries.[25] 'Theresa S.', Frances Theresa Schenzinger, was, like Ellis-Fermor, from London. By 1915 she figures in Brittain's diary as 'Schen', and was certainly a good friend; but so also was Katherine Wood (whom she doesn't mention in *Testament of Youth*), a student from Scotland who was interested in theosophy, and was one of the first people with whom Brittain became intimate enough to be on a given-name basis.[26] In January 1915, after Brittain had returned to Oxford from the Christmas holidays in which she had finally fallen in love with Roland Leighton, she felt close enough to Katherine to be able to discuss 'sex questions' with her.[27]

During this first year, with her circle of friends and acquaintances, Brittain enjoyed discussions, often late into the night, about College life, about the future, about her studies. She went shopping in the company of friends; boating on the river; and she played lacrosse. Sometimes, like the very young women they still were, she and her friends could enjoy interludes of childish rowdiness:

> After tea Dorothy, Katharine & I & a few others had a mad stampede in the little music-room, playing on the old piano that sounds like a trumpet. Then Miss Ellis Fermor & Dorothy & I played about in the Gym. for a bit. Just at a most unpropitious moment, when I with my shoes kicked off was half-way up a rope & Dorothy with her skirt tucked up round her waist was playing about on the vaulting-horse, Miss Hayes Robinson [Somerville's history tutor] elected to come through with two men. . . . We collapsed on the floor & laughed helplessly when they had gone through.[28]

For Brittain and her friends a subject of unfailing interest was the College's teaching staff. The female dons were important to their students not simply as teachers, but also as human beings and, specifically, as women whose lives offered a variation on the usual patterns for middle-class women. They were certainly important to Brittain who, during her first year, recorded in her diary minute and voluminous descriptions of the intellectual capacities, the mannerisms, the dress and general appearance of each member of Somerville's Senior Common Room. These women clearly played a large part in her thoughts and in shaping her feelings about the kind of adult woman she herself hoped to become.

She had an enormous respect for some of them, and a desire to gain their approval. In 1914, this was certainly the way she felt about Hilda Lorimer, a formidable woman, who was Somerville's Classics tutor from 1896 to 1937. Vera would say of her many years later:

> One of the most brilliantly eccentric of women dons, Hilda Lockhart Lorimer combined a thorough Scottish exterior, a ruthless mind, and a witty, sharp-edged tongue with a deeply compassionate heart. . . . For nearly sixty years the university knew, as part of its background, the indomitable little figure with frosty blue eyes, russet-apple cheeks, and golden hair which kept its colour almost to the end of her long life.[29]

That was much later. In 1914, Miss Lorimer was a source of fascination, fear, and the person Brittain most longed to impress, perhaps because she was the authority figure who, initially at least, was least impressed with her. At the time of their first interview, which took place the Friday that Brittain arrived at Oxford and shortly after she had been told that she would have to do Responsions Greek before she could proceed to the degree programme, Brittain records: 'I interviewed Miss Lorimer, who is a small, wiry, rather astringent person, & seemed to think me lazy because I had done so little Greek. Naturally she does not realise the conditions at home & seeing I *have* not done much Greek she has some reason for thinking me idle. She shall soon find out her mistake.'[30]

From then on, for the rest of that first term, one of Brittain's major goals was to do well enough to win Lorimer's respect. In her diary she admitted this frankly to herself: 'the more I try to please or at any rate not to displease her, the more antagonistic to me she becomes . . . the more she crushes & makes me feel small, the more interested in her I become'.[31]

But while she might admire 'the Lorie' (as she was soon referring to her) and others among the women dons, Brittain did not find them entirely satisfactory as alternative examples of ways to live a woman's life. While they did not embody the repressiveness of the Buxton matron, they represented the almost equally unappealing narrowness of spinsterhood. Much as she respected her Aunt Florence Bervon and Louise Heath-Jones, Brittain saw the life of the spinster school teacher as even drearier than the life of an upper-middle-class matron. The life of a don appeared to be only marginally preferable. To the conventionally pretty young woman Brittain was in 1914, the women dons represented dowdiness, and the entries she made in her diary reveal that, much as she respected them for their scholarship, she perceived most of them as failures as women, as the following entry about one of them, Miss Hayes Robinson, indicates:

> I cannot help feeling she has somehow missed her vocation in life . . . she ought to have been married. I should say she is very clever indeed & self-reliant, without being either violently original or aggressively independent, & these qualities . . . would have made her an excellent wife & really the ideal & equal companion of some brilliant man. . . . She is so far from being a typical don as to be quite unrecognisable as one if you did not know it; she is very far from sharing the donnish disregard of dress . . . To picture the Pen [Emily Penrose] soothing the wailing of a raging infant, or the Lorie [Hilda Lorimer] pushing a pram, is the kind of thing one could only imagine . . . in the wildest . . . dreams. But it does not seem ridiculous to imagine Miss Hayes Robinson doing any such thing. Perhaps she is nearer to the ideal type of woman – to the woman we hope the future will bring. . . . She is an instance of a woman who has spent her life in the pursuit & imparting of knowledge . . . without losing an atom of her womanliness or feminine attractiveness. . . . To see her is to feel that a don's life need not be a narrow routine & therefore a thing to dread.[32]

Brittain's comments about Hayes Robinson, with their condemnation of excessive originality in women and their acceptance of a 'womanly' ideal of equality, reveal the limitations of her youthful feminism. Although in 1914 she did indeed define herself as a feminist – for instance, when she joined the Oxford Women's Suffrage Society she wrote in her diary that she was 'very interested in it, as a small side of the enormous question of Feminism'[33] – her views about women's nature were much more conventional and constraining than they would later become. A decade later, when Brittain had become a staunch advocate of equal-rights feminism, she would publicly and privately reject the specious equality involved in limiting a woman's ambition to becoming the 'equal companion of some brilliant man'. But in 1914, while even then she used feminism to validate her own driving ambition, she had not yet had the opportunity to think clearly about what feminism might imply about several crucial areas of her life.

She was constrained, for example, when thinking about her own future. While in the privacy of her diary she did have grand hopes for her own literary success, they were vague. In contrast, her immediate ambition in 1914 and 1915 can best be described as timid, and as very much in consonance with her reveries about Miss Hayes Robinson's future as a wife. During her first year at Oxford, Brittain's immediate aspiration was to become a secretary to a distinguished literary man. Brittain had arrived at this goal after consultation with her old schoolmistress Edith Fry:

> She advised me to keep in mind all through that a secretaryship to a literary man – of course a well-known one for choice – would probably be a better way of launching myself into the literary world than any other, & it would only mean learning typewriting & shorthand after my college course. Literary secretaries are of course not mere shorthand & typewriting drudges, but have to do a considerable amount of research work, & get into the atmosphere of literary influence.[34]

The limitations of Brittain's thinking about feminism also contributed to her largely negative attitude, during this first year, towards her fellow students as a group and towards the College itself. While it is the case, as Martha Vicinus and others have argued, that the Oxford and Cambridge women's colleges did serve as communities of women, they were communities with ambiguous intentions. On the one hand, they provided staff and students with a refuge from the wider world in which women's intellectual merits were slighted and ignored or looked upon with disapproval. On the other hand, they had been founded not so much out of a wish to create a learned community of women independent of that of men, but because of the exclusionary policies of the men's colleges. A woman at one of the women's colleges could either feel a wholehearted sense of identification with her college as community, or feel that it was second-best and that she was there only because she had the misfortune to be born female.

For Brittain, who had at this time thought little about the issue of woman's solidarity, Somerville appeared distinctly second best, precisely because it was a woman's college. At twenty, Vera Brittain often defined herself as bored and irritated by other women. Her diary contains several entries expressing her feeling of distance from them. For example, she writes of the fact that she prefers her brother Edward's friends to her own, adding: 'as I really can't stand girls', and in another diary entry she writes of her 'detestation of women'.[35] And in a letter written in April 1915, as she was about to return to Somerville after a vacation, she comments: 'It is the feminine atmosphere I shall not be able to tolerate – strange how one can feel as I do about some women & be an ardent feminist still! . . . A feminine community is always appalling to anyone like me who gets on much better in the society of men. . . .'[36]

What did this rejection of the feminine community represent? Vera Brittain at twenty did not possess an awareness of a feminist point of view that would allow her to challenge the dominant perception that it was the world of men, not that of women, that offered excitement, wider horizons and challenges. In 1914 feminism meant for her not a sense of identification with other women, but rather a desire to enter the world of men. At this stage in her life Brittain associated femininity with a repressiveness epitomized for her by the Buxton matrons who in 1913 responded with raised eyebrows on hearing that she intended to go to Oxford. For them, she wrote, she was 'eccentric', 'ridiculous', a 'strong-minded woman', and she adds:

> It . . . is scarcely ever men who raise objections to a woman's being given what her talents deserve, but always other women. At first it seems extraordinary that women should be the retrogressive members just when the era of their true glory & justice is beginning to dawn. But I suppose it is that women are sharply divided into two classes, the old-fashioned, who can see nothing, & and the new-fashioned, who see all.[37]

For Brittain in 1914 and 1915, the claustrophobic nature of college life was exacerbated by the restrictions the College authorities placed on contacts between its women students and all males. Brittain was informed about the 'chap' or chaperone rules in August 1914, after she had passed the last of the examinations to gain her admission, and she was amazed by their restrictiveness.[38] Once at Oxford, she found that the restrictions extended even to her brother who, during the autumn months of 1914, was in Oxford participating in the Oxford Senior Officers' Training Corps. He could visit her rooms only under quite limited circumstances; and while she could meet with him in a café she was not allowed to go to his rooms.[39] The 'chap' rules did not in fact impede Brittain in any important way during her first year at Oxford, but for her and for other students they served as an irritant, one of the many reminders of the limitations of Somerville and of what the students often interpreted as the limiting and restrictive attitude of the College's academic staff.

This same restrictiveness also affected Brittain's experience of Somerville and Oxford as academic institutions. Brittain had quite genuinely come to university to learn, though as she wrote in her diary during her first exciting week, 'I again tried to do a little work, but work, for which I came here, seems at present to be what I am least capable of settling down to.'[40] However, within a few days, she was working, and working well, during that first year.

It was not, however, the sort of work she had hoped to do. Instead of studying literature and writing essays, she spent much of the year learning elementary Greek. Why was it necessary for her to undertake what was for the most part an arduous and largely thankless task? From the time of Emily Davies's founding of Girton, those involved with establishing the women's colleges at Cambridge and Oxford were divided about whether women students should be forced to follow the same curriculum as the men, a curriculum that was by the late nineteenth century widely acknowledged to be antiquated.[41] The argument against such a position was that it was absurd to force young women to jump through hoops that would soon be discarded. The argument for insisting that the women should do exactly what the men did was put forward most cogently by Emily Davies, who maintained that the women's movement would be able to convince a doubting world that women were indeed capable of pursuing education in the same fashion as men only if the women fulfilled exactly the same requirements as the male students.

In 1914, Somerville was taking an Emily Davies position. Emily Penrose and her staff knew that the battle over degrees for women would soon be won, and they were determined that as many of their students as possible would have completed the necessary work. It was for this reason that Brittain was given little choice about her own future: the College authorities were determined that Brittain, one of their entering Exhibitioners in 1914, would undertake the degree course. 'People who don't do the degree course seem to be looked down on somewhat & Exhibitioners are almost expected to',[42] Brittain noted with surprise in her diary after her initial interviews with Emily Penrose and other members of the college staff.

The regulations for the degree that affected Vera Brittain most acutely were those based on the assumption that the student came to university with a knowledge of both classical languages. Because of the examination requirements in Greek and Latin, in her first year at Oxford Brittain never in fact began to read English, the subject she had selected before entering. Instead, she had to prepare for and pass two examinations: Responsions Greek, which in 1914 was still required for a degree in a Humanities subject, and Pass Moderations, which involved a knowledge of both classical languages, and some mathematics.[43]

Since Brittain knew no Greek, the College provided her with a special tutor. She worked extremely hard and, fortunately, she succeeded.[44] She would say later that 'the fact that this was done on six week's study of that lovely language . . . testifies to the simplicity of Responsions as an examination'.[45] It also testifies to her capacity for sustained work and, as well, to her determination to win the approval of Hilda Lorimer. When the Responsions results were announced, the College authorities were delighted with her, and she found herself in January 1915 beginning her second term of studies basking in an atmosphere of warm approval. 'I met several people who all congratulated me about my exam', she wrote in her diary on the day of her return to Oxford. 'I hurried up to see the Pen, who also greeted me with a radiant smile & said she had been so delighted about what she was pleased to call my most brilliant performance.'[46]

Passing Responsions was only one hurdle. Pass Moderations remained. Brittain was finally able to work directly with Hilda Lorimer but the experience proved to be difficult and frequently dreary. After her first class she wrote: 'I cannot imagine how the mere prospect of belonging to it ever raised me to such a pitch of enthusiasm as it did last term.'[47] And although she recorded with pleasure that Lorimer 'smiled very kindly' at her during their first interview of the term,[48] on several subsequent occasions Lorimer unfairly criticized her for her weaknesses in Greek: 'The Lorie again used me as a safety valve (as the other P. Mods people say she does) in the unseen class . . . because I did not recognise a certain verb. . . . She cannot . . . realise that the constant practice the others have had in frequently meeting with these verbs fixes them much better in their minds than learning them from a grammar book ever can.'[49]

Brittain's arduous but dreary programme of studies allowed her little time for any of the reading she wanted to do, or for her writing, and any such activity was done in guiltily snatched intervals stolen from cramming. 'I got hold of Schopenhauer out of the library this evening and became very thrilled over the Essay on Genius – at the expense of my logic',[50] she wrote in October 1914. By 1915, she had become involved with the women's students' literary magazine, the *Fritillary*, but writing for it, like reading modern philosophy, had to be done in time snatched from her examination preparations:

> I meant to do such a lot of work today & did in fact manage to finish the Apology this morning. This afternoon however, instead of doing Homer I reviewed 'Sinister Street' Vol 2 for the Fritillary competition, and I also sent in another small poem. . . . I have not 'Sinister Street' with me, which made the review rather difficult, but I was determined to do it. . . .[51]

In spite of the anxiety and the limitations imposed by her examination preparations, this first year at Oxford did allow Brittain to expand her intellectual horizons. The formal work she did in logic and the classical languages was rigorous and challenging, if narrow. A few years later, when she returned to Oxford after her war service, she would be critical of Somerville and Oxford as educational institutions, but during this first year she accepted the hurdles she was set without questioning them deeply, and was able to benefit from exercising the self-discipline necessary for achieving success. And at least at Oxford the instruction she received was competent, in contrast to the home tutoring she had received in Buxton when she was preparing for entrance. Moreover, the possibilities for informal education, so much a part of Oxford life for women as for men, were of great benefit to her. Not only did she read widely, but for the first time in her life she found like-minded contemporaries with whom she could have intense discussions about a host of ideas and issues.

Oxford in 1914 also marked Brittain's first real step towards independent adulthood. She had, of course, been to boarding school, but when she became a Somerville student, both she and her family expected more autonomy. For example, although her father provided both the money for her tuition and her spending money, for the first time she controlled her finances. A few weeks before entering Somerville, she recorded proudly: 'I started a banking account in my own right this morning for the first time. Daddy went down . . . and paid in £100.'[52] And at Somerville she had her own space. Her room in college in 1914–15 was her first opportunity to experience 'a room of one's own' in Virginia Woolf's sense: as symbol and embodiment of genuine autonomy. In 1914 and 1915, Brittain took great pleasure in making her Somerville room both comfortable and an outward representation of her distinctive personality. The College furnished its rooms with only a minimum amount of furniture, and Brittain happily occupied herself with buying and arranging furniture, decoration and draperies.[53]

However, her new independence did not mean that she became isolated from her family. In the *Testament of Youth* account of her first year at Oxford, Brittain scarcely mentions her continuing ties to her family, but in fact they remained strong. She was, for example, eager to show off her room to her family. Her brother Edward – still stationed in Oxford – saw it first, on 15 October. Ten days later, Edith Brittain made her first visit to Oxford, and Vera was proud to offer her mother and brother tea in her rooms.[54]

Throughout her first year, letters from home were very important to her. For example, on 21 February 1915 she wrote to 'Dearest Mother & Daddy' in a mildly complaining tone, reminding them that she had received 'hardly' any letters that week: 'It is so delightful getting letters here, much more so than it ever is anywhere else; every time I go through the hall I look at my pigeon-hole to see if there is one.'[55]

Brittain's ties to her mother were especially strong. Although the plaintive letter just quoted was written to both parents, it was she and her mother who corresponded regularly, as they were to do for many years thereafter. It was to her mother that she confided intimate details about her day-to-day experience of college life. Her mother helped her decorate her room,[56] and and took charge of seeing to it that clothing Vera sent home was properly laundered and mended.[57] She remained concerned, as she had been when Vera was still at home, with her daughter's physical welfare. For instance, when Vera became ill with influenza in March 1915, she felt neglected by the offhand way in which she was cared for at Somerville ('They do not cater for ill people at Somerville', she wrote in her diary) and homesick for her family. When Edith realized that Vera was despondent about her condition, she went directly to Oxford and whisked her back to Buxton so that she could recover properly.[58]

In September 1914, on the eve of her departure for Oxford, when she had discovered that not only would her brother not be entering New College, but that Roland Leighton would not be beginning his studies at Merton, she had written in her diary: 'Going to Oxford will not be . . . the same for me if he is never there. The glamour will all fade from my college dreams. How much this terrible war has wrecked besides the lives of those which are exacted in its toll!'[59]

In fact, during her first term Brittain, as we have seen, was able to immerse herself in her new life as a woman student, and for the most part she thought little about the war, or even about her personal life outside of College. But inexorably, the war entered her personal consciousness as it did the consciousness of the University itself. After Christmas, her own feelings changed radically, when she and Roland fell truly in love. From January to June 1915, while she continued to work diligently for Pass Moderations (which she successfully passed in June), Oxford receded as the main focus of her attentions, to be replaced by her concern for her individual loved ones – Roland and her brother Edward – and by her gradually growing feeling that she herself must become involved in the war effort.

Oxford itself was changing, as increasing numbers of men students enlisted. In the summer term of 1915, the Somerville College buildings became a military hospital, and most of the students and staff were moved to Oriel College's St Mary Hall. As the war came closer, the Somerville community responded. Students and dons together participated in aid to Belgian relief, in entertaining wounded soldiers, and even in cooking classes. During these extraordinary times, some of the formality and distance between dons and students dissolved. Vera herself, along with a handful of other students, had been moved not to Oriel's St Mary Hall, but to Micklem Hall, where they were accompanied by Miss Darbishire, the English tutor. By May, as the end of her last term approached, Brittain had achieved a new level of friendship and even intimacy with Miss Darbishire. One evening, she and a friend were invited by Miss Darbishire to her rooms to see her Milton manuscripts where, Brittain recorded, Miss Darbishire became 'quite confidential over interviews with scholarship candidates'. She also introduced them that same evening to Rupert Brooke, whose *1914* she had just purchased from Blackwell's.[60] The evening ended with Miss Darbishire reading, at Vera's request, 'five sonnets by Rupert Brooke, the most promising poet of the younger generation, . . . who . . . died at Lemnos a week or two ago'.[61]

During this last term Brittain was the only remaining Somerville candidate for Pass Moderations, and even Miss Lorimer became less distant. In addition to their formal work together, she also met informally with her to discuss such questions as 'the different qualities of poetry and philosophy' and, on an even more intimate level, to discuss with Brittain her plans to seek leave from Oxford and take up nursing.[62] As these women became friends rather than mere authority figures, Brittain's admiration for them grew. For example, she pronounced a lecture that Helen Darbishire gave on Milton 'magnificent': 'It had that quality usually at present only found in lectures by men of getting a very great deal into a few words & yet telling you all you want to know about a subject.'[63] Thus it was not without regret and ambivalence that she left Oxford at the end of the summer term, to return only in 1919, after the war had ended.

5

Love in Wartime

'Men's wars are made of stories'[1] and stories about the First World War – the most literary of all wars in Western European history – have fascinated readers throughout our century. *Testament of Youth* was written as a *woman's* war story, and its initial success and enduring popularity derive in large part from its character as a war story. Brittain's most memorable achievement was her moving portrayal of her own youthful experience of grief over the loss of loved ones. She gave her readers both a touching recreation of her emotions and an analysis of them, filtered through her post-war re-thinking. The result is a powerful statement about war and about the relationship between love and war, romance and violence.

But precisely because Brittain's book recreates through narrative the experience of young people who supported the war when it was happening, its attitude towards war in general and the 'Great War' in particular is shot through with unacknowledged ambivalence. Because *Testament of Youth* is as much a classic war story as an anti-war statement, its author falls victim to the tradition in which war stories simplify moral and emotional realities. This is especially true of Brittain's treatment of the four young men who figure prominently in the book, and who were all killed in the war: her brother Edward, her fiancé Roland Leighton, and her two young friends Victor Richardson and Geoffrey Thurlow.[2]

In the *Testament of Youth* narrative, all four young men become the faultless heros of the traditional war story. Similarly, the woman who relates to them has to do so in an overly romanticized, unambivalent way. The Edward Brittain of *Testament of Youth* is a hero, because he dies on the Asiago Plateau: accordingly, the brother–sister relationship Brittain creates in her book is virtually free of conflict. But we have already seen that in reality Brittain had the ambivalent feelings toward her younger brother that one would expect a real person and not a war heroine to have. The death of that brother made it impossible to express these feelings or to write frankly about the real Edward.[3] Again, in tribute to the fact that he had died, she oversimplifies her romantic attachment to Roland Leighton. Vera was passionately in love with Roland in 1915, but it was a romance based largely on illusion. The two were victims of the war in that the war forced them to fall in love too quickly. After their initial attraction to each other, in April 1914, Vera was intrigued by the idea that Roland would be at Merton while she was at Somerville, but she was prepared to get to know him gradually, and she preserved the sense of detachment and the rationality that was so much a part of her pre-war personality. Later on, after the war was over, she realized that her knowledge of him – if not her feelings for him – had been insubstantial. She blurs this in *Testament of Youth*, to create a portrayal of star-crossed young love. This story of youthful love is poignant, but it is a perception of her experience that bears the marks of an entrapment in the traditions of the war narrative as much as it does of her feelings for Roland himself.

AUGUST 1914

In August 1914, on the eve of the First World War, Vera Brittain was a rebel in that she rejected the anti-intellectual provinciality of her family and defined herself as a feminist. But there her rebelliousness ended. In most ways she was a conventional 'provincial young lady'. This conventionality was especially marked when it came to politics and to ideas about social class and nationalism, aspects of life about which she had done little thinking. As she would explain it later: '"Current events" . . . represented something that must be followed rather reluctantly in the newspapers, but would never, conceivably, have to be lived. What really mattered to us were not these public happenings but the absorbing incidents of our own private lives – our careers, our ambitions, our games and our love-affairs. . . .'[4]

The outbreak of war was an event for which she was unprepared in every way, and initially she was able to respond to it only with the patriotic rhetoric of the newspapers and of government pronouncements. In the first months of the war, her diary is filled with entries about German culpability, English rectitude and the duty of everyone in England to contribute to the war effort: 'All the nations of this continent are ready with their swords drawn . . . Germany the aggressor . . . has broken treaty after treaty & disregarded every honourable tie with other nations.'[5] Only rarely did she express any realization about what the war would actually entail in terms of brutality and loss of life.

In the 1930s she would say that the war itself had made her a pacifist, and indeed her work as a nurse did contribute to her post-war internationalism and pacifism. But while the war was in progress that anti-war sentiment was expressed only in flashes. Even when she had become sceptical of the war's justice and critical of those responsible for it, she did not possess the language or the experience necessary for the formulation of a reasoned, sustained anti-war point of view that would have allowed her to act on such anti-war sentiment by refusing to participate further in the 'war effort'. Later, she would describe herself, during the final months of the war, as 'the complete automaton' existing in a state of 'numb disillusion'.[6] After the war, when she was able to reflect on what had happened to her and to others like herself, the evil use to which her youthful ignorance and idealism had been put engendered in her both a sense of outrage and a commitment to the better education of the young.

In her own subsequent analysis of the way in which her limited pre-war experience had made her vulnerable, she dwelt on her acceptance of England's moral superiority and on her overly ready adherence to conventional definitions of duty, honour and heroism. All these elements were present as part of the upper-middle-class patriotism that characterized her responses in 1914, but there was an additional factor that Brittain herself did not perceive, then or later: namely, the way in which the war caused her to subdue her feminist sentiments and to retreat to some extent into an acceptance of conventional definitions of masculinity and femininity. We know that Brittain was genuinely feminist in 1914, in that she had recognized in herself a legitimate ambition and perceived the conventional view of a woman's place as constricting and discriminatory, but we have also seen that she had thought little about the nature of femininity and still less about masculinity. Her views about the latter appear to have been shaped vicariously, through the experience of her brother Edward and the public-school values he absorbed at Uppingham. Her stance in relation to these values was crucial in determining her response to the outbreak of war.

Edward Brittain appears to have been, in most respects, a model public schoolboy who accepted without question the ethical and social principles that the school authorities were determined to instil in their pupils. Thus, in contrast to Robert Graves, for example, who recounts that he had resigned from the Officers' Training Corps at his public school as a protest against the school's attempt to connect manliness with militarism,[7] Edward was an enthusiastic member of Uppingham's OTC.

The OTC played a major part in inculcating what the public school mentality considered to be appropriate ideas about upper middle-class masculinity. It was there, even more than through sport, that conceptions of patriotism, bravery and duty were instilled. The OTC also brought home to the boys the fact that they were members of the governing classes, and that this membership brought with it the responsibility of leadership.

Edward appears to have accepted all these ideas, and in spite of the fact that Vera's feminism and ambition made her occasionally bitter, it never occurred to her to question the canons of masculinity. Instead, she was proud of them, and proud of her brother when he exhibited the appropriate behaviour. In July 1914, when Vera visited Uppingham for Speech Day, she was particularly thrilled by Edward's participation in the OTC: '[The Corps] were a fine sight as they stood for the Headmaster to inspect them', she wrote in her diary. In addressing the Corps, the Headmaster – whom Vera thought 'a splendid man' – offered the boys some precepts by which they should conduct themselves. 'I forget most of the precepts', she wrote, 'but I know the climax was that if a man could not be useful to his country he was better dead.'[8]

Vera and Edward Brittain, then, both accepted the conventional view of masculine upper middle-class duty. It is thus no wonder that they were extremely vulnerable to the propaganda the government immediately launched in August 1914, urging young men to volunteer; and it is no wonder that it was Vera, more than anyone else, who urged Edward to do so. In contrast, Arthur Brittain was at first adamantly opposed to the idea of Edward volunteering. In the family quarrels that ensued, with Edward and Vera on one side and Arthur Brittain on the other, subtle social class differences, between the middle-class father and his children, whose education had encouraged them to adopt upper middle-class values, played a part: 'Daddy worked himself into a thorough temper, raved away at us, & said he would not allow Edward to go abroad whatever happened', Vera wrote in her diary. 'Edward replied quite calmly that no one could prevent him serving his country in any way he wanted to . . .' Later on, Edward explained it in this way to Vera: 'Daddy, not being a public school man or having had any training, could not possibly understand the impossibility of his remaining in inglorious safety while others, scarcely older than he, were offering their all. . . .'[9] A month later, when Arthur Brittain was still refusing to let Edward volunteer, Vera wrote in her diary: 'After dinner we all discussed again Daddy's refusal to let Edward go into the Army, & the unmanliness of it, especially after we read in *The Times* of a mother who said to her hesitating son "My boy I don't want you to go, but if I were you I should!"'[10]

Vera Brittain's acceptance of public-school precepts about manliness, and of a woman's duty to urge 'manliness' on men in wartime, is clearly revealed in that comment. It is also revealed in her contemptuous attitude towards Bertram Spafford, her would-be suitor, who was not eager to volunteer. She saw him as a 'shirker', and as less than a gentleman, because he was concerned about the effect his volunteering might have on his business.[11] In the first months of the war, then, Vera's attitudes towards appropriate masculine and feminine behaviour in wartime were exactly those that were calculated to be of most use to military mobilization. Just a few months before, she had won an Exhibition to Somerville, the most austere and intellectual of the Oxford women's colleges; a few days after the war broke out, she took to knitting: 'the only work it seems possible as yet for women to do'.[12]

Brittain's narrative of her immediate responses to the outbreak of war in *Testament of Youth* corresponds in its essential points with the contemporary evidence, although she does minimize the extent to which she gave way to unthinking jingoistic patriotism. For example, in narrating the account of the dispute between her father on the one hand, and her brother (and herself) on the other, she says: 'My father vehemently forbade Edward . . . to join anything whatsoever. Having himself escaped immersion in the public-school tradition, which stood for militaristic heroism unimpaired by the damping exercise of reason, he withheld his permission for any kind of military training. . . .'[13] This description minimizes her own younger self's eagerness to embrace that public-school tradition. And nowhere does she disclose that she had been willing to pin metaphorical white feathers on men like Bertram Spafford, who were reluctant to immediately volunteer.

TRUE LOVE

Roland Leighton, Brittain's wartime fiancé, was a close friend of Edward Brittain's at Uppingham. He and Vera first became attracted to each other when he visited the Brittain family during the Easter holidays in April 1914. Roland at nineteen was good-looking and dashing. For Vera, he possessed a glamour deriving from his background, which had many of the features she sorely missed in what she felt to be her own irredeemably ordinary milieu. Roland's parents were both writers. While neither was a serious writer of the first or even the second rank, they had both fulfilled what had already become Brittain's most cherished secret ambition. They made their livings by their writing, and they were part of the London literary world.[14] Robert Leighton wrote adventure stories for boys, many with a 'wild west' theme, but the real power in the household belonged to the colourful, eccentric Marie Connor Leighton, who wrote melodramatic romantic fiction which was serialized in the Northcliffe papers and for which, in the years before the First World War, she was very well paid. In her reminiscences, Roland's sister Clare tells us that 'the entire household revolved around my mother's writings', while her father's work was 'not supposed to matter as much because he earned less'.[15]

The three Leighton children grew up in a family in which a raffish bohemianism was blended with Edwardian upper middle-class values. Thanks to Marie Connor Leighton's success as a writer, the family lived most of the year in a large house in St John's Wood, moving each summer to a seaside villa at Lowestoft in East Anglia. Both houses were perpetually untidy, the pace of life was frenetic, and tradesmen's bills were left unpaid, Marie Connor Leighton holding firmly to the principle that only the 'lower classes' bothered to pay on time.[16]

But while Marie Connor Leighton had a penchant for melodrama, she had not abandoned the values of her officer father and she intended that her children should be brought up 'most correctly'.[17] Roland, the eldest, was therefore sent to Uppingham, a most correct school, where, like his friend Edward Brittain, he became a conventional success, winning literary prizes but also excelling as a school leader, and participating enthusiastically in the Officers' Training Corps.[18]

In *Testament of Youth*, Brittain implies that she and Roland fell in love during his visit to Buxton in April 1914. 'Armed with my Somerville exhibition and my few months' seniority, I refused to be prospectively impressed by this person, but such equanimity was difficult to achieve',[19] she says. It was during this initial encounter that he first told her about Olive Schreiner's novel, *Story of an African*

Farm, which would later figure significantly in their wartime relationship.

'That Easter meeting with Roland had stirred a spring ferment in my blood', she says, quoting from her diary of 18 May: 'I could only gaze outside and long for someone strong and loving, a man in preference to a woman as most women annoy me, who would be intimate and understanding, so that I should not be any more alone . . . I so desire a sympathetic companionship, I do so want as Lyndall did in Olive Schreiner's book, "something to worship."'[20]

In *Testament of Youth*, this romance reaches its pre-war height at Speech Day at Uppingham. In creating the Uppingham Speech Day scenes, Brittain was both influenced by and at the same time was contributing to the post-war mythology surrounding the idyllic quality of the summer preceding the Great War, with its calm, sunshine and loveliness.[21] These were 'three radiant days',[22] she tells us, and it is clear that for Brittain and her readers in 1933, their radiance is enhanced by the fact that they are the 'lovely legacy of a vanished world'. For Roland and herself, the climax came the afternoon of the Headmaster's garden party:

> The afternoon was so hot, and our desire for conversation so great, that Roland and I were relieved when . . . we could lose ourselves in the crowd at the Headmaster's garden-party. I remember to-day how perfectly my dress – a frilled pink ninon with a tiny pattern, worn beneath a rose-trimmed lace hat – seemed to have been made for our chosen corner of the garden, where roses with velvet petals softly shading from orange through pink to crimson foamed exuberantly over the lattice-work of an old wooden trellis. But even if I had forgotten, I should still have Roland's verses, 'In the Rose-Garden', to renew the fading colours of a far-away dream.[23]

The visual cues Brittain employs here evoke a scene that could have been painted by any number of genre painters of the pre-war period. Her elegiac language conjures up an appropriate title – perhaps 'First Love: or In the Rose Garden' – and also the ornate gilded frame that would have served as the setting for such a painting, the frame securely walling off this irrecoverable experience from the post-war present in which she was writing. Brittain's diary entries for that 11 July are, in contrast, relatively prosaic. She does not in fact mention either her dress, or her hat, or the roses, but instead describes her conversation with Roland, including the banter that passed between them. I am not suggesting that Brittain did not experience that moment in the Rose Garden (indeed, her feelings for Roland and for the moment itself were probably stronger than the diary entries would suggest), but it was Roland's death in the war which lends to the *Testament of Youth* scene its melancholy intensity.

Brittain was certainly not exclusively or unequivocally in love with Roland in the summer of 1914, even though in creating the *Testament of Youth* narrative she felt she had to portray herself as being so. To that end she engaged in some judicious editing in her retelling. For example, when she quotes her 18 May 1914 diary entry, in which she says that, like Olive Schreiner's character Lyndall, she wanted 'something to worship', she implies that she was referring to Roland. In fact, if she was referring to any one individual, it was probably Joseph Harry Ward, the Fairfield curate. But while she exaggerates in the telling, she did find Roland attractive. He was a boy she could respect; she found his conversation stimulating; she thought him handsome; and she was intrigued by his literary London family, and especially by his mother, whom she was very disappointed not to meet at that Uppingham Speech Day.[24]

The attraction she felt for Roland did give her some encouragement that there might be more to heterosexual relationships than fending off kisses from over-eager Buxton boys at dances, or proposals of marriage from dreary suitors, or worst of all, avoiding the furtive intrusiveness of 'Old Cheese', her Latin tutor. But her feelings for Roland were not strong enough, even after their meeting at Uppingham in July, to cause Brittain to bring matters to a conclusion with Bertram Spafford. She continued to allow Spafford to believe that she might possibly relent, and on occasion she herself was confused about how she felt about him.

Moreover, explosive possibilities for confusion were present in the only partly acknowledged feelings of jealousy that existed between Vera and Edward Brittain concerning Roland. In *Testament of Youth*, Edward figures in the romance between his sister and his friend only as a benevolent, understanding sponsor of the relationship. In fact, the situation was more complicated. Roland was, after all, Edward's friend. He and Roland, along with a third boy, Victor Richardson, had become an intimate threesome at Uppingham. Edward was deeply attached to Roland, he admired him, he acknowledged him as his superior, both intellectually and in terms of his capacities for leadership. We can assume that he had invited Roland to Buxton in April 1914 so that he could enjoy his exclusive companionship. And then he had to share him with his sister – at least for the first week of the visit. Fortunately for Edward, Vera had earlier planned a visit to their paternal aunt and uncle in Windermere, and she left for the Lake District a few days before Roland's visit ended. In her diary Brittain wrote: 'Roland said to me most earnestly "Why *are* you going tomorrow?" . . . I suggested that perhaps my departure would induce him to neglect Edward less, & he said he certainly had given up his company for mine a good deal.'[25] Although Brittain says explicitly in *Testament of Youth* that Edward 'did not appear to object',[26] in fact she and Roland knew he was hurt.[27] He would certainly have been upset had he known that his sister and his friend discussed him and his personality in a critical way. Roland, it appears, was eager to talk about Edward with his sister. Perhaps because she herself was irritated with Edward just at that moment, Vera entered into this discussion, recording in her diary that 'Leighton finds "brick walls" in his [Edward's] intellect just as I do, & with me objects to the orthodoxy & general properness of his opinions'.[28]

By Speech Day, Edward had become openly despondent about his friendship with Roland. On the evening after the Headmaster's Garden party, Edward, Vera and Edith Brittain were alone, and, Brittain records, Edward 'made us all depressed by giving over to his melancholy feelings on leaving school . . . E. seemed somewhat depressed about [Roland] & not so sure as he is of Richardson. I asked him if he meant to drop Roland when he got to Oxford. He said "No, but he thought Roland would probably drop him". . . .'[29]

Edward's and Vera's affection for one another was unconditional, although they might at times become exasperated with one another. But each doubted his or her ability to retain Roland's interest. When they parted at Uppingham on 12 July 1914, Brittain wrote in her diary: 'I could not help wondering whether & when I shall see him again, & whether he will really drop Edward . . . and thereby more or less drop me.' At the same time, she acknowledged to herself that she was very attracted to him: 'I said goodbye . . . with more indifference than I felt. . . . He seems even in a short acquaintance to share both my faults & my talents and my ideas in a way that I have never found anyone else do yet.'[30]

Even if Edward's feelings for Roland were limited to a deep fondness, there was an undoubted element of triangularity in the relationship between these three young people in the summer of 1914, with the elusive, self-confident Roland at its apex. And the relationship between Edward and Roland may have involved more than friendship. Given that there is convincing evidence that Edward later was involved in a homosexual relationship,[31] it is plausible to assume that there may have been a homoerotic side to his feelings for this close friend in 1914. Roland may possibly have had similar feelings for Edward. In any case, in the spring and summer of 1914 he engaged in emotionally charged intellectual conversations with Edward's intelligent, attractive sister perhaps as a move towards heterosexuality. The feelings of all three of these sensitive, intelligent but inexperienced young people were more complicated than the conventional mythology about friendship and romantic love in which Brittain cast them in *Testament of Youth*.

Certainly Brittain was uneasy about sexuality, in large part because even then she realized that women had to pay a price for heterosexual involvement. Many years later she would become one of the interwar period's most vigorous and outspoken advocates of egalitarian marriage, but at this early stage in her life, while she viscerally rejected a dominant ideology that was fundamentally oppressive to women, she was too young to have devised alternative models. So, while she did on occasion daydream about romantic love with Roland that summer, and did feel that some of the excitement had been taken out of her Oxford adventure because neither Roland nor Edward would begin their studies, she was far more concerned with studying for (and passing) the Oxford Senior Local examination than she was with any possibilities of romance. In September, after attending the wedding of a Buxton acquaintance, she wrote in her diary: 'I do not think I am likely to marry as I am too hard to please & too difficult to understand . . . and I would be satisfied with nothing less than a mutually comprehensive loving companionship.'[32] In short, in the summer and autumn of 1914 Brittain shut the lid as firmly as she could on the Pandora's box of love and sexuality, and turned all her energies to preparing for Oxford.

If there had been no war, would Vera and Roland have fallen in love? Had they been able to get to know each other under normal circumstances, one suspects these two strong and competitive personalities might well have become quickly disenchanted with one another. It is impossible to say. What did happen was that the abnormal wartime situation encouraged them to proceed more quickly than they would otherwise have done in moving from an initial mutual attraction to intense love.

In the autumn of 1914 when Roland was negotiating to obtain a commission (at first unsuccessfully because of problems with his eyesight) he and Vera did correspond. He wrote as follows to Vera, the week before she left for Somerville, when it appeared that he had found a suitable regiment: 'I feel . . . that I am meant to take some active part in this war. It is to me a very fascinating thing – something, if often horrible, yet very ennobling and very beautiful, something whose elemental reality raises it above the reach of all cold theorising. You will call me a militarist. You may be right.'[33]

In answer, she expressed approval of his efforts to join up: 'There cannot be any question that you are doing the right thing, though even if you are unsuccessful you certainly cannot accuse yourself of cowardly shirking when you have done your best.' When she responds to his comments on militarism, some of the ambivalence she already felt towards the position into which the war had thrust women emerges, but she also echoes Roland's rhetoric about the glamour of war:

> I don't know whether your feelings about war are those of a militarist or not; I always call myself a non-militarist, yet the raging of these elemental forces fascinates me, horribly but powerfully, as it does you. I find beauty in it too; certainly war seems to bring out all that is noble in human nature, but against that you can say that it brings out all the barbarous too. But whether it is noble or barbarous I am quite sure that had I been a boy, I should have gone off to take part in it long ago; indeed I have wasted many moments regretting that I am a girl. Women get all the dreariness of war and none of its exhilaration.

A few days later, she put both the dreariness and the glamour behind her, and became immersed in the experiences of her first term. As she would say in *Testament of Youth*: 'It was all so thrilling that for the time being the neglected War . . . seemed quite out of the picture.'[34]

Her insulation from the war and romance ended abruptly with the Christmas vacation. She took the Responsions Greek examination on Wednesday, 9 December and immediately thereafter went home to Buxton where, in contrast to Oxford, she read the newspapers. The war news and the soldiers stationed in Buxton made her think of Roland.[35] Both Edward and Roland were by now 'gazetted'. Edward had left Oxford to join the 11th Battalion of the Sherwood Foresters at Frensham as a subaltern on 22 November, and Roland was in Norwich with the 4th Battalion of the Norfolk regiment. Both were steadfastly determined to get to the Front as soon as they could, and Vera had by this time given up the hope she had still retained in October that 'we may yet all be at Oxford together in spite of everything; and that things which used to count so much will begin to count again'.[36]

All during their autumn correspondence, Vera and Roland had remained quite formal with each other: Vera wrote her letters to

'Dear Roland' and signed them 'Yours ever sincerely, Vera Mary Brittain'. Roland began his without any salutation, and signed them 'Yours ever, R.A.L.'. But now, the pace of their relationship quickened. She and Roland agreed to exchange photographs, and Vera had one taken especially for him. Roland not only wrote but telephoned, asking her what she wanted for her twenty-first birthday, on 29 December. 'I suppose really I ought not to let him give me anything for my birthday, but, apart from the fact that, however much I insisted he ought not to, he would probably do it just the same, I simply *cannot* deny myself the joy of receiving a book both from him & inscribed by him',[37] she wrote in her diary.

Brittain was conscious of the importance this birthday ought to have ('It is a serious matter I suppose to be twenty one & responsible for oneself entirely'[38]) but her experience of coming of age was diminished by the sudden, spurious maturity with which both her brother and Roland were invested by becoming soldiers. '[I]t seems absurd', she wrote to Roland, 'not that I am of age . . . but that you are not; you seem so old for your age that I always feel younger, & now with your recent responsibilities & anxieties I suppose you will be more so than ever. Even beside Edward at Oxford I felt a mere child; he seems to have grown up absolutely & so suddenly.'[39]

Edward returned home for Christmas from his regiment a few days after Vera wrote that letter, and seeing him in person, now a real soldier who might soon see fighting, he became transformed for Brittain: 'he seems so tall & absolutely grown up . . . he really is a fit object of devotion'.[40] The fact that Edward her beloved, but still her *younger* brother, for whom in ordinary circumstances she felt a deep but not uncritical love had become 'an object of devotion' reflects the heightened state of Brittain's emotions during the final days of 1914. The drama and the poignancy of war were conspiring at this critical juncture to ensure that she would fall deeply in love with Roland. And that is exactly what happened when the two young people met in London. On 21 December, when writing in her diary, she could still be gently amused by Roland: 'The dear boy is so pedantic that I cannot help laughing at his letters',[41] she says. But on 28 December she received a letter from Roland, suggesting that she come up to town, to visit him and meet his mother. On 29 December, her birthday, she was touched to receive '*five* books' from him: 'I loved every single thing he sent me', she wrote.[42] On 30 December she travelled up to town (along with Edward who was going on to rejoin his battalion) and this New Year's meeting with Roland – the first time that they had met face-to-face since July – was when they truly fell in love. As she would say later, in *Testament of Youth*, she found a changed Roland, a boy who had been transformed into a man, a soldier in uniform.[43] She wrote at length in her diary about New Year's Eve, '[t]he most precious evening of my life thus far':

> Everything these two days had been dreamlike & incomplete; almost everything we could have said to each other had been left unsaid, but I knew the one thing that made all the difference in the world – that the feelings which, ever since I had known him I had thought might quite possibly arise between us, were no longer a dream but a reality.[44]

During their two days in London, Vera and Roland met, not alone, but in the presence of members of their families. Conventional middle-class mores – and the Brittains were especially observant of them – ensured that these two young people could have extended privacy only in their letters to one another. Vera's Aunt Belle, her mother's younger unmarried sister was, fortunately, a sympathetic chaperone (she was much more lighthearted than the formidable Aunt Florence). Aunt Belle sensed a romance as soon as she saw her niece and Roland together, and she was delighted to encourage their feelings for one another. It was she who reminded Vera that, given the circumstances of the war, their meeting 'might be for the last time'.[45]

'In this time of tragedy there can be no postponement.'[46] Falling in love had to be done quickly, because both of them realized that Roland might soon be killed. From that time until Roland's death a year later, love for him dominated Vera's being. Temporarily, at least, feelings of love diminished her ambition and her fierce desire for autonomy. As she wrote in her diary, after the poignant few minutes when they were actually alone together on New Year's Eve 1914: 'Beside these newly-born dreams of a possible future my old dreams & aspirations grew pale, as would the moon's cold splendour beside the passionate flames of the sun.'[47]

Brittain's language reflects the intellectual and psychological adaptation imposed by wartime circumstances. In the pre-war period, she had fashioned a self-definition that included assertiveness, ambition and a commitment to hard work, all of which violated Edwardian feminine stereotypes and also prevailing sentimental stereotypes about passion and emotion. The war caused her to retreat, to a certain degree at least, back into those feminine stereotypes. Having fallen deeply in love, the only way she could bear the intensity of her feelings was by adopting a traditional wartime role for women, that of hero's beloved.

On 21 April 1915, three weeks after Roland had left for the Front,

Brittain wrote in her diary: 'sometimes I can hardly believe I am I. I feel as if I were writing a novel about someone else & not myself at all. . . .'[48] Even as it was happening, the insubstantial quality of their relationship encouraged these two young people to fashion a romance that was always more real as a narrative about itself than it was as actual lived experience. Partly this was a result of the circumstances of war and distance. In all, Vera and Roland met on only seven occasions, for a total of some seventeen days. Only three of these occasions occurred after they had truly fallen in love.[49] And added to their limited opportunities for meeting and thus genuinely getting to know each other was the overpowering diffidence that both felt about sexuality. We know that such diffidence was not universal among youth during the First World War: there were 'war babies' born to unmarried mothers; and the problems of 'Khaki fever' and the dangers of wartime sexuality were matters of widespread public discussion.[50] Brittain herself commented on this question in her diary in April 1915, and her point of view is revealing: while she rejects harsh condemnation of such unmarried mothers, she also does not believe that such immorality (which she sees as a 'problem almost entirely connected with the working classes') should be easily condoned: 'These kind of people forget that the strength of a race lies in its chastity, that in our stronger moral fibre lies the whole source of our superiority over the French. . . .'[51]

Vera and Roland were never in any danger of producing a baby 'out of wedlock': indeed until their meeting in August 1915, which was to be their last, they had never even kissed each other.[52] Even in March 1915, when he visited her at Buxton during a brief leave, the closest they came to physical contact was when Roland kissed Vera's hand: 'He took my hand and kissed it again as he did in the train once before – but this time there was no glove upon it.'[53] About their parting that day she wrote: 'For a moment I wished he would have kissed me; many men would have done so and it would hardly have been a liberty at that solemn moment. But afterwards I was glad that he had not done so, but had remained characteristic of himself up to the last. . . .'[54] When he finally did kiss her, during their railway journey from Buxton to London in August 1915, it was clear to Vera that this was the first kiss Roland had given any girl. She writes: 'Suddenly he came over from his window & kissed me – with such a boyish shyness & awkwardness that I could have laughed – only I shivered instead. He had so obviously never kissed any other girl before me.'[55]

But the limited nature of their actual physical contact did not diminish the intensity of Vera's feelings for Roland. Because neither she nor he could allow the sexual part of their relationship to be actualized this literary young woman instead experienced the sexual passion she felt for her lover both through the power of literary allusion and through her own creation of a narrative of the experience as it was occurring. Her use of literature as a vehicle for sexual feeling can be seen in a diary entry made in April, after she had finished reading Turgenev's *On the Eve*, one of the books Roland had given her for her birthday. The love scenes between Elena and Dimitri, she writes, 'made me think of Roland & me – not what we have ever risen to in one another's presence, but what I believe we are both capable of rising to. All the rest of the day I felt wild with desire for him.'[56]

Months earlier, in December 1914, Roland had taken Vera and her Aunt Belle to see a play. Brittain tells us in *Testament of Youth* that it was *David Copperfield*,[57] but she does not include the fact that she and Roland both agreed that Steerforth was the 'finest character in the book'. Steerforth is Dickens's Byronic anti-hero. Passionate, selfish and sexual, he is not the sort of male character of whom Brittain usually approved, or to whom she was usually attracted. We can surmise that Steerforth's sexual energy and his capacity for tragedy represented in a covert way both the sexual feelings that Vera and Roland had for each other, but never felt free to express, and also Vera's wartime capacity to identify love with feminine self-sacrifice.

Dickens, Turgenev, Rupert Brooke all served as validating texts for these two young lovers, but none was as important to them as Olive Schreiner's *The Story of an African Farm*, which Brittain would refer to in *Testament of Youth* as 'the strange little novel which had become our Bible'.[58] We know that Brittain had encountered Schreiner's feminist *Women and Labour* at school, well before she had ever met Leighton. In *Women and Labour* Schreiner had written a reasoned plea for women's freedom. In *The Story of an African Farm* Schreiner is ambivalent about women's freedom. While the novel's heroine Lyndall is, as Joyce Berkman has said, 'a feminist rebel against gender norms' her story also illustrates the peril that freedom entails for women. Shreiner's heroine Lyndall dies making statements about women's disadvantaged position, but they are statements of despair and not hope, and she dies – as a result of bearing a child out of wedlock – seeking freedom not through autonomy, but through passion unfettered by convention.[59]

Roland had given Vera the Schreiner novel in April 1914, sending it after her when she had left Buxton to visit her relatives in

Windermere. On receiving it, Brittain had recorded in her diary: 'Inside the cover he inscribed "V.M.B. in gratitude for much. R.A.L." Queer boy! I wonder what he considered he is grateful for . . . He says he thinks Lyndall . . . is like me, only "sadder & less charmingly controversial". He wants me to write & tell him what I think of the book.'[60]

Brittain was not unmoved by *The Story of an African Farm* when she first read it, but the book and its characters came to have far more meaning for her after December 1914. From that time until Roland's death, references to it were woven into their courtship, through their own correspondence, through Brittain's diary, and through the correspondence between Brittain and Marie Connor Leighton, who had undoubtedly introduced her son to the novel in the first place.[61] There are several reasons why this book appealed so strongly to these young people. At times, the atmosphere of Schreiner's novel is one of overheated romanticism. Its themes include suffering, loneliness, and unfair persecution of the young by the old. It extolls high feeling, self-sacrifice and the beauty of death. In addition, although neither Roland nor Vera ever refers to it, there was the undoubted attraction of Lyndall's overt sexuality. While they restricted themselves to what Brittain in *Testament of Youth* refers to as 'what we both believed to be decent behaviour', Lyndall breaks through the barriers of conventional morality, and through her, so could they. Finally, the novel covertly supports feminine self-sacrifice. Normally, Brittain had rejected and would reject any such acceptance of female subordination, but in 1915, sustaining both a wartime romance and adhering to the principle of female autonomy was a difficult burden. Schreiner's Lyndall, who is punished by her creator for her assertiveness, provided Brittain with a seductive outlet for her confusing and conflicted feelings.

So also did her diary, in which during 1915 – and especially following March 1915, when Roland went to the Front – she created a narrative of her romance, describing her few actual meetings with Roland in detail; keeping account of their correspondence by frequently transcribing both her letters to him and his to her; and confiding her thoughts. In 1915, Brittain's 'Reflective Record', as she called it, is studded as never before or after with what critic Paul Fussell[62] has called the raised language of Victorian heroism.

This narrative already existed when Brittain came to write *Testament of Youth*. And while her purpose in the autobiographical study was to analyse heroism rather than simply to describe it, the impress of the very young woman who had sustained herself through an enormously difficult period by adopting the rhetoric and the emotions of conventional heroism can be seen even as the authorial voice of *Testament of Youth* treats that younger self with amused aloofness.

Both Vera and Roland were able on occasion to break out of this mould. In their correspondence, they were able both to be more frank than either could be in person about their feelings for one another and to be more matter-of-fact. For example, Roland's letters from Flanders are full of detailed and specific descriptions of his experiences. Vera's letters, once she began nursing, include accounts of her new work.

And when a climax in their relationship was reached during Roland's leave in August 1915, Vera's feminism, her fundamental allegiance to her principles concerning woman's autonomy, did in fact reassert itself. In *Testament of Youth* the informality of their engagement is presented as a joint decision, but it was Vera rather than Roland who declined to enter into a conventional engagement with an announcement in *The Times* or a formal request by Roland to her father for her hand. She records in her diary that she refused Roland's offer of an engagement ring:

> I told him emphatically that I would not be labelled, and he comprehending said he hated the obvious too. I have deep-rooted objections to wearing an engagement ring.... Certainly I have, owing to unfortunate heredity, a trace of conventional social instinct which makes me understand a certain amount of pleasure in wearing such a ring. But my best self refutes this instinct, for it recognises the custom as a survival of those days when woman was the possession of man, and the ring was the token of this. It is the symbol of the old inequality & therefore hateful to me.[63]

That 'best self' would reassert itself permanently after the war, but it is significant that it emerged here, at this critical juncture, even if only briefly.

What we know of the relationship between Vera Brittain and Roland Leighton does offer a profoundly moving example of young love in wartime. The two did have deep feelings for one another, and Brittain did experience intense grief after Roland's death. But the pressure of circumstance did deform their feelings and the fact that the war, like her wartime love, encouraged in Brittain a destructive romanticism was precisely one of the ways in which the war was a tragedy for her. In *Testament of Youth*, she struggled with only partial success to convey this reality.

After December 1914, the war and her love for Roland encouraged

Brittain to be dissatisfied with and hypercritical of Oxford. She continued to work diligently for Pass Moderations and to enjoy the intellectual and social stimulation of university life, but her feelings of detachment were considerably stronger after January 1915 than they had been during her first term. These feelings are, for example, reflected in her comments about the new clothes she had acquired over the holidays: 'I wish Roland, and not merely a pack of college women, could see me in these things', she says.[64] Between 31 March 1915,[65] the date of Roland's departure for the front, and the end of her first year at Oxford in June, Brittain decided to leave Oxford, at least temporarily, and take up nursing.

6

War Work

On 27 June 1915, wearing the grey uniform of an auxiliary Voluntary Aid Detachment nurse,[1] Vera Brittain took the short walk down the hill from Melrose to Buxton's Devonshire Hospital.[2] 'Behold, a new experience beginneth!' she wrote prophetically in her diary about what would turn out to be one of the most extraordinary periods of her life.[3] From June 1915, Brittain would nurse almost continuously until April 1919. After the Devonshire, she left Buxton in October 1915 to become a full-time VAD under contract with the British Red Cross Society at a London military hospital. Shortly after Roland's death in December 1915, she signed on for foreign service and was sent to Malta, where she nursed from October 1916 to May 1917. After a brief hiatus, she nursed at the 24th General Hospital in Étaples from August 1917 until April 1918, when she broke her contract to return home to care for her ailing mother. Her final nursing assignments were at London hospitals from September 1918 until her contract expired in April 1919.

By the spring of 1915, several factors conspired together to encourage Brittain to abandon her studies and become actively involved in war work. First, there was her response to increased public pressure. By 1915, labour shortages in a number of key areas caused the British government to launch a propaganda campaign encouraging the participation of women. Women's war work included factory and agricultural employment and office work, as well as nursing, and from 1917 would include participation in the women's paramilitary units. Women of all social classes were involved, although the majority of the greatly increased female labour force was working class.[4] For an upper middle-class young woman like Brittain, all the options mentioned were open. Some of her school and college contemporaries did become munitions workers; others worked on farms; some became office workers.[5] But the women who, like herself, nursed under the auspices of the Voluntary Aid Detachment programme have a special place among Britain's women war workers. To a greater extent than the far more numerous munitions workers or Land Army girls or the largely forgotten General Service VADs or even the trained nurses who served through the Queen Alexandra's Imperial Military Nursing Service Reserves and the Territorial Forces Nursing Service, the women who nursed as VADs have become part of the mythology surrounding the Great War.

The VAD programme, which was designed to provide voluntary aid to the sick and wounded, and to supplement the services provided by trained professional nurses, had been established before the war, but was greatly expanded in 1915, when it became clear that the devastating effect of trench warfare was creating a severe shortage of nurses.[6] From then on, in addition to the original volunteers – the women who managed auxiliary hospitals or worked as visitors in military hospitals on a part-time basis, and who received no pay and no allowances – thousands of women signed on under contract with the military authorities, who paid them a stipend, provided them with room and board, and in return were entitled to their services for the duration of the contract. It was these women who served on ambulance trains, and in British Expeditionary Force hospitals at home, or overseas in France, in Malta or the Middle East, and who became the VADs of wartime propaganda and of post-war memory. Dressed in a starched ankle-length uniform, with her white apron bearing a large red cross and her head covered in a scarf reminiscent of a nun's coif, the idealized VAD was 'The Rose of No Man's Land' who succoured the wounded and soothed the dying.[7]

There were, as well, negative images of the VADs. Especially at the outset of the war, the military authorities and the general public alike were sceptical about the motives of the women in volunteering, and about the value of their services, even as women were urged to contribute. Often the VADs were stigmatized and trivialized as idle, well-to-do women, meddling where they had no business to be and thoughtlessly seeking adventure in the midst of tragedy.[8] To some extent, the negative stereotyping of the VADs persisted throughout the war[9] although, as the need for their work was acknowledged, the alternative image of the VAD as heroine nurse outstripped it in emotional power.[10]

Historians of the First World War have seen women's participation in the war effort as significant both for the history of women and for the history of the war. Vera Brittain herself helped to construct that history, for in *Testament of Youth* she provided one of the most famous, most frequently quoted and, it is generally agreed, most reliable accounts of VAD nursing.

Because she was one of the most prominent exemplars of wartime nursing, and because in retrospect her choice of nursing appears to have been virtually inevitable, many commentators have overlooked the fact that Brittain came to nursing only reluctantly. Certainly the intensity of her meeting with Roland on 19 March 1915 and then his departure for France twelve days later did encourage her to focus on her wartime responsibilities, but at first she perceived it to be her duty to continue her studies: 'Hard manual labour would be easier; truly my sort of work is difficult now, when so much of intellectual life seems at a standstill and the war cry drowns the purer voices of the upper air. But that intellectual life & none other is the work for which I was made, & I must not shirk it & forget how urgently it is always needed . . . ,'[11] she wrote the day after Roland had left after his brief visit. Two days later she recorded that she'd 'tried to work . . . & with some success, realising that if I could not feel interested in my work I must do it without feeling interested. Such is the only form of courage I can practise.'

But the 'war cry' was indeed drowning out 'the purer voices of the upper air' and Brittain herself felt ambivalent about the course she ought to pursue. When she learned that two of her girlhood acquaintances were going out to France to nurse she wrote of her 'envy' of them, employing language that is unusually 'raised' and 'heroic' even for her 1915 diary: 'I envy people who nurse now – surely truth is to be found in such experience, even as it is embodied in all elemental things. I would like the stern labour for love's sake, for surely the soul grows thereby.'[12] In her entry for Easter Saturday, a week later, she reverts to her more authentic rationality. That Saturday, when Edith Brittain was assisting several other women parishioners in decorating the church, one of the other Buxton matrons proffered some pointed criticism of the fact that Vera was still pursuing her studies: why, this woman demanded of Edith, had Vera not considered taking up nursing, as had Leslie Duncan and Hilda Cox? In her diary, Brittain recorded her annoyance with the interfering Mrs Whitehead and, as well, her rational objections to undertaking nursing:

> As there has been no great call for nurses – voluntary & half trained I mean – her remark is hardly true. The need is still present, & will be greater after the war, of highly trained people to do important intellectual work. . . . In a year or two many of those who were capable of

> undertaking it will be dead. . . . Where will the supply exist . . . except largely among those women whose training is in process during the war?

She goes on to note that

> [j]ust lately there has been an appeal in the papers to women who are willing to work – clerical, armament or agricultural – & thus can set free a man to fight, to register either at the Head Labour Exchange or local ones . . . of course the appeal is chiefly to working women but others are wanted too, especially I should think, for clerical work. This sort of service appeals to me far more than merely to swell the number of superfluous housemaids.[13]

The 'elemental' pull of nursing won out: by the late spring of 1915 she had become convinced that nursing was the path demanding the hardest work and the greatest degree of self-sacrifice, and that it was through nursing that she could best live up to the sacrifice that Roland and her brother were both making as soldiers.

Other factors contributed to Brittain's choice of VAD nursing. First, there was the practical but significant fact that her initial stint at the Devonshire Hospital could be easily arranged with the help of her mother, on whom Brittain still remained very much dependent.[14] The Devonshire was a well-known Buxton institution. Even physically, its large, handsome dome was one of the dominating features of the town's landscape. The Brittains were subscribers,[15] they were friendly with members of its Board of Management, and they knew the Matron, Miss Hyland. The prospect of Vera's working there, in familiar surroundings, was considerably more appealing to her family than the other option she seriously considered, that of registering with a London Labour Exchange. She discussed this possibility with her friend Cora Stoop during a visit she made to Cora at the beginning of April. In London she and Cora consulted Vera's favourite uncle, William Bervon, and even Uncle Willie thought that the Devonshire would be the wisest choice, although he did help Vera to purchase a typewriter so that she could learn to type and thus prepare herself for office work.[16]

There were also powerful psychological reasons why Brittain chose nursing. Brittain, only twenty-one and deeply in love, wished to cast herself in both a heroic and a feminine mould, and wartime nursing had long since entered popular consciousness as both heroic and feminine, with a tradition extending back to Florence Nightingale's mission to the Crimea. By becoming a nurse, Brittain could share in this tradition. The VAD uniform, a transforming outward sign of her new status, was strongly appealing to her.[17] Even more appealing was the dream that, through nursing, she might actually be able to help Roland directly. As she said after she had decided to nurse:

> I told him . . . that if he *must* get wounded, he might postpone it till August, by which time I might be efficient enough to help in looking after him – that is one dream of mine – that he should come home wounded not too seriously, and that I should have had a little practice in nursing first, & be able to look after him & thoroughly spoil him.[18]

Finally, the question of social class entered into Brittain's choice. Members of the nursing units were meant to have the same status as male commissioned officers, and were to be of an equivalent social class: according to historian Arthur Marwick, '[t]he careful selection procedure and the use of references made clear that these women were, and were intended to be, very middle class or upper class in background'.[19] In terms of social class and education, Vera Brittain certainly conforms to Marwick's description of the sort of young woman sought out by Devonshire House, the London headquarters of the Joint VAD programme. She was unquestionably a lady, with impeccable social and educational credentials – and with no nursing training, aside from the First Aid and Home Nursing certificates which she had earned at the outbreak of the war. In fact, Brittain represented the Devonshire House ideal, rather than the reality, for in truth there is good evidence to suggest that many VADs did not conform to this upper middle-class pattern.[20] None the less, the image of VAD nursing was one with which both she and her family could be comfortable in 1915 when she began her work.

In several respects, then, Brittain's decision to become a VAD in 1915 represents a step backward, a retreat into the conventional femininity of her Buxton 'provincial young ladyhood'. Literary critic Sandra Gilbert, whose influential analysis of the phenomenon of male resentment of women war workers during the Great War – and specifically resentment against VADs – contains many references to Brittain, misses this essential point. While Gilbert perceptively reveals the misogyny inherent in the attacks on the VADs, she herself reinforces that misogyny when she claims that while the war stripped the soldier of power, it gave middle-class young women more power than they had ever had before. And Brittain's case simply does not support Gilbert's claim that the war 'liberated' women. She did not need the war to release her 'passionate energies', or to bring about a 'revolution in her economic expectations'. She had already paved the way for such achievements by becoming a student at Somerville.[21]

Brittain began nursing as an unpaid volunteer at the Devonshire Hospital during the summer and autumn of 1915. She worked a gruelling nine and a half-hour day, serving meals, making beds and cleaning.[22] By July, she was dressing minor wounds and dealing directly with the needs of patients. Brittain proved to be not only willing but competent, earning the respect of the trained nursing staff under whom she laboured. In *Testament of Youth*, she would say wryly: 'No doubt the staff was not unwilling to make the utmost use of so enthusiastic and unsophisticated a probationer.'[23] She took considerable pride in the fact that she took the work seriously, that she was no ordinary, frivolous VAD of the kind that the Devonshire's trained nursing staff had no use for: 'I heard a great many tales about the previous VADs who spent most of their time giggling in the Laboratory . . . who sat on the soldiers' beds & talked to them, who left all the dirty & unpleasant work to the nurses', she wrote in her diary after one August working day at the hospital.[24]

Why was it that Brittain threw herself so willingly into the drudgery involved in hospital work? Why did she tolerate the long hours and agree to take orders from those whom, given her upbringing, she could not help but regard as her social as well as her intellectual inferiors? It was of course in large part her love for Roland that inspired her, but there was more to Brittain's willingness to nurse than the eager romanticism of a girl in love. Such enthusiasm would probably have dissipated within a few weeks or months, and surely after Roland's death. She stayed on throughout the war not only because she quickly realized that she was useful and needed, but also because the work offered her possibilities for self-realization very different from anything she had hitherto experienced. Until her service as a VAD, her upper middle-class life had shielded her from any sustained contact with physical drudgery and unpleasantness – as she tells us in *Testament of Youth*, when she began nursing she literally did not know how to boil an egg.[25] Her war service called on her to put aside life-long habits of fastidiousness, to face up to material realities that were unpleasant at best, and at worst were both revolting and terrifying. And nursing was not only a formidable challenge, it represented the antithesis of her wartime experience with love: if her romance with Roland was largely based on fantasy sustained by literary illusion, nursing plunged her into forceful contact with blood, flesh, pain and dirt. She took justifiable pride in the fact that she did find the courage and the determination to commit herself to this work, no easy task for a young woman who had been squeamish since her childhood and who had expected other people – the servants, her mother – to arrange the material details of her life: 'I have never worked so hard in my life; it gives me a little insight into the lives of those who have always to work like this.'[26]

By early July Brittain had decided that she would not return to Oxford, and that instead she would sign on with the British Red Cross Society as a VAD under contract. At first, as was not uncommon, her offers were rebuffed: 'I had an unsatisfactory sort of letter from the Red Cross, talking vaguely of delays and numerous interviews', she wrote in her diary on 4 August. 'British authorities & their Red Tape are distinctly depressing. Strange that they should plead for volunteers and then make it as unpleasant as possible for you when you have volunteered.'[27] Brittain cut through the red tape herself, a week later. She and her mother went up to London where Vera, on the advice of Cora Stoop, decided to attempt to enroll on the spot in the same VAD unit (it was number 128) in which Cora had already enrolled, and in which Stella Sharp would also enroll. The three young women hoped at that time to be taken on together and posted as a group. Such group enrolments were not uncommon among VADs and were in fact encouraged by the VAD administration. Of VAD 128 Brittain wrote in her diary: 'It is about the best in England, as the Commandant is on the V.A.D. Selection Board; if they approve of you it does not take more than 10 minutes to be enrolled, but they have to see you before they will do anything.' At first it appeared that this impromptu visit would not succeed in its objective. When Brittain, her mother and Cora arrived at the office of VAD 128 in Paddington, neither the Commandant nor the Secretary was there, because they were both ill: 'Of course when I heard this I thought it was just what I deserved for trying to do things on Friday the 13th. However, I explained that I had come from Buxton on purpose to get enrolled if I could and was going back the same evening, also that I was a University student on leave from Oxford for a year and so wanted to get settled at something as soon as possible.' Brittain's academic credentials impressed the woman on duty in the office and so also, we may surmise, did the upper middle-class assurance that Edith Brittain, Cora and Vera herself would have displayed. Brittain was clearly a most desirable recruit: 'She seemed very impressed at my having come from Buxton, and still more so by the University student touch and said as I was such a special case she would ring up the secretary. . . .' The secretary, Mrs Wallace, agreed to see Vera, her mother and Cora at her home in Paddington and the interview took place in her drawing room: 'By this time I was hotter and more untidy than ever, but evidently I didn't create such a bad impression, as she said she would enroll me after a few minutes' conversation.'[28]

What followed was a period of waiting, but in October her orders finally came, and Brittain left Buxton for the 1st London General Hospital in Camberwell, the military wing of the great London hospital, St Bartholomew's. She and Stella Sharp (Cora did not in the end enroll with them) were part of the second group of VADs to arrive at the hospital. In *Testament of Youth*, Brittain would later describe in vivid detail her work and living experiences as a probationer at this hospital. While the hospital authorities accepted VAD help they did so only grudgingly. She describes the ambivalent suspicion to which the trained nursing staff often subjected the VADs who worked under them, and the inadequacy of the living conditions provided by the hospital, and also the idealism with which she and others overcame all these difficulties:

> Far from criticising our Olympian superiors, we tackled our daily duties with a devotional enthusiasm now rare amongst young women. . . . The temptation to exploit our young wartime enthusiasm must have been immense – and was not fiercely resisted by the military authorities.[29]

Brittain's experience with the trained nursing staff is echoed in that of other accounts of individual VADs and in the official record. One frequently occurring source of friction concerned the title to be given to the VADs: many of their soldier patients, unfamiliar with the hierarchy of titles for the trained nurse, called all the women who cared for them and who wore any sort of uniform 'Nurse', or sometimes even 'Sister'. Brittain herself was proud of the fact that by July patients at the Devonshire were calling her 'Nurse':

> It is delightful getting to know these people, which I never should if I had always remained Miss Brittain & never 'Nurse'. They look upon me here from quite a different point of view. I get nearer to 'the people' & find them so immensely interesting & intelligent. And I couldn't be treated more thoroughly as a nurse if I had been nursing for years. Of course the patients see very little difference between a V.A. Nurse & an ordinary hospital nurse.[30]

But among trained nurses, 'Sister' denoted a status earned only after several successful years in the profession, and therefore the informal conferring of that title on untrained VADs offended the trained nursing staff. Some Sisters, indeed, would not even permit the VADs working under them to be called 'Nurse'.[31]

Although the VADs as a group did unquestionably often suffer slights, unfair treatment and humiliation at the hands of the trained nurses under whom they worked, the hostility of the trained nurses is understandable. During the half-century between the end of the Crimean War and the outbreak of the First World War, nursing as an occupation had made enormous strides. As a result of the work of Florence Nightingale and others in the late nineteenth and early twentieth centuries, nursing had become a respected occupation for working and lower-middle-class women. But nurses still laboured under difficulties and faced uncertainties. It was only after the First World War that a nurses' registry was established. In the years before and during the war, there was still controversy about the function and the necessity of the customary three-year training, and there was still uncertainty about the nurse's professional status. And trained nurses were still exploited within the hospital setting.

No wonder, then, that as a group trained nurses were wary of the VADs. An Army Report of 1916 elaborating on the 'friction between trained nurses and Voluntary Aid Detachment members' pointed out that there was on the side of the VADs 'a tendency of the amateur to be impatient of . . . discipline', and on the side of the trained nurses 'a natural aversion of the professional from trusting the . . . beginner'. Moreover nurses as a group were afraid that after the war, women who had served as VADs would be competing with them for jobs and would not have to endure the 'drudgery, discipline and education' of the training school.[32]

The VAD administrators, for their part, had an ambivalent attitude towards the trained nurse. On the one hand, VAD Commandant Katherine Furse frequently reminded the VADs that they must 'never compete with trained nurses. Remember that the women who have trained for three years in order to obtain their certificates must be protected by us VAD members. . . .'[33] On the other hand, Devonshire House was at times very critical both of the nurses' behaviour towards individual VADs and of trained nursing as an occupation. One British Red Cross Society report criticized the trained nurses for what it called their 'trades union feeling' and for having lost their old commitment to service: 'What used to be a Profession of Devotion is now very often a money seeking profession. . . .' The report concludes by accusing the trained nurses of making a 'fetish of the three years' training'.[34]

Some of the friction between trained nurses and VADs may have been based on subtle but significant class conflict. As we have seen, at the outset of the war VADs were supposed to be patriotic volunteers, who worked without any kind of financial reward. Even after the Army instituted its salary of £20 per annum for full-time VADs in 1915, VAD work was still conceived of in the Lady Bountiful tradition of service which expected no reward. This was a distinctly upper middle-class tradition, and even though many – perhaps the majority – of VADs may in fact have come from middle- or lower-middle-class families, those who spoke for the organisation were upper-middle- or upper-class women. In contrast, while trained nursing was certainly a respectable and an eminently 'womanly' occupation by 1914, it was not seen primarily as an occupation for genuine 'gentlewomen'.[35] When the VAD hierarchy criticized the trained nurses for their 'trades union' attitudes, and for being 'money seeking' it was exhibiting an upper middle-class insensitivity to the situation of lower-middle-class and working-class women who had no choice but to earn their own livings.

Brittain's first probationary month at the 1st London General was so exhausting that she hardly had time to write in her diary. She worked a twelve and a half-hour day and, in addition to the gruelling work routine, she and the other VADs had to contend with the inadequacies of their housing: the authorities had billeted them 'in a distant, ill-equipped old house' whose cold bathroom and unreliable hot-water heater added to their miseries. After her month's probation, she signed on for six months. She was then paid the £20 a year VADs in military hospitals received, plus a laundry and uniform allowance. She recorded the landmark of signing on in her diary: 'after tea 15 of us VADs who came about the same time had to go to Matron's office & talk about signing on. We were very pleased because we were all asked to sign & no one was told she was unsatisfactory. . . . I had a sort of inward jubilation afterwards at having done something so irrevocable–something which I simply cannot get out of.'[36]

The first phase of Brittain's war experience ended abruptly and tragically on 27 December 1915. All during December, she had eagerly anticipated Roland's return home on a leave planned for the end of the month. Brittain spent Christmas on duty and on Boxing Day she travelled down to Brighton to be with her mother and father (who had by this time left Buxton)[37] and to await Roland's arrival. Instead, Roland's sister Clare telephoned on 27 December with the news that he had died of wounds on 23 December 1915.

On New Year's Day at the Leightons she wrote:

> This day last year was the first New Year's Day I had had with Him in my life. To-day is the first New Year's Day I have had with my life empty through the loss of Him. I am immeasurably richer than I was this day two years ago; I am incomparably poorer than I was this day last year. This year dawned differently from any other I have known . . . it marks the completion in the change of my outlook on life from a child's or even a girl's to a woman's. It is not years that have wrought this alteration . . . only a month ago in His letters He was calling me 'Dear Child'. But now that jeunesse d'orée with all its glory has gone down into the Abyss, and has taken my own youth with it – for ever and ever more.[38]

Roland's death was indeed a terrible blow. Brittain's love for him had become the centre of her emotional life, the spark that gave meaning to her exhausting and often dreary work as a VAD, and to have the hope of its fulfilment extinguished was almost unbearably painful. As she wrote to her mother towards the end of April, when she was recovering from an attack of German measles: 'The worst of the whole thing is that I get so very depressed; I haven't the energy to write much and reading for long at a time tires my eyes . . . so I lie for hours & think about Roland & go over & over in my mind all the times I saw Him & all the details of His death until there seems nothing worth having left in the future at all; it is a shame that everything worth while should come to an end so soon in one's life.'[39] She dealt with her grief by transfiguring Roland. In memory he became an icon of heroism. In her diary, and in her letters to her mother, to her brother and to Victor Richardson, Brittain refers to Roland as 'He', like Christ or God, and he becomes a touchstone for her when she is confused or discouraged. In transforming the dead Roland, Brittain was able both to give private expression to her grief and at the same time to contain it.

But although she grieved inwardly, outwardly she found it difficult to accept attempts to console her from anyone except her family, Roland's mother and Edward or Victor, and she made little public display of her grief. The engagement between herself and Roland had in any case been an informal and private one. (She did, however, purchase a mourning engagement ring, and wore it, even though she had refused to wear an engagement ring when Roland was alive.[40]) The hospital now irritated her intensely. 'Desperately lonely', she writes on her return to Camberwell. 'Hateful night-duty on officers' corridor.'[41] But the approach of a day-duty shift was even worse: 'Night-duty is bad enough, but I *loathe* the thought of day, never any time to oneself, never anywhere one can go to be alone, never the right person to go out with on one's times off.'[42] Clearly, after Roland's death, Brittain's desire to be the perfect VAD evaporated. The work, which had seemed like an offering to her love, now became hateful, and she began to chafe at authority, as she had chafed at school and at Somerville. As she wrote in a letter to Edward, who was at last about to be sent to the Front: 'The way they treat us like children here & make mysteries of trifles is too ridiculous for words.'[43]

At first, after Roland's death, Brittain seriously considered giving up nursing after the expiration of her contract. She discussed the subject with her uncle, William Bervon:

> He absolutely agreed with me that VAD work was a hopeless, depressing cul-de-sac for anybody, but for someone with my brains, let alone exceptional brains, quite intolerable. I was quite wasted on it, he thought, more especially as there seem to be more nurses now than are at all needed. . . . When I suggested a motor-driving scheme if I could not get anything more intellectual he thought it quite a good idea, promised to do all he could . . . [to] find out if any influence is obtainable in that direction.[44]

During March and April, Brittain vacillated about whether she would continue nursing or take a civil service position with the War Office. She went so far with the War Office plans that she made arrangements to rent a room in Bayswater. Describing it, she writes to Edward: 'It amuses me to think of living on my own in London, when a year ago I had to send a telegram to say I had arrived safely at Oxford, but such is War. . . .'[45]

But at the last minute she changed her mind again. As she explained in a letter to Edward, it was the memory of Roland that determined her choice: 'Although everything was so nicely arranged for me to leave, I changed my mind & like the erratic weathercock I may seem but really am not, almost at the last moment agreed, as they wished, to stay . . . no sooner had I decided to leave here than the growing conviction came over me quite against my reason, that somewhere He was living still, and knew and disapproved.'[46]

Gradually, Brittain's sense of overwhelming loss did pass and, while she continued to grieve for Roland, over the next months she recovered her natural resilience, her curiosity about life, and regained even the capacity for enjoyment. She also turned to the task of comforting and supporting the three soldiers closest to her who were still alive. First of all, there was Edward. In *Testament of Youth* she would later write: 'In the final months of intense, exclusive preoccupation with Roland, I had almost forgotten him, but now he returned quite suddenly to the chief place in my consciousness.'[47] Six weeks after Roland's death, on 10 February 1915, he left for France and the Front. The realization that her younger brother, whose welfare had always been of such importance to the Brittain family, was actually going to the Front, not to be trained for his own benefit, as he had been at his public school, in appropriate 'manly' behaviour, but to face the danger, the brutality and the chaos of trench warfare struck her forcibly: 'It is all unbelievable. He – to be standing in water & mud, when I can remember him in a brown holland overall, and everyone was always so careful to see that he didn't get his feet wet. . . .'[48] Edward saw action in July, at the Battle of the Somme. He was wounded in the left arm and right thigh on 1 July, and evacuated out to England, where by coincidence he was sent to the 1st London General. As Brittain wrote in her diary, which she managed to keep up sporadically even during this intensely busy period: 'There was an early morning convoy of officers into J . . . I saw Miss George, who ran up to me & said "Do you know your brother's in J?" *Edward* in J! . . . It was like some impossible novel that he should have come to *my* hospital.'[49] Edward spent three weeks at the Camberwell hospital recovering from his wound, and after his release was given extended leave. He was awarded the Military Cross for his 'conspicuous gallantry & leadership' during the battle on 1 July. His sister was enormously proud of him.

And then there was Victor Richardson, who had been Roland's and Edward's friend at Uppingham. Victor wrote Vera a touching letter of condolence in January, and they began seeing each other regularly for dinner on her off-duty Sundays. (Victor, who had contracted meningitis in 1915, was still recovering early in 1916 and had not been sent back to the Front.[50]) Finally, there was Geoffrey Thurlow, Edward's young fellow-officer, whom she had grown to like when Edward had brought him home on leave in October 1915.[51] Like Victor, Geoffrey also wrote Vera a heartfelt letter after Roland's death. When Geoffrey was wounded in February and sent to London, Vera visited him in hospital, where their friendship grew. After January 1916, Brittain's relationship with both Richardson and Thurlow was tinged with a subdued aura of romance. While they both figured in Vera's life as additional brothers, consoling her in her grief, in the background was the unstated possibility that, in time, either one might become more than a brother. Caring for them and for her brother, while it did not at first do much to relieve the sense of desolation she experienced after Roland's death, did provide both a sense of purpose about her personal life and some hope for the future.

MALTA: 1916–17

When Brittain decided to renew her VAD contract, she also decided to put her name down for foreign service. 'From here, it might be Egypt, Malta or Salonika, just as much as France.'[52] After a summer spent working hard at the 1st London General, where she helped to nurse the floods of wounded who arrived after the Battle of the Somme in July, she learned in September that her foreign posting would be Malta. On 24 September 1916 she and Stella Sharp, who had also been posted to Malta, departed with a convoy of Sisters and VADs aboard the SS *Britannic*. Brittain would later describe her Malta experience in *Testament of Youth* in a chapter with the resonant title 'Tawney Island':

> The memory of my sunlit months in the Mediterranean during the War's worst period of miserable stagnation still causes a strange nostalgia to descend upon my spirit. . . . Malta remains in my recollection as an interval of heaven, a short year of glamorous beauty and delight, in which, for the time being, I came to life again after Roland's death.[53]

The Army had established military hospitals on Malta to care for men wounded in the Gallipoli expedition, and later in Salonika. By March 1916, the military maintained some twenty-nine hospitals and convalescent homes there. The most intense demands for medical services on Malta came during the period from July 1916 to April 1917, with the peak in October, when there were 20,994 beds.[54] VAD nurses were well respected on Malta. As the Surgeon-General Director of Medical Services attested, 'I know of no weak points in the VADs . . . Here in Malta their work . . . has been wholly admirable.'[55]

Vera Brittain nursed on Malta from October 1916 until May 1917. She enjoyed her tour of duty there for several reasons. First of all the working conditions were good. At St. George's Hospital the professional nurses treated their VADs with respect, dispensing for the most part with the petty restrictions that had been so oppressive at Camberwell. As she wrote to her mother soon after she had begun active duty: 'The Matron is perfectly sweet, as different from my last one as anyone could be; she is not a bit stand-offish'. She reports that even the severe dress code, prescribed by VAD Headquarters at Devonshire House and vigorously enforced in military hospitals in England, was on Malta relaxed:

> We . . . wear soft low collars and panama hats, which you can buy here; no one seems to be very particular about uniform unless you meet the Principal Matron who of course has to be. The difference between the stiffness & starchiness of the Nursing Profession in England & the free & easiness here is quite remarkable. No one minds whether you come into meals in your mess-dress, your blouse & skirt & hat, or your ordinary indoor uniform . . .[56]

Best of all, was the fact that the hostility between regular nurses and VADs was reduced to a minimum: 'The Sisters treat you as friends & equals instead of as incompetent underlings.'[57]

This friendly relationship existed because VAD labour was indispensable and individual VADs had of necessity to be given considerable responsibility. As Brittain wrote in March 1917:

> I have just gone on night duty for a month. . . . I am in sole charge of the block; there is no one else but an orderly on it. At the lst London we used always to be on with a Sister . . . but they trust you much more here – in fact they have to, because there are not enough Sisters to go round. . . . Do you remember how afraid I used to be of thunder when I was little? Now I feel quite a 'Lady of the Lamp' marching along with the thunder crashing . . . to see if other people are afraid![58]

Brittain also found Malta's off-duty atmosphere congenial and familiar. As another VAD of similar social background wrote: 'Whatever type of home she had left behind her every girl in the great military hospitals . . . was living under strange and at first bewildering . . . conditions. . . . Life in a military hospital is a school within a school. Inside the big school of experience, there is a type of school life which is not unlike that which we lived in our 'teens, with its friendships, its "shops", its frenzied activities and its recreations. . . .'[59]

Brittain and her old school friend Stella Sharp experienced this 'school within a school' atmosphere. While Brittain was at times impatient with Stella Sharp's placid nature, the two women were very close on Malta and in addition both made friends with other women from social backgrounds similar to their own. In a snapshot from Vera Brittain's collection,[60] she and three other VADs stand on a bluff, on a windy day, with the sea behind them. The four young women are linked arm-in-arm. Over their VAD uniforms they wear loosely fitting cardigans and their collars are unbuttoned. Three of the four – including Brittain – wear the regulation headdress. One of them, however, does not, and her long uncovered hair blows in the wind.[61] The photograph captures very well the spirit of camaraderie and well-being that emerges from Brittain's letters home from Malta.

With Stella and with other VADs or Sisters, Brittain went shopping for herself and for gifts to send home, a gratifying activity on Malta even in wartime: 'The other day I went to the convent of the Good Shepherd at a little village called San Antonio', she wrote her mother on 18 November 1916. 'The nuns at this convent do the most exquisite embroidery and lace work . . . Don't be alarmed at the apparent expensiveness of the things I send; of course they would be very expensive in England, but here at these oriental bazaars', she says, the prices are low.[62]

In addition to shopping, Brittain also enjoyed such social occasions as picnics and garden parties – including one at the Governor's palace – with such congenial people as the 'lady-doctor' who had treated her for the illness she had contracted on the voyage out to Malta.[63] She also found time to learn some Italian. Of the woman who shared her Italian lessons she wrote to her mother as follows: 'She is half French-Swiss . . . plays both the violin & tennis very well, lived at Oxford for years & used to be in the Bach choir orchestra, and so of course knows heaps of people I know. . . .'[64]

That remark revealingly indicates the extent to which Brittain herself preferred working with women who shared her social background. A few months later, when she was nursing in France, she would tell her mother that 'I have never got on with the VADs so well anywhere before . . . more than half of them are ladies & the majority are quite free from the dreadful habit of talking shop'.[65]

In addition to feeling satisfaction with the work she did there, and with the milieu, Brittain enjoyed her posting to Malta because it was her first extended experience of foreign travel. Despite the dangers of war and her continued grief for Roland, the journey out and the sunshine and the flower-filled island itself aroused her sense of adventure and stimulated her powers of observation.

The adventure began with the voyage out on the *Brittanic*, a White Star liner converted to a hospital ship. Even as a hospital ship, the *Brittanic* retained the fittings of a luxury liner. On the day of departure she records: 'Soon after arrival we had dinner – a most sumptuous first class hotel meal in a beautifully furnished dining room.'[66] In

Testament of Youth she would comment on the incongruity between the luxurious fittings of the liner and the ever-present fear of enemy torpedoes. 'The expensive equipment of our cabins was illogically reassuring; those polished tables and bevelled mirrors looked so inappropriate for the bottom of the sea. "We are in danger!" I kept saying as I lay awake in the dark. . . .'[67]

On September 29 1916, when the *Brittanic* sailed into the Bay of Naples, Brittain put all troubles aside and revelled in the sights and sounds of the exotic and beautiful city. Her extensive diary entries reveal her enthusiasm, her openness and her resilience and, as well, the extent to which, even after a year at Oxford, she retained many of the stereotypical British prejudices about southern, Catholic Italy: 'In every little piazza there seemed to be . . . palms & cactus', she wrote. And 'even the beggars . . . were dressed in faded gay colours; nearly all seemed to be in some way halt, maimed, blind or diseased & to exhibit their defects almost with pride. Italy is a corrupt country, no doubt. All about the streets were mule-carts filled with vivid coloured vegetables, whose names I do not know, golden & scarlet & orange & brilliant green.' After an 'excellent lunch' they visited the Museum 'where we saw all the old Greek statues dug up from Pompeii. Pompeii itself was out of bounds for visitors as there was an epidemic raging there.'[68] The next day, from the top of San Martino, they saw the bay: 'the most glorious view I have ever seen on earth'.

Brittain left Malta in May 1917, after Victor Richardson was seriously wounded and Geoffrey Thurlow was killed in action. Although nothing she would experience in her life would ever devastate her in precisely the way that Roland's death had, Brittain's wartime experience involved multiple personal losses. Many thousands of readers of *Testament of Youth* have been touched by Brittain's portrayal of that sense of loss, of blow upon blow, beginning with Roland in 1915, then Geoffrey and Victor in the spring of 1917, and finally Edward in June 1918. During her tour of duty on Malta, Brittain corresponded regularly with both Geoffrey and Victor, and unquestionably she cared deeply about each of them. Was she aware at the time that there was an undercurrent of romance in her relationship with both young men? We know that she experienced some discomfort and confusion in this regard, because in December 1916 she wrote to her mother to ask her advice about whether or not it would be 'altogether correct' to send gifts of cigarettes to them, as well as to Edward. Edith Brittain evidently did think that her daughter's status as the woman who had been Roland's fiancée removed any impropriety, for Vera did send those cigarettes to Victor and Geoffrey.[69]

The news that Victor had been seriously wounded at Vimy Ridge on 9 April reached Brittain in Malta by cable. The cable, sent by Edward, who was at this time still in England, read 'Victor dangerously wounded; serious'. She was on duty when she got the cable. In the *Testament of Youth* narrative, she explains that she did not discuss the contents of the telegram with 'Betty' (Stella Sharp) or the other VADs on duty. They 'would not have understood why I should mind so much about someone who was not a *fiancé* or a brother or one of the other standard relationships'.[70] But that night, before going to bed, she wrote about Victor in her diary. During the period she was nursing on Malta, she turned to her diary only infrequently, recording her experiences instead through her letters home. The diary entries she did make concerning Malta itself and her work there are detailed and vivid but down-to-earth. The emotional crisis – the 'chaotic wretchedness', as she later would call it[71] – engendered by Victor's wounds caused her to revert back to the melodramatic, heroic style of the entries following Roland's death:

> I could so ill do without Victor; he always seems like the survival of a part of Roland, or rather, in his accurate, clear, & reverent memory of Him, Roland seems to me to live still. I remember how Victor and I last June in St. James' Park speculated about Edward's fate in the coming battle on the Somme, & he said only then that he thought he would never go to the front, & I that I was glad to know there would be someone left after the War & I should not be quite alone. . . . And now . . . he has 'made good' . . . and won through to the bridging of the gulf which he always felt lay between himself on the one hand & Roland & Edward on the other.[72]

In the heightened emotional state produced by the news of Victor's wounds, Brittain began to formulate the plan of returning to England to care for him:

> For us who cannot fight, it is a burden of debt almost more than we can bear to feel that we owe our safety to the lives & sight & strength of such as Roland, Victor & Edward . . . I feel that I would do anything for him – that I would give up all the things I ever meant to do & be if I could but repay him a little for what he has sacrificed. Maybe I shall have the chance & the choice – maybe not; who can tell? I feel as if Roland's sad eyes were entreating me out of Eternity to give to Victor some of the strength & comfort He would have given him if only He had been here. Poor motherless Tah![73]

When, on 1 May 1916, she received two pieces of bad news – that Geoffrey Thurlow had been killed in action and that Victor Richardson would certainly be blind – she determined to ask to be released from her contract. On 22 May she left Malta to return to England. As she wrote to her mother 'after all I have decided not to stay here for another 6 months, for I feel that, at any rate for a time, you all need me more . . . [W]hen I got your cables saying that Geoffrey was killed, I knew that I must try to come home . . . for I know that I can comfort [Edward] as no one else can. I am coming partly for your sake when he goes out again, partly because I may be of more help to Victor than any of you know, but chiefly for Edward. . . . If we were terribly busy here it would be different but we are not. . . .'[74] Her intention was to offer to marry Victor. In her diary entry for 1 May, she says: 'Sat out on the rocks edge in front of night quarters & suddenly something seemed to tell me to go home . . . decided to go home for Edward's sake & Victor's, & if he wishes it, to devote my life to the services of Victor, the only one (apart from Edward who is different) left of the three men I loved. For I loved Geoffrey. . . .'[75] It is only in *Testament of Youth*, not in the diary itself nor in her letters home, that she adds that as she sat on the rocks looking at the sea, she was reminded of the 'Agony Column' advertisement she had sent to Roland two years earlier as a curiosity: 'Lady, fiancé killed, will gladly marry officer totally blinded or otherwise incapacitated by the War',[76] and of her accompanying letter, speculating about the motives of the woman who had placed the advertisement. 'Quite an idea, isn't it?' she had written.

Brittain's plan to devote herself to a life of service to Victor was curtailed by his death on 9 June. As she says with great honesty in *Testament of Youth*: 'Only long afterwards, when time had taught me the limits of my own magnanimity, did I realise that his death had probably saved us both from a relationship of which the serenity might have proved increasingly difficult to maintain, and that I had always been too egotistical, too ambitious, too impatient, to carry through any experiment which depended for its success upon the complete abnegation of individual claims.'[77]

That was surely an understatement. In *Testament of Youth*, Brittain characterizes her feelings for both Victor and Geoffrey as atypical, even unconventional. They were different, she claims, from what she calls the 'standard relationships'.[78] But were they? How ought we to interpret Brittain's connection to Victor Richardson, to Geoffrey Thurlow and even to Edward, during these wartime years? The retreat into the familiar responses of conventional femininity and of the idioms of conventional heroism fostered in Brittain by the war and by her wartime romance with Roland Leighton continued to manifest itself in an attenuated fashion in her relationships to Victor, to Geoffrey and indeed to her brother. All three came to represent for her not merely themselves, but universal soldiers: for example, after Roland's death she uses the imagery of medieval chivalry to characterize Edward and Victor. They become the lost knights of a fallen lord: 'they both looked tall and fine and knightly, with their handsome faces grave with sorrow – like courtiers without a king', she wrote when she saw them at the Leighton's house just after Roland's death.[79] She compared Victor to Sir Galahad. We must of course remember and understand that she is using this language immediately after Roland's death when she was in the early stages of acute grief. None the less, it suggests a strongly felt need to cast her relationship with these remaining young men in the form of a familiar and therefore comfortingly predictable literary convention, that of medieval chivalry or, more accurately, Victorian England's version of medieval chivalry. Framed in this way, she and they could take their places in a story of love and war. Within the confines of this story, romantic feelings between herself and both Victor and Geoffrey became permissible: as the fiancée of a 'fallen' soldier she could love and be loved by his still remaining friends in a muted, symbolic fashion.[80]

And her relationship to all three young men was strongly coloured by her own role as a nurse. While on a day-to-day level, Brittain's approach to nursing included a sensible, realistic appraisal of the work involved and a disciplined willingness to undertake it, at the same time she was not immune to the influences of the imagery surrounding military nursing in general and VAD nursing in particular: the explicitly feminine image of the nurse as comforter of the wounded male.

In her analysis of Great War literary motifs, Sandra Gilbert suggests that, while the dominant image of the Red Cross nurse was that of the maternal ministering angel, behind the positive image there was a powerful, less openly acknowledged negative image of the nurse as the female devourer of male strength. In Gilbert's analysis, nurses like Brittain, in the course of caring for 'immobilized and dehumanized' men were seen to be, and even saw themselves as, appropriating the masculine strength of their patients for their own use.

Gilbert quotes extensively from *Testament of Youth*, claiming Brittain's experience as exemplifying the war's power to liberate women, and focusing on Brittain's statement that nursing contributed to her 'early release . . . from sex-inhibitions'.[81] Although, as I have suggested earlier, Gilbert fundamentally misinterprets Brittain's situation, her analysis of sexuality raises interesting questions about Brittain's relationship to sex, death and physicality during the years she worked as a nurse. For example, in *Testament of Youth*, Brittain makes the following statement about her nursing experience and her attitudes towards physicality and sexuality:

> Throughout my two decades of life, I had never looked upon the nude body of an adult male. . . . I had therefore expected, when I first started nursing, to be overcome with nervousness and embarrassment, but, to my infinite relief, I was conscious of neither. Towards the men I came to feel an almost adoring gratitude for their simple and natural acceptance of my ministrations. Short of actually going to bed with them, there was hardly an intimate service that I did not perform for one or another in the course of four years, and I still have reason to be thankful for the knowledge of masculine functioning which the care of them gave me, and for my early release from the sex-inhibitions that . . . beset many of my female contemporaries . . .[82]

Taken literally, and as I think Brittain meant us to understand it, this passage expresses Brittain's stance as a post-Victorian who has liberated herself from repressive 'Victorian tradition'. But how ought we now to interpret '[S]hort of actually going to bed with them, there was hardly an intimate service that I did not perform for one or another in the course of four years'? For Gilbert, this statement is evidence of the way in which nursing became eroticized for Brittain and, by extrapolation, for other VADs. In Gilbert's reading, all the 'services' that women perform for men offer the women 'erotic release', and given the men's weakness and the women's strength, the situation gives rise to an inversion of the traditional Victorian sexual power relationship. But with what we know of the young Vera Brittain's strong inhibitions concerning all physical aspects of life, and especially the human body and sexuality (remember that this is a young woman who in the intimacy of her diary mentions sexuality only as an acute problem, and never refers to any aspects of bodily functioning), it is Gilbert's analysis that ought to be inverted: Brittain's nursing 'ministrations', rather than being themselves eroticized, in fact drained sexuality itself of eroticism. Rather than offering sexual liberation, as Gilbert and as Brittain herself later suggested, the experience of nursing wounded and dying men postponed Brittain's need to confront her own erotic feelings because for the time being such feelings could clearly be more appropriately expressed as traditional feminine nurturance, as sisterly love.

This channelling of eroticism is most striking in the case of Roland himself. It is very evident in the diary entry she wrote in her first flush of enthusiasm, after her very first day at the Devonshire Hospital in Buxton in June 1915: 'Oh! I love the British Tommy! I shall get so fond of these men, I know. And when I look after any one of them, it is like nursing Roland by proxy. Oh! if only one of them could be the Beloved one!'[83]

Sadly, Roland remained for Vera the most disembodied of the four young men who figure in *Testament of Youth*. Roland died of wounds overseas in 1915. The only tangible evidence his loved ones at home received of his dying and death was the return of his kit. 'It was terrible', Brittain wrote. 'Everything was damp & worn & simply caked with mud. All the sepulchres and catacombs of Rome could not make me realise mortality & decay & corruption as vividly as did the smell of those clothes. I know now what he meant when he used to write "this refuse heap of a country" or "a trench that is nothing but a charnel-house".'[84]

In contrast, she was able to experience her brother and his friends Victor and Geoffrey as real wounded soldiers. Brittain visited Geoffrey in hospital in March 1916 and visited Edward regularly when he was assigned to her own hospital in July 1916. And in May and June 1917, after her return from Malta, she visited Victor up until his death. Seeing these wounded men to whom she had close ties emphasised both their physicality, and her need, as a woman and a nurse, to comfort them. Visiting Geoffrey, whom she then knew only slightly, at Fishmonger's Hall Hospital, she notices both that he was feeling the cold 'from the effects of shock' and how attractive he was: 'His hair was quite thick & soft – not close-cropped, like Roland's.'[85] Geoffrey talked freely to Vera and her mother, who had accompanied her on this 2 March visit, and it was from that time on that Vera and Geoffrey established a friendship independent of Edward. And when Edward was sent to the 1st London General, and Vera was given leave to rush to 'J' ward, she records in her diary in vivid detail the image of how he looked in bed: 'There was the dear, in bed, in blue pyjamas, struggling with a breakfast tray with one hand. The other sleeve was empty, & the arm below it stiff & bandaged.'[86] Writing about this later, in *Testament of Youth*, she adds: 'I noticed with relief, as I looked with an instinctively professional eye for the familiar green stain, that the outer bandage was spotless.'[87] Victor becomes '[p]oor motherless Tah' when she is returning home from Malta intending to marry him. There is no evidence in any of this of 'erotic release', either overtly or 'subtextually': rather, the war has transformed all Vera's lovers and potential lovers into brothers, men for whom she feels a gendered but non-sexual love, and for whom she will perform sisterly service.

In July 1917, after Victor had died and Edward had returned to France, Vera Brittain went back to VAD headquarters at Devonshire House, to join up once again. On this occasion, she tells us in *Testament of Youth*, she was met at first with harshness, for she had, after all, broken her previous contract. 'And why... did you leave Malta?', the Red Cross official who interviewed her demanded to know. When she explained that she had come home to marry a man who had been blinded at Arras, the woman was touched: 'To my surprise, for I had long given up expecting humanity in officials, a mask seemed to drop from the tired face before me. I was suddenly looking into benevolent eyes dim with comprehension....'[88] This time, at her own request, she was sent to France, to become a VAD on the Western Front.

As medical histories of the Great War attest, Voluntary Aid Detachment nurses served essential functions on the Western Front. The first VAD contingent went out to France in February 1915 to assist the trained nurses already serving in the military. At the outset the VADs were perceived as volunteer interlopers, but soon they were acknowledged to be indispensable and before long they were serving as paid nurses under the auspices of the army. These partially trained recruits were accepted so readily because military nurses were needed in unprecedented numbers in the First World War. The new technologies of war had on the one hand increased the numbers of wounded and the severity of their wounds, and on the other hand, new achievements in medical knowledge made it possible to save the lives, if not the limbs, of a greater number of the wounded.[89] A British Expeditionary Force (BEF) soldier wounded on the Western Front would be taken first to a regimental aid post, to be treated and classified by the battalion medical officer. From there, he would be sent to a casualty clearing station, where some treatment would be undertaken. Finally, if he was still alive, he would be transported, usually via ambulance train, to a stationary or base hospital, either in France or in England.[90]

In August 1917, Vera Brittain was sent out from England to serve in a BEF base hospital, the 24th General, near Étaples. She travelled from Dover to Boulogne, the north-east port which was the usual disembarkation point for medical personnel.[91] The next day, she travelled the short distance down the railway line to Étaples. Military regulations decreed that she could not tell her family exactly where the '24th General Hospital, BEF France' was located, but the censor did allow the following hint, included in the note she sent her mother from Boulogne, to stand: 'The place begins with the first letter of your Christian name; Edward was there on June 30th & I came through it on May 27th. Have mentioned it several times as a possible place.'[92] Shortly after her arrival at the base hospital she wrote home: 'Well, Malta was an interesting experience of the world, but this is War. There is a great coming & going all day long – men marching from one place "somewhere" in France to another; ambulances, transports etc passing all the time . . . Everything of war that one can imagine is here, except actual fighting & one can even hear the distant rumble of that at times. . . .'[93] She described the vast temporary establishment in which she was working: 'The hospital is about a mile out of the town', she informed her parents. 'It is all huts & tents. I am working in a hut & sleeping under canvas, only not in a tent but in a kind of canvas shanty, with boarded floor & a corrugated iron roof; . . . the camp bed is quite comfortable, and to have real Active Service conditions at last pleases me immensely.'[94]

The months that she nursed at Étaples were the most fulfilling, the most intense and the most exciting of her wartime experience. It was indeed 'Active Service'. The phase of the war on the Western Front known to military historians as the third battle of Ypres had begun on 31 July and culminated only with the taking of Passchendaele on 6 November. British losses during the period numbered some 240,000.[95] Brittain was part of the BEF effort to deal with the large numbers of wounded that resulted from this major offensive. She and the four VADs with whom she arrived on 4 August were immediately put to work. As she wrote to her mother: 'The hospital is frantically busy & we were very much welcomed.'[96] Medical personnel were pushed to the limit right through November. During one particularly taxing week, Vera wrote: 'Am frantically busy, & probably shan't be able to write a proper letter for days . . . Off-duty time non ext [*sic*] at present, convoys pouring in.'[97] 'Frantically': that word conveys the fear, pain and worry she experienced. But there was also exhilaration: the sense that she was participating in a great enterprise, and the sense of pride she gained from being able to rise to the occasion, to do this needed work successfully. As she points out in a key passage in *Testament of Youth*, the pacifist aim of abolishing war is so difficult not because of war's horrors, but because of its undeniable attractions:

> Since those years it has often been said by pacifists . . . that war creates more criminals than heroes; that, far from developing noble qualities in

> those who take part in it, it brings out only the worst. If this were altogether true, the pacifist's aim would be, I think, much nearer of attainment than it is. Looking back upon the psychological processes of us who were very young sixteen years ago, it seems to me that his task – our task – is infinitely complicated by the fact that war, while it lasts, does produce heroism to a far greater extent than it brutalises.[98]

Although Étaples did represent the apex of Brittain's wartime nursing experience, it was there also that she was exposed most starkly to the ugliness, to the monstrous irrationality of the war. On the strength of her experience in Malta, for her first assignment the Matron (whom she describes as 'the most delightful I have yet struck in all my manifold experiences of Matrons'[99]) assigned her to a ward devoted to German prisoners of war. In *Testament of Youth*, she would write:

> Before the War I had never been in Germany and had hardly met any Germans apart from the succession of German mistresses at St. Monica's, every one of whom I had hated with a provincial schoolgirl's pitiless distaste for foreigners. So it was somewhat disconcerting to be pitchforked, all alone – since V.A.D.'s went on duty half an hour before Sisters – into the midst of thirty representatives of the nation which, as I had repeatedly been told, had crucified Canadians, cut off the hands of babies, and subjected pure and stainless females to unmentionable 'atrocities'. I didn't think I had really believed all those stories, but I wasn't quite sure. I half expected that one or two of the patients would get out of bed and try to rape me, but I soon discovered that none of them were in a position to rape anybody. . . . At least a third of the men were dying . . .[100]

At the time, in writing to her mother, she did not acknowledge the sexual aspect to her initial discomfort which is so prominent a part of the *Testament of Youth* account. To her mother she says:

> You will be surprised to hear that at present I am nursing German prisoners. My ward is entirely reserved for the most acute German surgical cases; we have no cases but the very worst. . . . Of course no one nurses Germans all the time. I cannot, however, really say I dislike nursing the prisoners, though I should have expected to had I thought of it. To begin with the majority are more or less dying; never, even at the lst London during the Somme push, have I seen such dreadful wounds. Consequently they are all too ill to be aggressive, & one forgets that they are the enemy and can only remember that they are suffering human beings. My half-forgotten German comes in very

> useful, & the Sisters were so glad to know I understood it & could speak a little as half the time they don't know what the poor things want. It gives one a chance to live up to our motto Inter Arma Caritas, but anyhow one can hardly feel bitter towards dying men. It is incongruous, though, to think of Edward in one part of France trying to kill the same people whom in another part of France I am trying to save. . . . The less, however, one hates them the more one realises the tragedy of war; it seems so absurd that these men & ours should be bent simply on killing each other.[101]

She nursed the German prisoners until the second week in September, when she was abruptly removed from the prisoners' ward because her superiors believed that one of the patients was behaving in a sexually offensive manner toward her. Fifteen years later, when writing *Testament of Youth* she would characterize the incident as a 'bewildering rumpus' which she did not even then understand. '"I'm very sorry indeed, nurse, that you've been so much annoyed by that dreadful man," . . . the Matron amazingly began', she writes in the *Testament of Youth* account.[102] At the time, significantly, she gave no indication of the reason for her transfer when writing home to her mother, and one may surmise that she suppressed any direct awareness of the connection between sexual danger and the Germans.[103] The incident does however reveal that the nursing hierarchy – Matrons and Sisters did see the Germans, even as prisoners, as threatening and specifically as *sexually* threatening to women.

Pathetic, dying Germans were succeeded by pathetic, dying Tommies. On 30 November the German Army attacked near Cambrai, in an offensive that produced many casualties. Mustard gas had been used, and as she wrote in anguish to her mother after her first encounter with gassed cases:

> I wish those people who write so glibly about this being a holy war & the orators who talk so much about going on no matter how long the War lasts & what it may mean, could see a case – to say nothing of 10 cases – of mustard gas in its early stages – could see the poor things burnt and blistered all over with great mustard-coloured suppurating blisters, with blinded eyes . . . all sticky & stuck together, & always fighting for breath, with voices a mere whisper, saying that their throats are closing & they know they will choke. The only thing one can say is that such severe cases don't last long; either they die soon or else improve – usually the former; they certainly never reach England in the state we have them here, and yet people persist in saying that God made the War, when there are such inventions of the Devil about . . .[104]

Three months later, familiarity had made the gas cases no longer as horrifying: 'Our ward is quite busy with gassed cases now', she wrote in a letter home to her parents in February 1918, her matter-of-fact tone contrasting sharply with her initial response. 'I find the work quite interesting & it is conveniently regular – I mean the treatment is practically the same for everybody so you can simply go straight through it.'[105]

At the time she wrote that letter, the hospital was busy, but 'not so busy yet that I have to miss off-duty time'. A month later, at the time of the German offensive which began on 21 March 1918, the hospital was once again overwhelmed with wounded and dying men. To her mother on 31 March she wrote: 'I have been trying to find a moment to write to you all this week but there literally has not been one, we have been moving from morning till night, & meals a hurried scramble . . . I have never known anything like it before.'[106]

In *Testament of Youth*, she wrote of these days in March 1918 when the overwhelming tasks at hand seemed especially difficult because it appeared at first as if the Germans might be winning: 'However long I may be destined to survive my friends who went down in the Flood, I shall never forget the crushing tension of those extreme days.' In the *Testament of Youth* account, she juxtaposes the remembered reality with the calm elegance of the British Red Cross headquarters in Grosvenor Crescent, where she had gone to do research for the book's wartime chapters:

> Only a short time ago, sitting in the elegant offices of the British Red Cross Society . . . I read . . . the following words . . .'The V.A.D. members were not . . . trained nurses; nor were they entrusted with trained nurses' work except on occasions when the emergency was so great that no other course was open.' And there, in that secure, well-equipped room, the incongruous . . . picture came back to me of myself standing alone in a newly created circle of hell during the 'emergency' of March 22nd, 1918, and gazing . . . at the dishevelled beds, the stretchers on the floor . . . the brown blankets turned back from smashed limbs bound to splints by filthy bloodstained bandages. Beneath each stinking wad of sodden wool and gauze an obscene horror waited for me – and all the equipment that I had . . . in this ex medical ward was one pair of forceps standing in a potted-meat glass half full of methylated spirit.[107]

The horrors Brittain faced single-handed on 22 March 1918 represent the darkest picture of her service as a VAD on the Western Front. But she experienced lighter moments as well at Étaples, just as she had in

Malta. As she herself was aware, the quality of the sociability the nursing staff created for themselves was oddly reminiscent of her school and college days. 'We have little after-supper tea-parties here just like we used to at college', she remarks.[108] In another letter home, she writes of a Christmas entertainment the night staff 'are hoping to get up' and she asks her mother to send her some copies of Thackeray's *The Rose and the Ring* suggesting that she obtain the copies from St Monica's: 'I know St Monica's have several copies'.[109] The Thackeray play was planned as part of a programme to which Brittain herself was contributing the curtain-raiser: 'I have written a little skit on the hospital for the curtain-raiser in which the characters are an absurd Sister & a perfect little idiot of a V.A.D; it brings in all sorts of topical allusions, and ought to go down quite well.'[110]

Amateur theatrical performances; tea parties; a debating society (Brittain wrote home about this in February 1918: 'The nurses' club . . . has started a debating society . . . I have to second the motion on Monday night; it is about whether women should continue their present unusual occupations after the war or not. I don't know yet which side I have to take'[111]); weekly professional entertainment (in October 1917 she writes of attending a concert by the well-known performer Lena Ashwell[112]). All these activities provide evidence that the enormous effort that produced the temporary transformation of this part of northern France in the war years, the organisation that generated the network of base hospitals and ambulance trains, hostels and canteens, also gave rise to an evanescent but lively social structure which clearly did much to sustain the spirits of individual participants like Brittain herself. Women like Brittain were inducted into this new culture of Army life in small ways as well as larger ones. For example, VADs, as recipients of Army rations, received a weekly allotment of cigarettes. Vera Brittain, like many VADs, took up smoking during her war service.[113] As one VAD put it: '3 packets of cigarettes . . . a week . . . In face of that we could hardly be forbidden to smoke!'[114] Vera herself took to a tipped Russian brand called 'Ladies Russian Blend': they were one of the things, along with food and toiletries, that she regularly asked her parents to send out to her.[115] From its frequent and efficient postal service, to its social network, the BEF imposed an intricate, alternative structure on this part of the French countryside.

At Étaples, Brittain felt more at home with her fellow nurses – trained sisters and VADs alike – than she had in England or even in Malta. Partly, this reflected the middle- and upper middle-class origins of the particular group of women working at the 24th General Hospital. As she informed her parents during the first week she was in France: 'The charmingness of everyone is a great asset & I am quite friendly with one or two of the girls I came with, – all ladies, in fact most people here seem to be, even the Sisters.'[116]

During her tour of duty in France, Brittain made her only serious wartime friendship. The making of this friendship was probably facilitated by the fact that for the first time she was on her own, and not paired off with Stella Sharp. The friend was Faith Moulson, a trained nurse who had come out to France with the Queen Alexandra's Imperial Military Nursing Service.[117] Moulson was the Sister-in-Charge of the German prisoner-of-war ward in which Brittain's tour of duty at Étaples began. The attachment Brittain felt for Moulson developed quickly, after she recovered from an initial fear and antipathy arising from Moulson's exacting standards as a supervisor. On Brittain's part, this was a friendship based on admiration and respect: Moulson was eight years her senior, and of course had professional seniority. At its outset, as well, the friendship contained echoes of Brittain's earlier attachments to older, admired female figures: most notably to Edith Fry and to Hilda Lorimer. Like Fry and Lorimer, Moulson was an attractive, independent, assertive woman, a woman whose respect Brittain desired to obtain and whom she wished to emulate. She told her mother something of her feelings for Faith Moulson in the letters she wrote home:

> [M]y ward Sister is quite my best friend here – quite a different type from the usual trained nurse as not only is she very clever & original . . . but she comes from a very good family, mostly clerics & scholars some of whom I knew very well by repute at Oxford. Her uncle is the Bishop of Manchester. . . . She herself took up nursing because she couldn't stand the extremely clerical atmosphere of her family. She is quite young – about 32, not exactly pretty but has a very attractive face. . . . At first I was rather shy of going out with a striped sister but she says she sees no reason why we are not equals when off-duty . . . [Y]ou can't wonder that at last, after two years, I have found that hospital work can interest me, since I am doing really advanced work under an intellectual person I am extremely fond of, and who is not only willing but anxious to teach me everything I want to know.[118]

When she was off duty, Brittain explored the northern French countryside in which the base hospital was situated, with Moulson and with other friends. When she came to write about Étaples in

Testament of Youth, she entitled the chapter 'Between the Sandhills and the Sea', and that evocative phrase captures some of Brittain's feeling for the landscape. To her mother she wrote in August, soon after she arrived: 'Edward's description of this place is most unfair to it; outside the camps it is really lovely, especially on a stormy day, when the lights and shades on the sand hills with their little clumps of dark pines, & the long expanse of sand & the distant sea are most beautiful.'[119]

During the ensuing months, she went for long walks or drives and she and her companions enjoyed meals in restaurants and cafés. On 9 September she and Faith hired a fiacre and drove for eight miles 'through beautiful French country'. When they reached the coast, they dismissed the fiacre and walked along the shore for another five miles, ending up in a town where they enjoyed 'a very good omelette, & chocolate & red-current jelly' in a local café.[120] A week later, she and another VAD went for a twenty-mile hike through 'all kinds of fascinating French country, through two dear little villages, a common on the side of a hill, sand-dunes & a thick forest of mostly pines, till finally we came out again close to the coast. We had lunch – the usual good omelette & coffee – in a lovely old garden belonging to an ancient French house now used as a restaurant, and tea at a cottage beside a large mere surrounded by trees.'[121]

These passages from Brittain's letters home reveal that, even given wartime conditions, Brittain was eager to experience the sights, sounds and tastes of France. Her own curiosity and sensitive awareness enabled her to penetrate beneath the surface of the British Expeditionary Force establishment, and to enjoy glimpses of the real France that still lay underneath. Like many another twentieth-century member of the English middle classes, Brittain was delighted not merely with the countryside, but with the ambience of this foreign culture, with its language – she found time to take French lessons[122] – with its food, and with the style of French life. In fact, with the assumed sense of certainty characteristic of the very young woman she still was, she informed her mother in December 1917 that she never wished to live in England again:

> [A]part from the people in it, I have an intense distaste for England, nor do I think I am ever likely to settle permanently in it for any great length of time in my life. Now that I have seen a little of the world I have begun to realise how much more nearly every country appeals to me. Goodness knows why the cosmopolitan spirit is in me so strong, I can scarcely have inherited it from my untravelled ancestors – though there may have been a Wanderer among our forbears; who knows![123]

Brittain left France in April. She broke her contract because her mother fell ill and her parents – and most particularly her father – were insistent that she must therefore come home: 'As your mother and I can no longer manage without you . . . it is now your duty to leave France immediately and return to Kensington', he wrote.[124] In *Testament of Youth* Brittain described in retrospect the anguish that she and other women in her position felt under such circumstances, as they found themselves torn between Victorian and Edwardian middle-class patterns of feminine duty, in which the primary obligation of an unmarried daughter was to her family,[125] and the new circumstances produced by the war, in which daughters felt that not only personal preference, but duty as well meant that their primary obligation was to the war effort: 'Half-frantic with the misery of conflicting obligations, I envied Edward his complete powerlessness to leave the Army whatever happened at home. . . .'[126]

It was only in her later narrative reconstruction that Brittain was able to be open about her bitterness. While she did write with some heat to remind her mother that she was working under contract – 'Father appears to imagine that it rests entirely with *me* whether I come home to-morrow or in 6 months, but of course you understand differently'[127] – for the most part she repressed her annoyance, and reassured her mother that she was quite willing to come home.

The months following Brittain's return to care for her mother were in many ways the saddest and most discouraging of the war. The most grievous blow was Edward's death. He was killed in action in Italy on 15 June 1918. Brittain would say much later that Edward's was the bitterest of the war deaths for her. His death certainly was devastating for her parents. Arthur Brittain, in fact, never really recovered from the loss of his son. From then until his suicide in 1935 he suffered from recurrent periods of depression. After Edward's death, Vera herself was so numbed by grief and fatigue that she returned to Army nursing. This final tour of duty was especially disheartening. Because of a new Army rule that VADs who had broken their contracts while on active service could not be sent abroad without a 'retraining' period in a home hospital, she nursed from September 1918 until she was 'demobbed' in April of 1919 in two London hospitals. By 1918, she had energy left only for dogged endurance:

> Now there were no more disasters to dread and no friends left to wait for; with the ending of apprehension had come a deep, nullifying blankness, a sense of walking in a thick mist which hid all sights and

> muffled all sounds. I had no further experience to gain from the war; nothing remained except to endure it.[128]

∞

While the war and her war work did serve to dampen Brittain's feminist awareness (as she points out herself, she was not even aware of the passage in February 1918 of the Representation of the People Act, which enfranchised women over thirty[129]) even the war did not seriously alter her central ambition of becoming a writer.[130] During her active-duty service, her creative energies and observational powers were channelled primarily into her diaries and letters. During the war itself, the principle publishable work she produced was poetry. Inspired by Roland, who expressed his own literary gifts through poetry, and who composed poems about their relationship, Brittain wrote poetry throughout the war. In the poem 'Perhaps', she wrote movingly about her deep sense of loss after Roland died:

> Perhaps some day the sun will shine again,
> And I shall see that still the skies are blue,
> And feel once more I do not live in vain,
> Although bereft of You.[131]

'To My Brother', written in June 1918, just before Edward was killed, captures in these poignant lines her sorrowful recollection of the wounds he sustained in the Battle of the Somme:

> Your battle-wounds are scars upon my heart,
> Received when in that grand and tragic 'show'
> You played your part
> Two years ago.[132]

In the poem 'In the German Ward' she wrote about the complex and conflicting emotions she experienced while nursing enemy soldiers. By the autumn of 1917, when she wrote 'In the German Ward', she had begun to think about her war poems as a publishable group. She was sending them home to her mother to have them typed, in preparation for submitting them to a publisher,[133] and, as she told her mother in late September: 'Should like to publish soon'.[134] By October, when through the good offices of Mrs. Leighton, a publisher had been found, she asked her mother to send along the typescript of the collection.[135] The volume, entitled *Verses of a V.A.D.*, came out in 1918.

In *Testament of Youth*, Brittain would be dismissively self-deprecating about *Verses of a V.A.D.* (the volume was 'unobtrusively ushered into an indifferent world' she says, '[o]n some utterly forgotten date'),[136] but as the letters she sent to her mother concerning the poems and the volume itself indicate, at the time she was far from indifferent to this project which did, after all, launch her career as a professional writer. But while the publication of the verse was important to her, Brittain knew that her natural medium was prose, not poetry. The problem was that during the war she had no time to write anything substantial. In France, it was even difficult to find time for letters. However, she had not abandoned her determination to write in the future. In April 1918, just before her return home, when her mother was about to go into a nursing home because she was suffering from fatigue, Vera wrote: 'If I were in the same position I should of course write a novel – which I mean to do when I get home – about this place, before I forget the impressions.'[137]

She began that novel in 1918, soon after her return to England in April, and wrote a substantial part of it in July, when she and her family took a brief holiday during the bleak summer following Edward's death. The novel, 'Folly's Vineyard', was never published,[138] but it is of interest both because it was her first adult attempt at writing fiction and because it offers access to her thoughts and feelings about the war and about her wartime nursing when the experience was still fresh. The plot of 'Folly's Vineyard' revolves around the relationship between Sybil Beresford, a young VAD, and the formidable nursing sister, Hope Milroy. 'Sybil' and 'Hope' are of course Vera and Faith: for the most part, only the names are changed. But because the characters are so directly drawn from life, we learn from this fictional recreation just how important the friendship with Faith Moulson was to Brittain. As Sybil is about to leave for France, the reader is informed that:

> She suddenly felt sure that through going there she would meet some individual of an unusual type, with whom she would become intimate, and whose intimacy would influence her life . . . and her instinctive mind had no doubt that the impending personality . . . would be that of a woman. . . . Beyond one or two superficial school friendships and the warm regard of a don . . . women had not affected her at all up to the day she entered hospital.[139]

'Folly's Vineyard' suffers from what Brittain herself later characterized as 'lurid' touches,[140] and contains in its tone and style traces of the penchant for melodrama which infused the novelettes she had written as a young girl. For example, in one version of the novel, the character drawn from Faith Moulson becomes pregnant, and considers having an abortion. She eventually rejects that solution: 'To me it would be covering up one sin by another far worse – shirking shame by crime.'[141]

But in addition to its overheated touches, 'Folly's Vineyard' also contains some revealing passages which reflect Brittain's serious thinking about the meaning of war. For example, she writes movingly of her experiences nursing German prisoners. For the fictional character 'Sybil' and for her creator, the thoughts and emotions aroused by that work led to a condemnation of warmaking itself and of those in power on both sides: 'The more Sybil pitied them, the more acutely she felt the tragedy of war. It seemed to her that she and they alike were victims, broken by the desire for domination of that military caste which had plunged Europe into disaster.'

Between the neophyte effort 'Folly's Vineyard' and the mature *Testament of Youth*, Brittain wrote no major account of her wartime experiences. *Testament of Youth*'s qualities as a literary achievement are the subject of a later chapter of this book: in this chapter and the previous one, I have been concerned with the way in which the *Testament of Youth* narrative should be used in assessing Brittain's immediate experience of the war years. In the narratives of love, of her relationship to the men she knew who fought and died in the war, Brittain's portrayal, touching as it is, presents her experience through a distorted mirror. In *Testament of Youth* her love for her lover, for her potential lovers and for her brother are all seen through stereotypical assumptions about romance in wartime, about masculine bravery and feminine self-sacrifice. They are 'just warriors'; she is a 'beautiful soul'.[142]

In contrast, in narrating her work experience during the war, Brittain's purpose in *Testament of Youth* was to provide as much information, as much historical context, as possible, and accordingly those sections of the book are notable for their realism rather than their romanticism. But here too, *Testament of Youth* has some important limitations. In it Brittain presents herself as a typical VAD, and her account has been used to reinforce the belief that the VADs as a group were educated, upper-middle-class young women who joined up out of a sense of patriotic mission, that they 'were, and were intended to be, very middle class or upper class in background'.[143]

Many of the women who served as VAD nurses were indeed, like Vera Brittain, from solid middle- or upper middle-class backgrounds. Ruth Manning, for example, who served as a VAD at the 55th

General Hospital, Wimereux, from 1915–18, was the daughter of a Church of England clergyman.[144] Ida Haigh, from Bradford, who received her initial training as a VAD nurse at a hospital in Leicester, and then in Wales, and who did foreign service in Egypt and Palestine, was the daughter of a successful Bradford textile exporter.[145] May Wedderburn Cannan, from a very well-connected Oxford family, whose mother was the first Commandant of the No. 12 Detachment (Oxford University) in 1911, served in that Detachment before the war, worked part time as a VAD at an Oxford hospital, and then went out to France in 1918.[146]

But to these women compare Joanna Swarbrick, who served as a nursing VAD at Southwark Military Hospital from 1916–18. She was from what appears to have been a lower-middle-class Blackpool family, and had received a much more limited education than Brittain, Manning, Haigh or Cannan.[147] Or consider the case of twenty-three-year-old Miss Touzel who had trained as a nurse for fourteen months, but had been obliged to abandon her training because her mother had become ill. In November 1917 she was working as a clerk, but because of her 'passion for nursing' she wanted to do some after-hours work as a VAD. Touzel had an influential friend, feminist activist A. Maud Royden, who wrote to the VAD Chief Commandant on her behalf. Royden tellingly describes Miss Touzel's social status: 'She is an attractive young person – not a lady exactly – but *really* a lady, I think. . . .'[148] The evidence from Brittain's own letters home – although not from *Testament of Youth* – confirms that many of the women who served as nursing VADs were, like Miss Touzel, not 'ladies'. The many VADs with nursing backgrounds may, like Miss Touzel, have wished to be professional nurses, but had been prevented by financial hardship or other circumstances from completing their training. And we can assume that more often than not, those who served in the ranks, rather than with commissions, as General Service VADs – typically working as cooks, clerks and housekeepers – came from lower-middle-class or working-class backgrounds.[149]

It is a tribute to Brittain's success in creating a detailed, balanced and well-researched account of her war work that *Testament of Youth* has been so frequently cited as evidence for the VAD nursing experience. However, although she certainly never intended this result, Brittain's account has unfortunately also contributed to reinforcing some of the myths about VADs, and therefore to the continued exclusion from the historical record of a consideration of the experience of VADs of lower-middle-class or working-class origins.

CONCLUSIONS

Taken as a whole, the historiography dealing with women's experience in the First World War appears to be of three kinds. There is the naive optimism of the earliest accounts, echoed most recently in Arthur Marwick's *Women at War*, which argues that women's participation in new occupations during the war improved their status and advanced the cause of women's rights. Then there is the more critical approach exemplified by Gail Braybon's *Women Workers in the First World War: The British Experience*[150] which stresses how limited and how evanescent women's wartime progress was. Third and most recently, historians and literary critics influenced by cultural studies have developed what they themselves maintain is a more nuanced position, in which women as a group are seen to have made concrete advances, but at a painful price: women's liberation from the trammels of Victorianism, they suggest, gave rise to gender strife. This strife and the misogyny that accompanied it are seen as responsible for the emergence in the post-war period of a politics of 'sexual difference' among women activists themselves and a corresponding retreat from equal-rights feminism.[151]

Throughout the development of this historiography Brittain's *Testament of Youth* has frequently been used as evidence: Brittain, indeed, is part of the historiographical tradition. One purpose of Part II of this book has been to reflect on the way in which Brittain's experience both supports and refutes historical generalizations about British women and the First World War. What can we conclude? My analysis suggests that neither on Arthur Marwick's terms nor on Sandra Gilbert's did Brittain's war work serve to liberate her from the limitations of femininity: Brittain had already begun such a liberation before the war began, and the war years in fact had a retrograde effect on her feminism and on her professional career. However, her VAD experience was responsible for another sort of liberation. For a brief time it freed her, at least in part, from the expectations of her social class. Brittain would work all her life, but for most of her career she would be a worker by brain and not by hand. During the years 1915–19 she engaged in arduous manual work and she did so along side women and men who were not from her own upper middle-class milieu. The fact that she succeeded had long-lasting beneficial psychological effects. In the post-war period, Brittain would mature into a writer and social activist whose views would be sharply at variance with those of the young girl whose conceptions of 'Service and

Sanctification' had been formed in her Edwardian adolescence. But while she would later question some aspects of the moral framework within which she had been raised, at least she knew that she herself had possessed the inner strength to live up to its precepts.

Part III

'Lady into Woman': Friendship, Work and Marriage in the 1920s

7

Friendship and Feminism

In Part III of this book I examine the new life that Vera Brittain made for herself after the end of the war, tracing her journey from her numb despair on armistice morning in 1918 to the late 1920s. The 1920s were Brittain's years of literary apprenticeship. She published her first two novels (*The Dark Tide* in 1923 and *Not Without Honour* in 1924) and she developed her career as a writer of journalism and of book-length works on feminism and internationalism. By the end of the 1920s, she felt ready to turn to what she had long thought of as her most important literary project, the transformation of her wartime experience into literature, the work that culminated in *Testament of Youth*.

As a young girl, Brittain had longed for a personal life free from the burdensome rituals of bourgeois provinciality. When asked as an eighteen-year-old schoolgirl to write an essay describing 'A Sitting Room furnished on £25', she had envisioned a plain booklined room in a London flat, the antithesis of her parents' overstuffed Edwardian drawing room.[1] In the decade after the war, Brittain fashioned a personal life for herself that captured the essence of that girlhood vision. In the early 1920s she achieved financial independence and personal autonomy, as well as a deep friendship and working partnership with another woman, her fellow author and Oxford contemporary Winifred Holtby. In 1925 she married G.E.G. Catlin, and by 1930 they had two children, but she managed to be a wife and mother without sacrificing either her autonomy or her close ties with Holtby. Finally, in addition to her achievements as a writer and her construction of an avant-garde personal life, in the decade after the war she made her mark as an activist working in the cause of feminism and of internationalism.

The three chapters in Part III deal with Brittain as writer, as activist, and as friend, wife and mother during the years 1919–33. This chapter, 'Friendship and Feminism', is concerned with Brittain's post-war return to Oxford, with the formation of her friendship with Holtby and with her apprenticeship as a novelist. Chapter 8, 'Feminism and Internationalism', deals with her feminist and internationalist activism in the post-war period and her work as a journalist. The third chapter in Part III, 'Semi-detached Marriage,' is concerned with the public and private face of her experiment in feminist marriage.

OXFORD, 1919

In April 1919, just a few weeks after her final VAD contract had expired, Vera Brittain returned to Oxford. If we were to rely only on *Testament of Youth*, we would conclude that her first two post-war terms and the intervening summer were bleak indeed. She entitles the chapter in *Testament of Youth* in which she discusses this period of her life 'Survivors not Wanted', and in the sections dealing with the months from April 1919 until February 1920 she constructs a picture of herself as living in a state of 'interminable loneliness'.[2] After she concluded her last, grim stint as a VAD, she tells us that she had hoped for 'the spring of life after the winter of death'. But as the emotional and spiritual numbness of the last months of the war wore off, the Brittain of *Testament of Youth* is overwhelmed by acute and unrelenting psychological distress.[3] She went back to Oxford hoping that she would 'be comforted and restored'.[4] Instead, she meets with a wall of determined rejection.

The College staff wished to sweep her experience under the rug, and her fellow-students, she says, were no better. Neither her immediate juniors who had come up fresh from school nor those who had remained at Oxford during the war years were interested in hearing about the sacrifices she had made or the griefs she had suffered. They rejected her war service as pretentious or, worse still, foolish. In *Testament of Youth*, the climax of this period of humiliation and isolation is the Somerville Debating Society debate in Michaelmas term, 1919. When Brittain defends the motion 'That four years' travel are a better education than four years at a university' the other students turn on her, mocking her for her aloofness and making fun of her preoccupation with her war-time service:

> I didn't really care what they said or thought, my pride insisted, as the voting went unanimously against me . . . but afterwards, alone in my

cheerless lodging, I realised that I had minded dreadfully. Too miserable to light the fire or even to get into bed, I lay on the cold floor and wept with childish abandonment. 'Why couldn't I have died in the War with the others?' I lamented . . . I'm nothing but a piece of wartime wreckage, living on ingloriously in a world that doesn't want me![5]

After the debate, Brittain tells us, she simply buried her feelings about the war, and turned instead to what she explains she consciously and deliberately took on as an intellectual project in the immediate post-war period, the task of attempting to understand how it was that the war had happened. To that end, she had already made the decision that on returning to Oxford she would switch from English to History:

One of [my] half-found inspirations translated itself, trivially enough, into a determination to read History at Oxford instead of English, but the motive behind this superficial change of School was not really trivial. After the first dismayed sense of isolation in an alien peace-time world, such rationality as I still possessed reasserted itself in a desire to understand how the whole calamity had happened. . . . So, thus portentously, I decided to read History . . . [6]

In sharp contrast to the desolate picture presented in the autobiography, in Brittain's letters home during the year of her return to university we never see the exhausted, humourless, intensely sad, lonely and world-weary persona of *Testament of Youth*. The Brittain of these letters is in fact very much her pre-war self: she is lively, she is acutely observant of and intrigued by her surroundings, she is enthusiastic about Oxford and she is very much involved with friends and family.

In these long, chatty, frequent letters, written mainly to her mother but on occasion to her father, she vividly describes her surroundings, her friendships and her academic activities. The contrast between the tone of the letters and that of the autobiography written a decade later is marked.

Take the issue of her physical surroundings. On her return to Oxford, Brittain, as an upper-year student, lived in 'digs'. In *Testament of Youth*, every time that she mentions the room she occupied during 1919–20 in Keble Road, she uses imagery suggestive of physical coldness and spiritual loneliness. She refers to 'the solitude of my cold little room in Keble Road', 'my cheerless lodging', 'my desolate room', 'the chill room at whose door nobody ever knocked'.[7]

In contrast, the letters she wrote while she was actually occupying that room were clearly meant to convey the impression that her surroundings were cheerful: she sent her mother the following description, just after she arrived in October 1919: 'My room is very nice, quite large & on the first floor, & there is plenty of space to put things – except the wardrobe, which is rather small. . . . My landlady seems very nice & says I can have a fire every evening if I don't light it before 5 – which is really all I need as I shall probably be out on & off till then.'[8] True, the room may have been a bit chilly at times, since we find her thanking her mother for sending her a 'foot muff' a few days after her arrival[9] but any physical chill was compensated for by the physical and spiritual warmth provided by her mother's thoughtful gifts.

And in her letters home, Brittain displayed the same keen interest in decorating her private space that had been evident in her pre-war Somerville year. In April 1919, soon after her arrival, she had asked her mother to send on some pictures, their wartime themes – 'Verdun', 'Die Nacht am Rhein' – revealing that she wished through the display of these images to connect her new peacetime life with her wartime experience.[10] In October 1919 she asks her mother to try to find her a black screen decorated with gold storks which she intends to use to hide the washstand in her Keble Road room: 'You know the kind of thing, paper or canvas on a wooden frame that one could get for about 12/6 before the War. I can't get one here for less than 2 Guineas.'[11]

As for her academic work, her switch from English to History appears in a less portentous light than in *Testament of Youth*. She had already had the switch in mind in 1914, when she had discovered during her first term that, as a degree subject, History was thought to be more interesting and more challenging than English.[12]

Brittain's letters home in the spring and the autumn of 1919 indicate that, far from suffering unrelenting loneliness and isolation, during these months she quickly made several friends and found at least some people who were interested in hearing about her VAD service. In the spring of 1919 she lived in a house with five other returning students, including one with whose sister Brittain had nursed in France.[13] With Nina Ruffer, one of these five students, Brittain became intimate enough in the spring of 1919 to confide in her not only about the past, including her romance with Roland, but about the present. With Nina, Vera shared walks, cocoa parties and the amateur 'séances' which were then in vogue. With other fellow women students she shared bicycle rides. She was friendly with several undergraduates and she enjoyed the festivities during Eights Week.[14] In short, although in this term the Vera of *Testament of*

Youth is very lonely indeed, the Vera of the letters has become so busy by the end of May that she writes: 'Don't let Father come up here unexpectedly as now I know more people I am full up with engagements, so if he comes would like plenty of notice.'[15]

Nina Ruffer, who suffered from heart disease, died in the summer of 1919, just as she was preparing to meet Brittain for a summer session in Cambridge. Without Nina, Somerville was even more bleak for the Brittain of *Testament of Youth* in October than it had been in the spring:

> My real return to Oxford seemed to come the next term, when I found myself, lost and bewildered, amid a crowd of unfamiliar ex-schoolgirls in a semi-familiar Somerville. . . . Nobody knew or appeared to want to know me; one or two stared with half-insolent curiosity at my alien face, and my Classical tutor . . . invited me occasionally to tea in her study, but the majority disregarded me completely. . . . [N]ow there was no Nina to share the solitude of my cold little room in Keble road, and . . . I spent many hours of [the term] in lonely walks and in 'cutting' college dinner.[16]

Again, the letters home contain no trace of this forlorn despondency. Indeed they often directly contradict the gloomy picture that infuses the period from October 1919 to February 1920 in the *Testament of Youth* account. For example, in the passage quoted above, Brittain conveys the impression that Hilda Lorimer (her Classics tutor in 1914–15) was inviting her to tea because she felt sorry for her and was concerned about her lonely state. In contrast, the letters home suggest that in 1919 Hilda Lorimer, who was no longer directly involved in Brittain's academic life, was delighted to initiate a genuine friendship with her. Moreover, the friendship involved Brittain's mother. On Edith Brittain's frequent visits to her daughter at Oxford, the three women often had tea together.[17]

And while in *Testament of Youth* we are presented with a reclusive, even hungry, Brittain 'cutting' dinner, the letters present quite a different picture. She did 'cut' dinner but not because she felt like an outcast. Indeed, she frequently shared these unauthorized meals with others: 'I am having a supper party tonight – our supper on Sunday never being very extensive', she writes in early November.[18]

It was during autumn of 1919 that Brittain first met Basil Blackwell, the young Oxford publisher, and his sister. Miss Blackwell had a 'literary circle' on Saturday evenings, to which Brittain was first invited in October, and which she attended regularly thereafter. As she informed her mother in November:

> Miss Blackwell has been extremely kind to me & apart from that I am most anxious to make as much of the acquaintance as possible as her brother the publisher, who is getting on rapidly & knows heaps of literary people, has taken a great fancy to me & is very much disposed to help me in the future.[19]

Brittain's accounts of her first forays into Oxford literary society in her letters to her mother are full of gossipy detail and reflect the great pleasure she took from these new contacts. She enjoyed dressing up for the occasion ('I feel I really ought to wear an evening dress for Miss Blackwell's literary circle on Saturday evenings'[20]); she enjoyed Basil Blackwell's admiration, although she hastens to warn her mother that there is no possibility of romance ('He is married & has 2 little children so don't get excited'[21]); and, applying her Buxton categories, she offered her mother an assessment of the Blackwells' social status: ('You will not find much of the tradesman's daughter about Miss Blackwell, nor about Mr., who was at Merton!'[22]).

In *Testament of Youth* the great pleasure that Brittain took from these new literary contacts is largely suppressed. She does indeed mention her involvement with the *Oxford Outlook*, the *Oxford Chronicle* and *Oxford Poetry* in 1919–20 but her main purpose, once again, was to reinforce a desolate picture of her situation during the immediate post-war period. For example, her use of her own poem 'Boar's Hill' is designed to emphasise her melancholy state of mind:

> On Boar's Hill, where I wandered alone very often, the cherry-trees were turning to flame against the lowering greyness of the stormy October clouds. Had I actually walked there with Edward . . . or had he accompanied me only in spirit? With Roland, I knew, I had never been on the Hill, and yet it was as vivid with memories of him as though we had often seen it together. The two of them seemed to fuse in my mind into a kind of composite lost companion, an elusive ghost which embodied all intimacy, all comradeship, all joy. . . . Incessantly I tramped across the Hill, subconsciously pursuing this symbolic figure like a lost spirit seeking for its mate, and one dark afternoon, when I came back from a long walk to a solitary tea, followed by a lonely evening in the chill room at whose door nobody ever knocked, I endeavoured to crystallise the mood of that search in a poem which later, in *Oxford Poetry*, 1920, I called 'Boar's Hill, October 1919.'[23]

> Tall slender beech-trees, whispering, touched with fire,
> Swaying at even beneath a desolate sky;
> Smouldering embers aflame where the clouds hurry by

At the wind's desire.
Dark sombre woodlands, rain-drenched by the scattering shower
Spindle that quivers and drops its dim berries to earth –
Mourning, perhaps, as I mourn here alone for the dearth
Of a happier hour . . . [24]

In sharp contrast, in the letter home describing the same afternoon she writes: 'I went up to Boar's Hill yesterday: it was looking rather desolate but the colours were lovely; whereupon I wrote a small poem which I am sending to the Chronicle; if it comes out I will let you have a copy.'[25] And this is her final comment on this Michaelmas term from the letter she wrote two days later, on 30 October 1919: 'I shall be quite pleased to be home again & get sufficient food & warmth – tho' it has been quite a nice term.'[26]

How should we interpret the marked difference in tone between Brittain's 1919–20 letters home and the account of this period in *Testament of Youth*? I would suggest that both versions present incomplete pieces of the truth. If the *Testament of Youth* account is overly bleak, the letters home are overly cheerful and, moreover, they disclose less in reality than in appearance. An example of an unacknowledged silence in the letters concerns the Somerville debate which figures so prominently in *Testament of Youth*. Before the event, Brittain wrote to her mother and father in considerable detail: 'Next week we are having a most amusing debate which I have to propose; the subject is: "That four years travel are a better education than four years at a University." I am going to make a most revolutionary speech, ardently supporting travel & violently attacking the university, so if any dons are present they will probably get a shock.'[27] But significantly, in the two chatty, cheerful letters she wrote over the course of the next ten days Brittain did not mention the painful humiliation she experienced.[28] At this lowest point in her post-war Somerville experience, she clearly did not feel that she could turn to her parents for solace.

The reasons for the editing here and elsewhere in the letters home are complex, and Brittain herself may not have been fully aware of her own motives in presenting a steadily optimistic face throughout this correspondence. Brittain did suffer from moments of deep hopelessness and despair during this period, even at times fearing for her own sanity, and she would continue to suffer from such feelings recurrently over the next decades. We can speculate that there were at least three interrelated reasons for her silence concerning these feelings in her letters home.

The first arose from her own unresolved conflicts between her love for her mother and her rejection of her mother's way of life. Although not completely happy with her daughter's choices, in the years just before the war, Edith Brittain had been supportive of Vera's decision to become a university student. After the war her support for Vera was if anything stronger and less equivocal. And Vera clearly received much sustenance from Edith's abiding interest in the day-to-day details of her life, from her visits to Oxford during term-time, and from her practical assistance. It was her mother, for instance, who arranged in advance for a library ticket to the Kensington Library so that Vera could work there during the summer holidays in 1919, and who clipped stories from *The Times* about degrees for women in the autumn of 1919 for a story that Vera was writing for the *Oxford Outlook*.[29] But in spite of – or perhaps because of – this closeness, Brittain experienced a need to keep some emotional distance between her mother and herself. In part, even in her mid-twenties she had not completely banished the temptation to regress to an earlier dependent relationship with her mother and therefore felt compelled to resist such dependence vigorously. Again, sensing that her mother might, even in 1919, have preferred it had she made more conventionally feminine choices, she wanted to present the less-conventional choices she had made in the best possible light.

Then there was Edward's death which complicated the relationship between Brittain and her parents. Brittain, who had loved Edward deeply, missed him and grieved for his loss on her own account. But in addition, his death left her with the burdens that inevitably befall a surviving child, including the need not to disappoint her parents or add to their anxieties. Brittain was, for example, very conscious of her mother's continuing sadness about Edward and of her own need to act as her mother's comforter. On the anniversary of his death she writes: 'If I were you I should certainly go to the Melba concert next Sunday – Edward would like it, & I am not sure moreover that on the whole we don't allow ourselves to be too upset by "anniversaries".'[30]

Finally, there was her father's ill health which constituted the most pressing reason why she could not easily share her troubles with her mother. Brittain's letters home contain few details concerning this matter, but those few are revealing. In the autumn of 1919, for example, Arthur was suffering from influenza. It left him both exhausted and depressed. 'I am sorry Father is so depressed', Brittain writes. 'I wonder if he will improve at all when I come home.' 'He generally wants me home when I am away', she adds, but when she is there, he finds her 'more of a nuisance than anything else'.[31] Arthur Brittain's bouts of depression were to be a persistent affliction, culminating in his suicide in 1935.

Studies on the effects of clinical depression on members of the afflicted person's immediate family indicate that depression commonly has a constraining effect on the range of emotional expression other family members feel they can allow themselves.[32] During this period, Arthur's depression was, it appears, having this effect on Edith and on Vera Brittain. Edith Brittain, already anxious about her husband, appears to have become concerned at any hint that her daughter might also be suffering from depression. There is some evidence, for example, that she was worried about Vera's state of mind in September 1919. Because we do not have Edith's side of the correspondence we cannot know exactly what she said, but Vera's sensible reassurance about any unhappiness she might be feeling on her return to Oxford indicates that she is calming fears: 'Don't worry because I don't like college as much as I perhaps should have if I had come up before the War. Don't you know that the only people who ever do well at a University are the ones who aren't altogether happy there?'[33]

Given this combination of factors, it is not surprising that Brittain could not freely express her moments of despair to her mother and perhaps not even to herself. Later, Brittain would use her writing as a vehicle for acknowledging these feelings. She did so through fictional characters in her first published novel, *The Dark Tide*, and also more directly in *Testament of Youth* where, in certain key passages, she conveys with convincing directness flashes of the troubling feelings she experienced in the immediate post-war period. She does so, for example, when describing her reactions to Nina Ruffer's death in the summer of 1919. When the news of Nina's death arrived, Brittain tells us, she 'pushed the thought of her away . . . for I was sick beyond description of death and loss'. But the shock of this new, post-war death could not be completely repressed:

> I looked one evening into my bedroom glass and thought, with a sense of incommunicable horror, that I detected in my face the signs of some sinister and peculiar change. A dark shadow seemed to lie across my chin; was I beginning to grow a beard, like a witch? Thereafter my hand began, at regular intervals, to steal towards my face; and it had quite definitely acquired this habit when I went down to Cornwall in the middle of July to spend a fortnight with Hope Milroy and escape the Peace Celebrations.[34]

Brittain's feelings of 'incommunicable horror', the inner panic she suffered as she struggled to absorb the trauma of her wartime experience is vividly conveyed by that passage. The precise meaning of the image of witchlike transformation that Brittain so much feared here is left unexplained (probably because Brittain could not explain it herself) but intimations of death and decay are clearly present.[35] The confusion and horror evoked by the delusion of the shadow across the face have a ring of authenticity, as does her evocation of the intense loneliness and misery she experienced, alone in her room in Keble Road after the Somerville debate. The fact that she could not convey any of this when she wrote home to her family must have intensified her feelings of isolation.

Thus, it is not her bruised loneliness that is unconvincing in this section of *Testament of Youth*, but rather the unrelieved quality of desolation, the sense of utter exhaustion and weariness of the Brittain of *Testament of Youth*. The real Vera Brittain, while she suffered from bouts of loneliness and panic, of self-doubt and even of depression throughout her life, also possessed resilience and a good-humoured curiosity about the world. In the letters home, even during her bleakest moments, these capacities never fail to manifest themselves but they are conspicuously lacking in the weary post-war persona of *Testament of Youth*.

I have suggested that the overstated optimism of the letters home arose from Brittain's need to protect both herself and her mother from her feelings of depression. In contrast, the unrelieved gloom of the post-war section of *Testament of Youth* arose from Brittain's literary intentions. One of the primary purposes of *Testament of Youth* is to narrate Brittain's odyssey from the unreflecting patriotism of her youth to the anti-war internationalism she adopted in the post-war era. In the section of *Testament of Youth* dealing with the crucial year after the war, she wished to emphasise her sense of injury, isolation and anger, and her belief that those like herself who had served in the war and survived had been cheated, if not of their lives, then of their youth.

In emphasising her post-war anger, Brittain was of course not alone. As George Orwell would later put it: 'By 1918 everyone under forty was in a bad temper with his elders . . . At that time there was, among the young, a curious cult of hatred of "old men" . . . a revolt of youth against age, resulting directly from the war. . . .'[36] Orwell, who was born in 1903, was too young to have participated in the war, but not too young to have observed its effects. While Vera Brittain shared Orwell's anger against the old, in *Testament of Youth* she was more concerned to evoke the painful nature of the barrier between the war generation and its immediate successors, young people of Orwell's own age, who are represented most vividly in *Testament of Youth* by the students at the Somerville debate who mocked her war service. She would continue to believe for many years that there was a 'fundamental antagonism . . . between those who suffered deeply from the War, and the others who escaped its most violent impacts'.[37] It is because she wished to place this antagonism in the foreground that Brittain emphasised her own loneliness at Oxford in 1919, establishing it as the main motif by calling this chapter 'Survivors not Wanted' and by heading it with her poem, 'The Lament of the Demobilised':

> 'Four years,' some say consolingly. 'Oh well,
> What's that? You're young. And then it must have been
> A very fine experience for you!'
> And they forget
> How others stayed behind and just got on –
> . . .
> And no one talked heroics now, and we
> Must just go back and start again once more.
> 'You threw four years into the melting-pot –
> Did you indeed!' these others cry. 'Oh well,
> The more fool you!'
> And we're beginning to agree with them.

In that poem, as in 'Survivors not Wanted', Brittain does movingly articulate the antagonism between the war generation and post-war Oxford. But even Brittain, who believed that as a woman she could make a special contribution by speaking with a woman's voice, was only partially able to articulate the multifaceted isolation that arose from her unusual situation as a woman survivor. In sharp contrast to the men, women like herself were in a minority in post-war Oxford. In addition, post-war mythology did not validate their experience in the way it validated that of their male contemporaries. The returning soldiers were heroes, and even though that term came to have ironic overtones for many men of the war generation, those who had experienced combat did have an emotional and an intellectual bond with their fellows, one that was recognised both by them and by others. The women, in contrast, could not easily define themselves as genuine members of the 'war generation'. Brittain struggled to make a place for women's experience, both at the time (for example in an article she published in 1919 entitled 'The Point of View of a Woman

Student', in which she railed bitterly against Oxford's trivialization of her war service) and in *Testament of Youth* itself.[38] But even Brittain did not always clearly articulate the woman's perspective. The masculine voice often dominates this section of *Testament of Youth*. 'The Lament of the Demobilised' is written from a young man's point of view rather than that of a returning VAD: as she herself tells us, one reviewer said of it that it 'might have been produced by Godfrey Elton out of Siegfried Sassoon'.[39]

She tells her readers this without commenting on the fact that this male reviewer is responding to her poem as if it were written by a man. That she lets this significant fact pass indicates her own inability fully to confront the distinctive isolation she experienced as a woman survivor. We encounter this inability again when Brittain explains how hurtful it was to be seen by her fellow Somervillians as 'a figure of fun, ludicrously boasting of her experiences in an already *démodé* conflict'.[40] Returning soldiers, whatever other burdens they had to bear, were not seen as 'figures of fun'. VADs and their contribution had been belittled even during the war itself. No wonder that on occasion they suffered from such denigration after the war.

Brittain's failure fully to convey the distinctive situation of women like herself may account for some of the overstatement in 'Survivors not Wanted'. She may have exaggerated her own feelings to compensate for her inability to identify the systemic nature of the misogynist attacks to which she and the small number of women in her position were subjected.

THE '*ONE* HUMAN CREATURE AMONG MY OWN SEX'

In October 1914, just before she went up to Oxford, Brittain wrote in her diary of her wish for a deep friendship with another woman: 'Surely now . . . I may begin to *live* & to find at least *one* human creature among my own sex whose spirit can have intercourse with mine.'[41] At Oxford in 1920 she finally found that kindred spirit in Winifred Holtby, a fellow Somervillian from Yorkshire five years her junior, but with similar aspirations and a not dissimilar background. This friendship, which would endure until Holtby's tragic early death from kidney disease in 1935, was not only central to Brittain's actual experience. Because she wrote about it so often it became an intrinsic part of her self-presentation. The genesis of the friendship is the key turning point in 'Survivors not Wanted', and its blossoming and maturing are described in succeeding chapters. A different version figures in her first novel, *The Dark Tide* (1923),[42] and their friendship forms the primary focus of *Testament of Friendship* (1940),[43] Brittain's tribute to her friend, written after her death.

The Brittain–Holtby friendship has been extensively analysed in recent years by feminist literary critics and historians. Literary critic Carolyn Heilbrun, for example, has described the relationship between the two women as 'an exemplary love' and has called *Testament of Friendship* 'an ideal, rare counter example' in a literary tradition that has defamed women's friendships.[44] Jean Kennard's literary study *Vera Brittain and Winifred Holtby: A Working Partnership* discusses their friendship and comments perceptively on its connection with their respective achievements as writers.[45] The friendship has also been of particular interest to such feminist scholars of twentieth-century lesbianism as Lillian Faderman and Sheila Jeffreys.[46]

In the context of this book, with its objective of understanding the relationship between Brittain's experience and her representations of that experience, the multiple presentations of the Brittain–Holtby friendship, beginning with Brittain's own portrayals in her fiction and in her non-fiction, constitute both an opportunity and a challenge. Like other feminist scholars, I too am concerned with understanding women's friendships and the nature of women's sexuality. But, unlike Faderman and Jeffreys or Heilbrun, for whom Brittain and Holtby are of interest primarily because their lives illuminate general points with which those writers are concerned, I wish here to present this friendship in as rounded and nuanced a fashion as possible.

If we begin with Brittain's own portrayals, we find some significant points of development between 1923 and 1940. One feature is constant, however. In all three of her extensive representations of the friendship – in *The Dark Tide*, in *Testament of Youth* and in *Testament of Friendship* – Brittain emphasises that her relationship with Holtby began with animosity rather than mutual attraction. They met when they shared tutorial sessions with an Oxford male don: 'We did not, to begin with, like each other at all.'[47]

In both *Testament of Youth* and *Testament of Friendship* Brittain describes herself as exhausted because of her war experiences. In contrast, Winifred appeared full of vitality. In *Testament of Youth* Brittain describes her as '[s]uperbly tall, and vigorous as the young Diana. With her long straight limbs and her golden hair, her vitality smote with the effect of a blow upon my jaded nerves. Only too well aware that I had lost that youth and energy forever, I found myself furiously resenting its possessor.'[48] In the early fictionalized version of *The Dark Tide*, set at 'Drayton College', the thinly disguised Somerville which figures in several of her novels, the contrast between 'Virginia', the character who on the surface most closely resembles Brittain herself – she is elegant, self-possessed, cynical and weary from her four years of war service – and the gauche, blowsy 'Daphne', who resembles Winifred, is exaggerated to the point of caricature. In *The Dark Tide* the animosity comes to a head when Daphne deliberately ensnares Virginia into participating in a college debate. The Drayton debate, like the Somerville debate on which it was based, was on the subject 'A life of travel is a better education than a life of academic experience'; like the actual Vera, when Virginia argues for the affirmative, she is mocked by the audience.

The friendship itself is treated quite differently in each of the three versions. In *The Dark Tide*, Virginia and Daphne do eventually become friends, but never intimates or equals, and their relationship develops only after their college days are over. Brittain wrote this novel when she was strongly influenced by feelings of bitterness and disappointment about Somerville's limitations as an institution and when she was only beginning to be exposed to new ideas about feminism. At 'Drayton College' the cloistered intensity of college life is portrayed as unhealthy and emotionally damaging largely because within the college itself the students and dons live in an exclusively female world. Brittain's plot in *The Dark Tide* centres on an improbable, melodramatic portrayal of the relationship that the two female characters have with their reprehensible male tutor, Raymond Sylvester. Thwarted in his attempt to court the brilliant, beautiful Virginia, he marries the insecure, clumsy Daphne simply to spite Virginia. When the marriage ends in bitter unhappiness for Daphne, Virginia comes back to help her reassemble her shattered life. To the extent that *The Dark Tide* is concerned with friendships between women, it presents them in a negative fashion. Brittain demeans the intellectual rivalry that she and Holtby actually did experience when they shared tutoring sessions in 1919–20 with their male tutor C.R.M.F. Cruttwell by transforming it into the sort of sexual rivalry between women that is the mainstay of romantic popular fiction.

A decade later, she had moved away from the point of view of her young adulthood, in which she had linked her feminism to her feelings of alienation from the majority of women, and had incorporated into it a commitment to women's solidarity. Accordingly in *Testament of Youth* she emphasises that the relationship between herself and Winifred was a close and unusually successful friendship. She explains that their initial friendship began early in 1920 when Vera was ill, and Winifred visited her with the gift of a bunch of grapes.[49] An intimacy sprang up quickly after that and became 'an association that in thirteen years has never been broken and never spoilt, and today remains as intimate as ever'.[50] She narrates in detail not only the friendship's genesis and its emotional and intellectual importance to herself and to Holtby, but also the way in which the friendship became a partnership between two modern women, both daughters of conventional bourgeois families, who relied on each other as they fashioned new patterns of living and working as aspiring writers and social activists in the London of the 1920s.

In *Testament of Friendship*, she goes further still in eulogizing the friendship. Brittain explicitly acknowledges that one major purpose of her book about her dead friend is to validate women's love for each other. As she puts it in the book's prologue: 'From the days of Homer the friendships of men have enjoyed glory and acclamation, but the friendships of women . . . have usually been not merely unsung, but mocked, belittled and falsely interpreted.'[51] Brittain returns to the themes of women's friendship and of the depth and harmony of the specific friendship between herself and Holtby repeatedly throughout *Testament of Friendship*. She also continues the narrative of the friendship from the point just before her own marriage in 1925 where she had concluded *Testament of Youth*. In *Testament of Friendship*, she recounts the way in which her intimacy with Holtby deepened and even expanded after the marriage, and she describes the joint household that she, Holtby and her husband established in the late 1920s and sustained until Holtby's death in 1935. As she puts it in one frequently quoted passage:

> Those years with Winifred taught me that the type of friendship which reaches its apotheosis in the story of David and Jonathan is not a monopoly of the masculine sex. Hitherto, perhaps owing to a lack of women recorders, this fact has been found difficult to accept by men, and even by other women.[52]

Brittain's public portrayal of her friendship with Holtby ranged from the exploitative fictional rendering of 1923 in *The Dark Tide* to the representation a decade later in *Testament of Youth*, where the genesis of the friendship, the moment when animosity became love, becomes a powerful symbol for Brittain's post-war reawakening. For after Holtby's gift of grapes came conversation. Brittain learns, to her astonishment, that Holtby too had served in the war, as a member of the Women's Army Corps, and that like herself she wished to become a writer: 'After the interminable loneliness of the previous months, I felt like an icicle beginning to melt in the gathering warmth of the pale spring sunshine.'[53] What critics like Carolyn Heilbrun have overlooked about the version in *Testament of Friendship* is its raw underside of guilt. For not only is the book about Winifred and about the friendship between Winifred and Vera, it is also about Brittain's deep regret, when it was too late, that she had not been a better friend to Holtby, that in so much of their shared lives Winifred appears to have been the giver and she the receiver of love. 'Passionately as I desired Winifred's friendship', she writes, 'the building of it was her achievement rather than mine.'[54]

Clearly, even Brittain's own representations present us with a complex relationship. The picture becomes even more complex as we go beyond Brittain's public statements about Holtby and their friendship to the voluminous evidence – and, as well, the significant lacunae – in the private correspondence and diaries. To illustrate, I shall expand here on some aspects of their early years of friendship, including the nature of their intimacy at Oxford; their shared living arrangements of the early 1920s; and their partnership as writers.

Their correspondence confirms that there was initial hostility. Brittain, for example, writes to Holtby, who was visiting her family in Yorkshire, on 11 November 1921 commenting on the fact that this is the 'first Armistice Day since the original one . . . that I haven't spent with you in the Cathedral at Oxford'. But whereas the year before, in 1920, they had purposely gone together, about 1919 Brittain says: 'It was funny, wasn't it, how in . . . 1919 . . . our mutual hostility drew us into the Cathedral in spite of ourselves . . . even then the Gods were laughing at us and planning to turn our rather foolish rivalry into something really blest.'[55]

And then there is the evidence of the many letters that Brittain wrote home (mainly to Edith Brittain) in the autumn of 1919, which are virtually silent concerning Holtby. In these letters she gives plenty of information concerning her sessions with her 'man and woman coach' but not once until the very end of the term does she mention that she was sharing the coaching sessions with C.R.M.F. Cruttwell, Dean of Hertford College,[56] with another student. Holtby is mentioned only in the final letter, and then not by name: she is there only to underscore Brittain's main point in the letter, namely that Cruttwell and the Somerville authorities are very pleased with her work:

> We had reports to-day – my tutor Mr. Cruttwell gave me a lengthy eulogy which ended up with, 'on the whole I consider she is the ablest woman I have ever taught'! . . . 'A very good report, Miss Brittain' said Miss Penrose. . . . He didn't give a bit of a good report to the girl I coach with & yet she always strikes me as being quite good.[57]

Given what we already know about Brittain's reticence in her letters home concerning unpleasant or painful matters, we can take this omission of any mention of Holtby as a sign that there was indeed antagonism between them, both over their academic rivalry for approval from Cruttwell, a representative of the power and prestige of male Oxford, and over the debate. Brittain continued to harbour hurt feelings over the debate long after she and Holtby had become friends. Not only did she make the incident a focal point of her 1923 novel, she featured it again in *Testament of Youth*, where she goes out of her way to assert that the version in *The Dark Tide* had been 'substantially correct'.[58] But did Holtby view this incident in the way that Brittain did? In a letter written in 1933, just as Brittain was completing *Testament of Youth*, in response to a query from Brittain about whether or not the debate passages would be hurtful to her, Holtby replied, suggesting that Brittain tone down the debate scenes, not because she herself would be hurt or because the account was in any way faulty, but because of 'the sensitiveness of my friends'. And she goes on to give her own version of the incident, which was now, of course, nearly fourteen years in the past:

> I had meant the whole thing to be a 'rag' as we WAACS had instituted rags in the army . . . to rub off some of what seemed to me . . . your superiority towards all my fellow-students who had not been in the War. You have to remember my year of anguished indecision at Oxford, in which my *desire* was to join the army, my *duty* as presented to me by all the people I respected . . . was to stay at College. It always seemed to me then that I yielded to desire to join the WAAC, a desire in which my poorer contemporaries, who had to hurry through with their preparations to earn livings, could not indulge in. And I felt very tentative about my 'choice', and a little ashamed of flaunting it, as though it were a liberty bought by my parents' money . . .[59]

As that passage suggests, Holtby had indeed been offended by Brittain's air of aloof superiority in the autumn of 1919, by her inability to see anyone's perspective but her own, and by her failure to recognise her own privileged status. Her further statement that she had not arranged the debate out of revenge for her feelings of discomfort in the shared coaching sessions with Cruttwell does at least indicate that the tensions concerning the sessions were experienced by Holtby as well as by Brittain.

We can surmise that Holtby changed her mind about Brittain in the early months of 1920 because she realized that Brittain's aloof manner was a pose and she saw through to the needy and lovable if difficult and oversensitive person underneath. Throughout her adult life, Winifred had a gift for friendship and part of that gift involved a wholehearted commitment to seeing the best in any person to whom she gave her friendship. In January 1920 it was she who decided to reach out to Vera. They did quickly become friends, although the evidence from Brittain's letters home indicates that their intense intimacy did not develop as quickly as Brittain suggests in *Testament of Youth* and *Testament of Friendship*. These letters indicate that the friendship had indeed begun by January 1920 since by then Brittain begins to mention 'Miss Holtby' by name in her correspondence to her mother, but during this spring term, the letters indicate that Winifred was one of three new friends that Vera had made and that all three together, not Winifred alone, were responsible for the fact that she was much happier in this term than she had been previously. While in retrospect Brittain remembered Holtby as the most significant of the three, and of the other two, only Hilda Reid is mentioned in *Testament of Youth*, in fact at the time she was most friendly with Joyce Simpson, a physician's daughter from Brighton, who was doing 'Greats' and would later become a schoolteacher.[60]

But by the end of that term, certainly by the summer of 1920, Vera and Winifred had become intimate. They spent part of the long vacation together in Cornwall, and in August Vera made the first of many visits to the Holtby family home 'Bainesse', in Cottingham, Yorkshire, a suburb of Hull. Their next and final university year, containing triumphs and disappointments for both, cemented their friendship. They continued to share 'coachings' with Oxford scholars outside the College in preparation for the degree examinations in the History School. This time, they were coached by Dr A.L. Smith, the Master of Balliol ('It is supposed to be a great privilege even for a man to go to him', Brittain wrote proudly to her father[61]). They shared sessions with and observations about Maude Clarke, Somerville's brilliant but aloof history tutor whom both women respected but also feared. They shared a passionate interest in the 'profound revolution' which took place at Oxford in 1920: namely, the final triumph, the granting of degrees to women. Early in 1920, soon after they had become friends, they were among the very few students who attended

Congregation's debate on the issue.[62] And on 14 October 1920 they both attended and were much impressed by the ceremony in the Sheldonian Theatre when degrees were given to women for the first time. As Brittain put it in a memorable passage in *Testament of Youth*:

> Within the Sheldonian, rows of eager childish faces looked down, awed and marvelling, upon the complicated ceremony in the arena below; the excited atmosphere was tense with the consciousness of a dream fulfilled which had first been dreamt, years before these feminine Masters and Bachelors were born, by women long dead – women who did not care whether they saw the end so long as they had contributed to the means.[63]

Above all, they shared their literary aspirations with each other. In describing their first summer retreat together in Cornwall, in July 1920, Brittain explains that they each had brought along materials relating to their respective Special Subjects (Vera's was international relations; Winifred's the reign of Richard II):

> In the sitting-room of the cottage lent to us at West Pentyre, [Winifred] sat half concealed by huge dingy volumes of monastic chronicles written in the rambling dog-Latin of the fourteenth century, while I meditated upon the cynicisms of Machiavelli as a prelude to International Relations. It was the beginning of a shared working existence which was to keep us continuously together for the next five years, and was to last, with only one or two long intervals, to the end of Winifred's life.[64]

Already by the summer of 1920 they were sharing plans for their first novels, Vera's Oxford novel 'Daphne', published as *The Dark Tide*, and Winifred's 'Anlaby Wold', published as *Anderby Wold*. In 1922–3, when their literary careers began in earnest, Winifred was the first to gain a measure of success. But during their Oxford years Vera's talents were more recognised, while Winifred was self-deprecating about her literary abilities. She knew she wanted to write but she felt that her experience was insufficient ('I hardly know what it's like to live, and know not at all what it's like to suffer'[65]) and she was often ashamed of what she did produce: ('It's a loathsome thing, but I *had* to write it', she said of a short story she sent on to Vera during the summer holidays of 1920[66]). Vera, on the other hand, was five years older than Winifred, and both Winifred and Vera agreed that Vera had really suffered. In any case, she had had much better luck than

Winifred in placing her poems and articles in the numerous Oxford publications available to students with literary aspirations in the early 1920s.

The most significant literary achievement of Brittain's Oxford career was her involvement with the volume *Oxford Poetry, 1920* which she co-edited along with C.H.B. Kitchin and Alan Porter at the invitation of Basil Blackwell.[67] This was a distinguished issue of this important post-war poetry magazine. It included works by Robert Graves, L.P. Hartley and Edmund Blunden, among others, and as Brittain herself noted with pride in *Testament of Youth*, the later reputation of some of the contributors spoke well for the editorial decisions made by the three editors. The volume included three of Brittain's own works: 'Boar's Hill' and the 'Lament of the Demobilised', both of which she included in *Testament of Youth* and discussed at some length, and a third which she did not mention, perhaps because it was a much more cheerful poem. Entitled 'Daphne', it appears to have been written as a tribute to Winifred: 'Is she not part of them, golden and fair / and undaunted, / Glad with the triumph of runners / ahead in the race . . .'.

As soon as their friendship became established, Vera did several things to encourage Winifred's literary aspirations. For instance, we can assume that it was because of Vera's position as co-editor that Winifred's poem 'The Dead Men' is included in *Oxford Poetry, 1920*. And on Winifred's behalf, Vera also enlisted the aid of Roland's parents, Robert and Marie Connor Leighton, who were at this time her most knowledgeable literary contacts. Robert Leighton, indeed, was at this time Vera's chief literary mentor, a person of authority to whom she turned for advice about her writing and about building her literary career. In the autumn of 1920 she gave him a story of Winifred's to read. During the Christmas vacation she was able to let Winifred know that Leighton's remarks about her writing had been encouraging. 'She's capable – she writes well . . . And her psychology is unusually good', Vera reports him as saying.[68]

We know from a letter that Winifred wrote in July 1921, when she first met Robert and Marie Connor Leighton, that she was deeply grateful to Vera for providing her with this connection:

> I'm just getting to know literary people now. Yesterday Vera took me to tea at the Leightons. Robert Leighton, the ex-editor of the *Daily Mail*, and his wife Marie Connor Leighton, writer of amazing novels of crime and convicts and blue-eyed heroines, that sell by the thousand. They live in a queer little jumbled house, hanging on the side of its twin

> in St. John's Wood. . . . And how they talk! Hall Caine to Hardy, George Meredith to O. Henry, Andrew Lang to George Moore – they know them all. . . . And they say they'll help me. It's all Vera. She was engaged to Roland Leighton, who was killed in the war. They love her, and she has told them that I write, and they are interested in any of her friends.[69]

On a much more amateurish and playful note, Winifred and Vera were involved together in the spring of 1921 in Somerville's 'Going Down Play'. As Winifred wrote to another friend:

> Vera and I are writing the G.D.P. It is a musical comedy of the Chu Chin Chow variety, called *Bolshevism in Baghdad: A Somerville Night's Entertainment*, and is all about a sultan, weary of the frivolities of his Hundred Wives, who sends to Somerville for three enlightened young dons who come to turn the harem into a women's college. It isn't very funny, but has infinite possibilities of caricature and topical allusions, which are the main thing.[70]

In the production, Vera acted the lead female role, and Winifred the part of the Caliph.

Sharing the amusements of the Going Down Play must have been a welcome diversion during this final term, which would end with disappointment for both of them, when they received Seconds rather than the Firsts that were expected of them and which they expected themselves. As Brittain says in *Testament of Youth*, this was 'a bitter blow',[71] one she attributed in her own case partly to her change of Schools after the war, partly to the exacting standards of the examiners with whom they were confronted in that particular year, and partly to the accumulated exhaustion and nervous anxiety to which she was prone. In July, after the results were published, she wrote as follows to her mother:

> The results are most extraordinary. Of the 6 Somervillians who were supposed to be probable Firsts, 5 got Seconds & the 6th . . . only got a Third! . . . We're lucky to have Seconds with these examiners. . . . Of course it is a grievous disappointment – especially as any other year we would both probably have got Firsts quite easily. But fortunately it doesn't make much difference to us, as we can get the kind of jobs we want on a Second . . .[72]

Brittain and Holtby shared the examination ordeal together, and after the final stage of the 'Viva' they spent a few days with the Brittains in Kensington, and then went up to the Holtbys in Yorkshire. Brittain, in fact, was at 'Bainesse' when the results were published in *The Times*, and she saw their results as so closely entwined that she told her mother: 'I'm glad I've got a Second just for one reason, & that is that it makes things better for Winifred's people. They're very disappointed, even though she never was supposed to be as sure of a First as I, & if I had got one & she hadn't, my being here would have made it seem all the worse.'[73]

Finally, Brittain and Holtby shared 'digs' in Bevington Road during their last year at Oxford. While we have no day-to-day record of their life there,[74] Brittain's comments in *Testament of Youth*, while brief, are revealing both of the emotional turmoil from which she continued to suffer, and of the kind of emotional balance that the two women arrived at during this crucial first year of their friendship. Brittain's room was on the ground floor of the Bevington Road house:

> It contained five large mirrors and for this reason had been selected for me by the Bursar, who was amusedly aware of that vain interest in clothes for which my fellow-seniors were accustomed good-humouredly to tease me. This ground-floor habitation which faced due north and was invaded at night by armies of large, fat mice, soon became for me a place of horror; I avoided it from breakfast till bed-time and if ever I had to go in . . . I pressed my hands desperately against my eyes lest five identical witches' faces should suddenly stare at me from the cold, remorseless mirrors. Because of the mice and the constant watch on the impending witch's beard, I became progressively unable to sleep . . . I took to spending the nights on a couch in Winifred's attic. The next term, though the sleeplessness persisted, the hallucinations began at last slowly to die away; and for the fact that they did not quite conquer me, *Oxford Poetry, 1920*, and the objective, triumphant struggle for women's Degrees were probably, together with Winifred's eager and patient understanding, jointly responsible.[75]

'Winifred's patient and eager understanding' on the one hand, and Vera's emotional fragility and vulnerability on the other were, as this passage indicates, established as a strong undercurrent in their relationship before the two women left Oxford. Perhaps because their friendship began at a time when Brittain appears to have been suffering from a depression severe enough to be characterized as illness and Winifred had the sensitivity to be neither frightened nor annoyed by the symptoms,[76] both came to accept and expect that Winifred would see Vera as more needy than she was herself and that Winifred as well as Vera would put Vera's needs and wishes first. This aspect of the relationship was not dominant. For the most part, the two established a friendship characterized by genuine mutuality. But at certain crucial times over the next fifteen years – in 1923, when Winifred's first novel was accepted before Vera's; in 1924–5, when Vera married and Winifred was left alone; and from 1933–5, during Winifred's final illness – the undercurrent came to the surface, and Winifred found herself unequivocally giving more than she received. However, even during these periods Holtby herself never questioned the terms on which the friendship had been established.

Their decision to live together in London after their studies at Oxford was arrived at in the spring of 1921. Although Brittain does not mention it in *Testament of Youth* or in *Testament of Friendship*, where the living arrangement is presented as emblematic of their particular and exclusive intimacy, they had initially planned to share a flat with the aspiring painter Clare Leighton, Roland Leighton's younger sister.[77] Although Clare was to play an important part in both their lives in the early 1920s, as it turned out she found her own studio and Winifred and Vera found rooms and then a flat in Bloomsbury together where they lived from January 1922 until October 1923, when they moved to a larger flat in Maida Vale.

In Brittain's public accounts and, in turn, in recent critical assessment of the significance of the Brittain–Holtby friendship, this establishment of a joint residence independent of their families figures as important evidence both of the relationship's 'modernism' and its social significance. In *Testament of Youth*, writing of their 'determination to live independently together' Brittain says:

> From the moment that the War ended I had always known, and my parents had always tolerantly taken for granted, that after three years at Oxford and four of war-time adventure, my return to a position of subservient dependence at home would be tolerable neither for them nor for me.[78]

In *Testament of Friendship*, she says: 'Long before we actually started to look for a modest flat suited to our limited incomes, Winifred had agreed to share with me the adventurous, experimental London life on which we proposed to launch ourselves the following January.'[79]

The shared household that Brittain and Holtby established did represent an attempt to create a new pattern. Martha Vicinus has written of the way in which possibilities for independence for middle-class women expanded in the late nineteenth and early twentieth centuries. But while the single women who are the subject of her study claimed the right to independence and to honourable work, when they constructed living spaces for themselves they 'fell back on what they knew best – the family'.[80]

In contrast, Brittain and Holtby consciously and deliberately set out to establish a household that would represent a rejection of conventional middle-class mores, not a cosy feminine substitute for the bourgeois family. Brittain pointedly emphasises this aspect in her published descriptions, writing of the discomforts of the Doughty Street studio, but adding:

> Superficially it was a supremely uncomfortable existence – and yet I felt that I had never known before what comfort was. For the first time, I knew the luxury of privacy, the tranquil happiness of being able to come and go just as I wished without interference or supervision.[81]

Brittain and Holtby both wanted a disciplined life based on work and intimate companionship in which they would achieve freedom from the tyranny of social and domestic obligations that had inhibited the creativity of their mothers and grandmothers. This was a rare possibility for women even then and, as they both privately acknowledged, it was possible for them only because of the relative wealth of the Holtby and Brittain families. Unlike most of their Somerville contemporaries, they could take the route of becoming writers and lecturers rather than full-time teachers. Holtby frequently felt guilty about her privileged position, but as Brittain put it to her late in 1921, they had an obligation to benefit from their privileges:

> Yes, I agree – it does make one feel somehow guilty that one avoids [teaching] . . . through no merits of one's own – yet I think we should not only be absurd, but wrong, if we joined the great army. . . . People like you and me – intellectual, anxious to benefit the world, and yet possessed of sufficient means to choose the form of expression their intellectuality shall take, are very few & far between & yet very much needed. . . . I think it would be wrong not to take advantage of the fact that Fate has made one such a person.[82]

While Brittain was substantially correct when she emphasised that she and Holtby were seeking autonomy, her emphasis on the serious social significance of their living arrangements does result in some distortions in the telling. For example, she overstates their independence, leaving no room for their continuing attachment to and dependence on their families. The two young women spent considerable time between 1921 and 1925 at their respective parents' homes. Holtby often had to go back to Yorkshire, and when she did, Brittain invariably went to Kensington to stay with her mother and father. Both Brittain and Holtby continued to refer to their parents' homes as 'home'[83] and they were very much part of each others' families. Both Alice Holtby's relationship to Vera and Edith Brittain's to Winifred had elements in which each assumed roles approaching that of mother and daughter. Of the Brittain family Holtby wrote to her friend Jean McWilliam: 'They are very sweet to me, and treat me as if I belonged to their family. It's like having two families.'[84]

Even in choosing their first shared accommodation, their families were involved. Winifred first found the rooms at 52 Doughty Street[85] but the final arrangements were made by Vera and her mother, after Winifred had gone back to Yorkshire for the Christmas holidays. 'I went with mother yesterday afternoon to see the place', Vera wrote to Winifred just before Christmas; 'if it weren't for my perpetual dread of mice & beetles I couldn't wish for anything better anywhere . . . there is plenty of plate & everyday china . . . all we want is your Christmas present china for parties'.[86]

Because details such as her own willing acceptance of her mother's solicitous help, or the ingenuous pleasure she took in contemplating entertaining with Winifred's 'Christmas present china', or the lighthearted innocence reflected in Winifred's characterization of their arrangement as that of 'girls sharing digs'[87] (so much less portentous than Brittain's statement that she was rejecting 'subservient dependence') are omitted from Brittain's narrative of these years, part of the charm that this interval in both their lives genuinely possessed is lost. Neither was as serious or as mature or as sure about the present or the future as they both appear to be in *Testament of Youth* and *Testament of Friendship*, and for that very reason this early period of independence, of standing on the threshhold of their literary careers, was more genuinely an exciting adventure than it appears to be in Brittain's narratives.

At first, even keeping house could be fun. Perhaps because she did not wish to reveal the extent to which both she and Winifred were accustomed to the comforts of upper middle-class life, Brittain minimized the very real challenge that their new neighbourhood and the housekeeping they had to do presented to these two gently reared, upper middle-class young women. Doughty Street, even in 1922, was no slum, but it was far more urban and adventuresome than the Brittains' decorous Kensington mansion flat 'Oakwood Court', or the Holtby's well-managed Yorkshire house. In a letter Holtby wrote to Jean McWilliam we get a glimpse of the two as they settled into 'the Studio' at 52 Doughty Street:

> My brain and tongue both feel rather exhausted, as I have spent the morning cleaning our kitchen – the stimulus to this unwonted energy being a whole new tin of Vim – and simultaneously conducting with Vera a most heated discussion upon 'What is individualism?' She has to coach a candidate for an entrance examination at L.M.H. [the Oxford women's college Lady Margaret Hall] and, having set her an essay on 'The Age of Elizabeth was the age of Individualism' proceeded to thrash out her coaching first, as usual, over the O-Cedar mop and dusters.[88]

But Vim and dusters quickly palled. In November 1921, when she was still living with her parents at Oakwood Court, Brittain had been reading about Marxism for the first time, and she had written only half jokingly to Holtby: 'I am rapidly being converted to Bolshevism – "the abolition of female domestic slavery by the establishment of communal kitchens, laundries & mending houses run by professional domestic workers" sounds so nice, especially when one returns from a day's work . . . to the momentarily alien & overwhelming domesticity of one's home!'[89] Even their stripped-down Bloomsbury housekeeping took precious time away from their writing and as soon as they could afford it, they fell back on the traditional upper middle-class solution to the problem of 'female domestic slavery' and hired a servant. Indeed, the possibility of having sufficient space for a maid was one of the principal reasons for their move, in November 1923, to the larger flat in Maida Vale.[90] Having made that decision, even their relatively Spartan domestic arrangement gave rise to its own version of the perennial middle-class 'servant problem', with its class tensions between women. At first, they had difficulty in finding and keeping a servant and in hiring one who would suit their unusual ménage. For example, Brittain was out of town when their servant gave notice in April 1924 and they were forced to look for a replacement. 'Isn't it just like me to be away when these things happen!' she wrote from Scotland where she was lecturing. She added the following advice for Winifred, who in her absence was to engage a new servant: 'We do not want a lady, only, someone younger & less opinionated . . . a clergyman's daughter would suit us very well. Still one can't be too particular. . . .'[91] At this juncture, fortunately, their problem was solved when Winifred's old nanny 'agreed to come from Yorkshire to look after us', as Brittain later put it in *Testament of Youth*.[92]

In *Testament of Friendship* Brittain's central focus was the strength and harmony of the bonds of friendship between herself and Winifred. But at the same time she took pains to deny that the friendship was in any way homoerotic. In a passage concerned with the 1930s she writes:

> Some feminine individualists believe that they flatter men by fostering the fiction of women's jealous inability to love and respect one another. Other sceptics are roused by any record of affection between women to suspicions habitual among the over-sophisticated. 'Too, *too* Chelsea!' Winifred would comment amiably in after years when some zealous friend related the newest legend current about us in the neighbourhood.[93]

Recent Brittain–Holtby scholarship has not been satisfied by this disclaimer. Of the Brittain–Holtby friendship, Jean Kennard has written: 'It is not possible today to write about a female friendship such as this, and feel one has adequately treated the subject, without raising directly the question whether or not it was a lesbian one.'[94] And Kennard's view is that if we accept the current 'broader' definition of lesbianism advanced by historians Lillian Faderman and Carroll Smith-Rosenberg, the relationship 'was certainly lesbian'. In work already published, I have explained that I find this 'broader' definition of lesbianism unsatisfactory, believing that it obfuscates rather than clarifies, and that 'lesbian' should be reserved for overtly erotic relationships between women.[95] For this and other reasons, I categorize the Brittain–Holtby relationship as non-lesbian. Any definition of lesbianism, I would suggest, including the 'broader' formulations of Faderman and others, must include *some* element of eroticism. In the voluminous correspondence between Brittain and Holtby there is no evidence that Brittain had erotic feelings – overt or covert – for Holtby. Nor is there evidence that she had such feelings for any other woman. Indeed, there is evidence that she found lesbian sexuality repellent. In one of the few references to the subject in the Brittain–Holtby correspondence, she comments on the views of a mutual acquaintance:

> Had . . . a tremendous vehement argument . . . with M. – about feminism and homosexuality. I am not as you know a shockable person but her views on the latter subject are revolutionary in the extreme. She feels men to be such oppressors & such sources of evil that she says if she had a daughter she would deliberately urge her to enter into a homosexual relationship with another woman rather than seek marriage – which is far more likely to be disappointing and disastrous. I tell her that such views are dangerous in the extreme & if this is the logical outcome of feminism, feminists such as she will end by wrecking their own movement . . .[96]

For herself, Brittain accepted the medical model then currently fashionable, in which homosexuality was defined as 'inversion', just as she accepted the modern medical and psychoanalytical definition of heterosexuality, but this modernism was a veneer imposed on a sexual sensibility that remained fundamentally Victorian, and emphatically heterosexual.[97] The fact that she knew lesbian women, and that she was one of the more prominent defenders of Radclyffe Hall, should not be interpreted (as they are by Lillian Faderman) as evidence of her own personal sexual preference.[98] In the case of Radclyffe Hall's lesbian novel, *The Well of Loneliness* (1928), Brittain reviewed it supportively in *Time and Tide*,[99] she was present in the court at the book's 'obscenity' trial in October, and years later she would write an account of the case which clearly took Hall's side.[100] She gave Hall this support not because she too was a lesbian, but because she was a civil libertarian. Her reservations about lesbianism and about Hall are revealed in this comment written in 1929:

> I want to write a longish article called 'Who are the Feminists' – a reply to the oft repeated statement . . . that feminists come from the ranks of the inverted . . . my argument being based on an analysis of the anti-feminism of 'The Well of Loneliness' & 'Extraordinary Women' in contrast to the sexually normal sex qualities . . . of such leading feminists as Mary Wollstonecraft, Josephine Butler, & Olive Schreiner & Mrs. Pankhurst . . .[101]

And what of Holtby? While it is possible that Holtby did have erotic feelings for Brittain, it does not appear that she ever openly revealed them to Brittain herself, while Brittain's heterosexuality was always recognised and fully acknowledged. Moreover, Holtby too was uneasy with homosexuality. That unease is reflected, for example, in comments she made to Jean McWilliam about Oscar Wilde in 1922, when Frank Harris's life of Wilde had just been published. While Holtby liked Frank Harris's *Life* because it approached its subject with 'reverence and sincerity', her remarks about Wilde – she refers to his life as 'that sordid tragedy of wasted genius and fatal amiability' – reflect her discomfort with his sexual behaviour.[102] A similar discomfort is again reflected in comments she made in a letter to Brittain written in 1928 about Radclyffe Hall: 'Radclyffe Hall has taught me a lot. She's all fearfully wrong, I feel. To love other women deeply is not pathological. To be unable to control one's passions is. Her mind is all sloppy with self-pity & self-admiration. She's not straight in her mind.'[103] This remark might be interpreted as reflecting Holtby's awareness that she herself could feel 'passion' for another woman. It unquestionably reflects her belief that such passion should not be gratified.

Both the recent scholarly focus on the sexual orientation of the two women and Brittain's own narratives, with their emphasis on the modernism of the relationship between the two, have together functioned to obscure other more important issues. For example, few observers have noticed the extent to which each woman's own assessment of the attractiveness of her physical appearance and personality reflected Victorian and Edwardian mores. In common with all women of their class and period, both Holtby and Brittain had been subjected in girlhood to an assessment of their future attractiveness to men and their ultimate marriageability. Before the Great War, as Brittain herself so poignantly bears witness in *Testament of Youth*, marriage was still defined as a middle-class daughter's primary objective. However, middle-class families had always recognized that some daughters were unlikely to marry. The evidence suggests that Winifred Holtby's parents identified their shy, awkward younger child as such a daughter, and that it was for this reason that they chose to educate her at Oxford. We know that her mother decided that Winifred would go to university when she was still a schoolgirl, but that no such plans were made for her older sister Grace, who duly married young. In *Testament of Friendship*, Brittain suggests that Holtby's mother determined that higher education was suitable for Winifred and not for Grace because Winifred was more talented than her sister, but she probably overstates Alice Holtby's protofeminism. While the Holtbys did recognize Winifred's talents, we can also surmise that they saw Grace's marriageability as an asset, and hoped to compensate for Winifred's lack of conventional prettiness, for her clumsiness and shyness with men, by providing her with alternative opportunities.

But if Holtby was to some degree marked out for spinsterhood from girlhood, the reverse was true of Brittain. By her early adolescence, it was apparent that she was maturing into a woman whose delicate prettiness would conform closely to her period's prevailing notions of femininity, and from the time she was seventeen, she knew that she was attractive to men.

By the time Brittain and Holtby met as young women, their respective childhood and girlhood experiences had crystallized. Brittain felt self-confident about her physical appearance whereas Holtby felt awkward and unattractive. Her vulnerability is painfully evident, for example, in this comment written at Christmas in 1920:

> My new black dress has come. . . . Grace and I are on show tonight. It will be 'dear Grace', 'dear Winifred' – and when we've gone – 'My dear – that young girl of Alice's grows more gawky and weird every day. I don't know why Alice lets her go to this Oxford; she never did do her duty by her children.'[104]

Brittain's response to Holtby's evident pain was sensible and helpful. She encouraged Winifred to see the best in herself. Winifred always felt that she was both too tall and too large. Accordingly, Vera emphasised how attractive tallness and strength could be: Mrs. Leighton, Vera tells her, had admired 'the laughter' in Winifred. 'She said you impressed her as being so full of energy and strength and vitality – a regular young Viking.'[105]

Brittain's encouragement, like her support of Holtby's tenuous and unsatisfactory relationship with Harry Pearson, the Holtby family friend who would drift in and out of Winifred's life until her death in 1935, was kindly meant.[106] However, by acting as if Holtby were indeed physically attractive and successful with men, Brittain underestimated the psychic wounds Holtby continuously suffered, and the delicate and intensely private adjustments that she consequently made in all her relationships. Although Brittain presents her friend as a model of a modern, free woman, an important part of Holtby's self-concept was patterned instead, I would suggest, on an updated version of the Victorian spinster. Like the model spinster, Holtby learned to cultivate selflessness as a duty and to take vicarious pleasure in the romances, the marriages and the children of her sisters and friends while never expecting to enjoy such experiences herself.

This was certainly the case in relationship to her sister Grace. Winifred loved Grace for her gentleness and her conventional femininity. When Grace visited her at Oxford in November 1920, she wrote: 'I love having her. Her peaceful presence makes small things insignificant and big things more worth while. Also she does my shopping and makes my tea. This is not bathos!'[107] In 1923, when Grace became engaged, she was from the beginning eager to be friends with her physician fiancé, and hopeful that the marriage would take place soon. She wrote to Jean McWilliam: 'I do hope that they will soon marry and make me an aunt. It is a position I have always desired.'[108]

Of course, unlike most Victorian spinsters, Holtby could clearly articulate the advantages as well as the disadvantages of the unmarried state. To Jean McWilliam (who was also single) she could write as follows:

> I don't believe that marriage in the ordinary, middle-class comfortable way is really good for women. It seems to make them so complacent and dependent. Bernard Shaw says that marriage is all very well, but that it absolutely puts an end to the adventurous outlook on life. If one has a household and children, it's not easy to be anything but a housekeeper. I think it's better not to marry.[109]

But even her awareness of the advantages her own life afforded could not diminish the mortification and disappointment she felt about her own body. Being a bridesmaid, for example, was particularly painful: 'I've got to be bridesmaid to Grace. I love her getting married, but I *loathe* being bridesmaid and looking like a stuffed Amazon. . . .'[110] Two years later, when Vera married, she tried to put a better face on the ordeal, but her dissatisfaction with what we would now call her 'body image' was still strong: 'What a mercy that Vera is getting married. I'd never otherwise spend £13 13s 0d. on a dress. But oh, my feet! I take the poor things all over London to find pretty shoes for them. Says the young lady, 'Not in *that* size, madam,' and my poor feet grow more and more depressed . . . Then skirts are so short. There's no hiding the horrid facts of one's physique.'[111]

The fact that both Brittain and Holtby defined Vera as small and pretty and Winifred as large and plain was emblematic of many aspects of their relationship. It added weight, for example, to their mutual definition of Vera as emotionally fragile and Winifred as strong. From the small but significant fact that it was Vera and not Winifred who had a horror of mice, to the more noticeable circumstance that it was Vera and not Winifred who had experienced tragedy during the war, many factors contributed to establishing a pattern in which all too easily Winifred became the participant in Vera's life, rather than the reverse.

We can see this pattern manifesting itself during the trip abroad that the two women took together in the autumn of 1921. In *Testament of Friendship*, Brittain says of this six weeks' journey to Italy and France that it was 'the most perfect holiday of all my experience and, I believe, of Winifred's'.[112] Both Brittain's and Holtby's letters from Venice, Florence, Assisi and the other Italian towns they visited are full of the excitement and the pleasure of new experiences, and of their great enjoyment in travelling together.[113] For the most part, this was a lighthearted adventure in which they both could share equally. However, the journey had a sombre focus: the two made visits to Edward's grave on the Asiago Plateau in Italy and Roland's grave at Louvencourt. These 'two days of poignant sorrow'[114] take up most of

Brittain's description of the trip in *Testament of Youth*. Her visits to the war graves were wrenching experiences for Brittain. But Holtby, too, became intensely involved to a remarkable degree. During this journey, Vera's dead became, by proxy, hers as well.

In sum, then, beginning at Somerville in the early 1920s, Brittain and Holtby together created a deep and complex friendship which drew on patterns from their pre-war girlhoods as well as from their perception of themselves as modern young women. By January 1922, when they set up house in their Bloomsbury studio, they had come to rely on each other for day-to-day companionship, and for the mutual sharing of their most intimate thoughts and feelings. In addition they shared a concern with each other's work; and the extent to which the friendship was a partnership centred on work is noteworthy because in this more than in any other aspect, their relationship broke with the past. Historians of women's friendships in the nineteenth century have made much of the richness of the culture women created for themselves and have claimed that these friendships of the past were both satisfying and remarkably free from conflict.[115] But those 'bonds of womanhood' between nineteenth-century women derived their strength from women's acceptance of the Victorian ideology of femininity. Disciplined achievement directed at public performance with its inevitable competitiveness was only rarely part of the experience of Victorian and Edwardian women.

In sharp contrast, as educated women of the post-war period both Brittain and Holtby welcomed the fact that they would compete for success in a literary world that was for the first time genuinely open to women. Brittain frankly acknowledged her own need for self-fulfilment and for public recognition. Holtby, although much less consumed by a need for success than Brittain, also fully accepted the premise that feminism's success meant that women must compete fully in the public arena.

Thus, throughout their relationship, but especially in the early years, Brittain and Holtby saw themselves as partners in a joint enterprise. Part of the purpose of their friendship was to launch their two literary careers. To this end, they were committed to providing each other with encouragement and with practical support. For example, in 1921 several older friends advised them that part-time teaching and lecturing would leave them with more time to write than would a full-time school-teaching post. Among their advisers was Brittain's old St Monica's headmistress, Louise Heath Jones. As Brittain gathered information about employment agencies that could find her lecturing and tutoring positions, she shared this information with Winifred, assuming without question that she was seeking out opportunities for both of them. And to whom else could she confide her mingled feelings of anticipation and apprehension when she was about to meet the novelist Rose Macaulay for the first time:

> 'Winifred, I am terrified of that woman – terrified of meeting her on the 7th of Dec – terrified she'll see me for the egotistical little poseuse I know I am so often. Above all, I am terrified of writing a book she may someday review.'[116]

The practical assistance and emotional support Brittain and Holtby offered each other as they made their way as lecturers, journalists and part-time teachers was important, but they both considered that the help they could give each other as serious writers was of even greater importance. Each defined the other as her most devoted critic. To a considerable extent, the two were indeed able to perform this function for the other, but the mutuality of their supportiveness was not as complete as Brittain's reconstruction of the friendship suggests. As we know, Brittain herself publicly acknowledged that Winifred contributed more to the friendship than she did, and nowhere was this more apparent than in the way each confronted feelings of competitiveness and envy in relationship to their work. This pattern of inequality was established in the early 1920s when they were both writing and attempting to publish their first novels. *Anderby Wold* and *The Dark Tide* were both completed by the spring of 1922. Both were published in 1923, but *Anderby Wold* was accepted first and appeared before *The Dark Tide*.

Although both young writers drew on their own experience in writing these first published works, in *Anderby Wold* Holtby did so only obliquely. In contrast, *The Dark Tide*'s openly autobiographical qualities did hold the possibility of contributing to tension between the two friends. As discussed earlier, the novel has two central female characters, the self-conscious, insecure Daphne, who never knows what to do with 'her long legs and large, clumsy hands'[117] and the elegant, self-possessed Virginia, who, when they first meet, strikes Daphne as 'small and dark-eyed and pale' with a 'quiet perfection of style' which makes her feel like 'a vulgar barmaid in her Sunday best'.[118] Beneath the surface both Virginia and Daphne represent aspects of Brittain's own character more than either resembles anyone else, with Daphne reflecting Brittain's intense desire for recognition and her deep insecurity and Virginia her self-possessed 'ideal' for herself. But on the surface the character Daphne Lethbridge, with her height and golden hair, is very obviously drawn from Winifred. As a portrait of Winifred, Daphne, with her tactlessness, her misplaced ambitions and her physical shortcomings, is a cruel and ruthless caricature. It was certainly taken as such at the time by many who knew both women.[119] Why did Brittain believe that she had the right to use her friend in this manner, and how did her behaviour affect their friendship?

Throughout her career as a writer, Brittain derived her inspiration from her own experience, fashioning it either into autobiography or into autobiographical fiction. From the time she was nineteen, when she first planned a novel, she relied on her informal writing – her jottings, diaries or letters – as the initial inspiration for her published work. There is no evidence that she ever subjected the aesthetic or the ethical implications of the 'confessional' mode to critical scrutiny. She simply assumed that writers had the liberty to draw from experience and to distort it at will, and that those close to her would have to make the best of it. As she said in a letter to Holtby, in which she expressed irritation about Hilda Reid's objections to *The Dark Tide*'s treatment of Somerville: 'I wonder who ever wrote a book who didn't borrow from surroundings familiar to someone or other.'[120] In the case of the representation of Holtby in *The Dark Tide*, Brittain proceeded as if Holtby must of course understand the process whereby actual experience becomes transformed into fiction. Holtby never challenged Brittain's assumptions about the licence conferred by the demands of the writer's craft and both women openly acknowledged that, in creating Daphne, Brittain drew initially on the exterior qualities of Winifred herself and on the negative energy generated by Brittain's unkindest thoughts about her friend. Holtby absorbed without protest any anger or disappointment she may have felt, and at times even managed to joke about her resemblance to her friend's pathetic fictional character.[121]

Holtby's forbearance allowed Brittain to proceed unhindered; to assume that her friend was mature enough to endure the similarities between herself and the fictional Daphne, and wise enough to realize that the character was a creation, and was never meant to be an exact portrayal. As Brittain put it in a letter written in November 1921: 'Poor Daphne! I get more & more cruel to her. The chief consolation is she gets less & less like you.'[122]

But this evidence of openness between the two women should not obscure the fact that it was one-sided. If asked, both would have insisted that theirs was an even-handed relationship, but in fact it was not. Not only did Holtby exhibit unusual tolerance over the matter of

Daphne, neither then or later did she ask Brittain to deal with a similar situation. Holtby knew that while she could accept being caricatured as Daphne Lethbridge, Brittain would not be able to withstand such a cavalier appropriation of her personality, and she never did draw a full portrait of Brittain. In 1923, she couched her reasons for not doing so in characteristically self-deprecating language: 'I am too different, my dear, to try to draw anyone just like you. I should not succeed as well as you succeeded with Daphne. . . .'[123]

The negative characterization of Holtby represented only one opportunity for friction presented by the women's two first novels. Brittain's envy of Holtby when *Anderby Wold* was accepted for publication before her own book represented another. Brittain acknowledged this with considerable candour in *Testament of Youth*:

> To me . . . this event [*Anderby Wold*'s acceptance] was something of a psychological crisis; Winifred was considerably my junior, at Oxford she had followed modestly in my literary wake, and it had simply never occurred to me that her work could be preferred and published before my own. In Kensington, alone in my bedroom, I made myself face and acknowledge the hard fact that *Anderby Wold* was a better book than *The Dark Tide* . . .[124]

What Brittain does not fully disclose is that here again she asked much more of Holtby than she was able to give. She had never been as unstinting in her praise of *Anderby Wold* as Winifred had been of *The Dark Tide*, and when the novel was accepted she could not restrain herself from mingling her own hurt feelings with her congratulations:

> It is a kind book as well as a clever one, and has always inspired me with a secret envy. I think I pretended that it bored me because it gave me a despairing sense of my own inability to reach the same level . . . one who talks but never achieves, while you quietly achieve, but don't talk. You will be quite famous by the time you are my age. . . . Somehow the whole world seems subtly changed by your book getting taken. . . . Almost I think of you as if you were a stranger; we are not equals any more.[125]

Many people might have been irritated by such inappropriately timed, self-centred despair but Holtby responded characteristically, hastening to bolster Brittain's self-confidence:

> You must not really talk such nonsense, you know. You are perfectly right in saying that we are not equals. . . . I have always known how much keener and clearer and finer your mind is than mine . . .[126]

In all its aspects, then, but especially in relation to their serious writing, the friendship was sustained by Holtby's willingness to be extraordinarily tolerant of Brittain's outbursts of selfishness, envy and competitiveness and at the same time to forgo any expectation that Brittain would be able to offer her similar patience in return.

In underscoring this point, it is not my intention to portray Brittain as the villain of the piece and Holtby as the saint, but rather to understand this particular relationship and also to explore the wider significance of Brittain's – and of Holtby's – individual psychological characteristics.

Although Brittain's public persona projected self-confidence, self-doubt was an ever-present feature of her private personality. In the 1920s and early 1930s her most painful emotions coalesced around her conflicting feelings about ambition. During periods when she could see herself clearly as a hard-working, talented writer she experienced her ambition as affirming and empowering. At other times, during periods of self-hate, she perceived it as a consuming need and therefore as shameful. Her moods of self-rejection were reinforced by her awareness that people she wished to impress favourably were indeed often repelled by the raw, too obviously visible quality of her desire for success.

The negative reactions she did sometimes produce in others should not be seen as deriving from any unique deficiency in Brittain's character: instead, they reflect one unfortunate effect of the status and gender hierarchies that were part of the fabric of British society during this period. As a woman, Brittain inevitably struggled with the tensions produced by the dissonance between the prescriptions of Victorian femininity and those of post-war feminism. In addition she herself always insisted that she was hampered as a writer because of the 'obscurity' of her social origins.[127] From a late twentieth-century vantage point, such assertions may seem groundless, but in fact her perception that the provincial business background of her family was a handicap to a literary career did have some validity.[128] Its most evident unhappy consequence was that when her social insecurities were aroused, she could behave in ways that offended more securely established people, and – worst of all – she herself internalized their judgements.

In this regard, Holtby was able to offer Brittain one of the most precious gifts a friend can give: not merely love but sympathetic understanding of one's less-loveable self. It was to Winifred alone that Vera could confess that she was at times an 'egotistical little poseuse' who felt 'petty & parochial & conventional . . . a little vexed worrying gnat bragging impotently about unimportant things'.[129] Only to Winifred could she fully disclose her fervent desire for the limelight: 'I don't want to reveal to anyone else the unreasonable ambition which is arrogantly dissatisfied with anything less than the stars. . . .'[130]

While Brittain's emotional conflicts readily reveal themselves, Holtby's character is more opaque. There is no easy explanation for her unfailing patience with the difficult side of Brittain's character nor for her continual need to overpraise her friend. We do know that in the early years of their friendship Brittain herself was often openly worried that Winifred would realize this and abandon the friendship, and she would sometimes advise her directly to be more assertive. 'I wouldn't call it cowardice, but an excess of patience', she wrote once, commenting on Winifred's 'meekness'.[131]

By the summer of 1924, Holtby knew that very soon she would need to bring to her relationship with Brittain not only patience, but her ability to sacrifice her own happiness for the sake of that of her friend. G.E.G. Catlin, Brittain's future husband, had appeared on the scene. Winifred wrote to Jean McWilliam, characteristically suppressing her own sense of loss and emphasising her own pleasure in Vera's future happiness: 'Do you know, I think that my little Vera is going to be married after all', she says, and she goes on to write of Catlin in the warmest possible terms: 'I like, respect – I could say, love, him, and am very happy, though it means losing Vera's companionship and no one can tell what she has meant to me for these four years. But I covet for her this richer life.'[132]

A year later, when the marriage took place, neither Winifred nor Vera anticipated that in fact within two years they would be living together once more. What Winifred assumed she was confronting was the need, once again, to re-order her life: 'In June Vera will go, and I shall be on my own again. No one will ever know what I owe to her during these five years; but now comes the choice again – how shall I live?'[133]

8

Feminism and Internationalism

During their years together, both before and after Brittain's marriage in 1925, Vera Brittain and Winifred Holtby made their mark not only as creative writers, but also, working together and separately, as political journalists and activists. In this chapter I examine the public face of Vera Brittain's politics during the years 1919–33, at the centre of which was her commitment to feminism.

It is a fundamental premiss of this book that for Vera Brittain feminism was more than a cause she espoused. It was the central organizing principle of her personality, the belief that gave direction to her energies, that enabled her to make the best possible use of her talents as a writer, and through which she defined her personal relationships and her own sense of self. As discussed in Part I, Brittain was one of those women who was born feminist, in that she responded with a spontaneous sense of outrage when confronted with the confines of the feminine role. As soon as she discovered it, feminism allowed her to articulate that outrage. We have seen that she discovered it early, and that while her earliest feminist beliefs may have been limited, they were none the less both deep and authentic. Even though Brittain's active support for feminism receded so far during the war years that she was 'completely unaware that . . . the Representation of the People Bill, which gave votes to women over thirty, had been passed by the House of Lords'[1] a feminist consciousness remained a part of her being, if only in that it helped to sustain her sense of self-worth.

After the war, when her intellectual and political interests revived, she returned to a conscious commitment to feminism. She expressed this commitment for the first time in print while she was still at Oxford when she entered the debate over the issue of degrees for women, writing an article in 1919 for the *Oxford Outlook* supporting the cause in staunchly feminist language: 'To us the Degree is not a mere "titular distinction". It is the symbol of that abolition of unreasoning sex prejudice, of traditional fear and unsubstantiated distrust, which we look for from the coming years.'[2]

Brittain's vigorous defence of the importance of university degrees for women stands in sharp contrast to the approach of another feminist writer of the period, Virginia Woolf. In a striking image in *Three Guineas*, her feminist-pacifist essay of the late 1930s, Woolf conjures up a vision of a 'procession of the sons of educated men':

> There they go, our brothers who have been educated at public schools and universities, mounting those steps, passing in and out of those doors, ascending those pulpits, preaching, teaching, administering justice, practising medicine, transacting business, making money. It is a solemn sight always – a procession, like a caravanserai crossing a desert.

And what should educated women do, Woolf asks, now that 'trapesing along at the tail end of the procession, we go ourselves . . .'?[3] Her answer is that educated women must refuse to 'join the procession'. Only if women remain outsiders will they be able to use the power of their newly won education to transform society.

Brittain fundamentally disagreed with this approach. Not only is it obvious that she took great pleasure in 'joining the procession' – and she could well have said that this was a pleasure Leslie Stephen's daughter could more easily forgo than could she – she believed that only by joining, by participating fully in public life, could women not only achieve their birthright, but change society.

By 1921 the two most important feminist organizations of the inter-war decades, the National Union of Societies for Equal Citizenship (NUSEC) and the Six Point Group, had been established. Eleanor Rathbone, the leader of the NUSEC, was the leading exponent of the new feminism, a position challenging what its supporters claimed was the traditional feminist preoccupation with equal political rights, in favour of a greater concern with the special needs that working-class women had as mothers. The driving force behind the Six Point Group, the NUSEC's most important opposition, was Margaret Haig Mackworth, Lady Rhondda. Lady Rhondda was also the publisher of *Time and Tide*, the influential feminist weekly that began publication in 1920. The Six Point Group defined itself both as the voice of the younger generation of feminists and as the champion of a feminist position that placed equality for women at the centre of feminist belief and feminist activism.[4]

From the time that Brittain and Holtby were introduced to the Six Point Group in March 1922, both women identified themselves unequivocally with equal-rights feminism.[5] They were early and enthusiastic readers of *Time and Tide*, and by June 1922 they had met Lady Rhondda and become active participants in the Six Point Group. It was Holtby rather than Brittain who made a strongly favourable impression on Lady Rhondda, and Holtby's ties to *Time and Tide* were always stronger than Brittain's. However, Brittain did contribute regularly to *Time and Tide* in the late 1920s, and she was active both in the Six Point Group, serving on its executive from 1926,[6] and in the Open Door Council, an organisation formed in 1926 with the specific purpose of opposing all restrictive legislation directed at women workers.

Most historians who have written recently on the subject have emphasised the conservative nature of British feminism in the post-First World War period and have asserted that equal-rights feminism had become the viewpoint of a minority.[8] If one accepts this interpretation, then Brittain's advocacy of a feminism based on women's right to equality, and on the fundamental similarities between women and men, rather than on 'women's difference', takes on special importance. Not only should she be seen as a major feminist voice in the inter-war period, but as a minority voice speaking out unequivocally for feminist principles during a period of reaction.

Brittain asserted that her uncompromising, vigorous equal rights feminism had its origins in the way in which feminism had entered her consciousness during her girlhood. Writing in the 1920s, she likened her early introduction to feminism to a conversion experience, associating it specifically with the reading of Olive Schreiner's *Woman and Labour*: 'For many of us . . . "Woman & Labour" sounded with a note that had the authentic ring of a new gospel',[9] she wrote, and she was not exaggerating the extent to which Schreiner's work influenced her, both when she was a young girl, and during the 1920s and 1930s. Schreiner's championing of work as woman's right and as woman's liberator; her claim, on behalf of women, to 'take all labour for our province'; her condemnation of the narrow, confined 'parasitic' nature of the middle-class woman's role in modern industrial society, had spoken directly to the young Vera as she struggled to escape the confines of 'provincial young ladyhood', and continued to speak to the mature Brittain's belief that, while feminism was of course about the achievement of social and political equality for women, at its heart lay a commitment to woman's full autonomy and a rejection of Victorian notions of femininity. It was because of these beliefs that Brittain aligned herself squarely with equal rights feminism in the inter-war decades. The fact that she gave active support to the birth control movement, that she believed a better understanding of the needs of mothers was central to feminism, and that she became a member of the Labour Party (new feminism considered that it had a special link to Labour) underscores the fact that new feminism had, in reality, no monopoly on feminist support for social justice or for women's needs as mothers.

Brittain's feminist beliefs can best be traced through her feminist journalism, the main avenue through which she made her influence felt. In the interwar decades, Brittain's feminist journalism appeared in a variety of publications, including the *Yorkshire Post*, the *Manchester Guardian* and *Time and Tide*.[10] In this work, she most often took up issues that related directly to her own experience. As a professional woman, she was an incisive opponent of the barriers of law and custom that still confronted women in the post-war years, and, after her marriage in 1925, she wrote extensively about the difficulties educated middle-class women experienced as they attempted to combine motherhood with a career.

While she wrote about lingering prejudice and discrimination, the dominant tone of Brittain's feminism in the 1920s was one of optimism. Indeed, a large part of the hopefulness that characterized her outlook in the immediate postwar years sprang from the belief that while there were still battles to be fought, the barriers that had fallen offered women revolutionary new opportunities. As she and Winifred Holtby and others of their generation were demonstrating, women need no longer be confined to the narrow world of Victorian and Edwardian femininity. They now had both the right and the responsibility to participate fully in politics and in social, economic and professional life.

One major theme of Brittain's inter-war journalism was the assertion that it was work, above all else, that would allow women to enjoy these new opportunities: 'Work . . . has been the twentieth century's great gift to woman, it is dignified work which puts her, as far as the chance of happiness is concerned, upon the same level as men', she wrote in a 1927 article for *Time and Tide*.[11] Brittain knew from her own experience that work gave women a chance to test themselves, and to gain respect in the public arena. Work also brought with it independence, and if the first principle of Brittain's feminism was respect for work, the second was independence. In Brittain's view, it was the dependent position of the Victorian woman, as wife or as daughter, that had so often made her an idle and frustrated creature. But the successes of feminism meant that women need no longer be prisoners of the parasitic domesticity that had developed as a result of industrialization, a domesticity that had lead 'a whole generation of middle class women . . . [to produce] . . . vast debris of useless products . . . pathetic . . . crochet mats . . . waxflower models'.[12]

Brittain was appalled by the fact that even in the 1920s there were many women who clung to the false security provided by such outmoded definitions of femininity, and she developed in her journalistic writing an analysis of the dangers of an excessive preoccupation with domesticity. She was especially concerned to attack the internal and external pressures that led too many middle-class women in the 1920s to reject technological innovations that would simplify housework. Women who avoided such new possibilities were 'guarding themselves against life's problems by means of life's trivialities'.[13]

When discussing the burden that domesticity placed on women, Brittain was not insensitive to the fact that it weighed much more heavily on working-class than on middle-class women. In one of her most effective pieces, 'I Denounce Domesticity! A Protest Against Waste', published in 1932, she wrote:

> [T]he wage-earning classes of this country still live in badly planned, inconvenient little houses which harbour dirt, involve incessant labour, and are totally unequipped with the most elementary devices for saving time and toil. . . . [T]he home is the one place upon which sufficient capital has never been spent, with the result that . . . women with poor tools and no modern equipment fight a perpetual losing battle against the ever-accumulating detail of domesticity.[14]

In this critique of domesticity, and in her proposed solutions – that society should recognize the importance of improving the home, for the sake of women of all social classes, and that women themselves must no longer take a sentimental view of housework, and must be more open not only to technological change, but to collective solutions which might free them from unnecessary labour – Brittain reveals herself as an inter-war representative of a tradition that had its roots in early twentieth-century thinking, but that also anticipated mid- and late twentieth-century feminist analysis.

Brittain herself was well aware that in formulating her analysis she drew on Olive Schreiner. We know also that she was intrigued, when she first encountered it, by the socialist analysis of household work. From our vantage point, we can see that she looks forward as well, most obviously to the critique of domesticity offered by Betty Friedan in *The Feminine Mystique* (1963) but also to more recent feminist analyses of housework which point to the continuing influence of an association of domesticity with femininity.[15]

From the perspective of such recent work, Brittain's comments may appear flawed: for example, the belief that household technology would automatically serve to liberate women has been effectively demolished by such recent analysis. Again, Brittain did not address in print or in her own life the inherently exploitative nature of the relationship between domestic servants and their employers. None the less, in her critique of the sentimentalization of housework, of society's indifference to the waste of women's labour, and of the reluctance of men and women alike to seek collective or co-operative solutions to housekeeping, she was far-seeing.

After her marriage in 1925 and the birth of her first child in 1927 Brittain became especially concerned with the problems and the challenges women faced in 'combining marriage and a career'.[16] Indeed, she came to perceive the challenge of combining professional work with marriage and motherhood and of creating feminist marriages as the most important feminist task of the post-war era. In her journalistic writings, she opposed such specific barriers as the regulation that prevented the employment of married teachers in the state school system,[17] but she is at her most passionate and effective when she took on the even more damaging but still pervasive attitude that a married woman ought not to be gainfully employed. For Brittain, a wife's right not only to work, but to have her work regarded as equal in importance to that of her husband, was the key issue on which any genuinely egalitarian marriage must rest. Without full recognition of the married woman's need to work, women would be faced with what she called an 'intolerable' choice:

> [I]n effect it is this: Shall a woman who loves her work . . . continue it throughout her life at the sacrifice of marriage, motherhood and all her emotional needs? Or shall she marry and have children at the cost of her career, and look forward to . . . intellectual starvation and monotony? . . . Each normal person, whether man or woman, is endowed . . . with a mind and a body, and is intended . . . to fulfil the needs of both . . . the woman for whom mental atrophy has been the price of marriage is no more normal and complete than she who has forgone husband and children for . . . career . . . .[18]

Brittain formulated a definition of feminist motherhood and defended it against two different kinds of inter-war critics: the traditional anti-feminists, who clung to Victorian notions of maternalism, and the modernist anti-feminists who drew their support from newly powerful ideas in psychology, which they claimed provided 'scientific' proof that feminism was responsible for producing a new kind of woman, who was hostile to heterosexuality and to motherhood.[19]

In opposition to such biological determinism, whether 'scientific' or sentimental, Brittain offered a new alternative, a vision of the modern feminist mother. She believed that the primary role that educated professional women ought to perform for their children was that of moral and intellectual guide. Unlike the ideal mother of the nineteenth century, who had been a 'self-sacrificing . . . infant nurse', the twentieth-century mother, Brittain believed, would serve her children best by providing responsible professional care for them in infancy, and by continuing her own work. As a fully developed, productive member of society, she would then be a better mother, better able to oversee her children's development as they grew to maturity.[20]

Brittain not only advocated modern, feminist motherhood; she also advocated feminist fatherhood, believing that one solution to the modern woman's dilemma of combining employment with motherhood lay in greater participation on the part of men as husbands and fathers: 'The good husband of the future will be the man who understands how to play the part of equal comrade. . . . Such a husband will realise that, if life's prizes are to be accessible to men and women alike, the practical and domestic obligations of marriage must be reduced to a minimum for each by being shared by both.'[21]

Brittain also wrote frequently about the disabilities and the opportunities that confronted women, married or single, in the labour market. She was a vigorous defender of equal pay for equal work, and equal opportunity for education and employment; and she attacked the legislated inequality that women still faced, for example, as teachers and in the civil service. But she also insisted that young women must make wise occupational choices, and in 1928 she published a handbook, *Women's Work in Modern England*, to help them do so. Its primary objective was to encourage women to reject stereotypical definitions of women's work, and avoid 'overcrowded professions' by seeking out what today are called 'non-traditional' areas of employment.[22]

One enthusiastic reader of *Women's Work in Modern England* was Elizabeth Abbott, the Chairman of the Open Door Council.[23] The ODC's platform – 'To secure that a woman shall be free to work and protected as a worker on the same terms as a man, and that legislation and regulations dealing with conditions and hours, payment, entry and training shall be based on the nature of the work and not upon the sex of the worker'[24] – was one that Brittain wholeheartedly endorsed. She was an early supporter of the Council,[25] and remained a supporter right up into the 1960s.[26] She served on the ODC executive[27] and some of her most effective feminist pieces were written in support of the Council's position, a position which was clearly opposed to that of the 'new' feminists, who viewed legislation placing limits on women's work as 'protective' rather than restrictive.[28] Brittain effectively opposed this position, pointing out that it was based on 'a deep rooted misunderstanding of feminist aims'. Feminists, she explained, were not indifferent to the need for legislation controlling hazardous work. What they opposed was basing such legislation on sexual difference.[29] Brittain pointed out that the demand for the 'protection' of women was often based upon prejudice, not on knowledge, and she called for rational, 'scientific' investigation of problems relating to women's work:

> If we are bent on discovering whether a real need for restrictive legislation for women exists, such questions as the following . . . most readily occur. How many women, compared with men, have suffered from accidents due to the cleaning of machinery? How much physical weakness among women is due to natural disability, and how much to underpay and under-nourishment? How many women, compared with men, have been injured by carrying heavy weights?[30]

In the interwar decades, the issues of marriage, motherhood and women's work had both general and specific connections to debates among feminist groups. As we have seen, on all these questions Vera Brittain believed that women's autonomy and independence were of central importance. Where there were specific disputes – the best example being the debate over restrictive legislation – Brittain unequivocally rejected the maternalism of 'new' feminism and advocated the right to independence of women of all social classes.

Restrictive legislation divided feminists in the 1920s and 1930s. In the 1920s, one issue that united them was the unfinished business of franchise reform. The passage of the Representation of the People Act in 1918 had been a major but incomplete victory, the most glaring remaining inequity being the denial of the vote to women under thirty. It served as a useful rallying point for feminists in the 1920s,[31] with an active campaign being mounted from 1926 until the passage of the 'Flapper Act' in 1928.[32] This brief campaign provided the subdued feminist movement of the 1920s with the opportunity to revive some of the drama of the pre-war suffrage struggle, including the excitement of large-scale public demonstrations. Vera Brittain took an active part in this campaign,[33] and she believed an equal franchise to be of importance, but for her it was a symbolic rather than a substantive issue. As she put it in July 1927, on the occasion of one of the large franchise rallies held during these years:

> The vote, both before it was gained and after, was simply the symbol of equal rights and opportunities. . . . [I]t gave women for the first time the means of asking for what they wanted, but it did not thereby fulfil those demands. Women still hold political demonstrations because the incompleteness of the English franchise is again a symbol – a symbol of the incomplete recognition of women as human beings . . .[34]

And in a piece written in March 1928, she contrasted the impending passage of the Franchise Bill into law with the 'anti-feminist reaction' reflected in the refusal of some London hospitals to accommodate women medical students:

> The women's suffrage movement will achieve its final triumph with a bloodless victory. . . . Does [this final triumph] signify the final triumph of the feminist idea . . . or . . . is the acquiescence in equal franchise due more to a growing scepticism as to the importance of votes than to a growing conviction as to the justice of women's rights? Have we really rounded seraglio point? Or have we merely concluded that votes do not matter very much?[35]

For Vera Brittain, it is clear, 'rounding seraglio point' would occur only when women had achieved a thoroughgoing equality with men. The fact that women's gains in medicine were being eroded just as equal suffrage was finally becoming law – an erosion which she saw as dangerous not only for women doctors themselves, but also for their women patients – underscored the need for continued feminist activism.

In the 1920s, Vera Brittain was active not only as a feminist, but as an internationalist. Her first step in this direction was made while she was still at Oxford, when she decided to read History and to specialize in international relations, with the explicit intention of understanding how it was that the war had occurred. By the time she left Oxford, she was a firm supporter of the League of Nations, and a critic of the punitive portions of the Versailles Treaty. From the time she was working for her degree, she began a lifelong practice of thoroughly informing herself about current political affairs and their

Plate 1 The Brittain family sat for this portrait when they were on holiday in St Anne's-on-sea, *c.*1897; *left to right*: Arthur Brittain, Vera Brittain, Edward Brittain and Edith Brittain. The photograph was taken by Albert Wiggans of the Rembrandt Studio, St Anne's

Plate 2 The Brittain family, *c.*1904, in Arthur Brittain's motor car, with Glen Bank in the background. Vera is seated in the front, next to her father; in the back seat, *left to right*, is an unidentified woman (perhaps Aunt Florence Bervon), Edward Brittain and Edith Brittain

Plate 3 Vera Brittain in Buxton, *c.*1913

Plate 4 Vera Brittain and Edward Brittain in Buxton, *c.*1913

Plate 5 Edward Brittain, Roland Leighton and Victor Richardson (*left to right*), Uppingham School OTC camp, July 1914

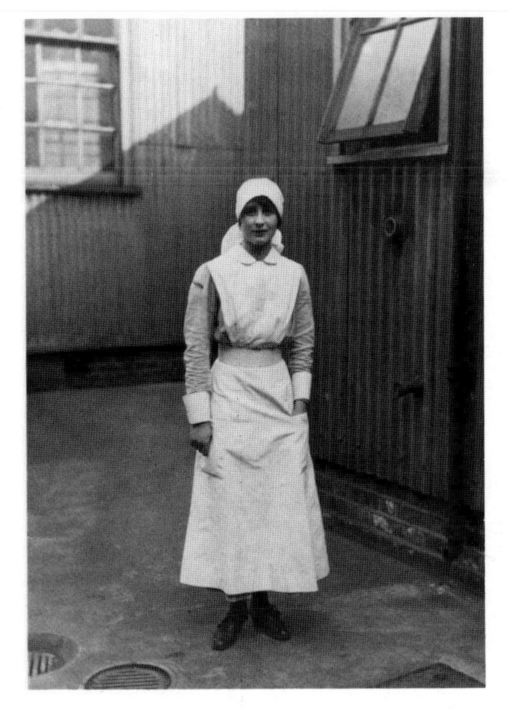

Plate 6 Vera Brittain as a VAD

Plate 7 In this group photograph of medical personnel, nursing sisters and VADs, Vera Brittain is in the third row from the front, and sixth from the left. Taken at the First London General Hospital, Camberwell, *c.*1915

Plate 8 Four friends, St George's Hospital, Malta, *c.*1917. Vera Brittain is third from the left

Plate 9 Winifred Holtby, *c.*1925

Plate 10 Vera Brittain and G.E.G. Catlin, in Ithaca, N.Y., *c.*1926

Plate 11 Vera Brittain with John Edward and Shirley, Sidmouth, August 1932

Plate 12 Studio portrait of Vera Brittain, *c.*1930; taken by Ellis & Fry, Baker Street, London

Plate 13 Vera Brittain with friend (possibly Cora Stoop?), *c*.1913

Plate 14 Geoffrey Thurlow in uniform

Plate 15 Roland Leighton in uniform

Plate 16 First editions of *Verses of a VAD*, *Humiliation with Honour* and *Testament of Youth*, together with the second edition of *The Dark Tide* and pages from the manuscript of *Testament of Youth*

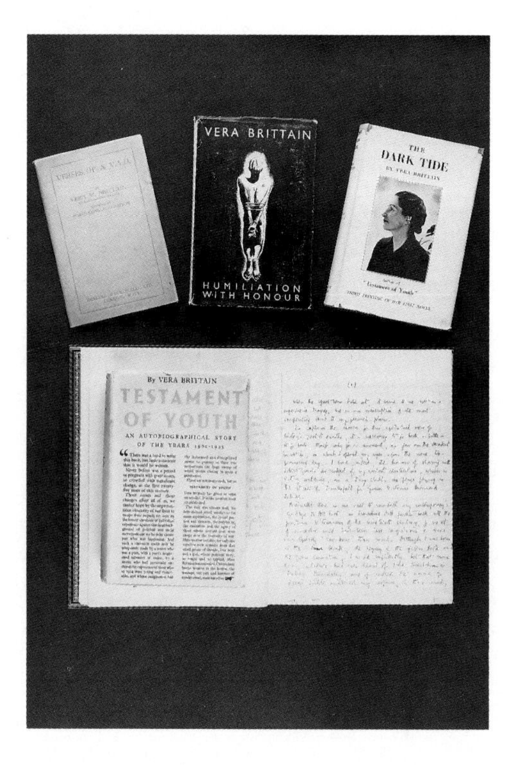

historical background. Her purpose was to create a well-formed perspective on social issues, one that would include both her commitment to feminism and her commitment to internationalism. Feminism and internationalism were, indeed, not separable for Brittain. For her, feminism meant the assertion of women's right to play a full and equal part in all aspects of life, and that brought with it both the right and the obligation to take as full and as responsible an interest in politics as men did. The war had taught her that men and women alike ignore politics to their peril: ignorance had not protected her in 1914.

Vera Brittain was a feminist well before she had even considered pacifism, and she remained a feminist all her life. What, then, were the connections that she saw between pacifism and feminism? Unlike many feminist pacifists, she avoided attempts to create a natural link between femininity and opposition to war, and only rarely made the claim that women, because they were mothers, had a natural interest in peace. She knew full well, from an examination of her own responses in 1914, that 'women are just as liable as men to be carried away by war-time emotion and deceived by the shining martial figure of patriotism'.[36] It was a rational rather than a sentimental link that Brittain wished to make between pacifism and feminism. Feminism, she believed, proclaimed women's equality with men. Feminism also gave women a responsibility to think about and to become involved in politics, and so, when she wrote about women and peace, her purpose was to exhort women to think about world affairs. What she objected to most strongly was the apathy of the non-feminist woman. She wrote of that 'terrible inert mass of lethargic womanhood', of the complacent woman who hid behind wifehood and maternity, claiming that those responsibilities left her time for no others:

> No argument will convince her that her first duty to her children is to watch the course of politics with a vigilant eye. She does not really believe that if this country . . . fails to support the League of Nations in putting up an effective resistance to the international aggressions of Italy, Germany and Japan, the ideal nursery and its inhabitants upon which so much of her time has been spent may be annihilated by enemy bombs within two or three years. So far, she has failed to perceive that the moral obligation . . . to keep her house clean and her children tidy is to-day infinitely less than the moral obligation to be intelligent about the future and its awful possibilities.[37]

In the 1920s and early 1930s Brittain worked to promote the League of Nations, and to encourage it to develop into a genuine force for peace.[38] To this end, she quickly allied herself with the most important English internationalist organization of the 1920s, the League of Nations Union, founded in October 1918.[39] The LNU supported multilateral disarmament and arbitration of international disputes through the League and it publicized and promoted the League's work in a variety of ways, including the sponsoring of lectures and study sessions.

Brittain became a League of Nations Union lecturer in 1922.[40] Like many other League speakers, she visited Geneva regularly, either for LNU summer school sessions, or to attend the annual September meeting of the League Assembly. She also wrote frequently about the League for such publications as *Time and Tide*.

During the early 1920s, Vera Brittain was optimistic about the possibilities for achieving lasting world peace through the League of Nations, and optimistic about the role that she and other educated people like herself could play in bringing rationality to world politics. As she put it in an enthusiastic letter to Winifred, written in November, 1921: 'I am so glad I did "International Relations", glad I am lecturing on them now, though in ever such a small way, glad to do anything, however small, to make people care for the peace of the world. It may be Utopian, but it's constructive.'[41] She remained, on balance, optimistic about the possibilities for lasting peace until the late 1920s, although frustrating disappointments with the League itself gradually dampened her optimism. The dangers inherent in the world situation, and in the half-hearted commitment to internationalism on the part of the Great Powers, impressed itself on her forcibly during a visit she made in 1924 to Geneva and then to occupied Germany. Germany frightened and disturbed her. The injustices of the Versailles Treaty, the oppression produced by the very fact of occupation struck her forcibly, especially in Cologne. In the undercurrent of hostility the Germans felt towards the occupying forces, Brittain saw the threat of a future war.[42] At a church service in Cologne cathedral, memories of the war and of the German prisoners she had nursed seemed to underline the evils of warfare: 'It was queer to stand in the midst of those Germans, all singing, and think of ten years ago; they made the war seem absurd and unnatural and caused me to feel more of a pacifist than ever . . . I am glad that what I did was so strictly neutral, even to nursing the Germans . . . .'[43]

But while Brittain could refer to herself in her diary as a 'pacifist' in the mid-1920s, she was still a strong believer in the need to work through the League in spite of its imperfections, and therefore remained a strong supporter of the LNU. For example, she commented as follows about the League's nay-saying critics: 'If the L. of N. can be said to have one weakness . . . they will not support it. Instead of themselves creating and improving the machinery of peace, they want other people to make it absolutely perfect. . . . As if their support would be needed for something that was perfect.'[44] Unhappily, by the late 1920s the League appeared increasingly ineffective in containing the alarming rise of Fascism, and for Brittain, as for many others, post-war optimism was giving way to increasing anxiety about the possibility of another world conflict.

In the late 1920s, Brittain also became involved with an international feminist campaign to make the League more responsive to women's rights. She regarded with dismay its lukewarm commitment to the equality of women, and she welcomed efforts to challenge its anti-feminist bias. For example, she, Holtby and her husband Gordon Catlin all acknowledged in private that the League had exploited the labour of women:

> Gordon put his finger on the matter when he said that five years ago the League was a 'volunteer' organization, associated in people's minds with 'voluntary work', which is usually done by women, and its sponsors were thankful. . . . But now it is seen to be successful, it is taken seriously . . . good, well paid jobs follow in its wake, men want them, and are trying to oust the women who stepped into the breech in the days of struggle . . .[45]

The chief specific goal of the campaign by feminist organisations was to secure passage by the League Assembly of an Equal Rights Treaty, whose main clause was to read: 'The Contracting States agree that upon the ratification of this Treaty, men and women shall have Equal Rights throughout the territory subject to their respective jurisdictions.'[46] In this campaign, the Six Point Group was the leader among British feminist groups.[47] Vera Brittain contributed to the campaign effort by producing two important statements about it, both of which became Six Point Group pamphlets,[48] by acting as a liaison between the American Woman's Party and the Six Point Group,[49] and in organising support for the Treaty among the English delegation to the League Assembly in 1929. On 10 August 1929 she organised and led a delegation of women to speak to Lord Cecil, the head of the British delegation to the Assembly, to encourage his support for the Equal Rights Treaty.[50] Her work for the Equal Rights International, which allowed her to combine her support for the League with her support for feminism, and thus link the two political causes that were of most importance to her, marks the high point of her involvement with feminist activism.

Brittain's writing on feminism and peace, her public speaking and the committee work she undertook between 1921 and 1933 represent first and foremost her contribution to strengthening both these causes. But there was another side to it. As a professional writer, expressing her cherished beliefs was also her business, and finding work was at times an exciting adventure and at other times an exercise in frustration and disappointment. In tracing Brittain's career-building activities, it is evident that her social and educational connections were of great importance. The first jobs she was successful in obtaining were part-time teaching and lecturing, first at St Monica's, and then at a girls' school in Kensington, where the headmistress 'seemed as much impressed by the fact that I had been head girl at St Monica's as that I had been to Somerville'.[51]

Brittain approached the League of Nations Union to offer her services as a lecturer in July 1921, right after completing her Oxford finals. To Holtby, who was in Yorkshire, she wrote giving the details of her initial telephone call and her prospective interview. As she excitedly explained to Winifred, Agnes Murray, Professor Gilbert Murray's daughter, who had been in her final year at Somerville when Vera went up in 1914, arranged the interview: 'It *is* Agnes & thanks to my first-year reputation she remembered me very well!' She went on to describe in vivid and precise detail what she intended to wear to the interview: 'I am going in my dark blue frock . . . a soft tulle & straw black hat of Mother's with a hanging lace veil & my best buckles on black suede shoes!'[52] Brittain's concern with dress here is characteristic. She loved clothes, and she took great pleasure in creating an appropriate impression. Her mixture of intellectual professionalism and love of dress is delightfully illustrated in her comments to Winifred about how she 'rehearsed' her early lectures: 'You would have been amused . . . if you could have seen me last night, dressed up in a hat and a fur, declaiming in front of the looking-glass! I am going to do it every day once, till I know the thing by heart and stop feeling a fool. . . .'[53]

But there were many disappointments as well. Brittain worked very hard, for example, to prepare a series of lectures for the LNU. But it was in fact several months before they called on her, and when she did obtain a place on their lecture circuit, much of the work was arduous and thankless and unpaid, or paid at a minimal rate.[54] She did the lecturing primarily for the same reason that she and Winifred travelled together each autumn to Geneva to attend the League of

Nations Assembly: because she believed in the cause. 'It may be Utopian, but it's constructive. It's better than railing at the present state of Europe, or always weeping in darkness for the dead.'[55] But it was also good experience and good publicity, and she hoped it would lead to commissions to write and lecture elsewhere.

She did get such commissions, but they never came easily enough to satisfy her, and throughout the 1920s and early 1930s she suffered from the anxiety that afflicts all but the most successful of freelance writers: the work she coveted most – for example commissions from *Time and Tide* – seemed elusive, and in any case, what she really wanted to do was write fiction:

> I want very much to get back to 'Daphne'. I'm afraid the thought of lectures rather bores me at present. I wish I could write something good enough to justify my sticking to 'that one talent' . . . it's the only thing in the way of work that really absorbs me. Only I feel in despair when I read Sheila Kaye-Smith and Rose Macaulay and find how good they are.[56]

In spite of such moments of self-doubt about her abilities, or about her worthiness and attractiveness as a person, Brittain accomplished an impressive amount in the 1920s, as a journalist, as a lecturer, as a writer of non-fiction books and even as a novelist. Even before her great success with *Testament of Youth*, while she had not achieved fame, she had, through hard work and judicious use of her Somerville qualifications and contacts, built herself a solid career.

9
Semi-detached Marriage

In July 1920, after the failure of the brief engagement she entered into at Oxford that spring and summer,[1] Brittain composed a bitter poem entitled 'The Superfluous Woman', in which she expressed her despair that all the lovers worthy of the women of her generation had died in the war.[2] A decade later, Brittain selected that poem as the heading for the penultimate chapter of *Testament of Youth*, in which she emphasises that when she and Winifred established their household, she assumed she was destined for lifelong spinsterhood. The final chapter of *Testament of Youth* is entitled 'Another Stranger'. For its heading, Brittain chose Roland Leighton's intensely romantic 'Hédauville. November 1915', a poem whose tone contrasts sharply with that of her own 'The Superfluous Woman'. 'Hédauville. November 1915' contains the lines: 'Unknowing you may meet / Another stranger, Sweet', and in this final chapter we are told that after she had firmly put all thoughts of marriage behind her, the 'stranger' of Roland's poem appeared, unforeseen. The narrative of *Testament of Youth* concludes just before her marriage to the man she refers to only as 'G.'.

Brittain herself was well aware that in *Testament of Youth* she provided only a fragmentary account of her courtship with the political philosopher and Labour Party activist George Edward Gordon Catlin. In part, the unsatisfactory and incomplete nature of the final chapter of the book has a straightforward, pragmatic explanation: in 1933, as she was finishing the manuscript, she and her husband quarrelled bitterly over her treatment of their relationship and she reluctantly agreed to cut much of the material, leaving only the truncated account that appears in the published version.[3] But even if Catlin had been less thin-skinned, it is unlikely that Brittain would have been able to construct the narrative of her courtship in *Testa-*

ment of Youth in a more nuanced manner, any more than she was able to present the many sides of the marriage itself in *Testament of Friendship*, in *Testament of Experience* or in her extensive writing on marriage, sexuality and childrearing in which she frequently used examples from her own life as illustrative material.

Brittain could never bring herself to be completely open about her marriage partly because the information was too intimate even for an autobiographer as committed to frank disclosure as she was. In addition, as an active participant in the interwar movement to construct a modernist perspective on marriage and sexuality – a 'new morality' as it was often called[4] – Brittain had an investment in presenting her own marriage as a successful experiment in the project of creating new feminist forms for heterosexual relationships. In many ways Brittain's marriage was just such a brave venture, but the tensions between herself and her husband and the inner conflicts she herself wrestled with were, not surprisingly, greater than she ever felt free to admit in public. After all, in common with other intellectuals who were constructing public discourse on marriage and sexuality, her own sensibilities (like Catlin's) had been shaped by bourgeois Victorianism. Given the strength of that older tradition, it is no wonder that on a collective, public level, as well as on a personal, private level, the 'new morality' of the 1920s and 1930s was shot through with dissonance and unacknowledged contradiction.

G.E.G. Catlin, who was married to Brittain from 1925 until her death in 1970, was an Oxford-trained political scientist, a few years younger than Brittain (he was born on 29 July 1896). Their relationship began by correspondence, when Catlin wrote a 'fan' letter to Brittain after the publication of her first novel, *The Dark Tide*. The correspondence blossomed through the autumn and winter of 1923–4, and when the couple actually met for the first time, in the summer of 1924, they became engaged in a few weeks, and were married a year later.

Recently, a perceptive critic has asked: 'Why did Brittain marry?'[5] This is a legitimate question, and not only because Brittain herself presents her marriage as an unplanned and not entirely welcome occurrence in her own narrative of her life. For it appears that in some ways, by her late twenties, she was genuinely satisfied by a life without men. She had a clear-eyed awareness of just how damaging sexual relationships could be to a woman who wished to pursue an independent career, and she had achieved with Winifred Holtby a rare balance between independence and companionship.

But actively refusing marriage has never been an easy choice for women: it is only rarely that a woman freely embraces the social difficulties and the loss of status entailed in permanent 'spinsterhood', especially if it is assumed that she will marry. And Brittain had been thought of as eminently 'marriageable' since her adolescence. Thus, while in retrospect Brittain presented the household she and Holtby established as an arrangement intended to be permanent, in fact their families, their friends and the two women themselves were fully aware that their sharing of 'digs' was most probably an interval between college and marriage – *Vera's* marriage. From the beginning of their friendship in 1921 until Brittain's wedding in June 1925, Brittain was rarely without a love interest. There was first of all her brief engagement during her last year at Somerville; by 1923 Catlin had established himself as a long-distance suitor, and during this same period she was carrying on a flirtation with an uncle by marriage who was just a few years older than she.[6] Holtby knew the most intimate details of all these relationships, because Brittain, in this as in other matters, relied on Holtby to be her confidante, supporter and adviser. Thus while Holtby was deeply saddened by the marriage and Brittain was genuinely concerned about the pain her own happiness brought to her friend,[7] she is unconvincing when she suggests that she had ever resigned herself to permanent spinsterhood. In truth, neither Brittain nor Holtby was surprised by Brittain's marriage, and if G.E.G. Catlin had not appeared on the scene, someone else would have done so. As Holtby had written, only half in jest, in 1923 about Brittain's feelings that if she made it to thirty without marriage, she'd be safe: 'how often have I warned you not to put your trust in being thirty . . . absurd idea that thirty years constituted an invincible armour against sex attraction. Forty won't with you. I should still walk cannily at fifty.'[8]

From its beginnings in their courtship and throughout their marriage the Brittain–Catlin relationship reflects both an acceptance and a defiance of conventional norms. The formal trappings of the courtship and wedding were both irreproachably upper middle class. The couple announced their engagement in *The Times* in July of 1924 and the ceremony itself, held at St James's Spanish Place[9] on 27 June 1925, was a fashionable white wedding. The best man was the Earl of Stamford, a college friend of the groom. Vera Brittain was at her most beautiful in her thirties and a wedding photograph reveals that she was an exquisite bride in her dress, tulle veil and orange blossoms.[10] In the photograph, Catlin, tall and handsome, makes an elegant groom. Arthur and Edith Brittain, Catlin's clergyman father and Holtby, in a large hat, complete a picture that could be used as a representative model for upper middle-class wedding styles in the mid-1920s.

But the couple was also breaking with conventionality in fundamental ways. Even before they met, Brittain had made it clear that if they were to have a relationship, it would be defined in feminist terms. Ten years earlier, Brittain's courtship with Roland Leighton had also been carried out largely by correspondence, and the reader will remember the role that Olive Schreiner's novel *Story of an African Farm* played in that correspondence. Brittain had passionately identified with the persona of the unfortunate Lyndall, whose desire for independence leads to her sexual ruin and death. In this far less passionate courtship of her maturity, Brittain's own *The Dark Tide* serves as the basis for a very different courtship motif. In her correspondence with him, Brittain emphasised to Catlin that the real Vera was even more committed to independence than her fictional creation Virginia, and that she would never sacrifice either her independence or her commitment to writing.

After they had become engaged, Brittain was free to be both frank and explicit about this, and she emphasised that she was not offering to be a traditional wife, that she was marrying him because she admired his mind, and trusted the genuineness of his respect for her work and her feminist convictions. She kept her birth name – a decision that took considerable courage and determination in the 1920s – and while she agreed to follow him to Cornell University in Ithaca, New York, where he had a post in the Department of Government, she had no intention of abandoning her own work.

Moreover, she made it clear to him that she was marrying him with a frankly acknowledged recognition that the marriage might not succeed: 'Let me tell you quite plainly that I regard the first year or so of marriage as an experiment – the most serious, the least wanton, experiment . . . but nevertheless an experiment. . . . Marriage vows are the expression of one's honourable intentions . . . .'[11]

After a honeymoon in central Europe, Brittain accompanied Catlin to the United States, where she spent much of 1925–6. As they launched their marriage in Ithaca, relations between the two of them started out auspiciously. Although she found the constraints of academic society at Cornell difficult right from the start (she loathed being a Cornell 'faculty wife'[12]) Brittain was touched and grateful that her new husband actually took seriously his stated commitment to equality in marriage. In October, when they were just settling in, she wrote proudly to Winifred: 'his feminism is genuine and deep-rooted; in fact he won't sit down to his work till I am able to, as it only makes him feel restless if he is not sharing the domesticity'.[13] But in spite of her undoubted marital happiness at this juncture, Brittain missed Holtby deeply. In November, she wrote:

> Gordon has never understood – I suppose in the nature of things he could not understand – how much I love you. One could hardly expect one's husband to understand the queer love that makes one able to give a freer devotion of the mind where there is no sexual connotation – just as I loved Edward better than Roland, though I didn't know it until I found, when they were both dead, that I missed him more.[14]

And even Brittain's sense that Catlin truly understood the obligations of a working partnership was not consistently sustained. By November, Brittain commented regretfully that Gordon preferred to do the talking rather than the listening. By February 1926 her dissatisfaction had become more acute: when she wished to talk about her writing, Vera reported to Winifred, Gordon would ignore her, or even start reading the newspaper, or worst of all, tell her he wanted to 'schedule' the discussion for later – as if it were a class and she were one of his students. On 24 February 1926, after she and Gordon had had a serious quarrel, Vera wrote mournfully to Winifred: 'I know that I owe "The Dark Tide" & "N.W.H." [*Not Without Honour*] mainly to your powers of listening and suggesting. . . . You are more necessary to me . . . because you further my work, whereas he merely makes me . . . happy. . . .'[15]

Although two days later Vera and Gordon were reconciled, it is clear that she did acutely miss Winifred's companionship and supportiveness. Moreover, although she did her best to establish herself, she achieved little success in her efforts to be accepted as a journalist in America, and she could not settle to more extended work. Although she was developing an idea for an autobiograpical novel[16] (revealingly, on the theme of 'a woman's development . . . shown by means of vignette sketches of her contacts with different men, who are only incidental to what she believes to be her real purpose in life'), she could not make progress with it in an atmosphere she experienced as alien. She missed London as well as Winifred, and she believed that she needed to live in England to further her career. She came home in August 1926 and she did not return with Catlin to America in September.

But this rupture in their living arrangements did not mean the end of the marriage. Instead, Brittain and Catlin, along with Holtby, worked out a compromise which preserved the marriage and also gave Brittain what she needed most: physical and emotional closeness to both Catlin and Holtby. At first, Vera simply moved back to the Maida Vale flat she and Winifred had shared before her marriage, with no definite plan for the future. By the summer of 1927, when Brittain was pregnant with her first child, the three of them had decided to set up a joint household, an arrangement they sustained until Holtby's death in 1935. During these years, Vera and the children – John Edward was born in 1927 and Shirley in 1930 – made London their permanent base, with Winifred there much of the time and Catlin joining them for part of the year.

For Brittain and for Holtby, and for their feminist associates, this arrangement was not merely a compromise but a modernist experiment. Holtby, for example, writing to Brittain in 1929, reports on Lady Rhondda's views on the marriage:

> She thinks what you & Gordon are doing supremely important. She says it may happen that you as an artist & thinker won't accomplish as much as you might have done unmarried, because so much of your time will be taken up in fighting for your career, but that only by doing what you are doing will it be possible for people in the future to live normal lives, and that it is immensely important to humanity.[17]

By the summer of 1927, Brittain was using her own experience as evidence in the writing she began to do during this period about the challenge of combining professional work with marriage and motherhood. She called the solution that she and Catlin had worked out 'Semi-detached Marriage':

> One of the most rigid of traditions is that which regards marriage as a day-by-day, hour-by-hour, unbroken, and unbreakable association . . . Nothing could be further from the free, generous, and intelligent comradeship which is the marriage ideal of the finest young men and women of today. . . . That is why many women, and many thoughtful men . . . are beginning to practise 'semi-detached marriage', with the children, for obvious reasons, under the care of their mother. They have found that the advantages of living under one roof do not outweigh the disadvantages of one partner being deprived of her beloved occupation, and being thereby made dependent, restless, and discontented.[18]

But while the Brittain–Catlin arrangement was a bold experiment, it was not an easy one. In the autumn of 1926 it began well enough. Brittain wrote to Catlin soon after he had returned to Ithaca to tell him about the burst of energy she was experiencing:

> pushing feminism, attacking new papers . . . proving that my career is doing better *after* marriage than it did before . . . fearing nothing, save only such circumstances as sap & devitalise the fountain of this intense energy. To have to 'get tea', make beds, be called on, return calls, be a 'Faculty Wife', be called 'Mrs Catlin' – God! how I hated it! But I love marriage, and I adore you. You understand so marvellously. 'What matters is not where you are, but what you are' – no sentence could have expressed more clearly my own idea of what marriage . . . should be . . .[19]

But Catlin could not sustain this understanding. He was lonely and deeply unhappy in Ithaca, and he could not resist writing letters in which, by implication at least, he blamed Brittain. Her letters, in turn, took on an impatient and defensive tone:

> Why should I . . . have a sort of moral obligation to see that you eat enough. . . . Much you would notice . . . if *my* appetite showed a falling off! Why men should endow themselves with a monopoly of this kind of helplessness I really don't know! . . . I know now that you are willing to keep our bargain, but I wish I felt that you were keeping it, if not as cheerfully . . . at least as graciously & as benevolently as you originally said you would. If you give a general impression . . . that I am here in London *against* your will, playing, not the part of a cooperator, but the undignified part of a truant wife . . . then indeed the value of the whole experiment as one solution of the difficulties of modern marriage, does disappear.[20]

As she would openly acknowledge many years later in *Testament of Experience*, they did very nearly separate late in 1926.[21] What she could not acknowledge was the extent to which both parties harboured bitterness towards the other as a result of their 'semi-detached' arrangement all through the 1920s and 1930s.

One aspect of their married life deeply affected by these years of bitterness was their sexual relationship. Sexuality was, in any case, the area of married life in which Brittain experienced the most acute tensions between the patterns of her youth and her commitment to modernism. Throughout her autobiographical writings, it is one aspect about which she says remarkably little.[22] This reticence reflects her deepest feelings: sexuality was one aspect of Brittain's life where modernism represented a thin veneer superimposed upon a fundamentally Victorian sensibility. The Victorian bedrock is revealed in the way in which Brittain handled Catlin's wish that they should become lovers before their wedding. Although she would write much later that on her wedding day, 'the long tulle veil with its crown of orange blossom was an inappropriate symbol of unsophisticated youth',[23] in the most obvious and direct way, the symbolism fitted: although she had been engaged twice and had had several relationships with men, when she and Gordon married, she had never had sexual intercourse. One evening during their courtship in August of 1924, they came close to doing so, but she refused. Afterward she wrote him a long letter, explaining her reasons: 'At my school I received singularly little of the physiological sex training which is now comparatively common; so little indeed that though I knew how children were born I did not know precisely how they were conceived until the crude enlightenment of my hospital days.'[24] But while she acknowledges that her ignorance may have been unfortunate, she emphasises her support for the attitudes towards sexuality that were inculcated by her upbringing: '[O]n the other hand, my school produced in me . . . an attitude towards sex that was reverent without being sentimental, & a consciousness that the controlled body was as sacred & as pure as the uncontrolled body shameful . . .' She tells her fiancé that her respect for 'purity' stood her in good stead during the war, which supplied

> the tragic . . . reverse side of the picture, with its plentiful examples [of] . . . the physical wreckage of over-indulgence. . . . If indeed I had not already desired purity . . . I should have reached it through my experience in the worst cases of venereal diseases . . . and of those more heartbreaking though less disgusting . . . nervous diseases & those temperamental weaknesses & fears due to a loss of control in boyhood.[25]

To Winifred she wrote: 'my education . . . bade me resist his worship of my body. . . .'[26]

In 1924, then, Brittain couched her refusal to make love with Gordon in the language of the late nineteenth-century social purity crusade. Her letters to Holtby, written a year later during her honeymoon, reveal a very different side. In contrast to the evangelical solemnity of the year before, Brittain's tone is now flippant and in these letters to her friend written in the first weeks of her marriage, she assumes a pose of cool detachment: '[P]ersonally I am beginning to find a queer fascination in it [sexual relations] but I still cannot understand why for this cause wars have been fought . . . much as I love my husband, I would not sacrifice one successful article for a night of physical relationship.'[27]

Perhaps Brittain made her honeymoon into an amusing story narrated for Holtby's benefit as a way of reassuring both Winifred and herself that Gordon had not really come between them: she might be travelling with him, and going to bed with him, but by sharing their intimacy with her friend, she could reassert the primacy of the bond between herself and Winifred, as she did explicitly in one of her honeymoon letters: 'Meanwhile I still have the persistent feeling that my beloved husband is a mere accessory, and that you, not he, belong to the real essentials of life.'[28]

During the months of their annual separations in the 1920s and 1930s, Brittain and Catlin corresponded regularly. Their letters offer a remarkably full record of their relationship. Throughout these years, Brittain continued to oscillate between modernity and tradition in her sentiments concerning sexuality. About marital fidelity, for instance, she took a public position that was markedly different from that of other progressives of the period. In contrast to both Dora and Bertrand Russell, for example, who during these same years each produced books supporting the right of both women and men to have sexual relationships with more than one partner, Brittain's position, most fully expressed in print in her book *Halcyon: or the Future of Monogamy*, was that freely chosen monogamy was the wisest, most mature pattern for egalitarian marriage.[29]

Unfortunately, in practice she and her husband did not agree on this issue. The correspondence between the two reveals that Catlin behaved as though he assumed that when he agreed to the 'semi-detached' living arrangement, he gained the moral right to have extra-marital affairs – as long as he told Brittain about them. Brittain was deeply troubled, hurt and confused by his disclosures and by his behaviour. On the one hand, she clearly did think he had the right to relationships with other women, if only because she accepted the notion that regular sex might be necessary for his health: 'I want you to put first considerations of health and work, & not hesitate to do whatever you feel impelled to do', she wrote him in January 1929, when he wrote to her that he was considering one such affair. 'I know . . . my theory of sex intercourse as the supreme experience reserved for the dearest person is hopelessly ideal. . . .'[30]

His threatened infidelity not only hurt her, it made her unsure about her own feelings and about the wisdom of taking a public position on an issue that aroused such profound conflicts in her, and in their marriage: 'Sometimes I feel like giving up [her book on marriage] altogether because it seems hopeless to write on sex and marriage when I don't know what I really think. . . . If only . . . one could completely rid one's self of all one had ever heard or been taught about sex, all prejudices, customs, traditions, preconceptions, and come afresh to the problem. . . .'[31]

When Catlin decided a few weeks later that he would not, after all, embark on this particular sexual affair, Brittain was deeply relieved, and not only because she had been saddened and hurt, but also because of her conviction that the success or failure of their marriage was more than a private matter:

> [T]he thing I perhaps fear most is something that might smirch or spoil or render less dignified or in any way cheapen our relationship, not only in our own eyes but in the eyes of the world. Our work – at any rate . . . my work – depends largely for its success, not only upon the fact that we are ideally happy together, but that we are known to be so. If it seems arrogant to say that the success of our marriage matters to the world, to society, to politics, to feminism, I can only reply that it is the kind of arrogance that one ought to encourage in one's self. Today – as in the past, one happily married wife and mother is worth more to feminism, and to the whole cause of social morals, than a dozen gifted and eloquent spinsters. . . . The words 'abnormal', 'masculine' . . . etc. etc. are flung about still with such wholesale vigour . . . that a position which renders their use obviously absurd in one's own case is of inestimable value. . . . [T]hat our experiment in 'semi-detachment' should succeed . . . this I think of the supremest importance . . .[32]

In her next letter, she continued the discussion, adding:

> as Winifred remarked the other day with regard to the theories of Dora & Bertrand Russell, they are naturally as much concerned to justify their own story to themselves as to lay down a philosophy of freedom for the world . . . this decision of yours [not to pursue his extramarital relationship] seems to confirm the thesis of my little monogamy book . . . that people's self-respect will lead them to prefer monogamy . . . voluntary monogamy based on complete freedom.[33]

In the course of her research for *Halcyon*, and for a larger book, 'The Liberation of Marriage', which she never completed,[34] research she did with Catlin's help, Brittain learned several new facts about the physiology of human sexual response. In April 1929, she was reading both D.H. Lawrence's *Lady Chatterley's Lover* (which made her miss Gordon intensely)[35] and *Sex in Civilization*.[36] 'I am a little perturbed on the whole subject of what should be the woman's proper physiological reaction in sex intercourse', she wrote, initiating a lively and frank exchange of letters between herself and her husband about their own sexual relations.[37]

From the perspective of the history of sexuality in the inter-war period, this exchange of letters between Brittain and Catlin during the spring of 1929 is revealing and significant. Ruth Hall, editor of a volume of selections gleaned from the thousands of letters sent to sex reformer Marie Stopes, points out that in the decade immediately following the First World War, 'society was in its most interesting transitional stage between post-Victorian reticence and repression and today's more permissive attitudes to sexual matters'.[38] She goes on to comment that Stopes's middle-class correspondents, in contrast to the working-class people who wrote to her, were likely to know about birth control. 'Their letters to Marie Stopes, unlike those from the lower classes, were therefore largely concerned not with birth control and requests for abortion, but with the problems created by a sexually repressive society.'[39]

Brittain, although far more knowledgeable than most of the correspondents whose letters comprise the Stopes collection, still fits Ruth Hall's description. She was not only a public supporter of birth control (she served on Marie Stopes's Executive Committee for a time in the early 1930s[40]), she herself obtained from her medical advisers the most effective form of contraceptive then available.[41] But information about her own capacities for sexual pleasure was less easy to obtain. As she said in one of the letters she wrote to Catlin, 'doctors with this kind of knowledge are hard to come by'.[42]

If this April 1929 exchange of letters illustrates the gaps in Brittain's knowedge about sexuality, it also reveals her modernism. Having discovered the literature of sexology, Brittain believed that she should inform herself concerning the latest 'scientific' opinions about physiology and she clearly believed that the information she had gathered in the course of her reading could improve sexual relations between herself and her husband.

A year later, she would write this revealing assessment of her own early and present attitudes towards sexuality: 'I am much relieved to hear that you don't find me a "frigid" wife. I read so much about "frigidity" in my various sex books that I begin to be alarmed about it; also in writing the early sections of my war-book, as I am now doing, it does amaze me to recall how infinitesimal, for a person of my degree of vitality, was my sexual curiosity in youth . . . my predominating concern always was, and always has been ambition. . . .' Writers on sex, she says, do not allow for the sublimation of sex by ambition in 'an energetic boy or girl'.[43]

In the course of their differences over the issue of infidelity in 1929, Brittain had warned Catlin that she was afraid that if one or both of them were to engage in extramarital affairs, eventually their marriage could not help but suffer.[44] Sadly, her worries were justified. As the years passed, Brittain buried her hurt feelings in an almost contemptuous aloofness. She did not intend to dissolve the marriage because of his extramarital affairs, nor did he intend to dissolve it because of Brittain's determination to continue an arrangement in which she steadfastly guarded her right to autonomy and to the time and space necessary to do her work, but each of them felt disappointed with the other, especially during the 1930s. Because of the capacities for self-discipline, loyalty and commitment that each of them possessed, Brittain and Catlin did make their 'semi-detached' marriage work, but the emotional costs were not insignificant.

Brittain and Catlin carefully and deliberately planned for their two children. During their courtship correspondence, both had agreed that children were an expected part of marriage but Brittain emphasised to Catlin that she intended to approach motherhood in an unsentimental fashion: 'I should feel conscientious towards them, but not much interested until they began to have ideas', she wrote, adding: 'I have really very little maternal instinct.'[45] For this couple, a primary reason for having children was that they believed that their offspring would be useful contributors to society. Brittain, who wholeheartedly supported the eugenicist thinking that was then so influential, made this point explicitly and repeatedly both in private and in public. To her future husband she wrote in 1925 that they should have children only when they could afford them: 'For people of our type it isn't safe to have a child under a *certain* £1000 a year. That sounds rather cynical . . . when the great majority have nothing like that.' But without that secure income, the wife becomes 'a general cook & bottle washer' and not only is this detrimental to her welfare, it is not good for the children.[46]

Two years later, just as she and Catlin were about to start their own family, Brittain expanded on this theme, explaining why she thought middle-class couples were wise to have small families:

> children, in those classes which maintain their own standard by means of an orderly home and a Public School and University tradition, are for at least twenty years a heavy financial liability . . . This situation precipitates the inevitable conflict between the future of the race and the present standard of life. Many would probably argue that for the sake of the future our young married couples should relax . . . the discipline of their tradition; that a permanent contribution to the next generation is worth temporary chaos. . . . [But] are we really working for eugenic birth control if we persuade our few thoroughly civilized individuals to descend even a little towards the standard of the slum-dweller? Is it not owing to their very tradition that we desire our middle classes to

> produce larger families? How else, save by children brought up in decency and order, and nourished upon the beauty and affection which complete control of circumstances alone makes possible, are we to leaven the national lump of mediocrity and inefficiency?[47]

Brittain and Catlin planned for their first child during the winter of 1926, when Catlin was in Ithaca and Brittain was in London. They agreed that Brittain would travel to America in the spring. In planning for the trip, Brittain explained to her husband that the timing of her arrival required considerable forethought:

> if we plan to submit ourselves to the chance of an infant as soon as we meet (and biologically this is by far the soundest plan) and succeed at once, if I came out in Feb. or March I should have to return across the Atlantic just when I was feeling most damnable and the risk of miscarriage already present. And it would mean the infant coming in November or December, which is the worst possible time not only for my work but for my and its health . . . I emphasise the physical aspect to an extent that may seem to you undue, because I think it is so thoroughly inefficient either to be very ill over the business one's self, or to produce a sickly infant. And keeping well under those conditions depends almost entirely on having . . . convenient circumstances. The last thing I want to feel myself, or make others think, is that motherhood is a work-destructive crisis bringing temporary chaos.[48]

> My great object . . . is to prove that work and maternity are not . . . mutually exclusive . . . this is a matter of principle which I care for more . . . than . . . motherhood itself.[49]

When Brittain went to America in April of 1927, this time accompanied by her mother, who had 'decided to give herself a break from my father and accompany me to America for the eight weeks' visit',[50] she became pregnant almost immediately.[51] Early in the pregnancy, although she experienced morning sickness ('It is disconcerting to be the slave of such small things', she wrote to Holtby[52]) she was determined to continue with her work as much as she could. 'I feel it to be . . . important to the women's movement to supply the fullest possible proof that one can be a normal woman as well as a good feminist. . . .'[53] In the early stages of pregnancy, she sometimes felt despondent about the coming responsibilities, a despondency she could only share with the absent Holtby, to whom she wrote: 'It's queer how it has been my fate to get married, and presumably to have children when all I really care for deeply is writing . . . and have so little forte for marriage & motherhood. You would have done both so much better. . . .' Sometimes, she says, she would like to 'cut all human relationships but yours & get back to the stage we were in at the beginning of 1923'.[54]

But that was a particularly bleak day, and both she and Catlin may have been feeling the strain of living in the small Ithaca apartment with Edith Brittain who, while well-meaning, could not control her fussiness. During these first few weeks of her first pregnancy, Brittain both welcomed her mother's presence and felt irritated by it. On the one hand, she was grateful that Edith offered in advance to help with child care.[55] On the other hand, it appears that Edith's presence intensified the inevitable day-to-day tensions between Gordon and Vera. That Edith was certainly conscious of these tensions is suggested by the fact that Edith wrote to Winifred about them: 'Vera is having her ups & downs and is particularly temperamental . . . yesterday a bad one & poor Gordon could not do anything right . . . she *will* expect the "mere man" to be what you are & have been to her & that is impossible. . . .'[56]

While this letter indicates that Edith may have been injudiciously entangled in the relationship between Vera and Gordon, she was correct about Vera's need for Winifred. And it was in May, during the early stages of her pregnancy, that Brittain wrote to Holtby to suggest that she and Gordon and Winifred (and the expected baby and its nurse) set up a permanent household together. Although in public Brittain would always emphasise the radical aspects of the shared household, in this letter of May 1927 she advances a much more traditional reason: the shared household won't be 'at all queer', Vera comments: 'Half the married couples in this town seem to have a sister living with them, and you are more to me than any sister.'[57] In effect, Brittain was suggesting that Holtby assume, albeit in a modern guise, the role of spinster sister living as maiden aunt in her married sister's household. Holtby accepted.

Brittain's first pregnancy was relatively uneventful – throughout it, she worked on the collection of essays that became her book *Women's Work in Modern England* – but John Edward, born on 21 December 1927, came three weeks early and his was a difficult birth, for both mother and baby. Brittain for years after harboured considerable anger at the way in which the birth was handled. She had decided when she first became pregnant that she would not have the baby at home, but in a nursing home or hospital.[58] The nursing home in which she gave birth appears to have been chosen by her parents. While it was fashionable and comfortable, Brittain felt that the handling of her labour was bungled by the nursing home staff and by the physician. For one thing, she did not receive anaesthesia, which she regarded as a medical advance to which as a modern woman she had a right,[59] and she also felt that the physician had taken insufficient care of the frail infant during his first three months, defeating her attempts to breast-feed him, and dealing inappropriately with his initial failure to thrive.

Fortunately, by the spring Brittain found in the Chelsea Babies Club an alternative to her parents' style of medical care. In an article she wrote for *Time and Tide*, Brittain called this well-baby clinic, staffed with a physician and a nurse, to which subscribers paid a fee of five guineas a year, 'the first welfare centre for middle-class mothers'.[60] To her personally it meant a great deal: she credited the care and advice she received there with saving John Edward's life.[61] Brittain's doubts about her 'maternal instincts', and her cool detachment towards maternity vanished with John Edward's birth. She loved both her children deeply, and during John's first troubled months she suffered what she herself described as 'anguish and anxiety'.[62] The Chelsea Babies' Club appears to have offered her not only guidance and medical advice she trusted, but sociability and a sense of connection with other mothers who, like herself, were attempting to fashion new patterns for motherhood.

The Chelsea Babies' Club represented for Brittain one crucial aspect of modern feminist motherhood: the recognition that it should be *informed*. She believed that the traditional view that motherhood was instinctive had been proved wrong. As she said publicly, 'mothercraft is a science which has to be taught'.[63] She pointed out that reformers had recognized the necessity of teaching working-class women how to mother and had set up infant welfare centres to assist them. Brittain insisted that middle-class mothers like herself also needed this help, and she not only used the Chelsea Babies' Club for both her children, she also publicized its work and served on its board of management.[64]

In our own era, when a mistrust of the medical profession and of the claims to expertise advanced by the social sciences is a dominant element in feminist discourse, and indeed in radical discourse generally, Brittain's faith in the value of professional expertise may seem naive and even conservative. But in the context of the 1920s and 1930s, it was part of the postwar revolt against Victorianism. Moreover, Brittain did not regard a reliance on professional expertise as an anti-feminist acceptance of a male-dominated intellectual establishment: she advocated that women not only use experts, but that they become experts; she herself sought out women professionals wherever possible;[65] and she believed that 'science' was on the side of advanced, feminist motherhood. For example, in the interwar years she was an advocate of Freudian and Adlerian psychiatry, believing that this new 'science' supported women's autonomy and the rights of mothers to independent careers:

> how many children have had a better education and a surer start in life owing to the income earned by their mother . . . how many children have suffered either physically or psychologically through the absence of their mothers for five or six hours of the day? How many have been injured even more by their mother's incessant, dominating presence? Answers . . . could very readily be provided through psychiatry, the newest science of child welfare, which is as yet little known in this country, though it is already practised to a considerable extent in America.[66]

Brittain also believed that an organization like the Chelsea Babies' Club represented women's voices in a male-dominated world. In a letter to her husband written in January 1932, she tells him that imperial politics are much less important than the needs of women:

> [W]hether we lose or help India matters much less than whether we establish a National Maternity Service. Biological values are far more important in the long run than political; though no man ever thinks so . . . My Babies' Club is not so trivial as you imagine: only it represents the application of female values in a world where all values that have been thought to matter have hitherto been male.[67]

From the time of John Edward's birth until her children were grown, Brittain not only wrote about but also successfully met the challenge of combining motherhood and career. However, the task was not without its conflicts and contradictions. As she wrote to Winifred soon after Shirley's birth in 1930 and when the family was just settling into the Chelsea house that Holtby, Catlin and Brittain had bought together in anticipation of the addition of a second child: 'If only I could eliminate the constant wish to work . . . and cease chasing work-periods which don't materialise. . . . I can imagine nothing much pleasanter and more satisfying than the care of these little things. . . .'[68]

The most difficult and obviously pressing of these conflicts arose not so much from motherhood itself, but from the burdensome tasks associated with creating a household suitable for children. When she and Winifred had lived together in Bloomsbury and Maida Vale and even when she and Gordon had lived together in Ithaca during the first year of their marriage, she had genuinely enjoyed a relatively austere style of housekeeping (austere, at least by her parents' standards) but the children made a difference. As we have already seen, Brittain believed that it was her duty to create for her future children a household informed by a post-war version of the Edwardian upper middle-class rituals of 'decency and order' and of intellectual and aesthetic 'civilization' that had been part of her own family of origin. Rearing children in 'chaos', as she had put it in her 1927 article on eugenic birth control, would be socially irresponsible.[69]

But how much 'order' did one need to produce 'decency' and avoid 'chaos'? This was a difficult personal dilemma for Brittain. On the one hand, she strongly believed that women in the post-Victorian age should free themselves from the trammels of an 'aggressive' domesticity that for their grandmothers and mothers had been an 'end in itself', rather than 'something to be disposed of and thankfully laid aside', as she put it in a 1927 *Manchester Guardian* article entitled 'Wasted Women: the Tyranny of Houses'.[70] But she herself had tendencies to fall back into the trap of just such an 'aggressive' domesticity. While she never saw domesticity as 'an end in itself', during the years when the children were young and she was at her most productive as a writer she often felt overwhelmed by household cares. In part, this was because she did indeed shoulder the primary responsibility for managing the household, but given the extensive household help she, Catlin and Holtby employed,[71] she was not faced with the 'double day' that most twentieth-century employed mothers have had to contend with. Why, then, did she so often feel so burdened? While Brittain, both as a public figure and in private, did genuinely wish to escape from the onus of the Edwardian standards of her youth, her memories of her childhood household and her adult relationship with her mother – who throughout these years lived in nearby Kensington, and continued there to maintain the elaborate household routine she had established in Buxton – made this difficult. For example, although Brittain as a young girl had hated her mother's ritual of spring cleaning, she continued it in her own household, completely turning everything upside down for a week or two, sending the children away if possible, and putting aside her own work to assist the paid help.[72] Thus, while she had radical ideas about household reform, supporting for example 'the substitution of co-operative housekeeping, nurseries and schools for the present wasteful system of small exclusive families',[73] and she might actually have enjoyed such an arrangement had it been available to her, she found it difficult in practice to escape from expectations – society's and her own – concerning the domestic role of the bourgeois wife.

There were also contradictions between Brittain's and Catlin's political ideology and the family's style of life: by the time they established their family, both of them had become Labour Party supporters[74] and they moved in Labour Party circles, but they employed domestic help and used fee-paying schools for their children. The contradiction between Brittain's and Catlin's support for Labour and their privileged lives was not, of course, unique to them. Historians agree that Britain in the 1920s and 1930s was almost as divided by class cleavage as it had been at the turn of the century. The contradictions between Brittain's beliefs about appropriate household arrangements and childrearing practices and her beliefs about social equality, as well as the contradictions between her beliefs and her actions, were typical of well-to-do intellectuals who were Labour Party supporters during the interwar decades.[75]

Brittain did at times wrestle with these contradictions. She was, for example, thoroughly aware of the fact that any domestic burdens she had to contend with were minor compared with those faced by working-class women. When John Edward was a baby,

> often . . . I thought to myself: This is what nine-tenths of the mothers in this country go through – not once, but again and again. Even now, I don't really know what they suffer. It was just a mistake that I was given no alleviation for the pain, and could come back to a pleasant home with people to help me. But they have to be up in a few days, and do everything for the baby and everyone else, and run badly-planned cottages better suited to animals than men. And government after government insists that we can't afford a national maternity service. . . .[76]

Brittain also suffered considerable ambivalence over planning for John's education, an ambivalence about which she found it impossible to be completely frank when narrating her own story. Only two years after John Edward's birth, both his parents were spending considerable energy worrying about his educational future. As Brittain put it in *Testament of Experience*, 'In our letters that spring [1929] G. and I discussed his [John Edward's] education with well-justified confidence that he would now grow up to need the best we could give him. . . .'[77] This comment comes in the midst of discussions of Brittain's participation in the 1929 Congress of the World League for Sexual Reform and her Labour Party activities. What it conceals is that 'the best we could give him' under discussion between the two of them was Eton, and that in 1929 both Catlin and Brittain went to considerable trouble to secure a place for John at a 'good' house at Eton.[78] As their correspondence reveals, this was not an easy project. While Catlin was an Oxford graduate and a respectable academic, his father had been an undistinguished clergyman and he himself had gone to St Paul's, which, while a good school, did not have the cachet of Eton, Harrow or Winchester, as Brittain herself noted:

> from what I can gather from discussing the matter in general with several people, it is quite a performance to get anyone whose father or family has no connection with them put down for either Eton, Harrow or Winchester. They are apparently quite different in this respect from the secondary public schools . . .[79]

Why did these two intellectuals, both Labour Party members, make such plans for their son? From their correspondence, it is clear that while they might object in principle to educational privilege, both parents believed that Eton, the country's most exclusive boys' public school, would offer their son the best possible opportunities for a successful life. Brittain herself, however, did have some doubts about the project. Her most serious questions concerned feminism, rather than class privilege:

> The one thing I fear most about Eton for John is that he will associate there with the sons of just the kind of men . . . who are traditionally contemptuous of and deceitful to their women – yet the one thing I want most is that he should grow up to know no difference (in status and respectworthiness) between women and men . . .[80]

During the ensuing years, Brittain considered a number of alternative schools for John,[81] continuing to be ambivalent about Eton. And she came out publicly against certain evils associated not merely with Eton but with boys' public schools in general. In 1935, when she was moving towards pacifism, she wrote an article on Officers' Training Corps:

> My views on the subject of Training Corps in public schools have become so definite that I cannot imagine any headmaster who advocates this insidious form of militarism as an education in 'manliness' welcoming me as a desirable parent. Nor can I picture myself, if my own wishes were the sole factor to be considered, sending my son to a school which regarded the O.T.C. as anything but an antediluvian though dangerous form of killing valuable time.[82]

But her own wishes were not 'the sole factor to be considered'. Clearly, his father at least was fearful of experimenting with his son's education. In 1938 Brittain and Catlin were still planning to send John to Eton. In the end, after he had spent three years during the war in America, he went to Harrow.[83]

Although Brittain suffered much ambivalence over John's education, she had fewer doubts about what she wanted for Shirley, and it appears that it was primarily she, rather than Catlin, who made the decisions about their daughter's education. She expressed her opinions on girls' education in an article written soon after Shirley's birth:

> At present the majority of girls' schools cater either for marriage or a job. So girls intended for marriage are turned into expensive parasites by private schools . . . while the future teacher or doctor goes to high school and college equipped with a felt hat, a macintosh, a hockey stick, and no frills. One type . . . specialises in charm at the expense of intelligence, and the other concentrates on intelligence at the expense of charm. Neither type . . . prepares its pupils for future motherhood . . . Success and appreciation await the school which will honestly prepare girls to make the best of both the worlds that men have always had, and women are now demanding.[84]

By 1932 Brittain had already begun to think that St. Paul's School for Girls, a London day school, with its reputation for providing its pupils with an excellent preparation for further education, would be suitable for Shirley; and after the children's wartime absence in America, this was indeed the school that Shirley attended.[85] Like the great majority of other left-leaning upper middle-class intellectuals of their period, Brittain and Catlin never seriously considered the possibility of using the state school system for either child.[86]

From 1927 until Winifred's death in 1935, Brittain, Holtby and Catlin lived in the joint household that the three of them had decided would be a solution to the needs of each. How did it work out in practice? In *Testament of Friendship* and *Testament of Experience*, the two autobiographical narratives that deal with this period, Brittain emphasises the joy that the arrangement brought to the two women: '[w]ith its babies, its books, its toys, its friends, and the companionship of both G. and Winifred, the household in Glebe Place was the nearest thing to complete happiness that I have ever known or ever hope to know. I believe that Winifred felt the same.'[87]

In *Testament of Friendship*, Brittain was also concerned to emphasise that the household was not a sexual *ménage-à-trois*:

> The unusual domestic arrangement which suited us so well gave rise, I was assured, to a plentiful crop of rumours. Chelsea is notoriously the home of the unconventional, but if most of its myths have as innocent an origin as those circulated about ourselves they are indeed tales told by an idiot, full of sound and fury.[88]

Brittain's intention was to present the arrangement as unusual, but in what she saw as its truest sense, namely as an experiment which provided all three adults with companionship; which provided her, as the mother of the two children, with a household arrangement that allowed her to work as well as to mother; and that provided stability and order for the two children.

The central figure in the household was Brittain. She was the one who lived in the flat in Nevern Place, Earl's Court, and then in the Chelsea house most of the time, using it not only as her home and the home for the children, but also as her work space. She was the one who was primarily responsible for the hiring of household help. Winifred did make her home with Brittain, Catlin and the children, but in fact she was often away, either travelling or visiting other friends or her family. Moreover, from the beginning of her illness in 1931 until her death in 1935, she spent a considerable amount of time either in nursing homes or living in the country. And throughout these years, Catlin was away from January to June in Ithaca.

The fact that it was primarily Brittain's house is reflected in the way in which it was financed. It appears that her father, Arthur Brittain, put up half the capital for the purchase.[89] The basic expenses were shared between Brittain, Catlin and Holtby, but Brittain normally assumed all of the burden of the Catlin–Brittain day-to-day expenses when Catlin was in the United States.[90] The Chelsea house was considerably larger than the Earl's Court flat to which they had moved in 1927 before John Edward's birth. In *Testament of Experience*, she would call it 'a tall ugly house with an attractive view of studios in Glebe Place, Chelsea'.[91] It was certainly big enough to allow room for several servants. By 1932 these included the housekeeper, Amy Francis. After she married Charles Burnett, the two worked as a couple in the household for many years. There was also a parlour maid, a nurse for the children when they were very young, and later a governess.

It was also big enough to allow for entertaining. When writing of their life during these years in *Testament of Friendship*, Brittain emphasised the social activity they generated in the Chelsea house: 'There were dinner parties and "At Homes" to which we invited crowds of a hundred and more....'[92] Who came to these parties? Brittain's own social and professional networks overlapped with those established by Winifred and Gordon. There were writers, mostly women and mostly active feminists, many of whom were connected with *Time and Tide*. These writers included Rebecca West, Naomi Mitchison, Storm Jameson and Phyllis Bentley. Then there were old acquaintances extending back to their Oxford years, or friends of even longer standing, like Clare Leighton. And there were social reformers: people like Maud Royden and Emmeline and Frederick Pethick-Lawrence; and Labour Party activists like Ellen Wilkinson and Monica Whately and Frank and Winifred Horrabin.[93]

Brittain enjoyed this social activity, but more than mere enjoyment was involved. As discussed in an earlier chapter, the Holtby–Brittain friendship was always to some extent a partnership through which the two women launched their respective literary careers. For Brittain and Catlin, and to a lesser extent for Holtby, the social life connected with literary London continued to be important as 'business'. All three of them believed that they were involved in a campaign to overcome the disadvantages of a relatively 'obscure' family background. Unlike Naomi Mitchison, who had been born a Haldane, or Virginia Woolf, the daughter of Leslie Stephen, Brittain, Holtby and Catlin were first-generation members of Britain's literary establishment. As a revealing comment from Brittain's diary indicates, all three of them were acutely aware of this fact. Brittain records having a 'long argument' with

> W. &. G. (re her first chapter in *Virginia Woolf*) about whether it was better to be born the member of a cultural aristocracy (like Virginia and Naomi) or to be like W. & myself, forced to make one's way out of a wrong environment into a right one & become a little vulgar in the process. Personally I cannot think it anything but an incomparable advantage to have been absorbing platonic philosophy & acquiring a respect for scientific truth at an age at which I was wasting my time & ruining my taste by reading Longfellow & Mrs. Henry Wood while W. endeavoured to find scope for the activity of her mind in lavatory copies of the *Ladies' Realm*.[94]

For herself, until 1933, Brittain regarded the creation of social and professional contacts as part of her strategy for achieving success. The greatly expanded circle to which she gained access after the 1933 publication of *Testament of Youth* would serve as an affirmation of her success.

If the association between Brittain, Holtby and Catlin was a triangular one in which Brittain occupied the apex, the triangle comprised three separate relationships: one between the two women, one between Brittain and Catlin, and one between Catlin and Holtby. By the late 1920s, the very stability of the living arrangement appears to have blunted the spiritual intimacy between the two women. Success was partly accountable for this diminished intensity. Even in their Bloomsbury and Maida Vale days, Brittain and Holtby had not had an exclusive relationship. Both had maintained friendships they shared and each had her own private relationships. However, then they had been two young outsiders looking in together on London's literary world. But by the late 1920s both had gained a foothold in a number of literary, political and professional circles, and this meant that they had less time for each other. By this time, Holtby seemed to Brittain to have more connections than she did:

> I have a strange feeling . . . that you and I now live week after week in the same house, I so absorbed in adoring a husband & son in the intervals of my work and you so absorbed in running round with friends of varying degrees of celebrity in the intervals of yours, that we never really see each other at all . . . You are much more self-confident than you once were, but then I am probably much more 'married' . . . which is even more objectionable.[95]

As we have already seen, in some ways Holtby's position in the household was reminiscent of the situation of a Victorian maiden aunt. But this similarity with earlier patterns should not be pushed too far. Brittain never wished or expected to exploit Holtby as she might have expected to exploit a dependent sister of an earlier generation. She respected Holtby's work, Holtby was of course not dependent in any material way on her, and, generous as Holtby was, she did not intend to be exploited in the traditional way. Still, in her narrative representations of the connection between Holtby and the children, Brittain does present Holtby as a surrogate aunt. 'No "childless spinster" was ever better acquainted with babies than Winifred', Brittain relates, and she goes on to describe Winifred's participation in John Edward's arrival:

> 'Oh darling! you are clever!' she cried with excited relief . . . and she and G. walked back arm in arm to Nevern Place to celebrate John Edward's arrival. On her next visit she picked up the human atom in her arms. . . . 'His head's just like a pussy-willow,' she observed . . . and from that moment she became his discreet but devoted slave.[96]

In part, in passages like these Brittain was at pains to counter the anti-feminist sentiments of the period which attempted to define the 'childless spinster' as neurotic and dangerous.[97] But there is also ample evidence to indicate that both Vera and Winifred did indeed assume that Winifred would be close to Vera's children: 'Won't you feel the baby is yours too?', Brittain asks in December 1926, when she was soon to give birth to John Edward.[98] And Holtby did in fact help with John and Shirley in essential ways, for example supervising the children's care when Brittain and Catlin went on holiday, or when Brittain toured North America in 1934 after the publication of *Testament of Youth*.

In the late 1920s and early 1930s, then, the friendship between Brittain, and Holtby was sustained, and each woman continued to be the other's most essential friend even though both felt free to seek out additional close friendships with other women. For Brittain the most important such additional friendship was with the novelist Margaret Storm Jameson. Born in Yorkshire in 1891, Jameson's childhood and youth had been far more painful and tumultuous than Brittain's. By the time she was twenty-four, she had entered into an early and unfortunate marriage and had given birth to her only child.[99] When Jameson first made overtures of friendship to Brittain in 1927, she was living in London with her second husband, the writer Guy Chapman. Jameson quickly became the friend with whom Brittain could share feelings of frustration about the difficulties of combining career with family life. Both women wrote about this topic for the popular press, and both knew that the challenges were greater than either could acknowledge in print. As Jameson put it in one of her early letters to Brittain:

> I suppose that by good management and by keeping enough of one's head and heart out of the career, one can manage a husband and even the most exacting of careers. I loathe domesticity myself and I couldn't even contemplate 'marriage as a career'. But add a baby to the affair, and . . . something has to go, either the career or the child. . . . You see, it's neither as easy as my smug articles in the Evening Standard pretend, nor so simple as the Time and Tiders imagine.[100]

From these beginnings the friendship flourished, and in the late 1920s and early 1930s Jameson offered Brittain something that even Holtby could not provide: comradeship with another woman writer who was attempting to combine marriage, motherhood and career.

During these same years, the marriage between Brittain and Catlin took shape. Because they each wrote long letters to the other during their annual periods of separation, their voluminous correspondence affords an extraordinarily intimate and extensive record of a marital relationship. They wrote to each other about books they had read, about feminism, about socialism, about peace activism. They wrote at great length about their relationship to each other, about household affairs, about their acquaintances and their friends, and about the children. In her letters, Brittain usually addressed her husband as 'Dearest' or 'Darling' (even when she was annoyed with him) and signed the letters 'Much love, V.' or 'Much love my dearest dear – Ever, Vera'. Catlin, who in public was a formal, even unapproachable person, had in private a sentimental streak. In his letters to his wife he used openings such as 'My darling and adored little love', and signed them 'Adoringly', to which he added not his name but his initials, 'G.E.G.C.'.

These letters, touching as they do on so many subjects, provide a wealth of information not only about this unusually intelligent, active and successful couple, but about the intellectual and social climate of the period. For example, during the winter and spring of 1929, when Brittain was at work on her 'marriage' books, she and Catlin carried on a vigorous correspondence about the nature of marriage and sexuality, interspersing their consideration of the intellectual issues with a frank discussion of their own relationship. (It was in the course of this series of letters that they had the exchange about sexuality, mentioned earlier in this chapter.) Brittain drew on Catlin's knowledge as an academic, asking him for suggestions about what she ought to read. In March 1929, for example, she remarks:

> Must I read Ellis' 'Sexual Psychology'? . . . I can't read everything. . . . I don't believe some of the writers – e.g. Mrs Russell – read anything much, but are simply acute observers. . . . But if you think Ellis really worth having, purchase . . .[101]

In the spring of 1930 they were still sharing information about each other's early experience of sexuality. For example, Vera writes on 19 May 1930:

> Darling love – I was much interested in your letter of May 7th, dealing chiefly with the question of adolescence – The actual technical information I had already acquired from Tenenbaum's 'Riddle of Sex' – a very useful book that – but much of your own experience was new to me, though some of it you had told me before – the episode of the cook undressing would not, I imagine, have made any impression upon you had you been quite accustomed to seeing your parents in a state of

> nudity or semi-nudity – a practice which Havelock Ellis & others recommend for parents & children . . .[102]

In the early 1930s, they often corresponded about Labour Party politics and socialism. Catlin comments to her in early January 1932: 'I never can persuade myself that socialism has any very real significance to you as a matter of passionate faith.'[103] She replies vehemently in the next letter:

> Why do you say that socialism has no significance to me as a matter of passionate faith? What – to be explicit – actually is socialism nowadays, and how does one express 'passionate faith'? The two 'causes' I care for most are the abolition of war and the further progress of feminism; neither one is compatible with the mode of privilege and dictatorship by persons with no responsibility towards society. It will always be to the interest of some capitalists to have war and to the interests of all capitalism to keep women a subject class, docile and inexpensive.[104]

One thread that runs throughout their correspondence is the deep concern each shared about their children. When they were babies, Brittain loved them in an intense and immediate way, and she touchingly tried to convey to their absent father her own closeness to them and the delight she took in them. In a letter written when John was a baby, she tells her husband that she accidentally pricked him with a 'nappie pin . . . a thing which I have always been afraid of doing' but says he was 'a perfect saint . . . he really is a beautiful child'.[105] Throughout the months of separation each year she sent him photographs of the children[106] and described what they were doing or saying.[107] Gordon, for his part, could write: 'Love the babas for me: they are nice babas. . . .'[108]

But their love for the children, while genuine, expressed itself often as anxiety. As we have already seen, as a journalist Brittain publicly affirmed that educated people ought to have children and that when they did, they had an obligation to instil in their offspring the upper middle-class virtues of order and 'civilization'. In private both she and Catlin placed great importance, as parents, on encouraging their children to achieve intellectual and social success. Their preoccupation with the public school that John would attend has already been noted, a preoccupation stemming in part at least from the fact that he was a boy, for while Gordon Catlin was avowedly feminist, he did harbour conventional aspirations for his only son: 'John I suspect may prove a child of intelligence', he writes somewhat pompously in

February 1932. 'There are some signs of it. He is worth taking trouble over and spending money on . . . I shall begin to take him in hand myself this year: he ought to be able to concentrate enough. And he should learn to ride, to swim, perhaps to play if he is musical, and be introduced to the great at an early age so that he will grow with natural poise.' Catlin does at least conclude here with a query about the real John, rather than his own projections about the ideal adult this five-year-old boy was to become. 'How goes the tricycle', he asks.[109] While Brittain was more deeply committed to sexual egalitarianism than Catlin and as concerned with Shirley's intellectual development as with John's, like their father she focused on the children's future much of the time, rather than on the present, and her ambitions for them were great: 'Tenenbaum's "Riddle of Sex" . . . contains some interesting facts', she writes. 'Did you know that half the world's leaders have been produced by only 1 per cent of the population (i.e. by families like the Haldanes . . . Mosleys, Galtons, Darwins, Huxleys) . . . I wonder if you & I, in spite of our undistinguished ancestry, have sufficient vital ability . . . to found a famous family. . . .'[110]

Another constant thread that runs through this correspondence is the annoyance and disappointment both parties felt towards the other because of their annual separations. Even in public, she called 'semi-detached marriage' 'not a universal solution but a possible one'.[111] In the intimacy of their private correspondence both acknowledged the stresses and strains: 'I do think that . . . the present arrangement is very unsatisfactory', Brittain writes in 1929. 'As you know, very few marriages would survive it; ours does so because you and I are an unusually successful partnership (at least I still think so and I hope you do). . . .'[112]

The damage to the relationship caused by Catlin's extramarital sexual activity has already been discussed. Another major cause of tension arose from Brittain's sense of grievance that it was she rather than her husband who bore the brunt of the responsibility for children and household. Brittain never expected a completely even-handed sharing of parenting responsibilities. Even in public, she assumed without question that if a couple attempted 'semi-detached' marriage the children would be 'for obvious reasons, under the care of their mother'.[113] But in practice she resented the freedom that Gordon enjoyed during his periods in Ithaca, and she resented his failure to recognize just how much time and effort she devoted to the care of children and household. They had a bitter exchange about this in January 1932, when she and Winifred went for a brief holiday together and Gordon took charge of the household. After Vera and Winifred had been away for a few days, he wrote a letter to Vera in which, while his intention was clearly to offer helpful advice, his tone was injudiciously complacent: '[E]verything has gone as well with you away as when you are here: children, meals, everything. My advice is to cut responsibilities to a minimum – they are often a form of giving oneself a good excuse from the travail of writing. . . .' Be 'careless and slovenly and slipshod' about the household, he urges: 'Middle class and artistic virtues are bluntly inconsistent and always have been.'[114] Brittain was infuriated. Anticipating Second Wave feminist analysis concerning gender and household responsibilities, she points out to him that he is ignoring the planning she had to do prior to her departure (for example spending 'a whole evening going carefully through the entire menu for 10 days with Amy . . . etc.') and ignoring the effort she devotes to working well with their household help: 'they regard me, not you, as their employer, and . . . therefore your slackness & indifference would make little difference to them, but mine would have immediate repercussions in inefficiency'. She also roundly dismisses his suggestion that she should let the household arrangements deteriorate into a Bohemian slovenliness. 'The solution does not lie in selective inefficiency', she says, 'but in so changing the system that the community itself shoulders three-quarters of the domestic jobs that now fall on individual women . . . I suppose I shan't be alive in that time though my writings may help to bring it about.'[115]

The couple also experienced conflicts over the furthering of their respective careers. Up until Brittain's success in 1933, building a career involved frustration and disappointment for both. While each was often supportive of the other and each remained committed to the other's achievements, in their letters both Brittain and Catlin often dispensed judgemental advice to the other, and on each side offence was often given and taken. Brittain not infrequently blamed her husband for at least part of her frustration and disappointment at having achieved less than she had planned. In January 1933 she wrote: 'Of the half-dozen books I was then [in 1924–5] planning to write, not one has materialised . . . since the spring of 1924 – *nine* years – I have published nothing but two glorified pamphlets. Conclusion; a husband & the production of a family demands a heavy price. . . .'[116]

Catlin too suffered from disappointment. From the perspective of distance, it is clear that Sir G.E.G. Catlin had a long and distinguished career as an academic. In addition to his years as a professor in the

Department of Government at Cornell University, he taught at McGill University in Montreal. Beginning with *The Science and Method of Politics* in 1927, he published continuously from the 1920s to the 1960s on political theory and political science. He also was an important Labour Party figure. He achieved a knighthood. But in the 1920s and 1930s he was a bitter and frustrated man. He felt exiled at Cornell, and he deeply desired an academic post in Britain: the fact that this never materialized he attributed to the opposition of his enemies, chief amongst whom he placed Harold Laski.[117] Years later, Brittain would publicly support her husband's perception that personal enmities had damaged his career and she too blamed Laski: 'Laski's subtle but determined opposition remained a permanent obstacle to G.'s chances of obtaining one of the few academic posts which England had to offer in his subject. . . .'[118] In private, she did much to defend his interests. She wrote letters, she advised and consoled him, she made contacts for him. In taking his part, she goes so far as to tell him in one letter that she has heard that Laski (who was Jewish) will not support him because 'whenever a post is going that you could fill, he has some Jew in mind for it and works for the Jew'.[119]

Although she did help him, Brittain frequently became exasperated with Catlin's feelings of disappointed entitlement. ('Oh, my love, why *cannot* you be lucid and explicit even where your own interests are most deeply concerned!' she writes, criticizing the draft of a letter he had written about a possible job opening.[120]) And while she followed up many of his requests to read his manuscripts; to get him books to review; to get his own books reviewed by the right people in the right places;[121] and in the 1930s to help him find a winnable Labour constituency, she did not hide from him that she frequently found his commissions irritating. 'Really, I am *not* your private secretary!!!'[122] she says in one letter.

In my discussion of the marriage of Brittain's parents in Part I of this book, I made the point that Arthur's and Edith's marriage was in part a business partnership designed to foster their upward social mobility as a couple and as a family. While Vera Brittain had no wish to recreate her parents' values, the old patterns reasserted themselves. Gordon and Vera, like Arthur and Edith, were acutely concerned with improving their social status. The Brittains had sent Edward to Uppingham: Gordon and Vera devoted considerable thought and effort to getting John Edward 'put down' for a good house at Eton. But for the younger couple, the issues surrounding status and social achievement were much more complex than they had been for the late-Victorian Arthur and Edith. The Brittains' progress up the social ladder had involved no ambivalence. Their goal had been to rise from the middle to the upper-middle class, and to achieve undisputed gentility. Their elegant, successful daughter was a supreme token of their success. But their daughter – and their son-in-law – did not desire anything so simple. Brittain and Catlin both wanted success and fame. Brittain wanted literary success, which not only meant publishing successful books, but also being accepted into the inner circles of English intellectual and literary life. Catlin wanted academic and political success, which meant achieving an academic post at the London School of Economics or somewhere equally prestigious, and gaining enough influence within the Labour Party to be offered a nomination in a constituency that would give him a genuine chance of election to the House of Commons. In the England of the interwar period, Brittain and Catlin quite correctly realized that the achievement of such goals did not depend entirely on talent, ambition and effort. Those virtues counted for much, but success and power were still inextricably linked to the older social order. The power that the hierarchies of class still wielded is reflected in the unpleasant snobbery that mars the private writings of Virginia Woolf, who, for example, used her wit to sneer at Winifred Holtby's social background, referring to her as 'the daughter of a Yorkshire farmer [who] learnt to read, I'm told, while minding the pigs'.[123] It is in this context that we must see Brittain's and Catlin's sometimes obsessive, often unseemly, scramble to achieve recognition from those they defined as powerful.

The third side of the triangular relationship in the shared household was that between Holtby and Catlin. The two did develop a close and amicable relationship, but it was never independent of the ties that each had to Brittain. In her published writings, Brittain encapsulated her portrayal of the connection between the two in an anecdote she relates in *Testament of Friendship* about how Winifred rescued Gordon's forgotten gloves after their wedding:

> One of the many small obligations was the recovery of the gloves which G. had left in church. Thanks to his incorrigible absentmindedness, Winifred's genuine affection for him had begun to acquire an almost maternal quality. Those gloves were the first of a long series of miscellaneous objects which she was to spend quite a large proportion of her life in helping him to retrieve.[124]

The tone of this symbolic vignette is not inaccurate. Winifred, while deeply unhappy at first about Vera's marriage, was determined to make the best of it. This meant not only a resolute commitment to seeing the best in Catlin, but the forging of an alliance with him in which Brittain became the fragile being who needed protection from both of them. Holtby's and Brittain's early private name for Brittain was 'very small very dear love', which Brittain abbreviated to 'vsvdl' when signing her letters to Holtby.[125] As early as their engagement in 1924, Winifred and Gordon – in their correspondence at least – wrote to each other as if they shared their 'very small very dear love'. In September, when Catlin had to return to America, Holtby telegraphed: 'Bon Voyage will keep good guard Winifred'.[126] In November 1926, when Gordon was in Ithaca enduring his first bleak winter alone, Winifred wrote:

> My dear Gordon. I marvel not at the gloom of your letter but at the frequent cheerfulness of yours to the child [Brittain]. I imagine this to be a damnable year for you. . . . Nevertheless, pas de resignation . . . or rather, resign, but don't be resigned. We must and shall get you home. The child longs for you, and is sometimes tempted to take the next boat out, but that would be a) impracticable when she is just digging herself in with the Children of This World among editors and the like – b) a surrender of those principles which she loves better than her peace of mind . . .

She urges him to come home, if at all possible – 'I cannot believe that Cornell can be completely good for you, and it is obviously fatal to Vera' – and concludes: 'with all my heart, I wish you home again. Partly because I want to see Vera happy. Partly because you are one of the few people who make the vulgarities and follies of humanity tolerable. Partly because as a feminist I want to see the audacious yet wholly sane experiment which you and Vera are making succeed triumphantly.'[127]

Holtby, it appears, managed at the same time to be intimate with Brittain and to forge links with Catlin and to do this while only rarely causing either Brittain to experience jealousy or Catlin to feel excluded. This was no easy achievement. Brittain, even though she wanted the two to love each other, did occasionally feel insecure about their friendship. Soon after their engagement, Brittain wrote to Holtby: 'You and Gordon both make me feel a little, superficial, suburban thing; something that has never really thought & felt, something immature in spirit, mind & body . . . How strangely you understand him',[128] and such feelings of doubt and insecurity would recur from time to time. But even though Winifred could make jokes to Vera about how 'if Gordon were a Mormon' they could both have married him[129] and could arrange with Gordon to buy birthday underwear for Vera on his behalf[130] and could be the invariable recipient of Vera's complaints about Gordon, she was able to act as a successful third presence in the marriage. As usual, this delicate balance was achieved because of Winifred's tact and determination, and it cost her some pain and, we may surmise, considerable self-repression.

It will be recalled that in writing of it, Brittain said that their time together in the Chelsea house in Glebe Place 'was the nearest thing to complete happiness that I have ever known or ever hope to know'.[131] The vicissitudes and contradictions documented in this chapter do not vitiate that conclusion. As Catlin wrote to Brittain in 1929:

> Have you noticed how tremendously we gain by living in a co-working and like minded group. – How Winifred supplies a cooler, detached element when our own relations grow too emotional and 'nervy' – how we gain rather than lose by departing from the 2+ children-in-a-household system.[132]

Catlin's and Brittain's experiment in 'semi-detached marriage' and the less self-consciously experimental joint household did genuinely represent a successful attempt to solve some of the personal and familial dilemmas with which educated professional women and men were faced in the interwar decades.

Part IV

'Having Crossed the Rubicon': the 1930s and After

10

The Writing of *Testament of Youth*

For nearly a decade I have wanted, with a growing sense of urgency, to write something which would show what the whole War and post-war period – roughly, from the years 1914 to about 1925 – has meant to the men and women of my generation, the generation of those boys and girls who grew up just before the War broke out.

Vera Brittain always intended to write about the First World War. Indeed, all through the war years she had written about it, either in her diary or in her letters home. As a young girl she took up writing because it came as easily to her as talking, and from 1912, when she began to keep her 'Reflective Record', writing was the main means through which she made sense of her experience. Her voluminous wartime diary and her letters home from Malta and France helped her to carry on during that extraordinary and difficult period. And she knew even then that, later on, they would become material from which she would fashion finished work.

In 1918, immediately after the war, she attempted to use her nursing experience at Etaples and her friendship with Faith Moulson as the basis for the novel 'Folly's Vineyard'. But, as described earlier, she was dissatisfied with it, and put it aside as a failed experiment.

Brittain did make an attempt to edit her war diaries sometime between 1922 and 1924, in response to a publisher's competition, but when 'Chronicle of Youth' was not selected she once again put the war aside as a literary subject.[2] Brittain hoped to write books of which she could be truly proud and which would bring her fame, but she was both hard headed and practical. As a professional she wrote to be read and she wrote to be published. Since publishers and the reading public did not appear to want wartime material she turned in her journalism and in her fiction to the many other topics that interested her and for which there was a market.

10
The Writing of *Testament of Youth*

For nearly a decade I have wanted, with a growing sense of urgency, to write something which would show what the whole War and post-war period – roughly, from the years leading up to 1914 until about 1925 – has meant to the men and women of my generation, the generation of those boys and girls who grew up just before the War broke out.[1]

Vera Brittain always intended to write about the First World War. Indeed, all through the war years she had written about it, either in her diary or in her letters home. As a young girl she took up writing because it came as easily to her as talking, and from 1912, when she began to keep her 'Reflective Record', writing was the main means through which she made sense of her experience. Her voluminous wartime diary and her letters home from Malta and France helped her to carry on during that extraordinary and difficult period. And she knew even then that, later on, they would become material from which she would fashion finished work.

Brittain wrote poetry during the war, publishing *Verses of a VAD* in 1918. Immediately after the war, she attempted to use her nursing experience at Étaples and her friendship with Faith Moulson as the basis for the novel 'Folly's Vineyard'. But, as discussed earlier, she was dissatisfied with it, and put it aside as a failed experiment.

Brittain did make an attempt to edit her war diaries sometime between 1922 and 1924, in response to a publisher's competition, but when 'Chronicle of Youth' was not selected she once again put the war aside as a literary subject.[2] Brittain hoped to write books of which she could be truly proud and which would bring her fame, but she was both hard-headed and practical. As a professional she wrote to be read and she wrote to be published. Since publishers and the reading public did not appear to want wartime material, she turned in her journalism and in her fiction to the many other themes that interested her and for which there was a market.

But towards the end of the 1920s, as Great War literature began to appear in profusion, the literary climate changed. The first volume of Sigfried Sassoon's autobiography, *Memoirs of a Foxhunting Man*, appeared in 1928, as did Edmund Blunden's *Undertones of War* and R.C. Sherriff's play *Journey's End*. Robert Graves's *Goodbye to All That* and Richard Aldington's *Death of a Hero* both appeared in 1929. With this outpouring of writing about the war, Brittain turned once again to an appraisal of her own wartime experience, partly because the wealth of discussion had the effect of stimulating her own thoughts on the subject, and partly because she realized that if she did not write her own war book soon, the moment for it would pass. As she wrote to Winifred Holtby, in late 1928, after reading Blunden 'I am reading "Undertones of War"; grave, dignified but perfectly simple and straightforward; why shouldn't I write one like that?'[3]

From her first thoughts about it in 1928, the book that became *Testament of Youth* was conceived of as a woman's book about the war. As an acute feminist observer, Brittain realized that she could produce a war book that would be substantially different from those that were receiving attention in the late 1920s, because even the best of them omitted any account of the experience of women. Some of them, indeed, made her very angry. In an article written in November 1929, she called attention to Richard Aldington's misogyny in *Death of a Hero*, which she characterized as pouring a 'cynical fury of scorn' on the wartime suffering of women.[4]

In Brittain's view a male writer, even if he were sympathetic, could not speak for women:

> The war was a phase of life in which women's experience did differ vastly from men's and I make no puerile claim to equality of suffering and service when I maintain that any picture of the war years is incomplete which omits those aspects that mainly concerned women.... The woman is still silent who, by presenting the war in its true perspective in her own life, will illuminate its meaning afresh for her generation.[5]

By 1931, when she wrote that comment, Brittain was hard at work on *Testament of Youth*. It is clear that she hoped she would be the woman who would illuminate the war's meaning, and that she would not have to be silent much longer.

Writing *Testament of Youth* took more courage, energy and time than anything she had yet attempted, but in it she redefined her ideas about serious writing, and in so doing she found an assured voice. Right through the 1920s Brittain thought of her prolific journalism as secondary to the more completely creative writing she hoped to do. This she had defined, from her first girlhood vision of herself as a writer, as the writing of novels, accepting the dictum that 'fiction is always greater than scholarship because it is entirely creative'.[6] She had written three novels, two of which had been published. Although *The Dark Tide*, with its Oxford theme, had a brief success as a 'sensation', she herself knew that both it and *Not Without Honour* were not what she had hoped they would be.

But while her goals remained unrealized, her thinking about the definition of the writer's craft and the relationship between writing and creativity was moving forward. Out of the experience of the war, and out of her commitment to feminism and peace, she had come to believe that all genuinely serious writing must serve a moral purpose, and moreover that it must do so not through sentimental moralizing, but through understanding and analysis. She knew that she wanted to bring her powers of understanding to an analysis of the connection between private experience and the wider historical context. When she explains in the Foreword to *Testament of Youth* that her intention is 'to write history in terms of personal life' she encapsulates the vision of autobiography that allowed her to release her creative energies.

Her working drafts of *Testament of Youth* reveal that she went about the task in a systematic way, assembling both historical and personal material. Brittain's Oxford training as an historian was of great value to her as she assembled the historical material, as was her League of Nations Union involvement through which she had developed a thorough acquaintance with politics and international affairs. She used her skills and knowledge in her preparation of the manuscript, doing research at the British Museum in newspapers and annual registers and at the British Red Cross Society. In assembling the personal material, she relied heavily on her own diaries and on letters she had written and received. Her notes reveal that as she planned chapters, she mapped out both a public and a private chronology. The book was indeed, as its subtitle indicates, an 'autobiographical study'.

Brittain began *Testament of Youth* in November 1929, completing the book early in 1933.[7] The writing was difficult not only in itself, but also because these years were among the busiest and most demanding of her personal life. There were the tensions in her marriage, there was Winifred's illness, and there were the children. She discovered she was pregnant with her second child soon after she began writing,[8] and consequently did little work on the book during 1930.

But by 1931, with the extended family now well settled into the Glebe Place house in Chelsea, she was working in earnest, and from then until its completion she was preoccupied with the book.

During much of 1931 and 1932 she felt discouraged, either about the circumstances under which she was working or about the book itself. Even with considerable household help she often felt overwhelmed by household cares. Writing to Winifred in 1931, from a holiday house in Sussex that she was sharing with another woman writer and her children, she says: 'My "Testament of Youth", if only I get the time . . . to do it properly, might be a great book. It is boiling in my mind and I shall become hysterical if I am prevented from getting down to it very much longer . . . if I am to continue sane I *must* have . . . a) a rest from the children & house and b) freedom & suitable circumstances to continue my book.' She adds that she must have a first draft done by Christmas, or she will be 'desperate'.[9]

Eighteen months later, even as she was actually about to finish the book, she writes, again to Winifred:

> My dear, I am more than ever convinced that . . . I ought *never* to have married, or at any rate never to have had children, and *certainly* not just at the age I did, if I ever wanted to achieve anything in this world. It's no good, I *cannot* organise a household: the management of maids simply paralyses me . . . my relations with Gordon seem all wrong because he completely disregards the extent to which it all worries me, wanting instead to add to the burden of domesticity (why can't he entertain in restaurants?) . . . and imagines I am cold and unresponsive to him when all that is really wrong is I am secretly meditating how to prevail on Amy to clean the steps without a devastating row . . . I *know* I can write . . . and instead . . . the one thing I can do gets dissipated and lost in a maze of small worries.[10]

1932 was the most difficult year and February the most difficult month. Gordon had left for his annual sojourn in America; Winifred, under orders from her physician, who had now diagnosed her illness as a serious form of kidney disease,[11] had gone to a cottage in the country; Brittain's father was suffering from an episode of depression;[12] and first John and then she came down with chicken-pox. 'I suppose with any luck my book will be finished about 1950',[13] she wrote mournfully to Gordon. But in spite of all this illness, worry and separation, between 20 January and 5 March she wrote a draft of the book's 'Malta' chapter.[14] On hearing of this accomplishment, Winifred wrote: 'I am coming to believe that much of the best work is done in spite of time, circumstance and discomfort'.[15]

Winifred was correct. Although these personal troubles were taxing, the worst moments were when she was revising the book in the summer of 1932, and came to doubt it. 'Absolutely in despair about "Testament of Youth" ', she writes in her diary for 22 August 1932. 'Just got to chapter I wrote last December . . . should never have thought I could write anything so inchoate & *bad*. Shall I *ever* finish the damned thing – will it be any good if I do?'[16] To Winifred, who was visiting her family in Yorkshire, she wrote a few days later: 'for good or ill, it must be finished . . . but I am *bored* with it, and have lost heart'.[17]

The tremendous pressure generated by writing *Testament of Youth*, combined with her worries over Winifred's health, her father's mental stability and her relationship with her husband caused her to embark in the spring and summer of 1932 on what proved to be an injudicious friendship with the Yorkshire novelist Phyllis Bentley,[18] whose novel *Inheritance* appeared in March 1932 to considerable critical acclaim. It was after its publication that Brittain sought Bentley's friendship. Unquestionably, Brittain initiated the friendship because of Bentley's success. The fact that *Inheritance* had been published by Victor Gollancz, whom she much admired, appeared to her to be a harbinger of what she hoped would happen to her own book.[19] So it was with a mixture of envy and genuine admiration and, as well, with an eye to what a friendship with this rising literary star might do to boost her own reputation that she initiated the friendship. As she records in her diary:

> In *Observer* saw magnificent review . . . of P.B.'s book . . . she is certainly 'made' as a writer. Decided to write to her & did so, even though I don't really know her & I haven't yet read the book – but I feel I have, because W. wrote yesterday saying *she* had finished it & thought it 'magnificent'. . . . mentioned my own 'Testament of Youth' to P.B. She mayn't be interested – but on the other hand she may; and Gollancz is her publisher.[20]

Brittain quickly followed this letter up by inviting Bentley to stay at Glebe Place.

In initiating this friendship, it must be admitted that Brittain behaved at times like a self-parody of her own picture of her worst self. First of all, Brittain was violating boundaries and behaving towards the absent and ill Holtby in a potentially hurtful fashion. Phyllis Bentley was Winifred's friend, not Vera's.[21] Winifred had known her well since 1930; Vera had met her once. Moreover, Vera took the liberty of inviting her to stay in the house – in Winifred's room –

when Winifred herself was too ill to occupy that room. Brittain's own diary entry reveals that even the long-suffering Winifred was 'surprised' by her behaviour.[22]

Towards Bentley herself, Brittain's motives were questionable. Brittain told herself that she was inviting Bentley to London to help her enjoy the fruits of her literary success: 'I feel, especially as she's had such a grey life, that she ought to get some enjoyment out of her success as well as capitalise on it with editors – & also that I'd like to have a hand in it'.[23] She added to Gordon that she hoped for Bentley's help with Victor Gollancz: 'Phyllis Bentley has definitely undertaken to interest Gollancz in my autobiography: she is very much interested in it herself & thinks he ought to publish it and as she is his best-seller of the moment she has a good deal of weight. . . .'[24]

For a brief period the arrangement did serve the immediate needs of both women. Bentley came up to London in May, and Brittain welcomed her with warmth and grace. She was flattering about *Inheritance*, and tactful in her suggestions about how Phyllis could improve her appearance. As a final gesture, just before Phyllis returned to Yorkshire, she held a party in her honour; after the guests had left, Vera records that Phyllis said to her: 'I've never been so happy as this in my life before'.[25]

The generosity Brittain and Bentley felt for each other was short-lived. During subsequent encounters the two women quarrelled bitterly about each other's personalities and, worse still, about their respective merits as writers. The friendship between Brittain and Bentley soured so quickly because the women had incomplete perceptions of each other. What Bentley saw in 1932 was the beautiful and accomplished career woman, wife and mother. What she failed to perceive was Brittain's solid core of seriousness, her deep commitment to writing, and her insecurities about her talent. Bentley's misreading of Brittain's personality: was understandable: Brittain after all, quite consciously played the role of beautiful social butterfly with Bentley, and remained seemingly unaware of the fact that her assumptions about the inadequacies of Bentley's life were presumptuous. Moreover, she made the mistake of assuming that Bentley would be as forgiving as Holtby was of her outbursts of irritation and of her habit of concealing her self-doubt behind a polished façade. During 1932 and 1933 both women made repeated attempts to repair their fragile friendship, with Winifred often drawn in as peacemaker, but as Bentley tactfully put it years later: 'We decided in 1933 that it would be wisest for us to stand at a little distance. . . .'[26]

Bentley's influence did play a role in the publication of *Testament of Youth*. In January of 1933, when Brittain had almost finished her manuscript, Winifred Holtby met Harold Latham, an editor with Macmillan of New York, at a dinner party and told him about the book. Macmillan were Bentley's publishers in America, and it was Bentley and Holtby together who persuaded Brittain that she should send the still unfinished manuscript to Latham.[27] Macmillan accepted it within a week, and on the strength of this strong vote of confidence, the manuscript was sent to Victor Gollancz. A week later, he too had accepted it with enthusiasm. The fact that the book was first accepted by the American publisher and that Victor Gollancz knew this to be the case when he read the manuscript, illustrates not only the interdependence of the publishing business in the two countries, but also the powerful influence that American taste wielded in Britain.

For his part, Victor Gollancz wrote: 'I have read *Testament of Youth* with the greatest admiration. It is a book of great beauty, and even greater courage, and I shall be very proud to publish it'. Brittain was overjoyed. She sent the good news to Gordon: 'After the discipline and the anguish of a book that's taken nearly 3 years or more, I can hardly believe that the effort is nearly over'.[28] To Winifred, still in Yorkshire, where her father was dying, she sent flowers along with a card which read: 'To my darling Winifred with deepest love & eternal gratitude for believing in my book.'[29]

Although *Testament of Youth*'s acceptance by both Gollancz and Macmillan was deeply gratifying to Brittain, there were still problems to overcome between February 1933 and the book's publication at the end of August. In personal terms, the most difficult concerned the conflicts between herself and her husband over the passages in which he appears. Catlin, who was upset enough to mark certain passages in the typescript she sent him as 'intolerable', insisted on changes to the original draft of Part III, asking Brittain to omit any references to him that would identify him. 'I am sorry if in changing any part I have seemed brutal', he wrote, 'but just because it is a great book and yet also very personal to ourselves I don't want any part of it to be something over which I should squirm . . . inevitably the spotlight must come on me . . . but I beg that this spotlight pass swiftly. . . .'[30]

'I'm sorry you want me to spoil my last chapter', Brittain replied. She explained to him that her conception of her book demanded references to their marriage: 'my method throughout this book has been to illustrate the tragedies of Europe and the story of our generation by the fortuitous symbolism of the events in my own life; and my marriage to you, my resurrection from the spiritual death of the war . . . are absolutely *essential* as illustrating Europe's struggles after a similar new self. . . .'[31] Reluctantly, she agreed to make most of the revisions he requested.

When *Testament of Youth* appeared at the end of the summer it was widely reviewed – far more widely reviewed than any of Brittain's previous books – and generally well received. The book was praised by reviewers on both sides of the Atlantic for its vividness, its honesty and its accuracy.[32] The hundreds of letters that Brittain received from the famous and from the obscure reflect the impact it made on a wide audience. Praise from distinguished people such as Beatrice Webb, who wrote that she had found it to be 'a wonderful story', and invited 'Mr and Mrs Catlin' to lunch[33] – meant as much to Brittain as the celebrity status she quickly achieved as the author of a best-seller. For Brittain, the publication of the book was indeed 'the Rubicon between unavailing obscurity and substantial achievement.'[34]

∞

For literary critics and historians of high culture, the post-First World War period was the era of modernism, of James Joyce, Virginia Woolf and T.S. Eliot, and of the new criticism of F.R. Leavis and his associates, whose journal *Scrutiny* was founded in 1932. But it was also the era of the 'best-seller' and the book club, of writers[35] who wrote successfully for a literary market made up of readers who, while they were educated and serious, were not likely to be responsive to literary experimentation.[36] In contrast to figures like Joyce or Woolf, such writers were not primarily concerned with transforming language or in developing new literary forms, but they were widely read and they often had an influence as personalities that extended beyond their writings.

Vera Brittain was just such an author and *Testament of Youth* was just such a book. It was reviewed and marketed as a 'best-seller': it was noticed in newspapers and magazines, but ignored, for example, by *Scrutiny*. And while historians have recognized its importance and it continues to move readers sixty years after its publication, it has never had a place in the 'literary canon'. Mainstream critics have ignored or dismissed it and, as a literary work, it has been largely ignored by feminist critics as well. The new feminist scholarship on Brittain has been more concerned with her life and her sentiments than with the literary merits of this particular work.[37]

It is easy to understand why the literary critics have ignored it. Their categories effectively identify the way in which a book such as

Testament of Youth is both flawed and unoriginal. What they overlook are the ways in which it does break new ground. The book's main weakness, the characteristic that threatens but never quite overwhelms Brittain's intentions, is also one of its strengths. Brittain never attempted to break the mould of conventional narrative: her literary models remained the Victorians, most specifically George Eliot,[38] whose influence is apparent both in the structure of *Testament of Youth* and in its tone of moral seriousness. *Testament of Youth*'s fidelity to traditional linear narrative makes for compelling reading, but it also at times obliterates nuance. In a playful letter to her niece Angelica Bell, Virginia Woolf wrote: 'Do you think it is possible to write a life of anyone? I doubt it; because people are all over the place.'[39] As I have attempted to show in earlier chapters, Brittain's strategy when confronted with the challenge of conveying emotions or events that were 'all over the place' was to force a resolution. Faced with the daunting task of recreating her ambivalent feelings about her mother, she simply eliminates most sides of their relationship. Faced with conveying the complex web of feelings she experienced as a young woman not only about Roland Leighton, but about sexuality, she creates a traditional love story.

The constraints inherent in the narrative form are accentuated by Brittain's practice of using traditional forms and allusions rendered ineffective through over-use. The epigrammatic excerpts she selected as signposts to mark each major transition in the book's three-part structure provide a good example of this tendency. They begin with the dedication, which reads: 'To R.A.L. & E.H.B. In Memory', followed by a quotation from Ecclesiasticus 44: 'Their bodies are buried in peace; but their name liveth for evermore.' Part I is then ushered in by a vignette from *The Pink Fairy Book*, in which Destiny offers the heroine the choice between a happy youth or a happy old age, and the heroine chooses the latter. For Part II Brittain selected two stanzas of verse by First World War poet and ex-VAD May Wedderburn Cannan about a woman who has lost her lover in battle. Part III begins with a quotation from Cicero in Latin, which translated means 'That long time when I shall not be moves me more than this short time.'[40] All four of these signposts are conventional, not merely in form but in content. The quotation from Ecclesiasticus expresses sentiments appropriate to one of the thousands of First World War memorial tablets placed in villages, towns and cities all over the Empire during these years. The passage from the *Pink Fairy Book*, while it nicely suggests the ironic contradiction between the settled security of pre-war upper middle-class life and the misery, danger and disorder of trench warfare, none the less prompts the reader to understand *Testament of Youth* through timeworn rather than fresh categories. Cannan's poem, 'When the Vision dies', which includes the line 'Know this is your War', is unimaginative in form and conventionally patriotic in sentiment. Finally, with the untranslated quotation from Cicero, Brittain calls in the weight of Classical tradition to authenticate her narrative. In short, these formal signs would have suited a far more conventional and much less interesting Great War book than *Testament of Youth*.

In his book *The Great War and Modern Memory*, an enormously influential work on the literature of the war, Paul Fussell discusses the use of euphemism and of 'raised' language – the legacy of the Victorian definition of the literary – that pervaded the language of the Great War. It appeared in government dispatches, newspaper accounts, and in the letters of officers and ordinary soldiers.[41] (For example, warfare becomes 'strife' and the dead become the 'fallen'.) Fussell's thesis is that the best of the Great War writers shattered this literary language. Clearly, Vera Brittain did not participate in this linguistic deconstruction, and it is primarily for this reason that her work has been ignored and even denigrated[42] by those who have formulated the critical categories creating the literary canon of the Great War.

But there are significant features of *Testament of Youth* that these categories cannot encompass. One such feature is the book's intellectual and analytic quality, its attempt to connect the public and the private, the past and the present, and to understand and explain the historical process. This analytic quality is not only a great strength, it is the characteristic that sets *Testament of Youth* apart both from the majority of books about the Great War and from the categories that literary critics of Great War literature have created.

The most famous of the Great War books – the works of Graves, Blunden and Sassoon – derive their power from a quality that reflected the course of the war itself. Their language and structure is designed to evoke the senselessness and confusion of trench warfare. As Edmund Blunden wrote, of an action in which he took part: 'The singular part of the battle was that no one, not even these, could say what had happened, or what was happening. . . .'[43] Blunden, indeed, revels in the unintelligibility of his subject. In the 'Preliminary' to *Undertones of War*, he writes:

> I know that the experience to be sketched . . . is very local, limited, incoherent; that it is almost useless, in the sense that no one will read

> it who is not already aware of all the intimations and discoveries in it, and many more, by reason of having gone the same journey. No one? Some, I am sure; but not many. *Neither will they understand* – that will not be all my fault.[44]

What Blunden is saying is that those who experienced trench warfare were bound together by its incomprehensibility. His book is successful because it puts into words not merely the hopelessness and the waste involved in the experience, but the futility of attempting to communicate or understand it. His purpose is to reveal, through epigram, the war's 'depth of ironic cruelty',[45] and it is for this ironic vision that he is praised.

But while the work of Blunden, Sassoon, Graves and similar writers is important because it replaced the language of traditional heroism with an ironic vision, it does not offer a coherent explanation for, or moral protest against, the war. In fact, taken as a whole, this literature retains many of the qualities associated with older visions of heroism in warfare. In the traditional vision, men in combat are bound together by a sense of loyalty and a commitment to a code of bravery and the ideals of glory. In the newer vision, the idea of glory is gone, but not the sense that those who fought together are initiates, are members of an exclusive coterie. Instead of sharing a precious commodity – heroism employed in a just cause – they share a sense of betrayal and a knowledge of the obscenity of pointless slaughter. None the less, Graves, Blunden and Sassoon accept their fate, and even embrace it.

In contrast to the literature of the trenches, Vera Brittain's *Testament of Youth* lacks the deft, understated irony that has become the hallmark of the 'best' Great War literature. But it has something to offer that understated irony does not: namely a reasoned analysis of why the war happened and of how to prevent a future war. Conventional thinking – including the thinking of mainstream literary criticism – assumes all too often that understanding is masculine whereas feeling is feminine. But Brittain had the courage to reverse such categories, and moreover she knew that in *Testament of Youth* she had done so. As she wrote to her husband in March 1932, in response to his complaint that she was too 'hard':

> Am I then so hard? Perhaps I am. I wasn't once. My book which is written so largely by way of explanation for you – describes the hardening process; after that, perhaps, no more retrospection; it is a 'Goodbye to All That' in more senses than Graves' book was. The queer and saddening thing is that, if I were a man, no one would

expect the particular kind of hard, logical intelligence that I have developed to have any other than the temperament I have got! Must I, being a woman, further handicap myself with a schism in personality? Must I always *show* love, understanding, pity? Isn't it enough that deep down I have them and that they are the mainspring of all I do?[46]

Furthermore, during the war itself, Brittain had grasped the correlative implications of the fact that the soldier's vision of the war was of necessity chaotic and fragmentary. Her correspondence with Roland in 1915 revealed to her that the men on the Western Front were in the very worst position possible for obtaining a genuine understanding of the course of the war. Roland's letters were full of vivid descriptions of what was happening in his immediate surroundings, but he had to ask her for information about the wider picture. As she put it herself, ruefully: 'they get very little news out there. Evidently they are intended to provide the news and not know it. . . .'[47] Brittain did not forget the irony that it was the men who were most involved in the war who were least well placed to understand its totality. In an article published in 1930 she wrote: a woman who worked with the armies can give a wider and more truthful picture of war as a whole than the active-service man whose knowledge was confined to a small corner of the front'.[48] In *Testament of Youth* itself, she laid claim to her authority, as a woman who had occupied a place midway between the non-combatants of the 'home front' and the exclusively male world of the trenches, to present such a picture.

Claiming 'a hard, logical intelligence' for herself as a woman writer took courage, but *Testament of Youth*'s most original contribution as literature lies in its vision of autobiography. In notes she made for the book she wrote:

I don't believe we are entitled to keep to ourselves any jot or tittle of experience the knowledge of which can in any way assist our fellow mortals . . . [experience] belongs to the collective effort of humanity. What really matters, for example, about a life like mine? It is that as many people as possible should know . . . that this is the effect of war . . . not that I should be able to say with smug satisfaction: this was my private life . . . and I've kept it to myself.[49]

As I suggest in the introduction to this book, Brittain's assertion of her right to write autobiography as a private person and as a woman was a significant achievement. Moreover, it anticipates the central project of late twentieth-century feminism, namely the recognition of the inextricable connection between the personal and the political. As such, it should be seen as a harbinger, an important early twentieth-century example of feminist political autobiography: a genre which has blossomed in the late twentieth century.[50]

11

'Having Crossed the Rubicon'

FAME

In 1939 Brittain recorded her memories of the February morning in 1933 when she came down to breakfast and found Victor Gollancz's letter accepting *Testament of Youth* for publication: 'I remember taking a walk by myself along the Embankment after breakfast & staring at the sun glittering on the water . . . somehow realising that this *was* the turning point of my literary career, and after so long a struggle I had at last crossed the Rubicon between obscurity & achievement.'[1]

The book's success would surpass her most optimistic expectations. Even before its publication, *Testament of Youth*'s fortunes took on an air of unreality. As she wrote to Gordon, just a few days after receiving the good news from Gollancz: 'Phyllis writes that she has just had a letter from Gollancz about my book, mentioning not only its "complete honesty" but also saying that it has the quality of "Greek tragedy". I must admit that these various judgments overwhelm me & make me feel that I'm someone else.'[2]

That gratifying but unnerving sense of amazement would resurface frequently in 1933 and 1934. Between February 1933 and the book's publication in August, she was occupied for the most part with practical matters relating to the final preparation of the manuscript. These included the painful process of revising the sections to which Gordon objected, and the arduous task of obtaining copyright permissions for passages from other authors quoted in the book. But from the last week in August, when the first pre-publication reviews of *Testament of Youth* appeared, and for weeks afterward, her diary entries reflect her emotions as she attempted to absorb the magnitude of her success: 'Oh, what a head-cracking week!' she writes. 'Reviews,

reviews, reviews, & reviews again. Never did I imagine that the *Testament* would inspire such great praise at such length or provoke – in smaller doses – so much abuse.'[3]

Suddenly she was in great demand as a public speaker. For example, the Six Point Group, by which she had always felt slighted, asked her to speak at their annual dinner as guest of honour,[4] and she derived particular pleasure from her warm reception in November at Oxford: 'Felt that I'd come full circle since days of *The Dark Tide* and been reinstated to favour. . . .'[5]

Testament of Youth made a significant difference to Brittain's finances. Before its publication only her journalistic writing had earned her any sizeable income. But from the signing of the contract with Gollancz, which carried with it an advance of £200[6] and promise of substantial royalties should the book be a success, *Testament of Youth* made money. It was profitably serialized in the *Sunday Chronicle*,[7] and Brittain was even offered $10,000 for the movie rights, but turned it down: 'They seem to think me mentally defective because I don't jump at the idea of selling my soul (to say nothing of other people's) for £2,000, but just think what Hollywood might do with "T. of Y.!" '[8] she wrote to Winifred.

Although Brittain resisted this American film offer, the climax of her experiences as a celebrity came not in 1933 and not in England, but in 1934 in America. The American edition of the book appeared in October 1933 and immediately became a best-seller.[9] Soon after its appearance Brittain found herself solicited by the American publicity agent, Colston Leigh, to do a speaking tour of the United States and Canada the following year. She accepted.

Brittain's 1934 American book tour[10] offers an example of what was then a frequent occurrence in Anglo-American cultural and commercial exchange. Throughout the twentieth century, middle- and upper-class British culture has had considerable cachet in the United States. In turn, those who produce and market such culture in Britain have been mindful of the need to appeal to 'transatlantic' audiences. The phenomenon persists today most noticeably in television programming, where British productions dominate the drama offerings on the non-commercial public television network. (For example, television viewers in the United States and much of Canada saw the the BBC serialized version of *Testament of Youth* on PBS's 'Masterpiece Theatre'.[11]) In the interwar decades, touring English authors offered a similar appeal. While a successful book was a prerequisite for an invitation, more than that was needed to guarantee the success of a book tour. To be received favourably by the book clubs, the school and university audiences, and the bookshop gatherings to whom the author would speak, the English author had to offer style, grace and just the right amount of Englishness. He or she needed to be elegant but not overbearing and to speak with a distinctly English accent, but at the same time be understandable to North American audiences.

Brittain herself was aware of these circumstances. Months before she was due to leave, she was already concerned about her reception. In the spring of 1934 she was preoccupied with the fact that Phyllis Bentley – with whom she was now definitely on bad terms – had not made a success of her tour to America. As she told Holtby: 'The rumor of Phyllis' unprepossessingness got about & kept the beauty-loving style-loving Americans away.'[12]

Brittain left for the United States, accompanied by Gordon, on 15 September 1934. They sailed on the *Berengaria*, a Cunarder, and they travelled first class, thanks to the money made from *Testament of Youth*. The previous day, Brittain had spent the morning at a beauty salon having her hair done, her face massaged, her eyebrows plucked and her hands manicured.[13] She records in her diary that for the departure she wore a 'black coat with grey fox collar, black dress with grey & red spotted bar, black Tyrolean hat with black & red feather' and her photograph was taken by Cunard's photographers as she boarded the boat train at Waterloo Station.[14] On the voyage, Brittain thoroughly enjoyed the 'palatial' first-class cabin ('It all seemed a very odd result of *Testament of Youth*') and the occasion to meet fellow first-class passengers, including Harold Nicolson who, along with his wife Vita Sackville-West, had also made a writers' tour of the United States organized by the Colston Leigh agency.[15] To Winifred she wrote of Nicolson and Sackville-West:

> I got the impression that . . . he and VSW had been difficile, insufficiently industrious in preparing their lectures . . . and tiresomely, aristocratically averse to doing anything openly commercial. They refused to give talks at bookshops. . . . Now *Why*? Delafield [E.M. Delafield] gave heaps. Presumably one writes books in the hope of selling them.[16]

When they arrived in New York on 21 September in the midst of a late summer heat wave, Macmillan's president, George Brett, and his wife Isabel were there to meet them. 'We are lucky to be with Macmillan', Brittain wrote to Holtby (whose *Mandoa, Mandoa!* was also published in the United States by Macmillan of New York). 'I have never imagined such publishers.' Macmillan had filled its Fifth Avenue window with red-jacketed copies of *Testament of Youth* ('what a gorgeous splurge of red'), and the Bretts were extremely kind and hospitable, taking Vera and Gordon up to their country place in Fairfield, Connecticut, the day after they arrived. She felt warmly welcomed. 'This life would be quite incredible if one weren't living it . . . I thought I knew New York; but being a celebrity in New York is like nothing else on earth.'[17]

She met Colston Leigh, the tour organizer, the afternoon she arrived in New York. Later and publicly she would describe him in relatively complimentary terms as a 'human dynamo' who was 'shrewd as a ferret and tough as a Brooklyn boy', but in her diary – perhaps because she was appalled to discover what would be expected of her over the course of the next three months – she reverted to an outburst of anti-Semitism, describing him as a 'pale, rather oily-looking Jew'.[18] 'My itinerary so far includes 34 lectures at 25 towns', she wrote to Winifred. She hoped she would not collapse under the strain.[19]

The tour took her as far west as Iowa and as far north as Toronto. She travelled in comfort, enjoying the luxury of Pullman train travel, in the 1930s still flourishing, with its well-appointed sleeping compartments and first-class dining car service. At her destinations she usually stayed in the fine hotels that were then part of the American urban landscape. Leigh had told her that he anticipated 'one of the most successful tours ever booked for a European writer',[20] and she did not disappoint him. With her elegant appearance, her stylish presentation and her thorough preparation, she was a great success with most of her audiences.

In contrast to 1926, when she had come to America reluctantly, in 1934 she liked the country and its people. In part, her changed attitude reflected her changed circumstances. Travelling as a celebrity was very different from living in Ithaca as a 'faculty wife'. But she also felt that the Americans had changed and that the Depression had improved them:

> Not only did the country seem different; I soon found that it was different. The American people, once so callous in their contempt for Europe's tragedies, had become humbler, kinder, less ostentatious; they understood now what chaos and sorrow meant because they had shared them.[21]

Of course, not every moment was glamorous. Brittain's itinerary included many small cities and towns. Towards the end of October, for instance, after lecturing to over 1,200 people in the Grand Ballroom of a big hotel in Detroit, she travelled on to Terre Haute,

Indiana: 'Then I caught the night train for this very different place – a little, black, dejected colliery town . . . the American equivalent of, say, Wolverhampton . . . I imagine that one would learn more about the depression from a few days here than from weeks in New York or Chicago. They only gave me $150 for my lecture instead of $200 or $250 as in all the other places.'[22] And from Wheeling, West Virginia, where she spoke to a women's book club, she wrote ruefully to Winifred: 'The Club greatly admired my frock and hat (the ones I wore at Foyle's), but the lecture was very tepidly received. It was the one on "Why I wrote 'Testament of Youth' ", but the trouble was that hardly anyone had read the book (this is not exactly a literary town). Since T. of Y is my only title to fame, I can't think why they chose either me or the subject.'[23]

For Brittain, the most exhilarating aspect of this 1934 American tour was her romantic involvement with George Brett. Flickers of sexual interest had passed between the two of them from the day she had arrived. She had wanted to buy something suitable for the sweltering September heat, and George had supplied her with some American currency and rushed with her to a shop where she purchased a light-weight blouse just at closing time. 'How many Englishmen would do this?' she comments to Winifred.[24] Within a week of her arrival, she writes that she had danced with George Brett, 'whom I find more attractive than is entirely convenient and dances divinely'.[25] A week later, from Virginia, she wrote: 'I could easily be a little in love with George Brett if I liked, but it probably wouldn't be a good idea.'[26] Winifred wrote back, approvingly: 'such gay virility should be very good for you . . . I don't want you to fall monumentally in love – but a little sunlit flirtation . . . it hurts no one & is . . . good for the nerves!'[27]

But by November she did feel – briefly – that she had fallen deeply and painfully in love with him: 'what anguish it is to be so much in love with someone!' she wrote Winifred after an encounter in Washington, D.C., where she and George had almost become lovers. Their passionate encounter came as she was saying goodbye to him in his bedroom compartment on the train to New Orleans: 'If there had been a chance of doing it on the train, I would have', she wrote Winifred. '[T]he sudden mutual abandonment of our defences is still all but unbearable in its results.'[28]

There are several reasons why Brittain may have felt a need for sexual reassurance at this juncture. Gordon, although he was largely supportive of Vera's success with *Testament of Youth*, was also envious of it, or at least disconsolate about his own perceived failures.

He continued in 1934, as he had earlier, to express his angry feelings indirectly, by telling Vera all about his attraction to other women.[29] In contrast, George was handsome and debonair, and their relationship was fresh and free from conflict. By admiring her as well as her work, he lifted her spirits.

It does not appear that Brittain and Brett ever became lovers. Brittain was committed to maintaining a monogamous marriage herself (whatever Gordon chose to do) and, moreover, she knew and liked Isabel Brett. But her feelings for George Brett, while painful as well as joyous, added immensely to the glamour of her 1934 American tour, and did have one important long-term result. Brett became a model for one of the main characters in her next book, the novel *Honourable Estate*.[30]

HONOURABLE ESTATE

In the spring of 1933, as she was completing *Testament of Youth*, Brittain had written to Holtby: [M]y mind seethes with plans for future work. . . .'[31] She was already thinking about *Honourable Estate*, the book she would write in the afterglow of her success with *Testament of Youth*. Although *Honourable Estate* did not achieve outstanding sales or great praise from reviewers when it appeared in 1936, of Brittain's five published novels it is the most ambitious in scope and the most successfully realized. It demonstrates that Brittain had achieved a new level of assurance and maturity as a writer of fiction and it deserves to be recognised as one of the major achievements of her literary career.[32]

Honourable Estate is an explicitly political, explicitly feminist novel. In the foreword, Brittain proudly and vigorously defends this political use of imaginative fiction: 'I make no apology for dealing in a novel with social theories and political beliefs, nor for the extent to which these are discussed by some of the characters . . . If large areas of human experience – political, economic, social, religious – are to be labelled inadmissible as subjects for fiction, then fiction is doomed as an organic art.'[33]

Concerning feminism, Brittain says, '*Honourable Estate* purports to show how the women's revolution – one of the greatest in all history – combined with the struggle for other democratic ideals and the cataclysm of the War to alter the private destinies of individuals.'[34] This statement from the book's foreword was no mere afterthought: *Honourable Estate* is inspired throughout by Brittain's faith in feminism. The novel's very title was designed to alert readers to its focus on feminism and the institution of marriage: 'The title of this story has not merely the obvious application derived from its origin in the Church of England Marriage Service. It stands also for that position of dignity and respect for which the world's women and the world's workers have striven since the end of the eighteenth century, and which, within my own lifetime, they have partly achieved.'[35]

In this novel of the 1930s, Brittain's analysis of the connection between individual experience and society's definitions of gender is remarkably farseeing. A generation after she wrote this book, 'second wave' feminist theory would define heterosexual relationships as a major point of intersection between the personal and the political, as the primary locus for sexual politics.[36] Although *Honourable Estate* was written more than three decades before the term was coined, an analysis of sexual politics is evident throughout.

Honourable Estate is a big book, with two intertwined narratives and a large cast of characters whose experiences span two generations. Much of the novel is set in the Derbyshire and Staffordshire of Brittain's youth, and in the course of writing it she revisited Buxton for the first time since the war and retraced the Brittain family history in neighbouring Staffordshire. For *Honourable Estate* she not only did her usual careful research, this time into matters as wide-ranging as the Staffordshire pottery industry and the history of suffrage militancy, she also brought a new richness of imagination to the writing. The result is a convincing, evocative recreation of the urban and rural landscape of the Midlands and of its people that is worthy of Arnold Bennett, the novelist of the 'Five Towns', whose work she had always greatly admired.

The book's characters include two couples, whose marriages begin in the 1890s. In Part I we meet the sadly mismatched Thomas and Janet Rutherston. Thomas is a conventional, timid Church of England clergyman who attempts to make up for his own emotional insecurities by a rigid adherence to patriarchal views about woman's place. When the novel opens, he is vicar of a church in Sterndale, Brittain's fictional recreation of the Buxton of the 1890s. Janet, seventeen years his junior, is one of *Honourable Estate*'s two feminist heroines. At twenty she becomes a mother unwillingly and she detests the role of clergyman's wife. As the years pass, she asserts herself, becoming active in the suffrage movement and entering into an intense friendship with an older woman writer, Gertrude Ellison Campbell. Janet and Thomas quarrel bitterly over her refusal to have a second child and over her feminism, and after years of painful disputes she eventually leaves the marriage in 1914 to devote herself to settlement work in London's Bethnal Green. But she has waited too long and her independent life is brief: she dies in December 1917 of an acute attack of a long-neglected chronic appendicitis.

The portrait Brittain creates of Janet Rutherston is of a woman whose temperament fitted her for achievement, but who is forced to conform to the limited model of Victorian wifehood. Her courage finally enables her to free herself, but her escape is paid for in bitterness, and her life story is a tragedy: neither her marriage nor her friendship with Ellison Campbell brings her happiness, and although she loves her son Denis and he loves her, it is a love always tinged with resentment. She has gained her autonomy, but at too great a price.

Part II of *Honourable Estate* tells the sharply contrasting story of Stephen and Jessie Alleyndene. On the surface, their marriage is successful, but here, too, there are underlying disappointments and misunderstandings. Stephen is the virile eldest son of a family which controls both a successful Staffordshire pottery firm and a family estate, Dene Hall. His wife Jessie, the daughter of a Cornish art teacher, had been the Alleyndene's family governess. Stephen falls passionately in love with Jessie, and she agrees to marry him, not out of love but because she wants the social and financial security he can offer her. Jessie is gentle and traditionally feminine, but she is frightened into coldness by her husband's robust sexuality, and at its deepest level the marriage is a disappointment to both, even though they prosper.

From her private notes and from her correspondence, and as well from the frank disclosure she makes in *Testament of Experience*, we know that Brittain based the character of Janet Rutherston on her husband's mother.[37] Gordon first told her about his mother, Edith Kate Orton, during their courtship in 1924. Brittain had been moved by her dead mother-in-law's feminism and by her bravery, and even before her own marriage she had sketched out a plan to incorporate Edith Orton's story into a novel. Stephen Alleyndene is based on her own father, and there are aspects of her own mother in the character of Jessie Alleyndene. But while actual people were her starting point, Janet, Thomas, Stephen and Jessie are all fully developed fictional characters, and in *Honourable Estate* Brittain demonstrates how much she had matured as a writer since her two earliest novels, *The Dark Tide* and *Not Without Honour*. Brittain brings both compassion and an awareness of nuance to the portrayal of these two Victorian marriages. Throughout, her intention is to show that the lives of these four people were not only shaped by their personal strengths and limitations, but also by their society's conception of gender.

Chief among *Honourable Estate*'s second generation of characters is the novel's younger feminist heroine, the Alleyndene's daughter Ruth, who is based on Vera Brittain herself. Like her creator, Ruth attends Oxford and serves as a nurse in the First World War. In the novel, Ruth's beloved younger brother Richard is killed in action in 1915. Two years later, when she is serving as a VAD in France, an American serviceman, Eugene Meury, appears without warning to deliver a letter that Richard had written to her the night before he was killed. In it, Richard reveals to his sister that he has become involved in a homosexual relationship with his old schoolfriend Valentine, that his commanding officer has discovered it, and that in order to avoid a court martial, he has decided to make sure that he will not survive the next battle.[38]

Ruth is devastated by this revelation and even though, like Brittain herself, she is uncomfortable with homosexuality, she blames society and her own parents rather than Richard: '"Surely it's a worse crime to be a statesman and involve a whole nation in war, than just to go in for some sort of unorthodox relationship which however wrong it may be in itself doesn't hurt anyone else."'[39] Ruth is comforted by Eugene and they fall deeply in love. Even though Eugene has a fiancée in America, and even though both young people have adhered in the past to conventional Victorian values concerning chastity, Ruth decides she must become Eugene's lover, and they make passionate love in a pine forest. Eugene, predictably, is killed in October 1918.

In the novel's concluding section, Brittain intertwines the Rutherston and Alleyndene narratives. After the war, Ruth Alleyndene and Denis Rutherston – whose memories of his own family life have made him into a committed feminist who is determined that he will 'never bring any woman unhappiness in marriage'[40] – meet and marry. Ruth and Denis have a twin boy and girl, and Ruth becomes involved in politics, running successfully for Parliament as a Labour candidate for the Staffordshire constituency in which she had been raised.

It is obvious that Ruth Alleyndene, like her predecessor Virginia in *The Dark Tide*, represents Brittain's 'best self', and that Denis is an affectionate but impossibly perfect portrayal of Gordon. But both characters also embody *Honourable Estate*'s mature and considered message concerning feminism: Ruth is able to achieve a life that encompasses Janet's unfulfilled desires because of the lessening of prejudice against feminist women. In Ruth, Brittain succeeded in representing through fiction that optimism about feminism that informed both her feminist journalism in the 1920s and her own life experience.[41]

As was the case with all her fiction and autobiographical writing, Brittain saw *Honourable Estate* as in part a way to explore the painful and puzzling dilemmas of her own personal life. In *Testament of Experience* she freely discussed the fact that in Janet Rutherston she could bring to life the mother-in-law she never knew but admired and pitied, and in Stephen Alleyndene she could pay tribute to her father. She was less frank about the private sources for the characters Richard Alleyndene, Eugene Meury and Gertrude Campbell. In private, however, she was explicit about the connections between her actual experience and these fictional characters, explaining to Holtby, her faithful literary confidante, that Eugene Meury was an idealized George Brett, that the failed friendship between Janet and Gertrude reflected her own failed friendship with Phyllis Bentley, and that Ruth's discovery of Richard's homosexuality was a way of working out a painful family secret:

> Well, thank God for books. In 'Mandoa' you gained . . . some measure of peace from your descriptions of Bill's fate & psychology. In 'Testament of Youth' I sought . . . a kind of peace & reconciliation with the War. But three things in my life remain unreconciled and maybe I can use 'Honourable Estate' . . . to find reconciliation for them – the failure of my friendship with Phyllis; what Colonel Hudson told me about Edward's last week in Italy (involving such fundamental doubts and speculations which can never now be answered); and now this involvement, unexpected & mainly . . . physical attraction to an American with whom I can never even correspond except about business. How I can reconcile two of them by drawing a portrait of George 20 years ago . . . and of Phyllis twenty years hence, and then killing them both off, only another writer could know, but you will understand![42]

Brittain never published an extensive account of her distressing failed friendship with Bentley or of her romance with George Brett. On the other hand, she never attempted to expunge either experience from the record: the letters and diaries available to researchers contain extensive references to both relationships. She was more guarded about Edward's story and about the way in which she came to know of it. The letter to Holtby quoted above is one of the few stray traces remaining in the archival record. In another letter, written to her husband in 1939, Brittain alludes to Edward's death in battle, and also mentions that her mother had found a diary of Edward's after his death 'making it quite clear' that he had been involved in 'homosexual doings at Uppingham'.[43] But what did Edith Brittain actually learn about Edward's sexuality after his death? When did Vera Brittain have the interview with Colonel Hudson which she mentions in the 12 November 1934 letter to Holtby? These remain unsolved mysteries.[44] However, the specific unresolved questions are less important than what this story reveals about the cruel and unrelenting nature of prejudice against homosexuality in the first half of the twentieth century. If, as seems likely, the fictionalized account of Richard's death in *Honourable Estate* is a retelling of what happened to Edward, then Edward's death was tragic indeed, for himself most of all, but also for his family. The inevitably corrosive effect of such a family secret does much to explain, for example, the deterioration in Arthur Brittain's mental health in the post-war period.

Brittain began *Honourable Estate* during a period of personal happiness and relative political optimism. By the time it was completed and published, the domestic and the international political scene had darkened, and as she concluded the writing in the autumn of 1936 she was acutely aware that the rise of Fascism and the return of militarism marked a reaction in politics, and that this reaction included a revived hostility not only to feminism, but to peace, social justice and democracy. But as she said in the book's foreword: 'the fact that we are now living in a period of reaction makes it the more important to contemplate that which was gained during the four decades which ended in 1930'.[45]

Fascism and the threat of war were mirrored in 1935 in her own personal life by a series of personal griefs, including her father's suicide and Winifred Holtby's death. From 1935 to 1940, these personal and political tragedies came together to produce another sea change in Brittain's life as profound as the one that had been brought about by the Great War.

1935: 'THE WORST, CRUELLEST AND SADDEST YEAR SINCE THE WAR'

The kidney disease that would kill Winifred Holtby in 1935 began to manifest itself in 1931. In the early stages of the illness, the doctors believed that Winifred was suffering from 'overwork'. Brittain was slow to realize the gravity of the situation, pushing her fears for

Winifred aside even after it was clear that her friend was gravely ill. Her inability to recognise that Winifred was dying can be explained in part by her preoccupation with her own work and family problems and in part by the confusing diagnoses that Winifred received from her physicians. But these factors do not provide a sufficient explanation for Brittain's inability to confront the truth. Unhappily, the longstanding patterns that had shaped the relationship did not easily allow for Holtby's illness. The friendship that began in 1920 with Winifred's appearance in Vera's Somerville sickroom with her bunch of grapes was defined as one in which Winifred was the stronger and Vera the more needy. In terms of physical illness specifically, up to 1931 if either of them were ailing, it would invariably be Vera. It appears likely that Winifred herself did not wish to alter the balance between them, even after she herself knew she was gravely ill. And so, throughout the years of the illness and indeed right up until her death, Brittain continued to rely on Winifred, just as she always had done: to rely on her support as she struggled with self-doubt over *Testament of Youth*; to rely on her understanding and tolerance when she attempted her ill-judged intimacy with Phyllis Bentley; and to rely on her practical help, whether it involved relatively small matters like fetching the children from Oxford in April 1934 so that Vera could enjoy two extra days of an Italian holiday,[46] or more extensive help, as when Holtby managed the household from September to December 1934. Up until the very end, Brittain simply could not accept the fact that Winifred now needed her more than she needed Winifred.

Occasionally, indeed, her anxieties did surface. In April 1932, after Winifred had been given grave news by her physician, Brittain wrote to her husband:

> I am so miserable that I keep on wanting to turn for comfort to – whom but Winifred herself! For twelve years she has always been there to turn to when anything troubled me, and I feel so lost when suddenly the one thing happens about which I can't seek comfort but must try to give it, while knowing so well how hollow all my suggested alleviations and compensations must sound, and how easily she must see through them – just as I should.[47]

Holtby's illness was not Brittain's only source of private anxiety during this period. Arthur Brittain's episodes of depression were becoming more and more frequent, and in May of 1934 he made a suicide attempt.[48] From then until his death in the following August, he was in and out of nursing homes. After his suicide attempt in May,

Brittain's mother wanted her to cancel her upcoming American tour. She resisted Edith's pleas, but only because both Winifred and Gordon insisted that she go as planned.[49]

It was Winifred who made the tour possible, by agreeing to manage the household and supervise the children. After Vera's return Winifred retreated to Yorkshire, where she worked steadily on her novel *South Riding*, knowing that the time left to her was limited. Brittain, distracted during this period by *Honourable Estate*, by tensions between herself and Gordon, and by worries that she might be pregnant, sent Winifred warm letters as always, but evaded her offer to visit Hornsea for an extended period, although Winifred asked her to do so. All she could spare for Winifred was a detour of a few days during a northern lecture tour.[50]

The Glebe Place household did plan a summer holiday in France in 1935. On 31 July 1935, Vera left for France along with John Edward and Shirley, the governess and two friends. Gordon was to join them within two days and Winifred in a week. On Saturday, 3 August, Winifred arrived unexpectedly:

> As we were sitting at lunch John suddenly called out, 'Look, there's Auntie!' and I turned to see Winifred in her tweed coat in the lounge of the hotel. As she wasn't coming till next Saturday and it was Gordon I was expecting I knew at once something dreadful had occurred . . . I went out to her at once & said 'Something's wrong.' she said 'yes' – I said 'Is it Gordon?' thinking he had been depressed about his book, but she answered 'No, it's your Father.'[51]

Arthur Brittain had disappeared during the night of 1 August, and on 5 August his body was recovered from the Thames. In the terrible aftermath of his death, Gordon dealt with the details relating to the inquest, and Winifred went back to France, where the children had been left in the care of their governess. When Gordon contracted a serious infection immediately following Arthur Brittain's funeral, she stayed there with them until the end of August.[52]

In a letter Gordon wrote to Winifred during this difficult time, he said: 'If you get ill, it will put the lid on. Take care of yourself.'[53] But Winifred was of course very ill, even as she made two trips across the Channel to help with this family emergency. Her final illness began on 10 September, and less than three weeks later, on 29 September 1935, she died.

Brittain's diary entries for September 1935 poignantly reflect her overwhelming grief. When Winifred died at 6:25 on a Sunday morning, the nursing home night nurse, Vera and Gordon were the only people present. Britain recorded later that as Winifred died she held her hand: 'It was strange, incredible, after all the years of our friendship & all that we had shared together, to feel her life flickering out under my hand.' The night nurse cut off a lock of Winifred's hair for Vera, and she and Gordon kissed Winifred goodbye. As they left the nursing home, it was still dark, but St James's Spanish Place (the Catholic church in which they had been married) was already open for seven o'clock Mass and they went in briefly. Brittain writes: 'I lit a candle for her soul, wherever it might have gone or whatever become.'[54]

Brittain's intense grief was particularly painful because it was mingled with guilt. 'We all exploited her', she would remorsefully write,[55] and there is no question that in the aftermath of Winifred's death she realized that in retrospect she had asked far too much of her during the family crises of 1934 and 1935. Winifred may always cheerfully have given more to Vera than Vera to Winifred. None the less, Vera had loved Winifred deeply and generously, the loss was a painful and permanent sadness, and the sense of failure was shattering.

In 1935, in addition to her father's suicide and Winifred's final illness and death, Brittain also had to cope with her husband's difficulties. In the mid-1930s, Gordon Catlin was often himself so depressed that Vera feared he might commit suicide. Brittain's success with *Testament of Youth* was a mixed blessing for Catlin. It was on the strength of the improvement in her income that he took the decision to resign from Cornell in 1934.[56] He resigned intending to run successfully for Parliament as a Labour Party candidate, an unrealistic goal in the mid-1930s when Labour was in disarray. Although his generous involvement in the grief and crises accompanying Arthur Brittain's suicide and Winifred's last illness would ultimately deepen the affection between himself and Brittain, in the immediate aftermath the two were irritable and uncertain with each other.[57] Brittain, for her part, while she had wished for years that he would resign, was quite rightly apprehensive about how he would fare without the stability of his Cornell appointment.

She had been relieved when, in June 1935, he was selected as a Labour candidate for Sunderland, a constituency which might have been winnable under different circumstances. The election was called soon after Winifred's death. Although initially Brittain could not rouse herself from her grief, she knew how important the election was to Catlin and as the 14 November polling day approached, she did participate in the campaign, using money from her royalties to help finance it,[58] and going to Sunderland in November to stump for him. But throughout this period, each found it difficult to be appreciative of the other. '"Don't be too ladylike"', he admonished her 'somewhat contemptuously' as she was about to make a speech at Miners' Hall. 'I take no notice of such remarks nowadays', she writes.[59] In the election, Baldwin's Conservative coalition won a majority, and Catlin was defeated. Catlin was bitterly disappointed and so was she. In a letter to a friend, she called the defeat 'our third major catastrophe' of 1935.[60]

On New Year's Eve, 'so thankful to get rid of 1935 that we wanted to do something to mark its passing', she and Gordon went to the watch-night service at St Paul's. Afterwards, she wrote in her diary:

> 1935 had really gone; what of 1936? Winifred in dying took with her that second life that she initiated for me just after the War; can I make a third? Can I, once more, begin again? . . . Does one make new friends when the thirties are over? Does love, orthodox and unorthodox, still abide? Time only can answer. . . . Goodbye to 1935; the worst, cruellest and saddest year since the War.[61]

A THIRD LIFE

After 1935, Brittain did indeed make a third life. The first life, her Edwardian girlhood, had been succeeded by the years in which she had struggled to achieve self-actualization through her writing. In sharp contrast, her third life was focused outward, on principled peace activism, when as a pacifist during the years of the Second World War she took on the difficult, disheartening and at times dangerous mission of protesting against the conduct of the war, and in the aftermath of war she continued to work for peace and social justice.

Initially, it was *Testament of Youth* which made Brittain a major spokesperson for peace in the 1930s. Because of the book's success, Brittain was asked to do extensive public speaking about peace. For example, the League of Nations Union, which had for many years undervalued her talents, now courted her, both as a speaker and as a 'prominent' voice, whose name could lend weight to the Union's cause.[62] This increased public exposure as a speaker on peace platforms came just when her own views on the subject were changing, and between 1933 and 1937 she moved from the espousal of internationalism to the much more radical position of pacifism.

On an organizational level, this transformation began with her dissatisfaction with the LNU. From the time of its founding, the Union had always had a wide spectrum of members and leaders, ranging from pacifists to those who were merely cautious supporters of internationalism.[63] In the 1930s, with the successive crises that began with Japan's invasion of Manchuria, it became clear that the League of Nations was losing its effectiveness as a voice for genuine internationalism. Accordingly, the role of the LNU became increasingly difficult: organized to support the League, what was it to do when the League began to falter? Should it support a policy of collective security that might involve a League war when it was clear that the Great Powers were not committed to working towards genuine internationalism through the League, or should it oppose the use of force? Tensions within the LNU surrounding the issue of collective security were never satisfactorily resolved. Vera Brittain, by the early 1930s, was among those original supporters of the Union who began to feel that it was no longer an effective voice for peace, and while she continued her affiliation with the Union right up until 1938, from the early 1930s she had increased her involvement with the Union for Democratic Control and the Women's International League for Peace and Freedom, both of which were more outspoken critics of big-power diplomacy than was the LNU.[64]

For Brittain, the decisive moment in her journey towards pacifism came in 1936, the year in which Hitler abrogated the terms of the Treaties of Versailles and Locarno and occupied the Rhineland, and in which the Spanish Civil War began. These events made it clear that liberal humanitarians opposed to war would face a painful dilemma. As Fascism grew in strength, how were anti-war activists to respond? Pondering this problem in March 1936, during the crisis precipitated by Hitler's remilitarization of the Rhineland, Brittain wrote:

> I fear War more than Fascism; anyhow I am sure you can't use Satan to cast out Satan: that Fascism which sprang from colossal injustice will only grow stronger if the injustice is rammed home. . . . The Press and all the people I meet seem to be divided into 1) those who hate murder in Germany but don't mind it in Russia; 2) those who hate murder in Russia but don't mind it in Germany; 3) a few minoritarians like myself who hate it anyway.[65]

Less than two weeks after she wrote that entry she and Catlin travelled to Germany as journalists, in time for the German elections on 29 March. Brittain deeply disapproved of Fascism but at the same time she retained considerable sympathy for the German people's resentment of the Versailles Treaty and the post-war occupation of their country. In Germany in March 1936 she was horrified – more horrified than she had expected to be – by the relentlessness of Nazi propaganda. In Berlin, confronted by banners, posters and staged demonstrations, she wrote: 'This vast, insistent, universal propaganda is terrifying in its skill and efficiency. . . .'[66] Brittain, who heard both Hitler and Goering speak, found Goering the more frightening of the two: 'Speech terrifying, like the letting loose of some enormous impersonal force – undirected, amoral, overwhelming, irresistible as a flood or an earthquake is irresistible. . . . No possibility of thought, reason, consideration here – only mass emotion on the largest possible scale. Thought of all the books I have ever read on herd-instinct & mob psychology.'[67]

But while she was frightened and repelled by the regime's perversion of democracy, it was only with some reluctance that she faced up to the plight of the German Jews. She certainly knew about the regime's anti-Jewish policies: she knew that Germans of Jewish ethnicity had been disenfranchised as soon as the Nazis came to power in 1933, and she knew about some of the effects of the Nuremburg Laws which had been passed in September 1935. But she felt reassured rather than sceptical when one informant, whom she describes as 'a very fair-minded man about [the] regime', defended the treatment of the Jews: 'Said the Jews *do* get the dole here the same as the Germans.'[68] And as a result of her long-standing, unexamined acceptance of the anti-Semitism so common in England in the inter-war decades, she was able to muster only a distant, uncomfortable sympathy rather than any genuine empathy, even when confronted by unmistakable evidence of Nazi anti-Jewish policy. In Frankfurt, three days after the 29 March election, she visited a Jewish café:

> Café gave one a queer feeling – the collective sense of humiliation was oppressive; marked admixture of classes who would normally not talk to each other driven together by common misfortune. . . . I felt as if I were among a gathering of Girondins under the Terror – or prisoners of War – or exiles in a foreign country.[69]

Two days later, Brittain and Catlin left Germany, travelling home by way of France: 'Sense of relief at being in France', she writes.[70] Perhaps it was just that sense of relief following on the fear and revulsion she had felt in Germany that elicited her rather flippant response to a film about conditions in the French Sudan that she and Gordon saw as they were travelling on to Verdun. They were in Metz on 4 April and, after enjoying 'quite a good meal' at the town's Grand

Hotel, they ducked into a cinema to escape 'torrents' of rain and to see the news. But first they had to sit through a Mickey Mouse cartoon and then a documentary, *Le Payes du Soif*. Brittain describes this film as follows: 'an incredibly long & dreary informative picture of the French Sudan . . . which went on for about 45 minutes, showing endless pictures of laden camels tramping across deserts, acres of sand, oases & natives who inhabited them, more sand, more natives. . . .'[71]

When Brittain used this passage later, in *Testament of Experience*, she edited out the references to 'natives', and moreover, she herself perceived in retrospect the irony involved in her reaction to drought when it was pouring rain outside: '[h]ere an extremely long and drearily informative film of the French Sudan . . . showed endless pictures of laden camels tramping over acres of sand where the superfluous water in the streets of Metz would have been a welcome gift.'[72]

In a paper discussing the nature of women's national identity, historian Joyce Berkman asks: 'What is specifically English in Vera Brittain's sense of self?' She perceptively analyses the way in which Brittain's self-identification with Anglo-Saxon Protestantism contributed to a 'complacent sense of nationality' and points out that Brittain never questioned her 'sense of ethnicity and nationality', her sense of Englishness. It is for this reason, Berkman argues, that Brittain slips 'with distressing ease . . . into vivid ethnic stereotypes'.[73]

In the comments quoted above, it is just that reassuring but fundamentally racist sense of Englishness into which Brittain retreats. By reducing the 'natives' to the same category as the camels or even the sand, she distances herself from the hardships they endure. That Brittain in her private discourse did at times construct Jews as 'the other' and 'natives' as objects is not to say that she was an intentional anti-Semite or racist. On the contrary, as a left-leaning humanitarian she was opposed to bigotry, and whenever she thought or wrote seriously about racial, religious or ethnic prejudice she spoke out for fairness and tolerance. What these 1936 remarks point to (as do examples quoted earlier in this book) was the extent to which even a progressive person like Brittain was influenced by the endemic racial and ethnic prejudices of the period.

Less than three months after this trip to Germany and France, when she was first exposed to Canon H.R.L. Sheppard and his pacifist Peace Pledge Union, Brittain began the transformation to pacifism that would not only alter her views on the issues of war and peace, but would profoundly shake her comfort with her own English sense of complacent superiority. When she wrote her final volume of memoirs, *Testament of Experience*, she would say of the great Peace Rally in Dorchester, held on 22 June 1936, that it was 'in retrospect . . . a turning point of my life'.[74] On this occasion she had been invited to appear on a platform with Sheppard himself and with George Lansbury. As she listened to the other speakers, and especially to Sheppard, she realized that she was hearing a message she had never encountered before and she was so overwhelmed that her usual assurance vanished:

> By the time that my own turn came I was panic-stricken. This Christian pacifist platform was like no other on which I had stood; here my customary little speech in support of collective security would strike a discordant note. Its basis was political, but the message of my fellow-speakers sprang from the love of God. Yet I had prepared nothing else. Struggling to my feet I quoted Bunyan, improvised a feeble little story about the pilgrimage of the *Anciens Combattants* at Verdun, and sat down – the biggest disappointment to thousands on that spectacular afternoon . . .[75]

Brittain was not quite ready to join the PPU in 1936, but she did so in 1937, becoming a sponsor of the organization. In 1938, when she broke her links with the LNU, her affiliation with pacifism, rather than internationalism, can be said to have been achieved.

As a pacifist, Brittain became part of a minority that would come to be regarded with increasing suspicion in the late 1930s. The unpopularity of principled pacifism was clearly brought home to her over the issue of the Spanish Civil War. Most of Brittain's friends and acquaintances, including her own husband, were active supporters of Loyalist Spain; but as her pacifist feelings deepened, the issue of Spain became a test. Because she had come to take an uncompromising position on war, she felt she had a moral obligation to take a publicly neutral position on the issue of Spain. In 1937, the *Left Review* produced a special pamphlet entitled *Authors Take Sides on the Spanish War*. Authors throughout Britain were requested to express their views about Spain, in answer to questions couched in such a way as to leave little doubt that those who did not express unqualified support for Republican Spain's war against Franco, would be considered as supporters of Fascism. The great majority of respondents to the *Left Review*'s questionnaire, even those most closely associated with the peace movement, gave answers that allowed them to be listed as supporters of the Spanish government. But Brittain did not equivocate:

As an uncompromising pacifist, I hold war to be a crime . . . whoever fights it, and against whomever it is fought. I believe in liberty, democracy, free thought and free speech. I detest Fascism and all that it stands for, but I do not believe we shall destroy it by fighting it. And I do not think we serve either the Spanish people or the cause of civilization by continuing to make Spain the battleground for a new series of wars of religion.[76]

Taking this unpopular position required considerable moral courage. Brittain's wartime peace work would demand even more. During the war years themselves, Brittain worked for the Peace Pledge Union's 'stop-the-war campaign', and its Food Relief Campaign,[77] and, most important of all, she became one of a handful of outspoken critics of the government's policy of saturation bombing. When writers in Britain were mobilized by the Ministry of Information, Brittain was immediately approached. On 7 September 1939 she writes in her diary: 'Letter from Ministry of Information asking me, as author valuable to them, to refrain from other national service till instructed. Could only reply that as pacifist can be useful only in so far as information contributes to peace.'[78] Even before she had received this official letter, she had already conceived a plan to employ her talents as a writer in the cause of peace. Beginning in September 1939 and continuing throughout the war years, she wrote a regular newsletter entitled 'Letters to Peace Lovers'. Initially the newsletter's 'business' office was in Dick Sheppard House, the PPU's Bloomsbury central office. It was housed in a bathroom because there was no other available space in the building.[79] While the PPU gave its support, this was Brittain's personal project. She conceived of it, she developed the mailing list, and she financed it. She also published the pacifist essay *Humiliation with Honour* in 1942, and, most controversial of all, her protest against 'area bombing', *Seed of Chaos: What Mass Bombing Really Means*, in 1944.[80]

Recently, in an introduction to *Testament of a Peace Lover: Letters from Vera Brittain*, a volume of selections from the 'Letters to Peace Lovers', Winifred Eden-Green, who assisted Brittain with the Letters, wrote as follows of her wartime pacifism:

Vera was a brave woman to undertake this venture. She could have continued her career as a successful writer; instead she placed it in jeopardy, standing by her own unpopular convictions and addressing the Letters not so much to the committed pacifist but to the doubters who could not reconcile their beliefs and ideas with the expediencies demanded by war. . . . I sometimes thought she looked back with nos-

> talgia at the heady days when *Testament of Youth* made her one of the leading writers of her time. She was egocentric, she liked popularity and she found criticism difficult to take; I do not think she enjoyed having to swim against such a strong tide of public opinion. She said she was a natural coward but she overcame her fear of the bombs, determined to carry on what she had set her hand to do. In a different context she quoted Van Dyke: 'True courage is not incompatible with nervousness and heroism does not mean the absence of fear but the conquest of it.'[81]

Winifred Eden-Green's assessment is not only fair and friendly, it is acutely observant, for it points to the genuine and deep-going spiritual transformation that accompanied Brittain's outspoken adoption of principled pacifism. Although there were many people within the peace community who continued to admire her, during the war years Brittain lost the glamorous aura of success which she had so deeply desired and then had achieved with the publication of *Testament of Youth*. Because of the position she took, during the war Brittain lost friends she valued; she endured vilification as a supposed Fascist sympathizer; she suffered police surveillance; she was denied the exit permits she needed to visit her children, evacuated to the United States in June 1940, or to attend the All-India Women's Conference at Mysore to which she was invited in December 1940 as a result of her involvement with the cause of Indian independence.[82]

Why was Brittain able to muster the strength she needed to take up this burden of unpopularity? First, the experience of success had been in itself a major and enriching turning point in her life. While Brittain would unquestionably have enjoyed a repetition of the acclaim she received after *Testament of Youth*, this single achievement was in her case liberating. It released her from her overwhelming need to seek fame and gave her the strength to face up to her own weaknesses and uncertainties. Second, Winifred Holtby's final illness and death, which followed so closely on the period of adulation she enjoyed in 1933 and 1934, caused Brittain to engage in painful soul-searching. Not only did she miss Winifred and mourn her, she experienced considerable guilt and remorse, because she knew that she could have been more attentive to her friend during the final year of her life and indeed throughout the years of their friendship. Finally, it seems likely that she did undergo something akin to a conversion experience when she encountered Dick Sheppard and his message of Christian pacifism at the Peace Rally in Dorchester on 22 June 1936.

Her published description of this event, written in the 1950s for *Testament of Experience*, is, as we have already observed, frank and detailed. Writing of her own emotions, she characterizes herself as 'panic stricken' when she could not speak effectively from a public platform, an accomplishment she had performed hundreds of times in the past. In striking contrast to the later description, her diary entry for that day is spare: it reads simply, 'Great Dorchester Peace Rally'.[83] Now, it is possible that she was so brief because it was only later that she realized the significance of the event. But it is more likely that this is one of several cryptic entries scattered throughout decades of diary writing. Although Brittain was normally a loquacious diarist, she would on occasion resort to saying little or nothing in the face of certain intense emotions, most particularly feelings of shame arising from a belief that she had embarrassed herself in public. On this occasion, however, because her uncharacteristic speechlessness arose from a genuine change of mind, her embarrassment had a transformative effect.

In the *Testament of Experience* account of the Dorchester Peace Rally, Brittain tells us that when she managed to struggle to her feet to say a few words, she 'quoted Bunyan'. This reference to the seventeenth-century author of *Pilgrim's Progress* is not accidental. No doubt she did quote Bunyan that June afternoon in 1936, but in addition, in the 1950s, when she was writing *Testament of Experience*, Bunyan was in the forefront of her consciousness. In 1948 she had published *In the Steps of John Bunyan: An Excursion into Puritan England*,[84] a project that she had initially taken on merely as a paid commission. But in *Testament of Experience*, Brittain explains that in planning the book she had come to see Bunyan not as a remote figure, but as 'the great conscientious Objector against orthodoxy and oppression'.[85]

In *Testament of Experience*, references to Bunyan appear as a leitmotif throughout Brittain's account of the Second World War. The chapter in which she discusses her difficulties as an outspoken pacifist in wartime is entitled 'The Valley of Humiliation', a phrase from Bunyan. Its main message is that Brittain saw herself, like Christian in *Pilgrim's Progress*, as taking up the burden of humiliation, represented in her case by her lost popularity, by the deliberate misrepresentation of her ideas, and by her frustration when she could not travel abroad. As she explicitly states, this burden altered her perspective, making her more empathic with victims everywhere:

> One October week-end [in 1940] I had walked through a country lane considering, with the ready indignation of a combative temperament, how I could 'get my own back' on the obstructive bureaucrats who had

> made such havoc of my personal life. Suddenly, in an empty valley covered with fallen leaves, something seemed to check the direction of my thoughts. Within my mind, an inconvenient second self addressed me firmly. 'Don't you realise that this is a spiritual experience? For the past few years you have had far more honour and appreciation than you deserve. Now you know what it is to be humiliated; and this gives you a new kinship with those to whom you have hitherto felt superior – prisoners, refugees, the unemployed, the down-and-outs and all the despised and rejected of men.'[86]

Brittain's use of 'humiliated' in this passage has great significance. As a young writer, she frequently employed the word 'honour' and its cognates, using them for example in the titles of two of her five novels, *Not Without Honour* (1924) and *Honourable Estate* (1936). 'Honour' for Brittain signified respect and recognition. 'Humiliation', in contrast, was a word that she avoided before 1936, using it only when referring to deeply painful, embarrassing personal experiences. In *Testament of Youth*, for example, one of the few times she uses the word 'humiliation' is in her description of the Somerville debating society incident: 'For years I believed that it had been deliberately planned with a view to my humiliation. . . .'[87] And in March 1936 she uses it about the Jews in the café in Frankfurt: it will be remembered that she wrote in the privacy of her diary that their 'collective sense of humiliation was oppressive'. For Brittain, then, 'humiliation' signified helplessness, embarrassment and shame.

It was in the summer of 1936, as she was finishing *Honourable Estate*, that the concept of humiliation began to take on an altered meaning for her.[88] The transformation is evident in the later sections of the novel, in which humiliation is presented as an emotion that can have unexpected spiritual benefits. As Ruth muses to herself in the novel's final pages: 'Some of us, perhaps, can never reach our honourable estate – the state of maturity, of true understanding – until we have wrested strength and dignity out of humiliation and dishonour.'[89]

Brittain continued to find resonance in the intertwining of humiliation and honour, making it the central theme of her pacifist essay of 1942, *Humiliation with Honour*. Brittain made sure that *Humiliation with Honour* would convey its point as soon as a reader picked the book up. It was she, rather than the publisher, who commissioned the artist Arthur Wragg to do the jacket cover illustration, and she approved the results: a kneeling, shackled figure, etched with a halo effect on a black background.[90] The jacket blurb drives home the message:

> Vera Brittain . . . has had to pay, in this second World War, a considerable price for holding convictions derived from her share in the events of the first. After much conflict she has come to realise that humiliation, like other forms of suffering, is a spiritual experience; and to recognise that this experience in itself provides a means by which she, and others in a similar position, should be able to bring consolation and strength to the many whose lives are to-day shadowed or broken by the catastrophes which power-politics have brought upon mankind.[91]

Brittain did not radically change her outward style of life after 1936, but her inner transformation was genuine and profound. She did reach her own 'honourable estate' of understanding and maturity and as a result she became a staunch and courageous advocate for peace and social justice. However, while this process involved spiritual growth, it also involved losses. After the publication of *Honourable Estate* in 1936, a book written when she was in her early forties and at the peak of her powers, Brittain relinquished her intense desire to claim a space for herself through her writing. Although she continued to be a prolific writer well into the 1960s, publishing two more novels, two more 'Testaments' and several significant contributions to pacifism and feminism, her work lost the fierce energy that had fuelled it ever since, as a girl of nineteen, she had planned her first novel.

This diminution in Brittain's creative energy is evident in *Testament of Friendship*, a book written too hastily and while her judgement was clouded by grief and remorse. Within a week of Holtby's funeral in October 1935, publishers were asking Brittain to produce an instant biography. 'I no more feel equal now to doing an immediate biography of Winifred than I felt equal to writing T. of Y. immediately after the War',[92] she wrote, but by the end of October she had agreed to do the book for Victor Gollancz, who at least did not expect her to complete it in a matter of months. With the respite granted by the Gollancz contract, Brittain was able to use 1936 to complete *Honourable Estate* and at the same time to fulfil her duties as Winifred's literary executor and shepherd *South Riding* into print. She did not turn her full attention to the biography until 1939. Early that year she began reading through Winifred's correspondence and personal papers. She embarked on the writing itself in March 1939[93] and completed the book in July.[94]

Virginia Woolf, who read *Testament of Friendship* soon after its publication, characterized it privately as a 'scrambling, gasping, affectionate book: and W.H. deserved a better'.[95] Woolf's is a harsh but acute assessment. While *Testament of Friendship* is a respectable, professionally written account of Holtby's life, as a work of literature it is only partially successful, largely because Brittain, in constructing the book, could not decide where to position herself and her own relationship to Holtby. Was the book to be a tribute to her friend and to their friendship, or was it to offer Brittain the opportunity for expiating her guilt? The contrast between the celebratory tone of the Foreword, with its well-known affirmation of the importance of women's friendships, and the raw guilt of the Epilogue encapsulates *Testament of Friendship*'s confused intentions. Unquestionably, the writing itself intensified Brittain's feelings of remorse. When she began reading Winifred's correspondence in earnest, early in 1939, she at first seized on the fact that Lady Rhondda had 'exploited' Winifred's generosity. But soon it was the evidence of her own selfishness which became painfully apparent. Brittain drafted the Epilogue before she began writing the book, 'being inspired to do so by all the evidences of exploitation (particularly by Lady R., her mother & me) in W.'s letters'.[96] In it, she asserts that Winifred was a 'saint' who served others: 'No one is especially blameworthy, for the simple reason that all of us . . . were cruelly and intolerably to blame. We all exploited her . . . According to our different standings and in our various ways, we, her most intimate and devoted admirers, made use of her magnanimity to further our personal ends.'[97] Critic Adrienne Rich has written: '[l]ying is done with words, and also with silence'. Because Brittain's own feelings were so unresolved, to a much greater extent than any of her other works, Brittain's *Testament of Friendship* is marred by 'lies, secrets and silence'.[98]

Originally, Brittain's biography was to have been entitled *A Woman in her Time: The Story of Winifred Holtby*. The decision to echo the title of *Testament of Youth* in *Testament of Friendship* and later in *Testament of Experience* was astute from the point of view of marketing the later books, but the similar titles should not obscure the profound differences between the three. *Testament of Youth* is Brittain's bold triumph, the book in which she claimed a space for her own still relatively obscure life, and thereby spoke not only for herself but for a generation of readers; *Testament of Friendship*, in contrast, suffers under the weight of guilty obligation. *Testament of Experience*, finally, was just what *Testament of Youth* was not: the memoir of a woman of great achievement, an eminent woman in her sixties who indeed 'ought' to have been writing her biography, and moreover a woman whose experiences had made her both more worthy and less bold than she had been in her youth. Thus, while it was and remains a major autobiography of the 1950s, both because it is a valuable record of the contributions of its author, and an important commentary on its period, it lacks the vigour and the single-minded creativity that suffuses *Testament of Youth*.

From the late 1930s up until her death in 1970[99] Brittain maintained her active life, working for peace during the war years, as we have seen, and after the war for famine relief, disarmament and support for a newly independent India. But what of feminism, the connecting thread that has been the primary focus of this study? Peace historian Y. Aleksandra Bennett writes that by 1936, pacifism 'had subsumed [Brittain's] socialism and her feminism, and informed every aspect and action of her life'.[100] In one important respect, Bennett is of course correct: after 1936, Brittain's activist energies were largely devoted to pacifist rather than feminist issues, and it is as a major pacifist figure that Brittain was best known from then until her death. But for Brittain, feminism was always more than a series of discrete issues, and a feminist commitment to woman's personhood – her own and that of all women – remained central to her self-definition and to her definition of the world until the end of her life. And indeed, Brittain's post-1936 activist concern with peace work developed directly out of her feminism. She had always believed that woman's personhood imposed on women the obligation to be politically active, and in the war-torn twentieth century that meant working for peace. As she wrote in 1936, speaking through her fictional character, Ruth Alleyndene:

> [T]he movement against war and the movement for better human conditions are bound up together, and the modern woman's movement is concerned with both. If only the women who now have votes on the same terms as men could realise what the abolition of war would mean to the wives and mothers still enslaved by intolerable living conditions, the end of poverty and injustice would be in sight. If only they would work for peace as their predecessors worked for their own liberation we should have no more of the monstrous folly which throws away a nation's resources on the destruction of mankind![101]

And while Brittain took up the challenge articulated by Ruth Alleyndene, she never ceased to speak out for feminism. For example, in 1953 she published a history of the women's movement with the evocative title *Lady into Woman: A History of Women from Victoria to Elizabeth II*.[102] This book bears witness to Brittain's abiding commitment to the cause of feminism.[103] Even in the 1950s, the nadir of feminism in our century, she was there as a voice in the wilderness, and as testimony to the fact that feminism never completely disappeared in the mid-twentieth-century decades. In *Lady into Woman* Brittain clearly enunciates her perception of the relationship between individual feminist issues and the wider meaning of feminism: 'It is therefore inevitable that the feminist movement should first have impressed itself on the public mind as a series of claims to equal citizenship. . . . But these practical claims add up, at a deeper level, to one demand; the recognition of woman's full share in a common humanity. Accept us, women say, as complete human beings, and we will be content.'[104]

As writer, as activist for peace and social justice, and as friend, wife and mother, Vera Brittain struggled throughout her life to become 'a complete human being', and to make the attainment of such personhood possible for all women and men. In 1935, when Winifred was dying, Frederick Pethick-Lawrence had written Brittain a touching letter in which he told her of the importance that both she and Holtby had for himself and his wife Emmeline:

> If you will forgive me for being very personal, may I tell you in what special way I regard herself & yourself & those others of your generation who are holding aloft with such courage and determination the noblest emblem of modern womanhood? . . . As we have no children of our body, so I always feel that those who fulfil the vision are children of our spirit.[105]

That assessment of Brittain's contribution to feminism by one of the major figures of the pre-war suffrage movement serves to remind us not only of the continuities in twentieth-century feminism, but also of the varied challenges that feminists have confronted throughout our century. Sustaining feminism in periods of vigorous activism – during the suffrage campaign, or during the passionate 1970s, the height of the 'second wave' revival – requires one kind of commitment. But an even deeper commitment is needed during those periods in which the very success of the women's movement generates opposition to feminism's core beliefs.[106] Vera Brittain did indeed 'fulfil the vision' of the early twentieth-century radical suffragists, and what is more, she helped to sustain it during the difficult interwar decades and into the anti-feminist 1950s and 1960s. At her best, she represents the best in the liberal, humanist feminist tradition.

12
Conclusion

In the dedication to 'My dear Daughter' with which *Lady into Woman* opens, Brittain writes: 'unlike many of your contemporaries you do not regard the women's movement as a bygone issue. Even from your brief experience you know that it is continuing, and still has far to go'.[1] Forty years later, the women's movement still has 'far to go'. Since *Lady into Woman*'s publication in 1953, women have been political leaders in countries as disparate as India and Norway, but in this final decade of the twentieth century, 85 million more boys than girls attend school, and violence against women is a problem everywhere, to enumerate just two cruel forms of injustice against women.[2] Moreover, even in the most advanced industrial democracies, women still face economic and social inequalities.[3]

And in our century, feminism's very success has brought with it new challenges. As part of the feminist revival, which began a decade after the publication of *Lady into Woman*, working-class women and women of colour have developed a body of feminist scholarship and social practice that accounts for race and class as well as gender, and that sharply questions the dominance of white, bourgeois feminist ideology. Moreover, in the 1980s and 1990s, the maturation of feminism has made divisions of opinion acutely visible. The significance of gender difference, for example, is vigorously contested terrain. Many contemporary feminists ground their feminism in a celebration of woman's 'special nature'; others insist that women's right to equality with men springs from the fundamental similarities all human beings share. It is partly because I ground my own feminist beliefs in a commitment to equality rather than difference that I have chosen to write about Vera Brittain, a leading feminist activist of an earlier period who was a staunch adherent of equal rights feminism. I have sought to demonstrate that in her struggles to develop a truly egalitarian vision of society she is representative of the successes and of the failures of liberal feminism in the mid-twentieth century.

By the 1950s, Brittain herself was keenly aware that in her early years she had been part of that 'eager generation of young feminists who were the first to inherit the freedom won for women by women'. She claimed for herself and others of her generation the 'privilege' of bridging the 'enormous gulf' between women like her mother, condemned to Victorian ladyhood, and women like her daughter, whom she hoped would enjoy adulthood as liberated women.[4] The interwar period was indeed one of significant but still insufficiently understood transition. Through my examination of the dilemmas with which Brittain struggled – combining friendship with work and competitiveness; constructing an egalitarian marriage; reconciling the responsibilities of motherhood with the demands of serious intellectual work – I have illustrated the continuities between early twentieth-century feminism and our own period. And through a discussion of the issues which Brittain avoided or only partially confronted – most notably the effect that her own privileged class, ethnic and national identities had on her experience – I have reflected, from a late twentieth-century perspective, on the limits of her feminist vision.

Brittain saw herself as a modern woman who had left the confinement and the hypocrisy of 'the Victorian tradition of womanhood' behind.[5] The contrast between the Victorian and the modern preoccupied her throughout her life, and her most important literary achievement, *Testament of Youth*, abounds with contrasts and comparisons between the prewar period, that 'unparalleled age of rich materialism and tranquil comfort'[6] and the tension and nervous speed of the modern era. Brittain designed *Testament of Youth* as a journey from that tranquil age with its comforts, but with its corresponding constrictions and prejudices, through the fiery furnace of the war and out the other side to the bleakness but also the liberation of 'post-Victorian womanhood'.

But while she proclaimed her modernity, Brittain was no modernist. As I argue in chapter 10 of this book, 'The Writing of *Testament of Youth*', *Testament of Youth* has been excluded from the standard literary canon largely because of Brittain's avoidance of modernist idioms. Brittain's lack of sympathy with modernism extends well beyond her use of literary forms. If we consider the two cultural constructs 'Victorianism' and 'modernism', the former describes Brittain more closely than the latter. 'Victorianism' has been defined as signifying in politics a liberal consensus characterized by a sober rationalism, a faith in representative institutions and a belief in progress; in social life, the dominance of a middle class that respected order, ritual and stability but at the same time encouraged individuals to 'improve' themselves through effective use of their talents and energies; in morality a commitment to Evangelicalism in its religious or in its secularized form, and a reliance on the primacy of the virtues of duty, effort and thrift and on the importance of the family; in culture, a respect for seriousness, for order, for rationality and for linear thinking.[7] 'Modernism', in contrast has been defined as questioning rationality, as rejecting stability in favour of movement for its own sake, but at the same time it placed no faith in 'improvement' or progress, and it ridiculed moral seriousness – as modernist Lytton Strachey did in 1918 in *Eminent Victorians*. Modernism's cultural forms emphasise dissonance and primitivism, and reject linear realism as superficial.[8] In her respect for reason rather than emotion, in her abiding faith in liberalism, in her sexual reticence, and in her adherence to Victorian cultural forms, Vera Brittain remained Victorian rather than modern.

Brittain's implicit rejection of modernism, while no doubt limiting in some respects, was at the same time an essential element in her feminist legacy. Throughout this book, I have referred frequently to recent historical writing which postulates that, in the period after the First World War, the women's movement in England turned away from equal-rights feminism towards an essentialist definition of gender difference. Susan Kent, for instance, takes up Sandra Gilbert's notion that the Great War set off a modernist sex war, and asserts that a conservative 'new' feminism emerged out of this sex war in the 1920s, a feminism that 'underscored not fundamental equality but the primacy of sexual difference'.[9]

If one rejects – as I do – all essentialist formulations of gender, be they modernist or traditional, Brittain's allegiance to equal rights feminism can be perceived as an enormously beneficial feature of her rejection of modernism. In the interwar decades, modernism may have seemed liberating, but with its penchant for the irrational and the primitive, it could and did lead to dangerously retrogressive ideas about women.[10] Vera Brittain represents the antithesis of the modernist identification of the feminine with the irrational. She was sober, disciplined and responsible. She placed duty before happiness, and while she bobbed her hair, wore short skirts and took an interest in psychoanalysis, she had little appetite for sexual liberation. And – it must be admitted – she was culturally unadventurous. Although she read D.H. Lawrence and admired Virginia Woolf's creativity, in her own writing she modelled herself on that most Victorianist of

Victorian writers, the rationalist, moralist George Eliot. Her ambitions as a writer never went beyond writing a good, realist, linear narrative. But her ambitions as a social reformer reasserted the most progressive aspects of the Victorian tradition of rational optimism and faith in the possibility of improvement.

Brittain's liberalism reveals itself nowhere more strongly than in her unquestioning belief in the existence of a transcendent self, expressed for example in her assertion that a central purpose of feminism is to ensure that women – and men – become 'complete human beings'. In the introduction to this book, I explain that I have found post-modernist theory helpful as I have attempted to expand the constraining boundaries established by Brittain's own narratives of her life. Post-modernist insights about 'representation' do challenge naive empiricism and do call attention to those things left unsaid in any narrative. But post-modernist theorizing about the primacy of 'representation' over 'experience' and about the 'decentred subject' is also dangerous, especially to historians and most especially to feminists. Although I do not claim to have recaptured the 'real' Vera Brittain, I believe that there was such a person, that she was born in 1893, that she died in 1970, and that between her birth and her death, she was alive. Yes, we can only know experience mediated through representation: none the less, it is experience that we are attempting to reveal. And feminists should be chary of theories that question the reality of human subjectivity. For much of history, patriarchy has denied women's subjectivity by constructing woman as 'other'. Feminism, in contrast, asserts women's claim to selfhood, but this claim is still fragile and incomplete and it is risky for feminists to embrace theories that question the legitimacy of the transcendent self or of experience. As Adrienne Rich has written, feminism means 'taking women seriously'.[11] It is because Vera Brittain took herself seriously that the nature and the development of her feminist consciousness is worthy of close examination.

Liz Stanley has written that 'in a sense it is *only* biography which can make available to us the detailed processes of historical change'.[12] Vera Brittain, good historian that she was, would have agreed with Stanley. It is because she believed so strongly that individual experience is essential to the study of history that she carefully left behind such a complete record of her own life and, as Winifred Holtby's literary executor, of Holtby's life. Brittain was fully aware that her private papers (and Holtby's) would reveal much that she omitted from her published writings and that some of what was revealed would contradict her public self-representation. Nine years after her death, her friend and future biographer Paul Berry wrote this perceptive tribute:

> The world is only as good a place as the people living in it choose to make it, and we should be grateful to Vera Brittain for her valiant fight to make it better, for her dedication to peace and the continuing liberation of women, for her passion for justice and her compassion for the oppressed, and, perhaps above all, for the shining example of her rock-like integrity.[13]

I write as someone who did not know Vera Brittain as a living person, but in so far as I do 'know' her through her writings and through my work as a researcher, Paul Berry's verdict concerning her integrity is one with which I would emphatically agree. The archival record does of course reveal aspects of her character that were not always wholly admirable and, as well, evidence of suppression and distortion. But we know about these distortions and unrevealed aspects because Brittain decided to allow researchers access to such a rich archival record. Brittain bequeathed her weaknesses as well as her strengths as evidence, and for this brave decision historians and a later generation of feminists should indeed be grateful.

Notes

The following abbreviated forms are used throughout the notes:

Brittain, *Testament of Youth* = Vera Brittain, *Testament of Youth: An Autobiographical Study of the Years 1900–1925* (London: Victor Gollancz; New York: Macmillan, 1933).

Holtby papers = The Winifred Holtby Collection, Hull Central Library, Hull, England.

VBA = The Vera Brittain Archive, William Ready Division of Archives and Research Collections, McMaster University Library, Hamilton, Ontario, Canada.

Full details of other references are given at first citation in each chapter.

CHAPTER 1: INTRODUCTION

1 *Observer*, 27 August 1933, p. 5: 'Tomorrow *Testament of Youth*: Vera Brittain's Autobiographical Study of the years 1900–1925.' A week earlier Gollancz had run a small but distinctive notice in bold lettering reading 'Ready today week: Testament of Youth' (*Observer*, 20 August 1933, p. 5).

2 See Brittain's diary entry for 29 August 1933: 'Lunched Cafe Royal with David Higham, who told me sales already amounted to 3,300.' Vera Brittain's manuscript diaries are in the Vera Brittain Archive, William Ready Division of Archives and Research Collections, McMaster University Library, Hamilton, Canada; hereinafter cited as 'VBA'. The diaries of the 1930s have been published in an excellent edition edited by Alan Bishop: *Vera Brittain, Dairy of the Thirties, 1932–1939: Chronicle of Friendship* (London: Victor Gollancz, 1986). Bishop has also edited Brittain's First World War diaries: Alan Bishop (ed.), *Chronicle of Youth: Vera Brittain's war diary, 1913–1917* (London: Victor Gollancz, 1981). With Y. Aleksandra Bennett he has edited the diaries of the 1940s: Alan Bishop and Y. Aleksandra Bennett (eds), *Vera Brittain, Diary 1939–1945: Wartime Chronicle* (London: Victor Gollancz, 1989). In this book, citations from the earliest diaries

are from the manuscript diary, the 'Reflective Record'. For the 1930s and 1940s most citations are from the published editions.

3 *The Sunday Times*, 3 September 1933, p. 8. The review was by the novelist Storm Jameson. Her friendship with Brittain is discussed on p. 214.

4 *The Diary of Virginia Woolf*, vol. IV: *1931–1935*, ed. Anne Olivier Bell (London: Hogarth Press, 1982). Entry is for Saturday, 2 September 1933 (p. 177).

5 Within six years, *Testament of Youth* sold 120,000 copies. Robert Wohl, *The Generation of 1914* (Cambridge, Mass.: Harvard University Press, 1979), p. 111.

6 From Brittain's diary, 19 Jannuary 1932, in *Chronicle of Friendship*, p. 30.

7 See Brittain to Holtby, 27 June 1921. The Brittain–Holtby correspondence is in the Winifred Holtby Papers, Hull Central Library, Hull, England; referred to hereinafter as 'Holtby papers', except where the letter appears in *Selected Letters of Winifred Holtby to Vera Brittain (1920–1935)*, ed. Vera Brittain and Geoffrey Handley-Taylor (London: A. Brown, 1960).

8 The Vera Brittain Archive is voluminous. The collection contains family papers, Brittain's diaries and notebooks, manuscripts, copies of her published and unpublished articles, and over 20,000 pieces of correspondence. There is a three-volume guide to the collection: *The Vera Brittain Archive*, parts I, II and III, *McMaster University Library Research News*, vol. 4, nos 3–5 (1977–9).

9 See Roland Leighton to Vera Brittain, 'In Billets: Flanders' and Monday, 26 April, from his dug-out, 25 April 1915, VBA. Roland also wrote a poem about this incident, which Brittain used to head chapter IV of *Testament of Youth*.

10 Vera Brittain to Edith Brittain from Somerville College, 14 February 1915, VBA.

11 From notes labelled 'Autobiographies' in folder labelled 'Vera Brittain Testament of Youth Holograph notes', A5 box 3, VBA.

12 Nancy K. Miller, 'Writing Fictions: Autobiography in France', in Bella Brodzki and Celeste Schenck (eds), *Life/Lines: Theorizing Women's Autobiography* (Ithaca, N.T.: Cornell University Press, 1988), p. 45.

13 Bella Brodzki and Celeste Schenck, 'Introduction', in *Life/Lines*, p. 1.

14 The phrase is Carolyn G. Heilbrun's. See her *Writing a Woman's Life* (New York: W.W. Norton, 1988).

15 Miller, 'Writing Fictions', p. 59. Other scholars have also offered intertextual interpretations of Brittain's fiction and autobiography. For example, Jean E. Kennard, *Vera Brittain and Winifred Holtby: A Working Partnership* (Hanover, N.H.: University Press of New England, 1989); and Rita Miriam Kissen, *Vera Brittain: Writing a Life*, PhD dissertation, University of Massachusetts, 1986.

16 Susan Groag Bell and Marilyn Yalom (eds), *Revealing Lives: Autobiography, Biography, and Gender* (Albany, N.Y.: SUNY Press, 1990), 'Introduction', pp. 1 and 2.

CHAPTER 2: ORIGINS, 1893–1911

1 Brittain, *Testament of Youth,* p. 31.
2 Ibid., p. 21.
3 Ibid., p. 20.
4 For parents' birth dates see 'Material belonging to Vera Brittain's parents', VBA. For information on Brittain's Ltd, see document in envelope marked 'In re Brittain's Ltd, re founders' bonus, etc.' in box marked 'Thomas A. Brittain/Edith Brittain, diaries and memorabilia of family', VBA.
5 For the firm's prosperity, see the above document which explains that the 'balance sheet . . . of 31 Dec 1907' shows that the 'concern in a very prosperous condition and amply capitalized'. For further information, see the material in box 'Material belonging to Vera Brittain's parents', VBA.
6 His will is in the box marked 'Material belonging to Vera Brittain's parents', VBA.
7 See John Edward Brittain Catlin, *Family Quartet* (London: Hamish Hamilton, 1987), p. 21.
8 There is information about John Bladder Inglis Bervon in various scrapbooks in a box labelled 'Material belonging to Vera Brittain's parents', VBA.
9 Brittain, *Testament of Youth*, p. 19.
10 John Bervon left £251.14.0 when he died. For his will, see box marked 'Thomas A. Brittain/Edith Brittain diaries and memorabilia of family', VBA.
11 Catlin, *Family Quartet*, p. 18.
12 Ibid., p. 19.
13 Vera Brittain, *Honourable Estate: A Novel of Transition* (New York: Macmillan, 1936).
14 I am surmising here from comments Brittain herself makes in *Testament of Youth*, p. 20.
15 See Vera Brittain, 'Reflective Record', 24 April 1913, VBA.
16 Brittain, *Testament of Youth*, p. 21.
17 The house is at 170 Chester Road. Thanks to Mr and Mrs Averiss, who lived there in 1992, for graciously allowing me to see the interior.
18 Brittain, *Testament of Youth*, p. 23.
19 Ibid., p. 21.
20 We know from a postcard she sent, dated 22 April 1905, that this servant had warm feelings for Vera Brittain; 'A happy Easter to you Dearie; I miss you dreadfully' (from Towby to Vera Brittain, in Juvenelia, VBA).

21 Brittain, *Testament of Youth*, p. 27. For her name, see Vera Brittain to her mother 24 September (no year, but probably 1904), with a post-script about the welfare of the children, written by 'A.M. Newby'. And see Vera Brittain to Winifred Holtby, 20 April 1933, in *Selected Letters of Winifred Holtby to Vera Brittain (1920–1935)*, ed. Vera Brittain and Geoffrey Handley-Taylor (London: A. Brown, 1960), p. 258.
22 Vera Brittain to Edith Brittain, 27 September 1903, VBA.
23 Edward Brittain to Edith Brittain, 27 September 1903, VBA.
24 Brittain, *Testament of Youth*, p. 27.
25 On this point, see the general discussion and some specific references to Vera Brittain in Carol Dyhouse, *Feminism and the Family in England* (Oxford: Basil Blackwell, 1989).
26 Vera Brittain to Edith Brittain, 24 September 1904(?), VBA.
27 Brittain, *Testament of Youth*, p. 24.
28 Vera Brittain to Edith Brittain, 18 September 1902, VBA.
29 On reading for girls, see Judith Rowbotham, *Good Girls Make Good Wives: Guidance for Girls in Victorian Fiction* (Oxford; Basil Blackwell, 1989); and Deborah Gorham, 'The Ideology of Femininity and Reading for Girls: 1850–1914', in Felicity Hunt (ed.), *Lessons for Life: Education and Gender 1850–1950* (Oxford: Basil Blackwell, 1987). On melodrama, see Joanne F. Thompson, *The Seduction, Rape and Untimely Death of Women in Fiction: An Educational Problem*, PhD dissertation, University of Toronto, 1988.
30 The childhood 'novels' are in Juvenelia (1), VBA.
31 Brittain, *Testament of Youth*, p. 27.
32 See, for example, Geoffrey Best, *Mid-Victorian Britain: 1851–1875* (New York: Schocken, 1972), p. 254.
33 For Buxton's history, see R. Grundy Heape, *Buxton under the Dukes of Devonshire* (London: Robert Hale, 1948).
34 Ibid., p. 73.
35 The house, 151 Park Road, which has in recent years been divided into flats, is a large, semi-detached, grey stone structure, set in a beautiful garden. I thank Mrs Katie Doyle-Davidson for kindly allowing me to visit the Doyle-Davidson flat, which occupies the first floor of the house.
36 Historians have explored the role of women in the construction of upward social mobility in some detail. See, especially, Leonore Davidoff, *The Best Circles: Society, Etiquette and the Season* (London: Croom Helm, 1973); and Pat Jalland, *Women, Marriage and Politics, 1860–1914* (Oxford: Clarendon Press, 1986), who explore upper-class and upper-middle-class patterns. For the earlier foundations of the relationship between gender and social status, see Leonore Davidoff and Catherine Hall, *Family Fortunes: Men and Women of the English Middle Class, 1780–1850* (London: Hutchinson, 1987).
37 Brittain, *Testament of Youth*, p. 20.

38 Ibid., pp. 27–8.
39 The Headmistress was Miss L. Dodd. See *The Buxton Directory* (1912) listing of schools, p. 9: 'The Grange school for Girls, The Park – Principal Miss L. Dodd. The staff consists of graduates of the various universities of the United Kingdom, trained for teaching; a foreign Mistress for languages, and teachers holding diplomas of the Royal Academy of Music.' (Directory held by the Buxton Public Library.)
40 See the report, signed Alice M. Aldorn, and dated 21 September 1905, in folder labelled 'Report cards' in box labelled 'Art work', Juvenilia, VBA.
41 Catlin, *Family Quartet*, p. 6.
42 See Vera Brittain to Edith Brittain, 8 October 1905 and 29 March 1906, VBA.
43 For Louise Heath Jones, see *St Monica's School Notes* (1931–2), an 'In Memoriam' issue, which discussed her career and reprinted her obituary from *The Times*. In Juvenelia, 'Art work', VBA.
44 No records appear to remain from St Monica's, but available evidence, including that from the school paper in VBA and from Brittain's early diary (her 'Reflective Record') and information from her daughter Shirley Williams, indicates that the pupils were from affluent backgrounds (interview with Shirley Williams, 3 June 1986). At Shirley Williams's kind suggestion, I had a telephone conversation, in June 1986, with Lady Joan Vickers, who had attended St Monica's, which further confirmed these surmises about the social status of St Monica's pupils.
45 For more information on the school, see my articles 'A Woman at Oxford: Vera Brittain's Somerville Experience', *Historical Studies in Edution/Revue d'histoire de l'éducation*, 8 (Spring 1991): 1–19; and 'The Education of Vera and Edward Brittain: Class and Gender in a Late-Victorian and Edwardian Family', *History of Education Review*, 20 (1), (1991):22–38.
46 My information concerning Florence Louise Bervon and Heath Jones is from *The Times* obituary of Louise Heath Jones reprinted in *St Monica's School Notes, 1931–2*, and from a piece written by Vera Brittain on Florence Bervon, which appeared originally in *The Times*, 22 May 1936, and which is reprinted in *St Monica's School Notes, 1935–6*. In Juvenelia, 'Art work', VBA.
47 Martha Vicinus, *Independent Women: Work and Community for Single Women, 1850–1920* (Chicago: University of Chicago Press, 1985), p. 7.
48 Brittain, *Testament of Youth*, pp. 36–7.
49 For more on St Monica's, see my 'The Education of Vera and Edward Brittain'. For middle-class girls' education, see Joan Burstyn, *Victorian Education and the Ideal of Womanhood* (London: Croom Helm, 1980); Carol Dyhouse, *Girls Growing Up in Victorian and Edwardian England* (London: Routledge & Kegan Paul, 1981); Felicity Hunt

(ed.), *Lessons for Life: The Schooling of Girls and Women, 1850–1950* (Oxford: Basil Blackwell, 1987); Deborah Gorham, *The Victorian Girl and the Feminine Ideal* (London: Croom Helm, and Bloomington, Ind.: Indiana University Press, 1982); and Felicity Hunt, 'Divided Aims: the Educational Implications of Opposing Ideologies in Girls' Secondary Schooling, 1850–1914', in Hunt (ed.), *Lessons for Life*.

50 While the school did offer some instruction in Latin, it is not clear that any instruction in Greek was offered during Brittain's years. Brittain's school reports indicate that the school offered scripture, arithmetic, geometry, geography, nature study, English literature, English history, French, German, Italian, Classics (primarily in translation), singing, drawing, handwork, cooking, gymnastics, dancing and games (Juvenilia, VBA).

51 See Brittain, 'Reflective Record', summer term 1911, VBA.

52 For details, see my 'The Education of Vera and Edward Brittain'.

53 Brittain, *Testament of Youth*, pp. 38–9. On the suffrage movement, see, for example, Sandra Stanley Holton, *Feminism and Democracy: Women's Suffrage and Reform Politics in Britain, 1900–1918* (Cambridge: Cambridge University Press, 1986); and Susan Kingsley Kent, *Sex and Suffrage in Britain: 1860–1914* (Princeton, N.J.: Princeton University Press, 1987).

54 Brittain, *Testament of Youth*, p. 40.

55 Ibid., p. 44.

56 Vera Brittain, 'Olive Schreiner', *Nation and Athenaeum*, 23 October 1926, G23 in VBA.

57 Brittain, *Testament of Youth*, p. 41.

58 Philippa Levine, *Feminist Lives in Victorian England: Private Roles and Public Commitment* (Oxford: Basil Blackwell, 1990), pp. 15–41.

59 Brittain, *Testament of Youth*, p. 38.

60 This is from the earliest portion of Brittain's 'Reflective Record': written in 1911, it summarises 1910 (VBA).

61 Vicinus, *Independent Women*, p. 187.

62 Vera Brittain, 'Reflective Record', from notes re Michaelmas Term 1910, VBA.

63 Brittain, *Testament of Youth*, p. 42.

64 Her St Monica's school essays are in Juvenelia, box 2, VBA.

65 Essay on More written in October 1911, in Juvenelia, box 2, VBA.

66 'Disciplined love' is Vicinus's phrase. See Vicinus, *Independent Women*, p. 187.

67 Brittain, *Testament of Youth*, p. 35.

68 Vera Brittain, *Not Without Honour* (London: Grant Richards, 1924).

69 Brittain, 'Reflective Record', 8 January 1911, VBA.

70 Ibid., summary of 1910, VBA.

71 Ibid., 14 February 1911, VBA.

72 Ibid.

73 Ibid., 11 February 1911, VBA.
74 See Ibid., 20 April 1913, VBA.
75 Brittain, *Not Without Honour*, pp. 10–11. Brittain's anti-Semitism was typical of the period. Her feminism did not preclude such views. On anti-Semitism in the women's movement, see Linda Gordon Kuzmack, *Woman's Cause: The Jewish Woman's Movement in England and the United States, 1881–1933* (Columbus: Ohio State University Press, 1990).
76 See Brittain, *Testament of Youth*, p. 35.
77 See Brittain, 'Reflective Record', *passim.*
78 Ibid., 28 March 1911, VBA.
79 From report card, Midsummer Term 1911, Lower VI, Juvenelia, box 2, VBA.

CHAPTER 3: 'PROVINCIAL YOUNG LADYHOOD', 1911–1914

1 For the significance of these rituals, see Leonore Davidoff, *The Best Circles: Society, Etiquette and the Season* (London: Croom Helm, 1973); and Pat Jalland, *Women, Marriage and Politics, 1860–1914* (Oxford: Clarendon, 1986).
2 An example of the business and professional elite would be the Coxes, who were friends of the Brittains; Dr J.J. Cox managed the Cottage Hospital and sat on the Board of the Devonshire Hospital. He was also President of the Chrysanthemum Society. Information about Buxton gathered from local newspapers; the Buxton Museum; the Buxton Public Library; the archives of the Devonshire Hospital.
3 See the memorabilia in the Buxton Museum. Pre-war performances included Arsene Lupin's *Passers By*, A. Conan Doyle's *The Speckled Band* and Gilbert and Sullivan's *Princess Ida*.
4 R. Grundy Heape, *Buxton under the Dukes of Devonshire* (London: Robert Hale, 1948), p. 124.
5 See, for example, the account of Mrs B. Ellinger speaking on 'Free Trade' to the Women's Liberal Club, *Buxton Herald*, 25 January 1911, p. 6.
6 See photo of Fairfield 1913 WSPU rally, Buxton Museum.
7 See *Buxton Herald*, 14 January 1914, p. 7: 'The Cottage Hospital Ball . . .', where 'Mrs Brittain' is listed as part of the Ladies' Committee, along with Lady Vaudrey, Mrs Cox, Mrs Ellinger, Dr F. Theobold, and others.
8 'Reflective Record', 4 January 1911, VBA.
9 For date of ball, see *Buxton Herald*, 27 December 1911, p. 5.
10 Brittain, *Testament of Youth*, p. 50.
11 For the Cottage Hospital Ball, see *Buxton Herald*, 8 January 1913, p. 5, and for the High Peak Hunt, see ibid., 15 January 1913, p. 5.
12 'Reflective Record', 4 February 1913, VBA.
13 Ibid., 29 January 1913, VBA.

14 Ibid., 2 June, 1913, VBA.
15 Ward came to Fairfield in January 1913. See 'New Curate Welcomed', *Buxton Herald*, 8 January 1913.
16 'Reflective Record', 27 May 1913, VBA.
17 Ibid., 29 May 1913, VBA.
18 For Ward and Fairfield, see the published version of the diary: *Chronicle of Youth: Vera Brittain's War Diary, 1913–1917*, ed. Alan Bishop with Terry Smart (London: Victor Gollancz, 1981), p. 350, n. 41.
19 On the arrival of Scott-Moncrieff, see *Buxton Herald*, 20 December 1911, p. 6. From circumstantial evidence, I assume that this was the church the Brittain family attended.
20 'Reflective Record', 19 January 1913, VBA.
21 Ibid., 15 November 1913, VBA.
22 Ibid., 23 November 1913, VBA.
23 Ibid., 30 November 1913, VBA.
24 Ibid., 1 January 1913, VBA.
25 Ibid., 18 October 1913, VBA.
26 Ibid., VBA.
27 An Exhibition was a minor scholarship.
28 Brittain, *Testament of Youth*, pp. 52–3.
29 Ibid., p. 58.
30 In fact, he came in the winter of 1913. See 'Reflective Record', VBA.
31 Brittain, *Testament of Youth*, p. 61.
32 Ibid., p. 63.
33 Vera Brittain, *Not Without Honour* (London: Grant Richards, 1924), p. 41.
34 Ibid., p. 77.
35 Ibid., p. 253.
36 Ibid., p. 226.
37 Ibid., pp. 274–5.
38 Ibid., p. 315.
39 Brittain, *Testament of Youth*, p. 32.
40 'Reflective Record', 23 January 1913, VBA.
41 Ibid., 5 February 1913, VBA.
42 Ibid., 5 May 1913, VBA.
43 Ibid., 31 May 1913, VBA.
44 Ibid., 18 October 1913, VBA.
45 Ibid., VBA.
46 Edith Fry to Vera Brittain, 26 October 1913, in General Correspondence, VBA.
47 'Reflective Record', 2 December 1913, VBA.
48 Brittain, *Testament of Youth*, p. 76.
49 Ibid., p. 70.
50 'Reflective Record', 25 March 1913, VBA.
51 Ibid., 25 March 1914, VBA.
52 The scholarly and popular work on motherhood and mothers and

daughters written from a feminist perspective has proliferated since the 1970s. For a perceptive analysis of the influential feminist writing on motherhood of the 1970s, see Nancy Chodorow and Susan Contratto, 'The Fantasy of the Perfect Mother', in Barrie Thorne and Marilyn Yalom (eds), *Rethinking the Family: Some Feminist Questions* (New York: Longman, 1982), pp. 54–75.

53 Brittain, *Testament of Youth*, p. 53.
54 'Reflective Record', 10 April 1911, VBA.
55 Ibid., 3 February 1913, VBA.
56 Ibid., 18 March 1913, VBA.
57 Ibid., 31 March 1913, VBA. See same entry for reference to 'the club'. Reference to the visit with Stella is 2 April 1913.
58 Ibid., 15 May 1913, VBA.
59 Ibid., 17 May 1913, VBA.
60 Ibid., 7 January 1913, VBA.
61 Ibid., 8 April 1913, VBA.
62 Ibid., 24 April 1913, VBA.
63 Ibid., 22 January 1913, VBA.
64 See ibid., 18 April 1913 and 26 May 1913, VBA.
65 Brittain, *Testament of Youth*, p. 73. 'G.F.S.' stands for the Girls' Friendly Society. The GFS and the Mothers' Union were two Church of England organizations.
66 'Reflective Record', 21 October 1913, VBA.
67 Brittain, *Not Without Honour*, p. 44.
68 'Reflective Record', 15 November 1913, VBA.
69 See, for example, ibid., 1 February 1914, 1 March 1914, 17 May 1914, VBA.
70 Brittain, *Not Without Honour*, pp. 24 and 26.
71 'Reflective Record', 25 May 1913, VBA.
72 This photograph is reproduced here as Plate 3.
73 See 'Reflective Record', 27 March 1911, VBA.
74 Ibid., 10 February 1913, VBA. (Presumably, these were 'debts' she owed her parents.)
75 See, for example, Edward Bristow, *Vice and Vigilance: Purity Movements in Britain Since 1700* (Dublin: Gill & Macmillan, 1977).
76 'Reflective Record', 12 March 1913, VBA.
77 Ibid., 1 January 1913, VBA.
78 Ibid., 15 November 1913, VBA.
79 Ibid., 15 February 1914, VBA.
80 Ibid., 24 April 1913, VBA.
81 Ibid., 7 January 1914, VBA.
82 Ibid., 19 March 1913, VBA.
83 Ibid., 9 March 1914, VBA.
84 Ibid., 25 March 1914, VBA.
85 For more on Edward and Uppingham, see my 'The Education of Vera and Edward Brittain: Class and Gender in an Upper-middle-class

Family in late Victorian and Edwardian England', *History of Education Review*, 20(1), (1991):22–38.
86 'Reflective Record', 23 January 1913, VBA.
87 Ibid., 27 March 1914, VBA.
88 Ibid., 24 April 1913, VBA.
89 Ibid., 8 April 1914, VBA.
90 Ibid., 16 February 1914, VBA.
91 Ibid., 12 April 1914, VBA.
92 Ibid., 2 January 1914, VBA.
93 Edward Brittain to Vera Brittain, 16 November 1913, VBA.
94 See 'Reflective Record', 10 and 15 April 1914, VBA.
95 Ibid., 4 January 1914, VBA.
96 Ibid., 1 May 1914, VBA.
97 Ibid., 26 June 1913, VBA.
98 Ibid., 11 July 1914, VBA.
99 See Brittain's letters to G.E.G. Catlin, her future husband, dated 26 August 1924, in VBA. I discuss Brittain's attitude toward sexuality at length in chapter 9.
100 'Reflective Record', 8 January 1913, VBA. Ernest and Maurice were two Buxton young men. Maurice was Maurice Ellinger; the Ellingers were close friends of the Brittains.
101 Ibid., 4 March 1913, VBA.
102 Brittain, *Testament of Youth*, pp. 58–9.
103 'Reflective Record', 23 June 1913, VBA.
104 Ibid., 25 June 1913, VBA.
105 Ibid., VBA.
106 Brittain, *Testament of Youth*, pp. 46–7.
107 Ibid., p. 47.
108 'Reflective Record', from St Monica's, 4 April 1914, VBA.
109 See references in ibid., for example 23 November 1913, VBA.
110 Ibid., 9 June 1914, VBA.
111 Ibid., 20 December 1913, VBA.

CHAPTER 4: SOMERVILLE, 1914–1915

1 Brittain, *Testament of Youth*, p. 17. This is the first sentence in ch. 1.
2 Ibid., p. 17.
3 On the significance of the campaign for the higher education of women, see, *inter alia*, Joan Burstyn, *Victorian Education and the Ideal of Womanhood* (London: Croom Helm, 1980); Martha Vicinus, *Independent Women: Work and Community for Single Women, 1850–1920* (Chicago: University of Chicago Press, 1985), ch. 4 and *passim*.
4 On women at Oxford: Vera Brittain, *The Women at Oxford: A Fragment of History* (London: George G. Harrap, 1960). On the history of Somerville College to 1921, see Muriel St Clare Byrne and

Catherine Hope Mansfield, *Somerville College, 1879–1921* (Oxford: Oxford University Press, 1922); Vera Farnell, *A Somervillian Looks Back* (Oxford: Oxford University Press, 1948). See also Susan Leonardi, *Dangerous by Degrees: Women at Oxford and the Somerville College Novelists* (New Brunswick, N.J.: Rutgers University Press, 1989).

5 For Brittain at Somerville, see also my 'A Woman at Oxford: Vera Brittain's Somerville Experience', *Historical Studies in Education*, 3(1) (Spring 1991): 1–19.

6 Brittain, *Testament of Youth*, p. 66.

7 See the Somerville College General Register for the Entering Class, October 1914, which lists age, religious affiliation, previous education and father's occupation. I thank Somerville College for permission to consult these records. The fees were £35 a term, which included board, lodging and tuition, with some smaller rooms at £31 or £28 'reserved for students who submit satisfactory evidence that they cannot pay the full fee'. See *Somerville College Report and Calendar* for 1913–14 and 1914–15. This was a considerable sum in 1914, when the average annual wage of an adult male industrial worker was £75, and that of a male salaried worker was £340. For these figures, see Arthur Marwick, *The Deluge: British Society and the First World War* (London: Macmillan, 1973), p. 23.

8 Vicinus, *Independent Women*, pp. 123–4.

9 A clipping from the *Lady's Pictorial* in the Somerville Log Book II, Hilary term 1920, describes the Senior Common Room for that year in detail.

10 Virginia Woolf, *A Room of One's Own* (1929; London: Hogarth Press, 1954), p. 27.

11 'Reflective Record', 8 October 1914, VBA.

12 Ibid., 11 October 1914, VBA.

13 Ibid., 12 October 1914, VBA.

14 Ibid., 10 October 1914, VBA.

15 Ibid., 12 November 1914, VBA.

16 For information about Helen Norah Hughes, see Somerville College Register for Entering Class, October 1914. Her father was a 'Commander, R.N. Retd' and she had been to Winchester High School. Norah Hughes left to do war work during the First World War and appears not to have returned to Somerville afterwards. She married in 1919.

17 'Reflective Record', 9 October 1914, VBA.

18 Ibid., 11 October 1914, VBA.

19 Ibid., 5 November 1914, VBA.

20 See Brittain, *Testament of Youth*, pp. 107–8, for a discussion of Ellis-Fermor.

21 See Somerville College Register for Entering Class, October 1914. Her father is listed as a 'Shorthand writer'.

22 'Reflective Record', 23 October 1914, VBA.
23 Ibid., 21 January 1915, VBA.
24 Ibid., 29 January 1915. VBA.
25 Brittain, *Testament of Youth*, p. 107.
26 'Reflective Record', 15 November 1914, VBA. See Somerville Register for Katherine Wood whose father was a 'merchant'.
27 'Reflective Record', 24 January 1915, VBA.
28 Ibid., 23 November 1914, VBA.
29 Brittain, *The Women at Oxford*, p. 91.
30 'Reflective Record', 9 October 1914, VBA.
31 Ibid., 27 October 1914, VBA.
32 Ibid., 8 October 1914, VBA. Miss Hayes Robinson did marry: see Byrne and Mansfield, *Somerville College*, p. 94.
33 'Reflective Record', 22 October 1914, VBA.
34 Ibid., 15 September 1914, VBA.
35 Ibid., 13 July 1914 and 6 February 1915, VBA.
36 Vera Brittain to Roland Leighton, 15 April 1915, in VBA.
37 'Reflective Record', 21 October 1913, VBA.
38 See Vera Brittain to Roland Leighton, 27 August 1914, VBA.
39 'Reflective Record', 16 October 1914, VBA.
40 Ibid., 12 October 1914, VBA.
41 The standard histories appear to agree that modern Oxford dates from the Commission of 1877 and the second University Reform Act (1877). For the reforms, see V.H.H. Green, *A History of Oxford University* (London: B.T. Batsford, 1974); and Charles Edward Mallet, *A History of the University of Oxford*, vol. III (1927; reprint, New York: Barnes & Noble; and London: Methuen, 1968). A.J. Engel, *From Clergyman to Don: The Rise of the Academic Profession in Nineteenth Century Oxford* (Oxford: Clarendon Press, 1983), chs 4 and 5, discusses the limitations of the reforms.
42 'Reflective Record', 9 October 1914, VBA.
43 For Pass Moderations, which was established in 1850, see Mallet, *History of the University of Oxford*, vol. III, p. 29.
44 See 'Reflective Record', 16 January 1915, VBA.
45 Brittain, *Testament of Youth*, pp. 111–12.
46 'Reflective Record', 16 January 1915, VBA.
47 Ibid., 19 January 1915, VBA.
48 Ibid., 16 January 1915, VBA.
49 Ibid., 13 January 1915 and 2 February 1915, VBA.
50 Ibid., 15 October 1914, VBA.
51 Ibid., 25 January 1915, VBA.
52 Ibid., 26 September 1914, VBA.
53 Ibid., 12 October 1914, VBA.
54 Ibid., 15 October and 28 October 1914, VBA.
55 Vera Brittain to Edith and Arthur Brittain, 21 February 1915, VBA.
56 For example, Vera Brittain to Edith Brittain, 24 January 1915, VBA.

57 For example, Vera Brittain to Edith Brittain, 14 February 1915, VBA.
58 'Reflective Record', 8–14 March 1915, Buxton, VBA.
59 Ibid., 30 September 1914, VBA.
60 See Brittain, *Testament of Youth*, p. 155.
61 'Reflective Record', 12 May 1915, VBA.
62 Ibid., 15 May 1915, VBA.
63 Ibid.

CHAPTER 5: LOVE IN WARTIME

1 On men, women and war stories, see Nancy Huston. 'Tales of War and Tears of Women', *Women's Studies International Forum*, 5(3/4), (1982): 271–82.
2 Victor Richardson, like Leighton and Brittain, had been at Uppingham. Geoffrey Thurlow was Edward's friend; he met him after he had joined up. See 'Reflective Record', 27 March 1915, VBA.
3 On relationships between sisters and brothers, including a perceptive analysis of Vera and Edward Brittain, see Angela Woollacott, 'Sisters and Brothers in Arms: Family, Class, and Gendering in World War I Britain', in Miriam Cooke and Angela Woollacott (eds), *Gendering War Talk* (Princeton, N.J.: Princeton University Press, 1993).
4 See the lecture delivered at a Luncheon Club meeting, 30 November 1932, VBA.
5 Vera Brittain, 'Reflective Record', 4 August 1914, VBA. For an account of government propaganda in the early months, see Arthur Marwick, *The Deluge: British Society and the First World War* (London: Macmillan, 1965), ch. 1.
6 Brittain, *Testament of Youth*, p. 458.
7 Robert Graves, *Good-bye to All That* (1929; New York: Doubleday Anchor Books, 1957), p. 58.
8 'Reflective Record', 11 July 1914, VBA. For Brittain's later opposition to the OTC, see chapter 9.
9 Ibid., 7 August 1914, VBA.
10 Ibid., 2 September 1914, VBA.
11 Ibid., 6 September 1914, VBA.
12 Ibid., 6 August 1914, VBA.
13 Brittain, *Testament of Youth*, pp. 101–2.
14 For the Leightons, see, in addition to *Testament of Youth*, Clare Leighton, *Tempestuous Petticoat: The Story of an Invincible Edwardian* (London: Victor Gollancz, 1948).
15 Leighton, *Tempestuous Petticoat*, p. 11.
16 Ibid., pp. 12–14.
17 Ibid., p. 37.
18 See the Uppingham material in files relating to Edward Brittain, VBA.
19 Brittain, *Testament of Youth*, p. 81.
20 Ibid., p. 85.

21 Robert Wohl offers a perceptive discussion of the mythology surrounding the idyllic summer: Robert Wohl, *The Generation of 1914* (Cambridge, Mass.: Harvard University Press, 1979).
22 Brittain, *Testament of Youth*. p. 87.
23 Ibid., p. 90.
24 'Reflective Record', 11 July 1914, VBA.
25 Ibid., 20 April 1914, VBA.
26 Brittain, *Testament of Youth*, pp. 83–4.
27 See Vera Brittain to Roland Leighton, 17 July 1914, VBA.
28 'Reflective Record', 20 April 1914, VBA.
29 Ibid., 11 July 1914, VBA.
30 Ibid., 12 July 1914, VBA.
31 For this aspect of Edward's story, see chapter 11.
32 'Reflective Record', 7 September 1914, VBA.
33 Roland Leighton to Vera Brittain, 29 September 1914. VBA.
34 Brittain, *Testament of Youth*, letter to Roland quoted on p. 104: 'It was all so thrilling . . .', p. 110.
35 'Reflective Record', 14 December 1914, VBA.
36 Vera Brittain to Roland Leighton, 1 October 1914, VBA.
37 'Reflective Record,' 16 December 1914, VBA.
38 Vera Brittain to Roland Leighton, 19 December 1914, VBA.
39 Ibid.
40 'Reflective Record', 23 December 1914, VBA.
41 Ibid., 21 December 1914, VBA.
42 Ibid., 29 December 1914, VBA.
43 Brittain, *Testament of Youth*, p. 121.
44 'Reflective Record', 31 December 1914, VBA.
45 Ibid., 30 December 1914, VBA.
46 Ibid.
47 Ibid., 31 December 1914, VBA.
48 Ibid., 21 April 1915, VBA.
49 Once in 1913; in April 1914; Speech Day, July 1914; December 1914; 16 January; 19 March; 18 August 1915: See Brittain, *Testament of Youth*. p. 197, where Brittain quotes Roland's letter which mentions seventeen days.
50 See Angela Woollacott, '"Khaki Fever" and its Control: Class, Gender, Age and Sexual Morality on the British Homefront in World War I', *Journal of Contemporary History*, 29 (April 1994): 325–47; and Philippa Levine, '"Walking the Streets in a Way No Decent Woman Should": Women Police in World War I', *Journal of Modern History*, 66 (March 1994): 34–78. See also the chapter 'Peace and War' in Sheila Fletcher, *Maude Royden: A Life* (Oxford: Basil Blackwell, 1989).
51 'Reflective Record', 19th April 1915, VBA.
52 Ibid., 8 April 1915, VBA.
53 Ibid., 19 March 1915, VBA.

54 Ibid.
55 Ibid., 21 August 1915, VBA.
56 Ibid., 18 April 1915, VBA.
57 Brittain, *Testament of Youth*, p. 117.
58 Ibid., p. 132.
59 Joyce Avrech Berkman, *The Healing Imagination of Olive Schreiner: Beyond South African Colonialism* (Amherst, Mass.: University of Massachusetts Press, 1989), p. 145. In her perceptive chapter on 'The Androgynous Vision', Berkman stresses Lyndall's strength, but even she agrees that at times Lyndall 'exudes self-pity and despair' (p. 145). Olive Schreiner, *The Story of an African Farm*, was first published in 1883.
60. 'Reflective Record', 23 April 1914, at Windermere, VBA.
61 Alan Bishop makes the case that the novel, even more than *Woman and Labour*, influenced the young Vera: see his '"With Suffering and Through Time": Olive Schreiner, Vera Brittain and the Great War', in Malvern van Wyk Smith and Don Maclennan (eds), *Olive Schreiner and After: Essays on Southern African Literature in Honour of Guy Butler* (Cape Town: David Philip, 1983), pp. 881–92. While I think Bishop makes an important point about *The Story of an African Farm*, the Schreiner of *Woman and Labour* was again of great importance to her after the war.
62 Paul Fussell, *The Great War and Modern Memory* (New York: Oxford University Press, 1975).
63 'Reflective Record', 23 August 1915, VBA.
64 Ibid., 13 January 1915, VBA.
65 Brittain, *Testament of Youth*, p. 135.

CHAPTER 6: WAR WORK

1 Brittain had volunteered through the Buxton chapter of the Red Cross. Auxiliary VADs working in local hospitals were entirely unpaid and supplied their own uniforms. The Military Hospital VADs, whether serving at home or abroad, signed a six-month renewable contract, worked full time, received room and board and an allowance of £20 per annum.
2 Right after the outbreak of war, Buxton's Devonshire Hospital offered 150 beds for military use to the government. See Devonshire Hospital, Buxton, Minute Book, 1908–21, 11 August 1914. The minutes of 10 September 1914 indicate that the military intake was to be at the expense of female patients: 'Recommended that the admission of female patients be limited to bad cases only'. The Devonshire was largely a hospital for rheumatic complaints. Minute books indicate that the 1,111 soldiers they took in by the end of 1915 were men suffering from rheumatic complaints. See Annual Report, Devonshire Hospital, 1915, p. 21. I thank the Devonshire Hospital for allowing me to use the Hospital archives.

3 'Reflective Record', 27 June 1915, VBA.
4 On women's war work, see Gail Braybon, *Women Workers in the First World War: The British Experience* (London: Croom Helm, 1981); Angela Woollacott, *On Her Their Lives Depend: Munitions Workers in the Great War* (Berkeley, Cal.: University of California Press, 1994); and Arthur Marwick, *Women at War, 1914–1918* (London: Croom Helm, 1977). See also relevant articles in Margaret Randolph Higonnet et al. (eds), *Behind the Lines: Gender and the Two World Wars* (New Haven, Conn.: Yale University Press, 1987); Ruth Roach Pierson (ed.), *Women and Peace: Theoretical, Historical and Practical Perspectives* (London: Croom Helm, 1987); and Miriam Cooke and Angela Woollacott, *Gendering War Talk* (Princeton, N.J.: Princeton University Press, 1993).
5 For an interesting collection of descriptions of upper middle-class women's war work, see the edition of the *St Monica's School Notes* filed under 'Published articles' as 'G4' in VBA. Some were VADs, some were agricultural workers, some were clerks, and one was a munitions worker. The Somerville Junior Common Room 'Log-Book' reflects a similar range of wartime occupations.
6 For the early history of the Voluntary Aid Detachments, see Anne Summers, *Angels and Citizens: British Women as Military Nurses* (London: Routledge & Kegan Paul, 1988).
7 'The Rose of No Man's Land' was a song. It has been used recently as the title of a book about the VADs: Lyn MacDonald, *The Roses of No Man's Land* (London: Michael Joseph, 1980).
8 For example, in her reminiscences, May Wedderburn Cannan recollects that '[w]hen the V.A.D.'s were first formed there was a good deal of a kind of mocking opposition. . . . The uniform was ugly and what *did* we think we could do?' ('Reflections of a British Red Cross VAD', in Women's Collections, Imperial War Museum, London).
9 See, for example, MacDonald, *The Roses of No Man's Land*, p. 73.
10 Histories of medical care during the war make it clear that the VADs served an essential function on the Western Front. The first VAD contingent of nurses was sent out to France in February 1915, to aid the trained nurses sent out through the QAIMNS and the Territorials. From being at first dubiously regarded volunteers, they became recognized as necessary, and, as the VAD authorities themselves put it, 'it was decided that the Army would employ paid nursing VADs in Military hospitals' (Rachel Crowdy, 'The Advent of VADs in France', BRCS 12/2/1, London; Women and Work Collection, Imperial War Museum, p. 6). The VADs served at rest stations, detention hospitals, hostels for relations of wounded soldiers, convalescent homes for nurses and VADs, recreation huts, sick bays for QMAACS, and Red Cross hospitals (BRCS 12/1/6).
11 'Reflective Record', 20 March 1915, VBA.
12 Ibid., 26 March 1915, VBA.
13 Ibid., 3 April 1915, VBA.

14 For the arrangements, see ibid., April–May 1915, *passim*, VBA.
15 See the Devonshire's published reports (Devonshire Hospital Archives).
16 'Reflective Record', 8 April 1915, VBA.
17 See ibid., 26 May 1915, VBA. She mentions sending measurements home so that her uniform could be made.
18 Ibid., 11 April 1915, VBA.
19 Marwick, *Women at War*, p. 84.
20 For example, one statistical study of the occupations of 200 VADs undertaken by the British Red Cross Society itself indicates a range of occupations, including dressmaker, governess and telephone operator. The most frequently mentioned previous occupation was nursing. See 'Analysis of 200 Cases of Selected Members Taken at Random' (n.d., BRCS, 10/5/4, 'Women and Work' Collection, Imperial War Museum, London).
21 See Sandra M. Gilbert, 'Soldier's Heart: Literary Men, Literary Women, and the Great War', *Signs*, 8(3), (Spring 1983): 422–50, and the revised version, in collaboration with Susan Gubar, as a chapter in Sandra M. Gilbert and Susan Gubar, 'Soldier's Heart: Literary Men, Literary Women, and the Great War', in *No Man's Land: The Place of the Woman Writer in the Twentieth Century*, vol. 2: *Sexchanges* (New Haven, Conn.: Yale University Press, 1989), pp. 258–323.
22 'Reflective Record', 27 June 1915, VBA.
23 Brittain, *Testament of Youth*, p. 164.
24 'Reflective Record', 15 August 1915, VBA.
25 Brittain, *Testament of Youth*, p. 166.
26 'Reflective Record', 16 July 1915, VBA. Interleaved in her diary for December 1915 is this clipping from the *Spectator*: 'Our VAD's: Thousands of girls who had led easy and cloistered lives, remote from everything that was not pretty and agreeable and smooth, have been pitchforked, after only a few weeks hurried training, into hospitals full of men maimed and disfigured by terrible and repulsive wounds. They have not quailed.'
27 'Reflective Record', 4 August 1915, VBA.
28 Ibid., 13 August 1915, VBA.
29 Brittain, *Testament of Youth*, p. 210.
30 'Reflective Record', 14 July 1915, VBA.
31 See Macdonald, *The Roses of No Man's Land*, p. 112.
32 From the *Report of an Advisory Committee Appointed by the Army Council to Enquire into the Supply of Nurses*, William Bridgeman, Chairman, 14 November 1916 (British Red Cross Society 'Women and Work' Collection, Imperial War Museum, London). Quotation is from p. 8 of the report.
33 Lady Katherine Furse, 'Letter to VAD Officers & Members', n.d. BRCS 10 1/3 'Women and Work' Collection, Imperial War Museum, London).

34 *Foundation of Present Difficulties in the VAD's Service*, no author, n.d. (BRCS 10 4/8, 'Women and Work' Collection, Imperial War Museum, London).
35 On nursing, see Lee Holcombe, *Victorian Ladies at Work: Middle-class Working Women in England and Wales* (Newton Abbot, Devon: David & Charles, 1973); and Martha Vicinus, *Independent Women: Work and Community for Single Women, 1850–1920* (Chicago, Ill.: University of Chicago Press, 1985).
36 'Reflective Record', 25 November 1915, VBA.
37 The Brittains had by this time moved from Buxton. A year later, they had settled into Oakwood Court, a mansion flat in Kensington, where they lived until 1934.
38 'Reflective Record', 1 January 1916, VBA.
39 Vera Brittain to Edith Brittain, 28 April 1916, VBA.
40 For the 'mourning engagement ring – in pearls –', see letter to Edward Brittain from Vera Brittain, 16 February 1916, VBA.
41 'Reflective Record', 4 January 1916, VBA.
42 Ibid., 30–1 January 1916, VBA.
43 Vera Brittain to Edward Brittain, 24 January 1916, VBA.
44 'Reflective Record', 26–7 January 1916, VBA.
45 Vera Brittain to Edward Brittain, 12 April 1916, VBA.
46 Vera Brittain to Edward Brittain, 19 April 1916, VBA.
47 Brittain, *Testament of Youth*, p. 244.
48 'Reflective Record', 17 February 1916, VBA.
49 Ibid., 5 July 1916, VBA.
50 For his letter of condolence, see ibid., 30–1 January 1916, VBA; and for their dinners at the Trocadero restaurant, see Brittain, *Testament of Youth*, pp. 249–50.
51 First mention of Geoffrey Thurlow is in 'Reflective Record', 27 March 1915, VBA. See also 10 October 1915.
52 Ibid., 6 March 1916, VBA.
53 Brittain, *Testament of Youth*, p. 290.
54 The British Red Cross Society papers contain an account of 'Military Hospitals in Malta: a Short Account of their Inception and Development', by G.A. Bruce, Capt. RAMC (n.d. but presumably 1918; see BRSC 16/2/2 in 'Women and Work' Collection, Imperial War Museum, London).
55 And he saw fit to add: 'Generally speaking they come from a very good social stratum' (memo to the Governor of Malta re VADs, dated 31 July 1917, M. Yarr, Surgeon-General Director of Medical Services, Malta: BRSC 16/2/3).
56 Vera Brittain to Edith Brittain, 25 October 1916, VBA. Note that the VAD authorities did not approve. Commandant Katherine Furse said, when she toured France: 'I am very sad about the irregularity of uniform among the military members . . . many of them have taken to low necked blouses' (from her 'Tour of VADs in France', August 1917,

p. 10, BRCS 12/2/1, 'Women and Work' Collection, Imperial War Museum, London).

57 Vera Brittain to Edith Brittain, 25 October 1916, VBA.

58 Vera Brittain to Edith Brittain, 19 March 1917, VBA.

59 Reminiscences of K.M. Barrow, 'A VAD at the Base' (BRSC 12/1/15 'Women and Work' Collection, Imperial Museum, London).

60 See mention of the snapshops in letters home: Vera Brittain to Edith and Arthur Brittain, 27 April 1917 from Malta, VBA. On women and amateur photography, see Diana Pedersen and Martha Phemister, 'Women and Photography in Ontario', in Marianne Gosztonyi Ainley (ed.), *Despite the Odds: Essays on Canadian Women and Science* (Montreal: Véhicule Press, 1990), pp. 88–111.

61 This photograph is reproduced as Plate 8.

62 Vera Brittain to Edith Brittain, 18 November 1916, VBA.

63 See Vera Brittain to Edith Brittain, 3 November 1916, VBA.

64 Vera Brittain to Edith Brittain, 13 February 1917, VBA.

65 Vera Brittain to Edith Brittain, 25 September 1917, VBA.

66 'Reflective Record', 23 September 1916, VBA.

67 Brittain, *Testament of Youth*, p. 296.

68 'Reflective Record', 29–30 September 1916, VBA.

69 See Vera Brittain to Edith Brittain, 2 February 1917, VBA.

70 Brittain, *Testament of Youth*, p. 340.

71 Ibid.

72 'Reflective Record', 18 April 1917, VBA.

73 'Tah' was Victor's nickname among his school friends: ibid., 22 April 1917, VBA.

74 Vera Brittain to Edith Brittain, from Malta, 4 May 1917, VBA.

75 'Reflective Record', 1 May 1917, VBA.

76 Brittain, *Testament of Youth*, p. 343.

77 Ibid., p. 359.

78 Ibid., p. 340.

79 'Reflective Record', 1 January 1916, VBA.

80 Geoffrey Thurlow, of course, did not know Roland, but he came to know him through Vera.

81 Gilbert, 'Soldiers' Heart', *Signs*, p. 436.

82 Brittain, *Testament of Youth*, pp. 165–6.

83 'Reflective Record', 27 June 1915, VBA.

84 Ibid., 13 January 1916, section entitled 'Les Événements', VBA.

85 Ibid., 2 March 1916, VBA.

86 Ibid., 5 July 1916, VBA.

87 Brittain, *Testament of Youth*, p. 282.

88 Ibid., pp. 366–7.

89 'Much of the wounding produced by the weapons of trench warfare, to say nothing of its volume, was new to surgeons.' The 'high-velocity conical bullet', according to this authority, changed the nature of wounds in warfare: 'Unlike the musket ball which, moving at slow

speed and without rotating, merely drove a clean path for itself through soft tissue, the high-velocity conical bullet . . . could produce inside the human body a variety of extremely unpleasant results' (John Keegan, *The Face of Battle* (London: Jonathan Cape, 1976), p. 265).

90 For the system, see Keegan, *Face of Battle*, pp. 266–7; and *The Times History of the War*, vol. 1: *The Battlefield of Europe*, American edn (New York: Woodward & Van Slyke, 1914–21), pp. 145–7.

91 For similar experiences, see Women's Collection, Imperial War Museum, London. Reflections of Charlotte Louise Fitzgerald Dalton and Ruth Manning.

92 Note from Vera Brittain to Edith Brittain, Boulogne, 3 August 1917, giving the mailing address to be used: 24th General Hospital, BEF France, VBA.

93 Letter from Vera Brittain to Edith and Arthur Brittain, 5 August 1917, VBA.

94 Letter from Vera Brittain to Edith and Arthur Brittain, 5 August 1917, VBA.

95 See, for example, Cyril Falls, *The First World War* (London: Longmans, Green, 1960), pp. 280–6.

96 Vera Brittain to Edith Brittain, 5 August 1917, VBA.

97 Vera Brittain to Edith Brittain, 7 August 1917, VBA.

98 Brittain, *Testament of Youth*, pp. 369–70.

99 Vera Brittain to Edith and Arthur Brittain, 5 August 1917, VBA.

100 Brittain, *Testament of Youth*, p. 374.

101 Vera Brittain to Edith Brittain, 5 August 1917, VBA.

102 Brittain, *Testament of Youth*, p. 280.

103 See letter from Vera Brittain to Edith Brittain, 12 September 1917, VBA.

104 Letter from Vera Brittain to Edith Brittain, 5 December 1917, VBA. Quoted in Brittain, *Testament of Youth*, p. 395.

105 Vera Brittain to Edith and Arthur Britain, 23 February 1918, VBA.

106 Vera Brittain to Edith Brittain, 31 March 1918, VBA.

107 Brittain, *Testament of Youth*, p. 410.

108 Vera Brittain to Edith Brittain, 23 October 1917, VBA.

109 Vera Brittain to Edith Brittain, 30 November 1917, VBA.

110 Letter from Vera Brittain to Edith Brittain, 30 November 1917, VBA.

111 Vera Brittain to Edith and Arthur Brittain, 9 February 1918, VBA.

112 Vera Brittain to Edith Brittain, 12 October 1917, VBA.

113 See letter from Vera Brittain to Edith Brittain, 19 September 1917, VBA.

114 From letter of Ida Haigh to her parents dated 30 July 1918 from the 69th General Hospital (Palestine). Like Vera, Ida also was fond of receiving sweets from home. Ida Haigh served as a VAD in Cairo and in Palestine. Her revealing letters home are housed in the Imperial War Museum, 'Women and War' Collection 80/41/1.

115 See letter from Vera Brittain to Edith Brittain, 19 September 1917, VBA.
116 Vera Brittain to Edith and Arthur Brittain, 5 August 1917, VBA. In a similar vein, see Ida Haigh: 'Strangely enough there are very few VADs whom I find really "sympatique": Most of them seem to have little else to talk about but tittle-tattle. It is astonishing how ill-read & uncultured most people are': Haigh's letter to her parents, 10 May 1917, from Kinmal Camp, Rhyl, in North Wales (Imperial War Museum).
117 For Moulson's membership in the QAIMNS, see Vera Brittain to Edith Brittain, 19 September 1917, VBA.
118 Vera Brittain to Edith Brittain, 5 September 1917, VBA.
119 Vera Brittain to Edith Brittain, 29 August 1917, VBA.
120 Vera Brittain to Edith Brittain, 9 September 1917, VBA.
121 Vera Brittain to Edith Brittain, 15 September 1917, VBA.
122 Vera Brittain to Edith Brittain, 30 November 1917, VBA.
123 Vera Brittain to Edith Brittain, 12 December 1917, VBA.
124 This letter is quoted in Brittain, *Testament of Youth*, p. 421. Brittain says it arrived 'early in April' but in fact must have been written some time in March. See her letter to her mother dated 31 March 1918, in which she refers to the letter from her father.
125 See my own discussion of this pattern: *The Victorian Girl and the Feminine Ideal* (London: Croom Helm; and Bloomington, Ind.: Indiana University Press, 1982). Philippa Levine finds similar conflicts between opposing views of women's duty among wartime women police: see her '"Walking the Streets in a Way No Decent Woman Should": Women Police in World War I', *Journal of Modern History*, 66 (March 1994): 77.
126 Brittain, *Testament of Youth*, pp. 422–3.
127 Vera Brittain to Edith Brittain, 31 March 1918, VBA.
128 Brittain, *Testament of Youth*, p. 458.
129 Ibid., p. 404.
130 Although she claims in *Testament of Youth* that it did: see pp. 399–400.
131 Vera Brittain, 'Perhaps', in *Testament of Youth*, p. 239.
132 Vera Brittain, 'Scars upon my Heart', in *Scars upon my Heart: Women's Poetry and Verse of the First World War* (London: Vivago, 1981).
133 See Vera Brittain to Edith Brittain, 15 September 1917; 19 September 1917; 3 October 1917, VBA.
134 Vera Brittain to Edith Brittain, 25 September 1917, VBA.
135 Vera Brittain to Edith Brittain, 24 October 1917, VBA.
136 Brittain, *Testament of Youth*, p. 447.
137 Vera Brittain to Edith Brittain, 9 April 1918, VBA.
138 See Brittain, *Testament of Youth*, p. 447, where she discusses taking Mr. Leighton's advice not to try to publish it.
139 From the 'Folly's Vineyard' typescript, ch. 1 (unpaginated), VBA.

140 Brittain, *Testament of Youth*, p. 447.

141 'Folly's Vineyard', ch. 16, VBA. In some versions the Moulson character is 'Sister Hope'. At other times she is 'Sister Lorraine'.

142 Ruth Roach Pierson, 'Beautiful Soul or Just Warrior: Gender and War', *Gender and History*, 1, (Spring 1989): 79–86.

143 Marwick, *Women at War*, p. 84.

144 See the Miss Ruth B. Manning Collection, consisting of three MS diaries and typescript reminiscences plus memorabilia, 'Women and War', Documents Section (80.21.1), Imperial War Museum, London.

145 Ida Haigh Gould wrote to me in 1986, when she was 94, kindly giving me information about her education, family background and life after the war. About her background: she said that she was born in 1892; that her father Stephen Haigh was 'an exporter of Yorkshire textiles'; that she attended Bradford Girls' Grammar School until she was eighteen. She considered attending university, but instead her parents sent her to France where she had 'a very happy year with a French family who specialized in foreign students', followed by less-happy experiences in Germany and Italy. 'Then the war came, and in that day nursing was the first thing a girl thought of' (letter from Ida Gould, Rothwell Grange, Lettering, Northants, 29 June 1986, in my possession).

146 May Wedderburn Cannan, 'Recollections of a British Red Cross Nurse', Imperial War Museum, Documents section. Like Brittain, she wrote poetry. Brittain used one of her poems as an epigram in *Testament of Youth*.

147 Joanna Swarbrick, miscellaneous papers relating to her service as a VAD at Southwark Military Hospital, 1916–18 (Imperial War Museum, Documents Section). References in the file indicate she attended Bispam Endowed School, Blackpool. The grammar used on a postcard she received from a friend Lilly Danoon, who also was a VAD, indicates that Danoon had only a limited education; so also does the grammar in a letter written by Swarbrick herself when later, as Mrs Joanna Porter, she served as a nurse assistant in the Second World War.

148 See the letter from A. Maude Royden to Katherine Furse, November 1917 (BRCS 10/8/72 'Women and Work' collection, Imperial War Museum). On Royden, see Sheila Fletcher, *Maude Royden: A Life* (Oxford: Basil Blackwell, 1989).

149 Document written by Rachel Crowdy, 'The Advent of VADs in France' (BRCS 12/2/1) indicates that the General Service VADs date from 1917 (the year in which the QMAAC was set up). Crowdy says of the GS VADs: 'At first, many of them were treated, by the army sisters and nursing VAD . . . members as though they brought disgrace and not credit . . . the one blot on the VAD escutcheon was this attitude and only the General Service VAD . . . knows what hardship she had to put up with' (pp. 15–16).

150 Marwick, *Women at War*; and Braybon, *Women Workers in the First World War*. Woollacott, *On Her Their Lives Depend*, argues that the war did offer women new opportunities, but these were shaped by factors of class as well as of gender.
151 In addition to the work of Sandra Gilbert, already cited in this chapter, that of Susan Kingsley Kent has been especially influential: see her 'Gender Reconstruction after the First World War', in Harold L. Smith (ed.), *British Feminism in the Twentieth Century* (London: Edward Elgar, 1990), and her book *Making Peace: The Reconstruction of Gender in Interwar Britain* (Princeton, N.J.: Princeton University Press, 1993).

CHAPTER 7: FRIENDSHIP AND FEMINISM

1 Essay in 'Juvenelia', VBA.
2 Brittain, *Testament of Youth*, p. 494.
3 Ibid., p. 468.
4 Ibid., p. 475.
5 Ibid., pp. 489–90.
6 Ibid., pp. 471–3.
7 Ibid., pp. 485, 490, 494.
8 Vera Brittain to Edith Brittain, 12 October 1919, VBA.
9 Vera Brittain to Edith Brittain, 18 October 1919, VBA.
10 Vera Brittain to Edith Brittain, 27 April 1919, VBA.
11 Vera Brittain to Edith Brittain, 14 October 1919, VBA.
12 See 'Reflective Record', 30 November 1914, VBA.
13 See Vera Brittain to Edith Brittain, 27 April 1919, VBA.
14 For these accounts, see 'Reflective Record', VBA, *passim*, and correspondence with her mother.
15 Vera Brittain to Edith Brittain, 25 May 1919, VBA.
16 Brittain, *Testament of Youth*, pp. 484–5.
17 For example, see Vera Brittain to Edith and Arthur Brittain, 12 October 1919, VBA.
18 Vera Brittain to Edith and Arthur Brittain, 2 November 1919, VBA.
19 Vera Brittain to Edith Brittain, 8 November 1919, VBA.
20 Vera Brittain to Edith Brittain, 18 October 1919, VBA.
21 Vera Brittain to Edith Brittain, 8 November 1919, VBA.
22 Vera Brittain to Edith Brittain, 18 November 1919, VBA.
23 Brittain, *Testament of Youth*, p. 485.
24 The poem is reproduced in ibid., pp. 485–6.
25 Vera Brittain to Edith Brittain, 26 October 1919, VBA.
26 Vera Brittain to Edith Brittain, 30 November 1919, VBA.
27 Vera Brittain to Edith and Arthur Brittain, 2 November 1919, VBA.
28 Vera Brittain to Edith Brittain, 8 and 11 November 1919, VBA.
29 Vera Brittain to Edith Brittain, 15 June 1919 and 26 October 1919, VBA.

30 Vera Brittain to Edith Brittain, 8 June 1919, VBA.
31 Vera Brittain to Edith Brittain, 18 November 1919, VBA.
32 See, for example, Demitri F. Papolos and Janice Papolos, *Overcoming Depression* (New York: Harper & Row, 1987).
33 Vera Brittain to Edith Brittain, 26 October 1919, VBA.
34 Brittain, *Testament of Youth*, p. 484.
35 For alternate interpretations, see Susan Kingsley Kent, 'Experiencing the Great War: the Consequences for British Feminism', unpublished paper, North American Conference on British Studies, Boulder, Col., October 1992; and Susan J. Leonardi, 'Brittain's Beard: Transsexual Panic in *Testament of Youth*', *Literature Interpretation Theory*, 2(1), (July 1990): 77–84.
36 The quotation is from George Orwell's *The Road to Wigan Pier* (1937), quoted in Samuel Hynes, *The Auden Generation: Literature and Politics in England in the 1930s* (New York: Viking Press, 1972), p. 19.
37 Brittain, *Testament of Youth*, p. 489.
38 Vera Brittain, 'The Point of View of a Woman Student', *Oxford Outlook* (June 1919): 122, VBA.
39 Brittain, *Testament of Youth*, pp. 490–1.
40 Ibid., p. 493.
41 'Reflective Record', 8 October 1914, VBA.
42 Vera Brittain, *The Dark Tide* (New York: Macmillan, 1936; first published by Grant Richards in 1923).
43 Vera Brittain, *Testament of Friendship: The Story of Winifred Holtby* (1940; London: Fontana, 1981).
44 Carolyn G. Heilbrun, *Writing a Woman's Life* (New York: W.W. Norton 1988), p. 99.
45 Jean E. Kennard, *Vera Brittain and Winifred Holtby: A Working Partnership* (Hanover, N.H.: University Press of New England 1989), pp. 6–7.
46 For example, Lillian Faderman, *Surpassing the Love of Men: Romantic Friendship and Love between Women from the Renaissance to the Present* (New York: William Morrow, 1981); Sheila Jeffreys, *The Spinster and her Enemies: Feminism and Sexuality, 1880–1930* (London: Pandora, 1985); Pam Johnson, '"The Best Friend Whom Life Has Given Me": Does Winifred Holtby have a place in lesbian history?', in Lesbian History Group, *Not a Passing Phase: Reclaiming Lesbians in History, 1840–1985* (London: The Women's Press, 1989). I discuss these works and others in my '"The Friendships of Women": Friendship, Feminism and Achievement in Vera Brittain's Life and Work in the Interwar Decades', *Journal of Women's History*, 3(3), (Winter 1992): 44–69.
47 Brittain, *Testament of Friendship*, p. 93.
48 Brittain, *Testament of Youth*. p. 487.
49 Ibid., p. 494.

50 Ibid., p. 495.
51 Brittain, *Testament of Friendship*, p. 2.
52 Ibid., pp. 117–8.
53 Brittain, *Testament of Youth*, p. 494.
54 Brittain, *Testament of Friendship*, p. 119.
55 Brittain to Holtby, 11 November 1921, in *Selected Letters of Winifred Holtby to Vera Brittain*, ed. Vera Brittain and Geoffrey Handley-Taylor (London: A. Brown, 1960).
56 Vera Brittain identifies him as such in *Testament of Friendship*, pp. 90–1.
57 Vera Brittain to Edith Brittain, 15 December 1919, VBA.
58 Brittain, *Testament of Youth*, p. 488.
59 Holtby to Brittain, 14 April 1933, Holtby papers.
60 See Vera Brittain's correspondence with Edith Brittain, *passim*, VBA.
61 The letter is quoted in Brittain, *Testament of Youth*, p. 494.
62 Brittain, ibid., p. 506.
63 Ibid., p. 507.
64 Brittain, *Testament of Friendship*, pp. 100–1.
65 Winifred Holtby to Jean McWilliam, 20 October 1920, in Winifred Holtby, *Letters to a Friend*, ed. Alice Holtby and Jean McWilliam (New York: Macmillan, 1938), p. 22. Winifred Holtby met ex-Somervillian Jean McWilliam in 1918, when she was serving in the WAAC. After McWilliam went to South Africa to work as a teacher in 1920, she and Holtby maintained an active correspondence.
66 Winifred Holtby to Vera Brittain, Summer 1920, in *Selected Letters*, pp. 1–2.
67 *Oxford Poetry, 1920* (Oxford: Basil Blackwell, 1920) was edited by 'V.M.B., C.H.B.K., and A.P.'.
68 Brittain to Holtby, 15 December 1920, *Selected Letters*, pp. 2–3.
69 Holtby to Jean McWilliam, 25 July 1921. In *Letters to a Friend*, pp. 52–3.
70 Winifred Holtby to Jean McWilliam, Sunday, Easter Term, 1921, in *Letters to a Friend*, p. 40. 'Bolshevism in Baghdad' was subtitled 'A Psycho-analytic Experiment'. See the programme reproduced in *Letters to a Friend*, pp. 42–3.
71 Brittain, *Testament of Youth*, p. 517.
72 Vera Brittain to Edith Brittain, 30 July 1921, VBA.
73 Vera Brittain to Edith Brittain, 30 July 1921, from Bainesse, VBA.
74 For the period between March 1920 and March 1921, the correspondence between Brittain and her mother is unavailable. This missing year of correspondence is one of the few significant lacunae in either the Vera Brittain or the Winifred Holtby archives. Possibly, Brittain wished to remove traces of an incident to which she refers only briefly in *Testament of Youth* and of which she was clearly ashamed: namely her engagement in the spring and summer of 1920 to a man she does not even mention by name. (He was Roy Anthony; see, for example, the reference in Vera Brittain to Gordon Catlin, 26 April 1932, VBA.)

75 Brittain, *Testament of Yourth*, p. 500.
76 On Brittain's self-awareness concerning depression: 'I dread depression more than sickness – as you know, it always takes the form of feeling I've never done anything worth doing & never been anything worth being . . . never mind, you will write & cheer me up, as only you can' (Brittain to Holtby, 4 November 1921, Holtby papers).
77 For example, see Holtby to Jean McWilliam, 10 April 1921, in *Letters to a Friend*, p. 46; and Brittain to Holtby, 5 July 1921, in *Selected Letters*, p. 9.
78 Brittain, *Testament of Youth*, p. 536.
79 Brittain, *Testament of Friendship*, p. 108.
80 Martha Vicinus, *Independent Women: Work and Community for Single Women, 1850–1920* (Chicago, Ill.: University of Chicago Press, 1985), p. 38.
81 Brittain, *Testament of Youth*, p. 546.
82 Brittain to Holtby, 23 November 1921, Holtby papers.
83 See, for example, Brittain to Holtby, 6 April 1923, Holtby papers.
84 Holtby to Jean McWilliam, 5 February 1922, in *Letters to a Friend*, p. 91.
85 See Holtby to Jean McWilliam, 3 December 1921, ibid., p. 72.
86 Brittain to Holtby, 23 December 1921, Holtby papers.
87 See Holtby to Brittain, 18 August 1921, in *Selected Letters*, pp. 11–12.
88 Holtby to McWilliam, 15 January 1922, in *Letters to a Friend*, p. 85.
89 Brittain to Holtby from Oakwood Court, 22 November 1921, Holtby papers.
90 For date of move to Maida Vale, see Holtby to Jean McWilliam, 9 October 1923, in *Letters to a Friend*, p. 223.
91 Brittain to Holtby, 6 April 1924, Holtby papers.
92 Brittain, *Testament of Youth*, p. 574.
93 Brittain, *Testament of Friendship*, pp. 117–18.
94 Kennard, *Vera Brittain and Winifred Holtby*, pp. 6–7.
95 See Gorham, '"The Friendships of Women"'.
96 Brittain to Holtby, from Geneva, 5 September 1929, Holtby papers. Significantly, while part of this letter appears in *Selected Letters* (p. 179), Brittain chose to omit this portion. M – was a friend who lived in an open lesbian relationship; Brittain and she continued to be friends after this argument. It was a political, rather than a personal, disagreement.
97 See my discussion of this point in my '"Have We Really Rounded Seraglio Point?" Vera Brittain and Inter-war Feminism', in Harold L. Smith (ed.), *British Feminism in the Twentieth Century* (Upleadon, Glos.: Edward Elgar, 1990), pp. 84–103, and in chapter 9, 'Semi-detached Marriage', in this book.
98 Faderman, *Surpassing the Love of Men*, p. 310.
99 The review appeared in the issue of 10 August 1928. In VBA.
100 See letter from Radclyffe Hall to Brittain thanking her for being

present at the trial: letter of 15 November 1928, in VBA. And see Vera Brittain, *Radclyffe Hall: A Case of Obscenity*? (London: Femina Books, 1968).

101 Brittain to Catlin, 5 February 1929, VBA.

102 Holtby to Jean McWilliam, 23 April 1922, in *Letters to a Friend*, p. 102.

103 Holtby to Brittain, 21 August 1928, from Bainesse, Holtby papers. Significantly, Brittain omitted this passage from *Selected Letters*.

104 Holtby to Brittain, Christmas vacation, 1920–1, in *Selected Letters*, pp. 3–4.

105 Brittain to Holtby, 16–17 August 1921, from Oakwood Court, in ibid., pp. 10–11.

106 Pearson appears in Brittain's published accounts as 'Bill'.

107 Holtby to Jean MacWilliam, from Bevington Road, 22 November 1920, in *Letters to a Friend*, p. 24.

108 Holtby to Jean McWilliam, 27 May 1923, in ibid., p. 181.

109 Holtby to Jean McWilliam, 5 February 1922, in ibid., p. 90.

110 Holtby to Jean McWilliam, 5 June 1923, in ibid., p. 186.

111 Holtby to Jean McWilliam, 9 May 1925, in ibid., p. 331.

112 Brittain, *Testament of Friendship*, p. 111.

113 See, for example, Vera Brittain to Edith Brittain, 4 and 13 September 1921, VBA. Also see Holtby to Jean McWilliam from Assisi, 2 October 1921, in *Letters to a Friend*, pp. 62–4.

114 Brittain, *Testament of Youth*, p. 521.

115 See my article '"The Friendships of Women"' for a discussion of this historiography. But see also the discussion of nineteenth-century feminist friendships in Philippa Levine, *Feminist Lives in Victorian England* (Oxford: Basil Blackwell, 1990), ch. 4, and Levine's 'Love, Friendship and Feminism in Later 19th Century England', *Women's Studies International Forum*, 13(1/2), (1993): 63–78.

116 Brittain to Holtby, 4 November 1921, Holtby papers.

117 Brittain, *The Dark Tide*, p. 24.

118 Ibid., p. 82.

119 See, for example, Brittain to Holtby, 30 December 1923, Holtby papers.

120 Brittain to Holtby, 16 November 1921, Holtby papers.

121 See Holtby to Brittain, from Cottingham, 30 June 1921, Holtby papers.

122 Brittain to Holtby, 5 November 1921, Holtby papers.

123 Holtby to Brittain, 28 July 1923, Holtby papers.

124 Brittain, *Testament of Youth*, p. 597.

125 Brittain to Holtby, 21 August 1922, Holtby papers.

126 Holtby to Brittain, 22 August 1922, Holtby papers.

127 See Brittain, *Testament of Youth*, p. 31.

128 The unpleasant comments made by Virginia Woolf in the privacy of her diaries and letters provide a good example of the persistence of

social snobbery in the literary world. Of Brittain she comments, when reading *Testament of Youth*: 'I have still to read how she married the infinitely dreary Catlin & found beauty & triumph in poor, gaping Holtby' (*The Diary of Virginia Woolf*, vol. 4: *1931–1935*, ed. Anne Olivier Bell (London: Hogarth Press, 1982): entry for Saturday, 2 September 1933, p. 177). And see this comment about Holtby in a letter to Hugh Walpole of 26 October 1932: 'No, I've not read Miss Holtby. . . . She is the daughter of a Yorkshire farmer and learnt to read, I'm told, while minding the pigs – hence her passion for me (Virginia Woolf, *The Sickle Side of the Moon: The Letters of Virginia Woolf*, vol. 5: *1932–1935*, ed. Nigel Nicolson (London: Hogarth Press, 1979), p. 114).

129 Brittain to Holtby, 4 November 1921, Holtby papers.
130 Brittain to Holtby, 28 October 1921: signed 'yours to reprove, Vera', Holtby papers.
131 Brittain to Holtby, 22 October 1921, Holtby papers.
132 Holtby to Jean McWilliam, 15 July 1924, in *Letters to a Friend*, p. 263.
133 Holtby to Jean McWilliam, 28 October 1924, in ibid., p. 289.

CHAPTER 8: FEMINISM AND INTERNATIONALISM

1 Brittain, *Testament of Youth*, p. 404, and see diary entry, 23 June 1932, in Alan Bishop (ed.), *Vera Brittain, Diary of the Thirties, 1932–1939: Chronicle of Friendship* (London: Victor Gollancz, 1986), p. 58.
2 *Oxford Outlook*, November 1919, G1 in VBA.
3 Virginia Woolf, *Three Guineas* (1938; London: Hogarth Press, 1952), pp. 111–13.
4 For Lady Rhondda, see Shirley M. Eoff, *Viscountess Rhondda: Equalitarian Feminist* (Columbus: Ohio State University Press, 1991). For *Time and Tide*, see Dale Spender, *Time and Tide Wait for No Man* (London: Pandora Press, 1984). I have discussed Brittain's feminism in my '"Have We Really Rounded Seraglio Point?" Vera Brittain and Feminism in the Interwar Period', in Harold L. Smith (ed.), *British Feminism in the Twentieth Century* (Upleadon, Glos.: Edward Elgar, 1990), pp. 84–103. For an analysis and overview of post-war feminism, see Harold Smith, 'British Feminism in the 1920s', and Susan Kingsley Kent, 'Gender Reconstruction after the First World War', both in ibid.; and Susan Kingsley Kent, *Making Peace; The Reconstruction of Gender in Interwar Britain* (Princeton, N.J.: Princeton University Press, 1993). See also Olive Banks, *The Politics of Feminism: 1918–1970* (Aldershot, Hants.: Edward Elgar, 1993).
5 Brittain, *Testament of Youth*, p. 583.
6 The Six Point Group Collection at the Fawcett Society Library, London, is sparse for the 1920s, but correspondence confirms that

Brittain was a member of the executive; for example, in a letter of 8 May 1927 from Brittain to Miss Vernon, Brittain mentions her membership (VBA).

7 See the Open Door Council and the Open Door International files in VBA. The Open Door International was formed in 1929. Its papers (sparse for the 1920s) are housed in the Fawcett Society Library, London. For Brittain's membership on the ODC Executive, see Brittain to Holtby, 25 September 1928, Holtby papers.

8 Susan Kingsley Kent, for example, has written extensively on 'the conservative nature of feminism after the Great War' ('Gender Reconstruction . . .', in Smith (ed.), *British Feminism*, p. 66). Harold Smith agrees that equality feminists met with strong resistance in the postwar period (see his 'British feminism in the 1920s', in ibid.), but his forthcoming book, *Gender and Pay: The Equal Pay Issue since 1888*, confirms that equality feminism did continue to be an important force in Britain in the interwar decades.

9 Vera Brittain, 'Olive Schreiner', *Nation and Athenaeum*, 23 October 1926, G23 in VBA.

10 For an excellent selection of Brittain's and Holtby's journalism, along with helpful commentary, see Paul Berry and Alan Bishop (eds), *Testament of a Generation: The Journalism of Vera Britain and Winifred Holtby* (London: Virago, 1985).

11 Vera Brittain, 'Woman's Place: the Passing of the Married Woman's Handicaps', *Time and Tide*, 25 November 1927, G79 in VBA.

12 Vera Brittain, 'The Girl Baby Has Her Day', *Yorkshire Post*, 2 December 1927, G82 in VBA.

13 Vera Brittain, 'Wasted Women and the Tyranny of Houses', *Manchester Guardian*, 10 June 1927, G55 in VBA.

14 Vera Brittain, 'I Denounce Domesticity! A Protest Against Waste', *The Quiver*, August 1932, G385 in VBA. Reprinted in Berry and Bishop (eds), *Testament of a Generation*.

15 See, for example, Ruth Schwartz Cowan, *More Work for Mother: The Ironies of Household Technology from the Open Hearth to the Microwave* (New York: Basic Books, 1983).

16 Vera Brittain, 'The Leisured Woman of America', *Yorkshire Post*, 12 November 1926, G25, VBA.

17 For example, Vera Brittain, 'Prejudice or Knowledge? Fields for Women's Research', *Manchester Guardian*, 28 June 1927, G58, VBA.

18 Vera Brittain, 'Semi-detached Marriage', *Evening News*, 4 May 1928, G107, VBA.

19 Charlotte Haldane, *Motherhood and its Enemies* (London: Chatto & Windus, 1927) provides a good example of the latter. Brittain wrote a witty and perceptive review of this book: 'Mothers and Feminists', *Time and Tide*, 18 November 1927, G97, VBA.

20 Vera Brittain, 'What Is a Good Parent? Changing Motherhood', *Manchester Guardian*, 6 May 1927, G46, VBA.

21 Vera Brittain, 'Future Husbands and Fathers', *Manchester Guardian*, 1 February 1929, G179, VBA.
22 Vera Brittain, *Women's Work in Modern England* (London: Noel Douglas, 1928), pp. 1–2.
23 See Elizabeth Abbott to Vera Brittain, 29 April 1928, VBA.
24 The statement of policy appears on ODC letterhead. See Elizabeth Abbott's correspondence with Vera Brittain in 1933, VBA.
25 See Vera Brittain, 'Woman's Record in 1927', *Yorkshire Post*, 30 December 1927, G88, VBA.
26 See the Open Door Council and the Open Door International files in VBA.
27 For her membership on the executive, see Vera Brittain to Winifred Holtby, 25 September 1928, Holtby papers.
28 On 'new' feminist support for such legislation, see, for example, *Time and Tide*'s report of the March 1926 meeting of the NUSEC's Council: *Time and Tide*, 5 March 1926, 220–1.
29 Vera Brittain, 'Women in Industry: Restrictive Legislation Again', *Manchester Guardian*, 13 December 1927, G85, VBA; reprinted in Berry and Bishop (eds), *Testament of a Generation*.
30 Vera Brittain, 'Of Prejudice or Knowledge? Fields for Women's Research', *Manchester Guardian*, 28 June 1927, G58, VBA.
31 Referring to the NUSEC, Jane Lewis says, 'The extension of the suffrage to women on the same terms as men continued to rally the whole membership' (Jane Lewis, 'Beyond Suffrage: English Feminism in the 1920s', *Maryland Historian*, 7 (Spring 1975): 1–17, esp. p. 4). Accounts in *Time and Tide* make it clear that from 1926 a wide-ranging spectrum of groups and individual feminists supported this last suffrage activism; see, for example, *Time and Tide*, 2 July 1926: 605.
32 On opposition to the extended enfranchisement, see Noreen Branson, *Britain in the Nineteen Twenties* (London: Weidenfeld & Nicolson), pp. 203–8.
33 In the early months of 1926, Brittain was in the United States, but she was involved in planning for the 3 July rally, at which she was asked to speak and serve as a marshall on behalf of the Six Point Group. See her letter to Winifred Holtby, from Ithaca, N.Y., 28 March 1926, Holtby papers.
34 Vera Brittain, 'Political Demonstrations: Why Women Still Hold Them', *Time and Tide*, 26 July 1927: 686. The article appeared first in the *Manchester Guardian* on 14 July 1927.
35 Vera Brittain, 'Women, the Vote and the Hospitals', *Nation and Athenaeum*, 31 March 1928, G99, VBA.
36 Vera Brittain, 'Women and Disarmament', *Highway*, February 1934, G445, VBA. On Brittain's pacifism, see Muriel Mellown, 'One Woman's Way to Peace: the Development of Vera Brittain's Pacifism', *Frontiers*, 8(2), (1985); Yvonne Aleksandra Bennett, *Testament of a Minority in Wartime: The Peace Pledge Union and Vera Brittain,*

1939–1945, PhD dissertation, McMaster University, 1984; and see her 'Vera Brittain and the Peace Pledge Union: Women and Peace', in Ruth Roach Pierson (ed.), *Women and Peace: Theoretical, Historical and Practical Perspectives* (London: Croom Helm, 1987); Abigail J. Stewart, 'The Role of Personality Development in Shaping Vera Brittain's Feminism and Pacifism', paper presented at *Testament to Vera Brittain*, Vera Brittain Centenary Conference, 15–16 October 1993, McMaster University, Hamilton, Ontario. See also Stewart's discussion of Brittain, in Carol E. Franz and Abigail J. Stewart (eds), *Women Creating Lives: Identities, Resilience, and Resistance* (Boulder, Col.: Westview Press, 1994).

37 From Vera Brittain, 'Women and the Next War', *British Legion Journal*, April 1936, G509, VBA.

38 On women and the League, see Carol Miller, *Lobbying the League: Women's International Organizations and the League of Nations*, DPhil, University of Oxford, 1992.

39 One authority calls it 'the largest and most influential peace society after the mid-twenties': Martin Ceadel, *Pacifism in Britain, 1914–1945: The Defining of a Faith* (Oxford: Clarendon Press, 1980), p. 317.

40 For information on her LNU involvement, see the papers relating to the LNU in the correspondence file, VBA.

41 Brittain to Holtby, 9 November 1921, Holtby papers.

42 'This country frightens me . . . I see a war in 20 years time' (Brittain's 'Travel Diary', 14 October 1924, VBA).

43 Ibid., 5 October 1924. See also her pieces, 'A City of Sorrow and Hate', *Weekly Westminster*, 10 January 1925, and 'The Transformation of Krupps', *Nation and Athenaeum*, 3 January 1925, G18 and G19, VBA.

44 Brittain, 'Travel Diary', 8 October 1924, VBA.

45 Brittain to Holtby, 30 July 1926, Holtby papers.

46 See Vera Brittain, 'A Memorandum Showing the Connection Between the Status of Women and the Relations between Countries, Published by the Six Point Group' (n.d. [but 1929]), p. 8, G264, VBA.

47 The Equal Rights Treaty was drafted at a conference in Paris in 1926 by a group of English and American women, including Lady Rhondda and American women from the National Women's Party. See 'The Six Point Group Makes History', *Woman Teacher*, 22 November 1929: 51 (clipping in the Holtby papers). See also the Equal Rights International collection, Fawcett Society Library, London (clippings and correspondence in box 331).

48 One is cited above. The second, which first appeared in two parts in *Time and Tide*, as 'Feminism at Geneva', parts I and II, on 25 January and 1 February 1929 (they are G177 and G178, VBA) was reprinted as a Six Point Group pamphlet entitled *Geneva–the Key to Equality*.

49 That she was involved as a liaison with the Americans is clear from

Brittain's correspondence when she was visiting her husband in Ithaca, New York in 1927. See Vera Brittain, writing from Ithaca to Miss Vernon [of the National Woman's Party], 8 May 1927, VBA. See also Lady Rhondda to Vera Brittain, 20 August 1928 and 4 September 1928, VBA.

50 This effort is fully described in her letter to Lady Rhondda dated 11 August 1929, VBA. However, Brittain's active involvement with the Equal Rights International apparently ended in 1929. See the letter to Helen Archdale from Winifred Mayo, dated 9 November 1930. Letter in 'Foundation File', Box 331, Equal Rights International Collection, Fawcett Library.

51 See Brittain to Holtby, 21 November 1921, Holtby papers.

52 See Brittain to Holtby, 12 July 1921, Holtby papers.

53 Cited in Brittain, *Testament of Youth*, p. 539.

54 See material in the LNU files in VBA.

55 Quoted in Brittain, *Testament of Youth*, p. 539.

56 Brittain to Holtby, 4 November 1921 in *Selected Letters of Winifred Holtby to Vera Brittain*, ed. Vera Brittain and Geoffrey Handley-Taylor (London: A. Brown, 1960), p. 16.

CHAPTER 9: SEMI-DETACHED MARRIAGE

1 See Brittain, *Testament of Youth*, p. 580 and ch. 7, n. 79.

2 Each of its three stanzas ends with the refrain: 'But who will look for my coming?'; 'But who will seek me at nightfall?'; 'But who will give me my children?' Clearly, the poet's answer is: no one.

3 See, for example, Brittain to Catlin, 10 April 1933, VBA.

4 For example, by 1929 the successful 'Today and Tomorrow' series published in Britain by Kegan Paul, Trench Trubner and in the United States by E.P. Dutton, which promised its readers 'a survey of numerous aspects of modern thought', had nine titles in its 'Marriages and Morals' section. For information on the series, see the end papers included in Vera Brittain, *Halcyon: Or the Future of Monogamy* (London: Kegan Paul, Trench, Trubner, 1929).

5 See Jean E. Kennard, *Vera Brittain and Winifred Holtby: A Working Partnership* (Hanover, N.H.: University Press of New England, 1989), p. 75.

6 For this flirtation, see Brittain's letters to Holtby, 1 August 1923, 5 August 1923, 27 December 1923, Holtby papers.

7 See Brittain to Catlin, 4 November 1924, VBA.

8 Holtby to Brittain, 29 December 1923, Holtby papers.

9 This is a Roman Catholic Church. Catlin had converted to Catholicism.

10 For this photograph, see Alan Bishop (ed.), *Vera Brittain, Diary of the Thirties, 1932–1939: Chronicle of Friendship* (London: Victor Gollancz, 1986), p. 3. On wedding styles, see John Gillis, *For Better,*

For Worse: British Marriages, 1600 to the Present (New York: Oxford University Press, 1985).

11 Brittain to Catlin, 4 January 1925, VBA.
12 See Vera Brittain, *Thrice a Stranger* (New York: Macmillan, 1938).
13 Brittain to Holtby, 15 October 1925, Holtby papers.
14 Brittain to Holtby, 29 November 1925, Holtby papers.
15 Brittain to Holtby, 24 February 1926, Holtby papers. See also Brittain to Holtby, 29 November 1925 and 24 February 1926, Holtby papers.
16 For her sketch for this novel, see Brittain to Holtby, 28 February 1926, Holtby papers.
17 Holtby to Brittain, 'Sunday' [August 1929], Holtby papers.
18 Vera Brittain, 'Semi-detached Marriage', *Evening News*, 4 May 1928, G107, VBA.
19 Brittain to Catlin, 15 October 1926, VBA.
20 Brittain to Catlin, 6 December 1926, VBA.
21 Vera Brittain, *Testament of Experience* (London: Virago, 1979), p. 46 (first published London: Gollancz, 1957).
22 Contrast Brittain, for example, with her acquaintance and contemporary, the writer Naomi Mitchison. In Mitchison's *You May Well Ask: A Memoir, 1920–1940* (London: Victor Gollancz, 1979), she is frank not only about her extramarital affairs but about her feelings about sexuality.
23 Brittain, *Testament of Experience*, p. 19. See also the unpublished 'Honeymoon in Two Worlds', VBA.
24 Brittain to Catlin, 26 August 1924, VBA.
25 Ibid.
26 Brittain to Holtby, 29 August 1924, Holtby papers.
27 Brittain to Holtby, 2 July 1925, Holtby papers.
28 Ibid.
29 Brittain, *Halcyon*; Dora Russell, *Hypatia, or Women and Knowledge* (Folcroft, Pa: Folcroft Library Editions, 1976: reprint of the 1925 edition); Bertrand Russell, *Marriage and Morals* (London: Allen, 1929).
30 Brittain to Catlin, 16 January 1929, VBA.
31 Brittain to Catlin, 23 February 1929, VBA.
32 Brittain to Catlin, 8 March 1929, VBA.
33 Brittain to Catlin, 27 March 1929, VBA.
34 See outline and rough draft in VBA.
35 Brittain to Catlin, 15 April 1929, VBA.
36 Brittain mentions only the title in her letter to Catlin of 19 April 1929, VBA. But I assume this is V.F. Calverton and S.D. Schmalhausen (eds), *Sex in Civilization* (New York: Macaulay, 1929).
37 See, for example, Brittain to Catlin, 15 April 1929 and 19 April 1929, VBA.
38 See Ruth Hall (ed.), *Dear Dr Stopes: Sex in the 1920s* (London: André Deutsch, 1979), p. 10. On this question, see also Jane Lewis, *Women*

in *England, 1870–1950* (Brighton, Sussex: Wheatsheaf Books, 1984), pp. 124ff.

39 Hall (ed.), *Dear Dr Stopes*, p. 156.
40 See diary entry for 29 January 1923: *Chronicle of Friendship*, p. 31.
41 See e.g. Brittain to Catlin, 19 April 1929, VBA, where she mentions that she uses a diaphragm.
42 Brittain to Catlin, 19 April 1929, VBA.
43 Brittain to Catlin, 14 March 1930, VBA.
44 Brittain to Catlin, 23 February 1929, VBA.
45 Brittain to Catlin, 21 January 1925, VBA.
46 Ibid.
47 Vera Brittain, 'Our Malthusian Middle Classes', *Nation and Athenaeum*, 7 May 1927, G47, VBA.
48 Brittain to Catlin, 26 October 1926, VBA.
49 Brittain to Catlin, 22 October 1926, VBA.
50 Brittain, *Testament of Experience*, p. 48.
51 See Brittain to Holtby, 21 May 1927, Holtby papers.
52 Brittain to Holtby, 5 May 1927, Holtby papers.
53 Brittain to Holtby, 8 May 1927, Holtby papers.
54 Brittain to Holtby, 19 May 1927, Holtby papers.
55 See Brittain to Holtby, 21 May 1927, Holtby papers.
56 From Edith Brittain to Winifred Holtby, from Ithaca, 26 May 1927, addressed to 'My Dearest Winifred' and signed 'Your second mother', Holtby papers.
57 Brittain to Holtby, 21 May 1927, Holtby papers.
58 Brittain to Holtby, 5 May 1927, Holtby papers.
59 On this and other aspects of maternity and child care in the interwar period, see Jane Lewis, *The Politics of Motherhood: Child and Maternal Welfare in England, 1900–1939* (London: Croom Helm, 1980), pp. 128–9.
60 Vera Brittain, 'Welfare for Middle-class Mothers', *Time and Tide*, 30 March 1928, G97, VBA.
61 'John might well have succumbed to the after-effects of his catastrophic arrival but for my providential discovery of the Chelsea Babies' Club' (Brittain, *Testament of Experience*, p. 51).
62 Brittain to Catlin, 24 May 1929, VBA.
63 Brittain, 'Welfare for Middle-class Mothers'.
64 For her membership on the board of management, see Vera Brittain, Diary, 24 April 1932, in *Chronicle of Friendship*, p. 37.
65 For her public advocacy, see, for example, her 'Maternal Mortality and Medical Women', *Nation and Athenaeum*, 31 March 1928, G98, VBA. For her private advocacy, see, for example, her letter to Catlin, 23 February 1929, VBA, where she mentions using a woman insurance agent. Her dentist and physician were both women.
66 Vera Brittain, 'Prejudice or Knowledge? Fields for Women's Research', *Manchester Guardian*, 28 June 1927, G58, VBA.

67 Brittain to Catlin, 1 September 1932, VBA.
68 Brittain to Holtby, 31 August 1930, in *Selected Letters*, pp. 180–1.
69 Brittain, 'Our Malthusian Middle Classes'.
70 Vera Brittain, 'Wasted Women: the Tyranny of Houses', *Manchester Guardian*, 10 June 1927, G55, VBA.
71 By the early 1930s these included Amy and Charles Burnett, a parlour maid, a nanny or a nanny/governess and a secretary. See *Chronicle of Friendship*, *passim*, and especially Alan Bishop's helpful notes.
72 See, for example, Brittain to Holtby, 14 April 1932, Holtby papers.
73 Vera Brittain, 'Women Who Were Young in 1914', *Good Housekeeping*, June 1931, G347.
74 Brittain says, in *Testament of Experience*, p. 57, that she joined the Labour Party in 1924. But it was in fact somewhat later. For example, see Brittain to Catlin, 14 February 1925, VBA: 'Have quite decided to join the Labour Party.'
75 'For most intellectuals . . . to see themselves as allies of the workers and the labour movement was something altogether new. It must be remembered that . . . the living standards and way of life of professional and middle-class people . . . were much more sharply cut off from those of workers than they are today' (Jon Clark, Margot Heinemann, David Margolies and Carole Snee (eds), *Culture and Crisis in Britain in the Thirties*, London: Lawrence & Wishart, 1979). This is why Marvin Rintala's claim that Brittain's socialism was fraudulent is excessively harsh and misses the point: Marvin Rintala, 'Chronicler of a Generation: Vera Brittain's Testament', *Journal of Political and Military Sociology*, 12 (Spring 1984). On Brittain and class, Y. Aleksandra Bennett is not only more just, but much more perceptive. While she maintains, correctly, that 'Brittain's writings . . . were arguably often clouded by deeply engrained class perceptions', she does not regard this failing as unique to Brittain; see Yvonne A. Bennett, 'Vera Brittain: Feminism, Pacifism and the Problem of Class, 1900–1953', *Atlantis*, 12(2), (1987): 18–23.
76 Brittain, *Testament of Experience*, pp. 51–2.
77 Ibid., p. 57. She does say, much later in the book, when she deals with John's return to England in 1944, 'we had visited Eton where G. had registered him soon after his birth' (p. 317).
78 See correspondence between Brittain and Catlin, *passim*, in VBA.
79 Brittain to Catlin, 23 February 1929, VBA.
80 Brittain to Catlin, 4 March 1930, VBA.
81 All fee-paying, but some progressive schools, for example Dartington Hall; see Brittain to Catlin, 12 April 1932, VBA.
82 Vera Brittain, 'What Shall I Do if my Son Wants to Join the Officers' Training Corps?', *Congregational Quarterly*, July 1935, G496, VBA.
83 Brittain, *Testament of Experience*, p. 317.
84 Vera Brittain, 'How Shall I Educate My Daughters?', *Daily Express*, 8 August 1931, G350, VBA.

85 For early mention of St Paul's as suitable for Shirley, see Brittain to Catlin, from Glebe Place to Ithaca, 18 February 1932. And for her attending the school, see *Testament of Experience*, p. 324.
86 The diary indicates that Shirley may have attended London County Council school for a very brief period: 'Shirley went back to L.C.C. school' (Brittain, Diary, 10 January 1939, in *Chronicle of Friendship*, p. 327).
87 Vera Brittain, *Testament of Friendship: The Story of Winifred Holtby* (1940; London: Fontana, 1981), p. 291.
88 Ibid., p. 292.
89 For example, see letter Brittain to Catlin, 20 March 1932, VBA.
90 In terms of income she was receiving in 1932 £300 p.a. from her father, plus her own private income 'which originally came from him' of £225 per annum (Brittain to Catlin, 20 March 1932, VBA).
91 Brittain, *Testament of Experience*, p. 61, and she continues: 'though G. and I lived there for seven years he never became acclimatised to its third-rate architecture, but I loved and still miss the small sunny back-garden, which proved to be an ideal place for writing. It was a real joy after the "unutterable Earl's Courtishness" of Earl's Court' (p. 61). Nevern Place was no doubt quieter and less grimy in the late 1920s than it is today, but there is no question that the move to Chelsea was a great improvement. While the Cheyne Walk house to which Brittain and Catlin moved after Holtby's death is older and more elegant, 19 Glebe Place is not only large and to my eye anything but 'third rate', it is in a lovely, quiet cul-de-sac.
92 Brittain, *Testament of Friendship*, p. 292.
93 The Labour Party connections were made primarily through Gordon Catlin. For the 1930s, Alan Bishop's notes and comments in *Chronicle of Friendship* are invaluable.
94 Brittain, Diary, 15 October 1932, in *Chronicle of Friendship*, p. 96. Holtby was at that time working on her book on Virginia Woolf.
95 Brittain to Holtby, 25 September 1928, Holtby papers.
96 Brittain, *Testament of Friendship*, p. 277.
97 See Sheila Jeffreys, *The Spinster and her Enemies: Feminism and Sexuality, 1880–1930* (London: Pandora, 1985). For an interesting analysis of feminist and non-feminist discourse on 'spinsterhood,' which includes a discussion of Holtby's writings, see Alison Oram, 'Repressed and Thwarted, or Bearer of the New World? The Spinster in Inter-war Feminist Discourses', *Women's History Review*, 1(3), (1992): 413–34.
98 Brittain to Holtby, 29 December 1926, Holtby papers.
99 Autobiography of Storm Jameson, *Journey from the North*, vol. I (1969; London: Virago, 1984), chs 1 and 2. I discuss the friendship between Brittain and Jameson at greater length in my '"The Friendships of Women": Friendship, Feminism and Achievement in Vera

Brittain's Life and Work in the Interwar Decades', *Journal of Women's History*, 3(3), (1992).

100 Typescript of Jameson letter to Brittain of 8 October 1927 in VBA.

101 Brittain to Catlin, 8 March 1929, VBA. 'Mrs Russell' is Dora Russell, whose *Hypatia* had recently been published by Kegan Paul, Trench Trubner in the 'Today and Tomorrow' series.

102 Brittain to Catlin, 19 May 1930, VBA. Reference is to Joseph Tenenbaum, *The Riddle of Sex: The Medical and Social Aspects of Sex, Love and Marriage* (New York: Macaulay, 1929).

103 Catlin to Brittain, 31 January 1932, from the *Bremen*, VBA.

104 Brittain to Catlin, 12 February 1932, VBA.

105 Brittain to Catlin, 16 February 1929, VBA.

106 For example, Brittain to Catlin, 22 April 1933, VBA: 'I enclose three charming photographs which Aunt Florence took of the babes'.

107 For example, in a letter of 18 March 1932 she says of John: 'by the way he said quite spontaneously the other day, & apropos of nothing: "I do want my Daddy to come back"' (Brittain to Catlin, VBA).

108 Catlin to Brittain, 7 January 1932, VBA.

109 Catlin to Brittain, 10 January 1932, VBA.

110 Brittain to Catlin, 20 February 1930, VBA.

111 Brittain, 'Semi-detached Marriage'.

112 Brittain to Catlin, 2 March 1929, VBA.

113 Brittain, 'Semi-detached Marriage'.

114 Catlin to Brittain, 11 January 1932, VBA.

115 Brittain to Catlin, 12 January 1932, VBA.

116 Brittain to Catlin, 30 January 1933, VBA.

117 Harold Laski, (1893–1950) was a political scientist and Labour Party activist.

118 Brittain, *Testament of Experience*, pp. 49–50.

119 Brittain to Catlin, 7 April 1932, VBA. To their discredit, in private and sometimes even in public, Brittain and her circle were not free from the ugly anti-Semitism so prevalent in this era. However, their letters, diaries and published writings are less marred by this and other forms of racism and xenophobia than is the discourse of many other writers and intellectuals of the era. And to their credit, Brittain, Holtby and Catlin altered their perspective with the rise of Nazism.

120 Brittain to Catlin, 7 April 1932, VBA.

121 For example, he asked for her help in reviewing Elie Halévy's book on the Enlightenment for *Time and Tide* (Brittain to Catlin, 18 March 1929, VBA).

122 Brittain to Catlin, 24 March 1932, VBA.

123 Virginia Woolf, *The Sickle Side of the Moon: The Letters of Virginia Woolf*, vol. 5: *1932–1935*, ed. Nigel Nicolson (London: Hogarth Press, 1979), p. 114.

124 Brittain, *Testament of Friendship*, p. 168.

125 For example, Holtby to Brittain, 4 October 1925, Holtby papers.
126 Telegram sent by Holtby to Catlin, 12 September 1924, VBA.
127 Holtby to Catlin, 7 November 1926, VBA.
128 Brittain to Holtby, 29 August 1924, Holtby papers.
129 Holtby to Brittain, 29 July 1926, Holtby papers.
130 'Milanese silk knickers, plain, are about £1.1, embroidered, which I recommend, about 25/ . . . I wait for further instructions . . . Debenhams or one of the French shops might have garments of suitable frivolity' (Holtby to Catlin, 7 November 1926, VBA).
131 Brittain, *Testament of Friendship*, p. 291.
132 Catlin to Brittain, 18 March 1929, VBA.

CHAPTER 10: THE WRITING OF *TESTAMENT OF YOUTH*

1 Brittain, *Testament of Youth*, p. 11.
2 She tentatively entitled the selection 'Chronicle of Youth'. It is in VBA, filed with her own note: 'Predecessor to Testament of Youth. Consists of extracts from my 1913–1916 diaries (with names changed), submitted for an autobiography competition about 1924, which it did not win. Naive, amusing, pathetic . . .'.
3 Vera Brittain to Winifred Holtby, 26 December 1928, Holtby papers.
4 Vera Brittain, 'Their Name Liveth: Forgetting Women's War Work', *Manchester Guardian*, 13 November 1929, G248, VBA.
5 Vera Brittain, 'A Woman's Notebook', *Nation and Athenaeum*, 24 January 1931, G321, VBA.
6 See letter from Brittain to Holtby, 27 June 1921, Holtby papers. I refer to this letter in the Introduction to this book.
7 For the date she began the book, see the 'Foreword' in the resumed diary, 1932, in *Vera Brittain, Diary of the Thirties, 1932–1939: Chronicle of Friendship,* ed. Alan Bishop (London: Victor Gollancz, 1986), p. 29.
8 Vera Brittain, *Testament of Experience* (1957; London: Virago 1979), pp. 59–60.
9 Brittain to Holtby, 24 August 1931, Holtby papers.
10 Brittain to Holtby, 28 December 1932, Holtby papers.
11 See Brittain, *Testament of Experience*, p. 70.
12 For Arthur Brittain's depression, see Brittain, *Testament of Experience*, p. 71, and Brittain to Holtby, 4 March 1932, Holtby papers.
13 Brittain to Catlin, 23 February 1932, VBA.
14 Brittain to Holtby, 5 March 1932, in *Selected Letters of Winifred Holtby to Vera Brittain*, ed. Vera Brittain and Geoffrey Handley-Taylor (London: A. Brown, 1960), p. 202.
15 Holtby to Brittain, 7 March 1932, from Monks Risborough, in *Selected Letters*, p. 205.
16 Vera Brittain Diary, 22 August 1932, in *Chronicle of Friendship*, p. 78.
17 Brittain to Holtby, 26th August 1932, in *Selected Letters*, p. 222.

18 Bentley, a year younger than Brittain, was from a family of solid, successful West Riding textile manufacturers. As the youngest child and only girl it was always assumed that she would accept the role of dutiful daughter. This she did. She was unmarried and she lived with her mother. See her delightful autobiography: Phyllis Bentley, '*O Dreams, O Destinations': An Autobiography* (New York: Macmillan, 1962). I have discussed the significance of this friendship at greater length in my article ' "The Friendships of Women": Friendship, Feminism and Achievement in Vera Brittain's Life and Work in the Interwar Decades', *Journal of Women's History*, 3(3), (1992). See also Alan Bishop's perceptive analysis in his excellent introduction to *Chronicle of Friendship*, and Hilary Bailey's valuable discussion in her *Vera Brittain* (Harmondsworth, Middx: Penguin, 1987).

19 See Brittain, Diary 22 March 1932, in *Chronicle of Friendship*, p. 33.

20 Brittain, Diary 3 April 1932, in ibid., pp. 34–5.

21 Holtby and Bentley met in 1930. See Brittain's Diary, 31 March 1932, in *Chronicle of Friendship*, p. 34, and the Holtby–Bentley correspondence, which begins in 1930, Holtby papers.

22 Brittain, Diary, 7 April 1932, in *Chronicle of Friendship*, p. 35.

23 Brittain, Diary, 7 April 1932, in ibid., p. 35.

24 Brittain to Catlin, 10 May 1932, VBA.

25 Brittain, Diary, 9 May 1932, in *Chronicle of Friendship*, pp. 39–40.

26 Bentley, '*O Dreams, O Destinations*', p. 179.

27 Brittain describes the process by which the book was accepted, first by Macmillan of New York and then by Gollancz, in *Testament of Experience,* pp. 83–5.

28 Brittain to Catlin, 21 February 1933, VBA.

29 Brittain to Holtby, signed VSVDL, 21 February 1933, Holtby papers.

30 Catlin to Brittain, 8 May 1933, VBA.

31 Brittain to Catlin, 10 April 1933, VBA.

32 Included among the positive reviews was Compton Mackenzie's, who called it 'not merely profoundly moving . . . but also extremely accurate . . . the charity of the book never fails' (*Daily Mail*, 31 August, 1933); Storm Jameson said: 'Its value as an experience and as literature, is above commendation' *(Sunday Times*, 3 September 1933); R.L. Duffas wrote, in the *New York Times Book Review*, 15 October 1933: 'Of all the personal narratives covering the World War . . . there can have been none more honest, more revealing . . . or more heartbreakingly beautiful . . . .' Not all reviewer response was completely positive. The reviewer for the *Listener* (6 September 1933), for example, while generally favourable, commented, as did several others, that the last section of the book was less effective than the first two-thirds of the book; and one Marxist critic called Brittain a 'muddled egoist' with insufficient 'consciousness of the existence of such people as working men [the reviewer does not mention working women], on whose labours society is wholly dependent for that surplus

product which is the economic foundation of university life' (C. Norman, *New English Weekly*, 5 October 1933). All the above are in the Review Scrapbook for *Testament of Youth*, in VBA. And Phyllis Bentley, while instrumental in paving the way for Macmillan's reading of the manuscript, wrote in April 1933 a pre-publication review of the book for Gollancz which was less than favourable. It was not used for publicity purposes, and it permanently damaged the friendship between Bentley and Brittain. See Brittain to Holtby, for example 7 April 1933, Holtby papers. Brittain discusses the positive and negative responses to the book in *Testament of Experience*, p. 93.

33 Mrs Sydney Webb [Beatrice Webb] to Vera Brittain, 28 September 1933, VBA

34 Brittain, *Testament of Experience*, p. 85.

35 There are several writers who could be included in this category with whom Vera Brittain was intimate or friendly at one time or another – such as Storm Jameson and Phyllis Bentley, both of whom she knew well, but quarrelled with, Naomi Mitchinson, and of course, Winifred Holtby; and others, such as J.B. Priestley, whom she knew less well. Marion Shaw has interesting points to make about inter-war women writers and experimentalism. See her 'Feminism and Fiction Between the Wars: Winifred Holtby and Virginia Woolf', in Moira Monteith (ed), *Women's Writing: A Challenge to Theory* (Brighton, Sussex: Harvester Press, 1986), pp. 175–91.

36 On the implications for cultural history reflected in the rise of such a readership, and specifically on the rise of the book club, in an American context, see the illuminating article by Joan Shelley Rubin, 'Self, Culture, and Self-culture in Modern America: the Early History of the Book-of-the-Month Club', *Journal of American History*, 71(4), (March 1985): 782–806. The Book-of-the-Month club was created in 1926. John Feather, in *A History of British Publishing* (London: Croom Helm, 1988), explains that the book club came to Britain from America: 'The first British book club, The Book Society, was founded in 1929. It followed the American example to some extent' (p. 187).

37 I would maintain that this is true of Carolyn Heilbrun and Lillian Faderman (both cited in chapter 7 of this book), for example. Jean Kennard, in *Vera Brittain and Winifred Holtby: A Working Partnership* (Hanover, N.H.: University Press of New England, 1989), does provide perceptive analyses of the writings themselves, but she too is more interested in the lives than in the works, as I am myself. Some recent critics writing from a 'gendered' perspective have been hostile or indifferent to Brittain, for example, Claire Tylee, *The Great War and Women's Consciousness: Images of Militarism and Womanhood in Women's Writings, 1914–1964* (London: Macmillan, 1990). Tylee thinks the book is a 'failure' in number of major ways (pp. 209ff). Margaret R. Higonnet, in a recent article on women's First World War fiction does not mention Brittain at all: see her 'Not So Quiet in No-

Woman's Land', in Miriam Cooke and Angela Woollacott (eds), *Gendering War Talk* (Princeton, N.J.: Princeton University Press, 1993), pp. 205–26.

38 For example, see this early reference: 'I finished *Felix Holt* after dinner. How George Eliot's books do inspire me; they make all good seem worthwhile' ('Reflective Record', 29 January 1913, VBA). There are many others.

39 Virginia Woolf to Angelica Bell, Sunday, 18 November 1935, in *The Sickle Side of the Mood: The Letters of Virginia Woolf*, vol. 5: *1932–1935*, ed. Nigel Nicolson and Joanne Trautmann (London: Hogarth Press, 1979), p. 445.

40 '*Longumque illud tempus, quum non ero, magis me movet quam hoc exiguum*' (Cicero, *Ad Atticum*, Book 12, Letter 18). Thanks to my colleague, Professor Roland Jeffreys, Department of Classics, Carleton University, who translated the passage for me and explained the context: Cicero, who grieves for his daughter, demonstrates his faith in building for the future by concerning himself with the monument he will build to commemorate her. Brittain, in using the quotation, means to convey that her monument to her lost loved ones – her work for feminism and peace – must console her for their loss.

41 Paul Fussell, *The Great War and Modern Memory* (New York: Oxford University Press), ch. 5.

42 Robert Wohl is particularly dismissive: '*Testament of Youth* was too self-indulgent, too self-pitying, and too lacking in self-irony to be good literature' (*The Generation of 1914* (Cambridge, Mass.: Harvard University Press, 1979), p. 111). Modris Eksteins, *Rites of Spring: The Great War and the Birth of the Modern Age* (Toronto: Lester & Orpen Denys, 1989), mentions Vera Brittain only in passing, and does not discuss her work at all.

43 Edmund Blunden, *Undertones of War* (London: Richard Cobden-Sanderson, 1928), p. 10.

44 Ibid., p. vii.

45 Ibid., p. 266.

46 Brittain to Catlin, 29 March 1932, VBA.

47 Reflective Record', 20 April 1915, VBA.

48 See her review of Mary Lee, *It's a Great War, Time and Tide*, 17 January 1930, G268, VBA.

49 Notes for *Testament of Youth*, VBA.

50 For example, of the many works to which it can be seen as a forerunner, there is Carolyn Kay Steedman, *Landscape for a Good Woman: A Story of Two Lives* (London: Virago, 1986). Although Steedman's late twentieth-century work is concerned with very different kinds of experience and reflects a nuanced, late twentieth-century understanding of narrative, none the less she, like Brittain, seeks to connect the personal with the political and to 'write history in terms of personal life'.

CHAPTER 11: 'HAVING CROSSED THE RUBICON'

1 See Brittain's notes made 6 February 1939 about 21 February 1933, Holtby papers.
2 Brittain to Catlin, 26 February 1933, VBA.
3 Brittain, Diary, Monday, 28 August–Sunday, 3 September, in *Vera Brittain, Diary of the Thirties, 1932–1939: Chronicle of Friendship*, ed. Alan Bishop (London: Victor Gollancz, 1986), p. 148.
4 Brittain, Diary, 17 October 1933, in ibid., p. 159.
5 Brittain, Diary, 1 November 1933, in ibid., p. 162.
6 See Brittain to Holtby, 21 February 1933, Holtby papers.
7 Vera Brittain, *Testament of Experience* (London: Virago, 1979), p. 94, says she received a 'substantial sum'.
8 Brittain to Holtby, 22 May 1934, in *Selected Letters of Winifred Holtby to Vera Brittain*, ed. Vera Brittain and Geottley Handley-Taylor (London: A. Brown, 1960), pp. 286–7.
9 See *Chronicle of Friendship*, p. 158.
10 For the tour, see Vera Brittain, *Thrice a Stranger* (New York: Macmillan, 1938), and the published and unpublished correspondence with Holtby.
11 The BBC dramatization was by Elaine Morgan. See Claire Tylee, *The Great War and Women's Consciousness: Images of Militarism and Womanhood in Women's Writings 1914–1964* (London: Macmillan, 1990), p. 209.
12 Brittain to Holtby, 12 May 1934, Holtby papers.
13 Brittain, Diary, 14 September 1934, in *Chronicle of Friendship*, p. 167.
14 Brittain, Diary, 15 September 1934, in ibid.
15 Brittain, Diary, 15 September 1934, in ibid., pp. 168–9.
16 Brittain to Holtby, 20 September 1934, Holtby papers.
17 Brittain to Holtby, 29 September 1934, in *Selected Letters*, pp. 300–2.
18 The public statement is from Brittain, *Testament of Experience*, p. 112; the diary entry is for 21 September 1934, in *chronicle of Friendship*, p. 171.
19 Brittain to Holtby, 24 September 1934, in *Selected Letters*, pp. 297–8.
20 Letter quoted in Brittain, *Thrice a Stranger*, p. 155.
21 Ibid., p. 149.
22 Brittain to Holtby, 27 October 1934, in *Selected Letters*, pp. 314–16.
23 Brittain to Holtby, 6 October 1934, in ibid., p. 306.
24 Brittain to Holtby, 24 September 1934, Holtby papers.
25 Brittain to Holtby, 29 September 1934, Holtby papers.
26 Brittain to Holtby, 6 October 1934, Holtby papers.
27 Holtby to Brittain, 17 October 1934, Holtby papers.
28 Brittain to Holtby, 28 November 1934, from Washington, D.C., Holtby papers.
29 See their correspondence, *passim*, VBA.

30 Vera Brittain, *Honourable Estate: A Novel of Transition* (New York: Macmillan, 1936).
31 Brittain to Holtby, 17 March 1933, in *Selected Letters*, pp 241–2.
32 The novel has never been republished, and little has been written about it. An exception is Lynne Layton, 'Vera Brittain's Testament(s)', in *Behind the Lines: Gender and the Two World Wars*, ed. Margaret Randolph Higonnet et al. (New Haven, Conn.: Yale University Press, 1987). Layton does discuss the novel briefly, as does Rita Kissen, in *Vera Brittain: Writing a Life*, PhD dissertation, University of Massachusetts, 1986, pp. 228ff.
33 Brittain, *Honourable Estate*, p. xiii.
34 Ibid., pp. xi–xii.
35 Ibid., p. xiv.
36 Kate Millett, *Sexual Politics* (New York: Doubleday, 1970).
37 See Brittain, *Testament of Experience*, p. 124.
38 Brittain, *Honourable Estate*, pp. 340–3.
39 Ibid., p. 346.
40 Ibid., p. 467.
41 Brittain says this explicitly: see *Testament of Experience*, p. 124.
42 Brittain to Holtby, 12 November 1934, Holtby papers.
43 Brittain to Catlin, 21 July 1939, VBA. Edith Brittain had destroyed the diary. I thank Abigail Stewart for calling this letter to my attention.
44 The fact that nearly a year of Brittain's diary (November 1933–September 1934) is missing from the Vera Brittain Archive might indicate that she made her discoveries about Edward some time after the publication of *Testament of Youth*. But we cannot know with certainty what Brittain knew of this family secret or when she acquired the information.
45 Brittain, *Honourable Estate*, p. xiii.
46 See Brittain to Holtby, 15 April 1934, from Portofino, in *Selected Letters*, pp. 275–7.
47 Brittain to Catlin, 18 April 1932, VBA.
48 See Brittain to Holtby, 5 May 1934, Holtby papers; and *Testament of Experience*, p. 111.
49 See Brittain to Holtby, 5 May 1934, Holtby papers.
50 Brittain to Holtby, 17 February 1935 and 26 February 1935, Holtby papers.
51 Brittain, Diary, 3 August 1935, in *Chronicle of Friendship*, p. 191.
52 On these arrangements, see, for example, Brittain to Holtby, 26 August 1935, Holtby papers; also Catlin to Holtby, 20 August 1935, Holtby papers; and Holtby to Catlin, 23 August 1935, from Wimereux, Holtby papers. Hilda Reid, Holtby's and Brittain's friend from Somerville, went with Winifred.
53 Catlin to Holtby, 23 August 1935, Holtby papers.
54 Brittain, Diary, 29 September 1935, in *Chronicle of Friendship*, p. 218.
55 Brittain, *Testament of Friendship*, p. 441.

56 See Brittain to Holtby, 26 November 1934, Holtby papers.
57 Brittain, *Testament of Experience*, p. 133.
58 Brittain, Diary, 25 October 1935, in *Chronicle of Friendship*, p. 230.
59 Brittain, Diary, 3 November 1935, in ibid, p. 231.
60 In Brittain, *Testament of Experience*, p. 138, she explains that she wrote this in 'a letter to New York'.
61 Brittain, Diary, 31 December 1935, in *Chronicle of Friendship*, pp. 235–6.
62 For the LNU's attitude towards Brittain, before and after the publication of *Testament of Youth*, see file of LNU correspondence, VBA. It was only after the publication of the book that she was asked to perform functions such as serving as a vice-president of the Youth Movement.
63 For tensions within the LNU, see Donald Birn, 'The League of Nations Union and Collective Security', *Journal of Contemporary History*, 9(3), (1974): 131–59; and J.A. Thompson, 'Lord Cecil and the Pacifists in the League of Nations Union', *Historical Journal*, 20(4), (1977): 949–59.
64 Vera Brittain was critical in public of LNU policy as early as 1933: see the letter she co-signed with Winifred Holtby in the *Manchester Guardian*, 6 July 1933 (clipping in VBA). For her involvement with the UDC and the WILPF, see the correspondence files relating to each organization in VBA.
65 Brittain, Diary, 16 March 1936, in *Chronicle of Friendship*, p. 256.
66 Brittain, Diary, 'Germany and France March–April 1936', in *Chronicle of Friendship*, p. 260.
67 Ibid., p. 265.
68 Ibid., p. 270. The informant was a Reuter's correspondent, Captain Charles Bennett.
69 Ibid., p. 276.
70 Brittain, Diary, 3 April 1936, Strasbourg, in ibid., p. 277.
71 Brittain, Diary, 4 April 1936, Metz, in ibid., p. 279.
72 Brittain, *Testament of Experience*, p. 157.
73 Joyce Berkman, '"Inter Arma Caritas": Issues of National Identity in the World War One Experience of Vera Brittain and Edith Stein, Volunteer Nurses on Opposing Warfronts', paper presented at *Testament to Vera Brittain*, Vera Brittain Centenary Conference, 15 and 16 October 1993, McMaster University, Hamilton, Ontario. My thanks to Joyce Berkman for permission to quote from this unpublished paper.
74 Brittain, *Testament of Experience*, p. 165.
75 Ibid. The work of Yvonne Aleksandra Bennett provides a thorough analysis of Brittain's involvement in the PPU: Yvonne Aleksandra Bennett, *Testament of a Minority in Wartime: The Peace Pledge Union and Vera Brittain, 1939–1945*, PhD dissertation, McMaster University, 1984; and see her 'Vera Brittain and the Peace Pledge Union:

Women and Peace', in Ruth Roach Pierson (ed.), *Women and Peace: Theoretical, Historical and Practical Perspectives* (London: Croom Helm, 1987). Also on the PPU, see Raymond A. Jones, *Arthur Ponsonby: The Politics of Life* (London: Christopher Helm, 1989), pp. 201–11.

76 'Authors Take Sides on the Spanish War', *Left Review*, 1937, copy in VBA.

77 For a perceptive brief overview of Brittain's wartime activities, see Y. Aleksandra Bennett's 'Introduction' to the wartime diaries: Alan Bishop and Y. Aleksandra Bennett, *Wartime Chronicle: Vera Brittain, Diary, 1939–1945* (London: Victor Gollancz, 1989).

78 Vera Brittain, Diary, 7 September 1939, in ibid., p. 29.

79 'With a board across the bath it served adequately as an office for several months': Winifred Eden-Green, 'Foreword' to the reprint edition of Vera Brittain, *England's Hour* (London: Futura, 1981), p. 7.

80 Vera Brittain, *Humiliation with Honour* (London: Andrew Dakers, 1942); Vera Brittain, *Seed of Chaos: What Mass Bombing Really Means* (London: New Vision Press, 1944); see Bishop and Bennett *Wartime Chronicle*, p. 331, notes.

81 Winifred Eden-Green's introduction to *Testament of a Peace Lover: Letters from Vera Brittain*, ed. Winifred and Alan Eden-Green (London: Virago, 1988).

82 On Brittain and India: Y. Aleksandra Bennett and Frances Montgomery, 'Brittain and India': paper presented at *Testament to Vera Brittain*, Vera Brittain Centenary Conference, 15 and 16 October 1993, McMaster University, Hamilton, Ontario.

83 Brittain, Diary, 22 June 1936, in *Chronicle of Friendship*, p. 291. In his notes, Alan Bishop identifies this as the meeting discussed in *Testament of Experience*.

84 Vera Brittain, *In the Steps of John Bunyan: An Excursion into Puritan England* (London: Rich & Cowan, n.d. [1948]).

85 Brittain, *Testament of Experience*, p. 438.

86 Ibid., p. 291.

87 Brittain, *Testament of Youth*, p. 488.

88 Brittain was working on *Honourable Estate* when she went to Germany and France in March. She resumed work after her return, finishing the novel on 2 August 1936: see Brittain, Diary, 2 August 1936, in *Chronicle of Friendship*, p. 292.

89 Brittain, *Honourable Estate*, p. 598. Brittain quotes this passage in *Testament of Experience*, p. 291, and it also appears on the end papers of Brittain, *Humiliation with Honour*.

90 See Brittain, Diary, 23 July 1942, in *Chronicle of Friendship*, p. 163.

91 From blurb for Brittain, *Humiliation with Honour*. For the jacket illustration of *Humiliation with Honour*, see Plate 16.

92 Brittain, Diary, 13–20 October 1935, in *Chronicle of Friendship*, p. 227.

93 Brittain, Diary, 20 March 1939, in ibid., p. 347.
94 Because she had a falling out with Gollancz, the book was published by Macmillan.
95 Letter 3579 to Ethel Smyth 16 January [1940], in *Leave the Letters Till We're Dead: The Letters of Virginia Woolf*, vol. 6: *1936–1941*, edited by Nigel Nicolson with Joanne Trautmann (London: Hogarth Press, 1980), p. 379. On Composer Ethel Smyth, see Elizabeth Wood's forthcoming biography, to be published by Bloomsbury Press, London.
96 Brittain, Diary, 23 February 1939, in *Chronicle of Friendship*, p. 339.
97 *Testament of Friendship*, pp. 440–1.
98 Adrienne Rich, *On Lies, Secrets, and Silence* (New York: W.W. Norton, 1979), p. 186. (Rich speaks generally here. She is not commenting directly on Brittain.)
99 Vera Brittain died on 29 March 1970. One evening in the autumn of 1966 she fell, while hurrying to give a lecture at St Martin-in-the-Fields in London. She never completely recovered from the after-effects of the fall and during the last four years of her life she was ill much of the time. See Paul Berry's touching account of her last years and her death in his introduction to the Virago edition of *Testament of Youth* (London: Virago, 1979).
100 Bennett, *Wartime Chronicle*, p. 12.
101 Brittain, *Honourable Estate*, p. 566.
102 Vera Brittain, *Lady into Woman: A History of Women from Victoria to Elizabeth II* (London: Andrew Dakers, 1953). Other feminist works of her later years include *The Women at Oxford: A Fragment of History* (London: George G. Harrap, 1960). The very last commission she undertook was a book on the Radclyffe Hall case, which she did for Femina Books, a newly established women's press which was a harbinger of the revival of feminism and which approached her, as a distinguished woman author, to write a book about the obscenity trial of *The Well of Loneliness: Radclyffe Hall: A Case of Obscenity?* (London: Femina Books, 1968).
103 Others disagree about Brittain's abiding commitment to feminism; see, for example, Martin Pugh, *Women and the Women's Movement in Britain, 1914–1959* (London: Macmillan, 1992), pp. 262–3. Pugh confuses activism with fundamental feminist beliefs. See also Olive Banks, *The Politics of Feminism: 1918–1970* (Aldershot, Hants.: Edward Elgar, 1993), p. 25. While it is true that her activist efforts were primarily devoted to peace work after 1937, both the Six Point Group files at the Fawcett Society and the Six Point Group correspondence in VBA indicate some continued involvement, and certainly no hostility. Two other examples of her continued feminist involvement (and of her commitment to an equal-rights formulation) include her work for the Equal Citizenship (Blanket) Bill campaign, during the Second World War: see Harold Smith 'The Effect of the War on the

Status of Women', in Harold Smith (ed.), *War and Social Change: British Society and the Second World War* (Manchester: Manchester University Press, 1986), p. 224, and her involvement with the Olive Schreiner Centenary celebration in London in 1955, documented in VBA and elsewhere. (Thanks to Joyce Berkman for calling my attention to the latter involvement.)

104 Brittain, *Lady into Woman*, p. 8.

105 F. Pethick-Lawrence to Vera Brittain, 28 September 1935, VBA.

106 Work by Dale Spender, Jane Lewis, Susan Kent, Harold Smith and many others has effectively demolished the older view that the women's movement in Britain disappeared after the First World War. Nobody would deny, on the other hand, that the movement was less visible and less strong in the interwar decades and in the aftermath of the Second World War than it was before the First World War or in the 1970s. On the fluctuating fortunes of feminism, see Dale Spender, *There's Always Been a Women's Movement This Century* (London: Pandora, 1983); and Susan Faludi, *Backlash: The Undeclared War Against American Women* (New York: Crown Publishers, 1991).

CHAPTER 12: CONCLUSION

1 Vera Brittain, *Lady into Woman: A History of Women from Victoria to Elizath II* (London: Andrew Dakers, 1953), p. xiii.

2 On educational disparities, see Population Action International's report, *Closing the Gender Gap: Educating Girls*, study reported in the *Toronto Globe and Mail*, 31 January 1994, p. A5. On violence, see, for example, Mimi Wesson, 'Digging up the roots of violence', *Women's Review of Books*, 11(6), (March 1994): 1, 3.

3 See, for example, Susan Faludi, *Backlash: The Undeclared War Against American Women* (New York: Crown, 1991).

4 Brittain, *Lady into Woman*, p. 1.

5 Brittain, *Testament of Youth*, p. 655.

6 Ibid., p. 50.

7 Defining 'Victorianism' was a post-Victorian phenomenon. For the definition sketched above, I draw heavily on G.M. Young, whose *Victorian England: Portrait of an Age* (London: Milford, 1936) was enormously influential.

8 All this and more is expressed or at least adumbrated in George Dangerfield's *Strange Death of Liberal England* (London: Constable, 1936) and it is noteworthy that these same traits are ascribed to modernism in Modrus Eckstein, *Rites of Spring: The Great War and the Birth of the Modern Age* (Toronto: Lester & Orpen Dennys, 1989).

9 Susan Kingsley Kent, 'Gender Reconstruction after the First World War', in Harold L. Smith (ed.), *British Feminism in the Twentieth Century* (Aldershot, Hants.: Edward Elgar, 1990), pp. 70–1.

10 One specific example would be the praise bestowed by the writer Henry Miller and others on the self-indulgent work of Anaïs Nin, a literary figure and personality who was taken up by some enclaves in the women's movement in the 1970s. In 1937, Miller praised Nin's as yet unpublished diaries for their 'illusion of submergence', and their 'female honesty'. See Claudia Roth Postgate, 'Sex, lies and thirty-five thousand pages', *New Yorker,* 1 March 1993. As Postgate points out, in Nin's case, her self-definition as a modernist masked the weakness in her writing. It also masked the essentialism, the embracing of irrationality and the covert misogyny in her thinking about women.

11 Adrienne Rich, *On Lies, Secrets, and Silence* (New York: W.W. Norton, 1979).

12 Liz Stanley, *The Auto/biographical I: The Theory and Practice of Feminist Auto/biography* (Manchester: Manchester University Press, 1992), p. 234.

13 Paul Berry, 'Introduction' to the Virago reprint edition of *Testament of Experience* (London: Virago, 1979), p. 13.

Index

INDEXER'S NOTE: For the purpose of this index only, Vera Brittain is abbreviated to VB; *Testament of Experience* to *Experience*; *Testament of Friendship* to *Friendship* and *Testament of Youth* to *Youth*. Authors are only given for works not written by Vera Brittain.